WESTERN MISSO

EAST →

Adam-ondi-Ahman

Gallatin   Millport

LIVINGSTON
COUNTY

DAVIESS COUNTY

Haun's
Mill

Grand

River

Shoal Creek

CALDWELL COUNTY

CARROLL COUNTY

Crooked

River

To St. Louis

DeWitt

RAY COUNTY

RICHMOND

L.B.Lee

Missouri

River

McIlwaine's
Bend

Lexington

LAFAYETTE COUNTY

THE
WORK
AND THE
GLORY
Truth Will Prevail

Arriving in Preston, England

VOLUME 3

THE
WORK
AND THE
GLORY

Truth Will Prevail
A HISTORICAL NOVEL

Gerald N. Lund

BOOKCRAFT
Salt Lake City, Utah

THE WORK AND THE GLORY

Volume 1: Pillar of Light
Volume 2: Like a Fire Is Burning
Volume 3: Truth Will Prevail
Volume 4: Thy Gold to Refine
Volume 5: A Season of Joy

Library of Congress Catalog Card Number: 92–73810
ISBN 0–88494–853–6

9th Printing, 1994

Printed in the United States of America

For behold, this is my work and my glory—to bring to pass the immortality and eternal life of man.

—Moses 1:39

Preface

With the coming forth of *Truth Will Prevail*, the third volume in the series *The Work and the Glory*, the reader can continue the saga of a fictional American family acquainted with Joseph Smith and caught up in the grand events associated with the restoration of the Church of Jesus Christ to the earth. Volume 3 carries on an attempt to help the reader feel what it must have been like to live during the events that Latter-day Saints of the twentieth century look back on with some awe and considerable wonder. And, as with the earlier volumes, it is hoped that, through this novel, readers who are not of the Latter-day Saint faith may come to a better understanding of the Church's beginnings and of the events that so stir Church members' hearts.

In the prefaces to the previous two volumes much was said about the nature of this work and its avowed purposes. A brief word or two in addition to those comments seems appropriate here.

First, while the various historical sources together give a remarkable picture of what was happening during the period of Church history covered in this third volume (1836 to 1838), they do not always agree on specifics. The novel makes no effort to resolve these disputed points, which are generally of little or no consequence to the story. In giving priority to presenting a coherent story line, the author has sometimes opted for vagueness on historical details or has chosen to accept one historical source over another. Occasionally, too, literary license has been taken to vary placement of minor events or of persons, especially when historical evidence is not conclusive. Chapter notes at the end of this book—a feature first introduced in volume 2 of the series—indicate when events depicted in the novel are based on actual historical occurrences and also provide a few relevant source citations.

Second, the early history of the restored Church is filled with well-documented miraculous experiences that are part of the rich spiritual legacy of the Latter-day Saints; indeed, it would be surprising to find it otherwise (see Mark 16:16–18). Therefore, in this and previous volumes in the series the author has placed the fictional family, the believing Steeds, in the midst of that environment.

As with the first two volumes, there are many acknowledgments to be given for help in preparing this third volume. No novel, however proprietary, is ever the product of one person. An immeasurable debt is owed to the cluster of Latter-day Saint historians who have provided such a rich cornucopia from which a writer can draw out the backdrop for his characters. A researcher who spends hours so that the writer can spend minutes is also one to whom much is owed. Then there are readers who read and critique the manuscript and knock off those corners that, if left, would later have proved to be embarrassments. There is the secretary who files and indexes and types and then does it all over again. An editor with an eye for detail coupled with a respect for the writer's individuality moves the manuscript from rough and sometimes inaccurate stages to the polished and (it is hoped) precise final product. There are designers and artists who attractively package the book and add to readers' pleasure by helping them visualize certain scenes or events. There are marketers and advertisers and warehouse staff and bookstore sales personnel. Truly, in the publishing of a book, as in so many other of life's endeavors, "no man is an island."

In previous volumes I have expressed appreciation for all of the above kinds of people in more detail. But again I say: To Rick Huchel and Calvin Stephens, to Deena Nay and Shawn Stringham and Garry Garff, to Robert Barrett and Lester Lee and Cinda Morgan and Jana Erickson and Russell Orton and Cory Maxwell and all the staff at Bookcraft—again, a most special thanks to each of you. Surely you can share generously in those moments when readers say, "I have been reading *The Work and the Glory*. Thanks."

Even a special thanks is not adequate for the contributions of my wife, Lynn, and of Kim and Jane Moe. Without their support, encouragement, and vision, the series would still be languishing somewhere in the back recesses of the mind, perhaps never to move from the shelves of imagination to the tables and desks and laps of tens of thousands of readers of many ages and occupations and interests.

One final thing needs to be said. Any grandeur that this series conveys, any emotions that it may stir, any uplift that it may bring are ultimately due to the work and the glory of God's great plan of restoration and redemption. It is to the Father and the Son that we look with gratitude and humility when we consider all that has been and will yet be unfolded in our behalf. And it is because of them that we can, even in the darkest of times, be moved in our hearts to exclaim, "Truth *will* prevail."

GERALD N. LUND

Bountiful, Utah
August 1992

Characters of Note in This Book

The Steed Family

Benjamin, the father and grandfather.

Mary Ann Morgan, the mother and grandmother.

Joshua, the oldest son; about twenty-nine as the book begins.

Jessica Roundy, ex-wife of Joshua; nearly thirty-two.

Rachel, daughter of Joshua and Jessica; four years old as the story opens.

Nathan, the second son of Benjamin and Mary Ann; about twenty-seven.

Lydia McBride, Nathan's wife; age twenty-six.

Joshua Benjamin, older son of Nathan and Lydia; nearly five years old.

Emily, daughter of Nathan and Lydia; thirteen and a half months younger than Joshua.

Nathan Joseph, younger son of Nathan and Lydia; six months old.

Melissa Steed Rogers, older daughter of Benjamin and Mary Ann; twenty-five.

Carlton Rogers, Melissa's husband.

Rebecca ("Becca"), younger daughter of Benjamin and Mary Ann; age eighteen as the novel opens.

Matthew Steed, the youngest son of Benjamin and Mary Ann; two years younger than Rebecca.

Note: Melissa and Carlton ("Carl") have two sons, but they do not figure prominently in the book.

The Smiths

* Joseph, Sr., the father.
* Lucy Mack, the mother.
* Hyrum, Joseph's elder brother; almost six years older than Joseph.
* Jerusha Barden, Hyrum's wife.
* Joseph, Jr., age thirty as the story opens.
* Emma Hale, Joseph's wife; a year and a half older than Joseph.
* William Smith, a younger brother of Joseph's; about five years younger than Joseph.

Note: There are other Smith children, but they play no part in the novel.

Others

* Oliver Cowdery, an associate of Joseph Smith's; one of the Three Witnesses to the Book of Mormon.
* Martin Harris, one of the Three Witnesses to the Book of Mormon.
  Derek Ingalls, a factory worker in England; nearly nineteen.
  Peter Ingalls, Derek's younger brother; almost twelve.
* Heber C. Kimball, friend of Brigham Young's and a member of the Quorum of the Twelve Apostles.
* Newel Knight, an early convert to the Church.
  Caroline Mendenhall, a woman of Savannah, Georgia.
  William Donovan Mendenhall, Caroline's son; twelve.
  Olivia Mendenhall, Caroline's daughter; about three and a half years younger than William.
* Warren Parrish, an associate of Joseph Smith's in Kirtland.

*Designates actual people from Church history.

* Parley P. Pratt, an early convert and a member of the Quorum of the Twelve Apostles.

Clinton Roundy, Jessica's father; saloon keeper in Independence.

* John Taylor, an Englishman residing in Toronto, Canada.

* David Whitmer, one of the Three Witnesses to the Book of Mormon.

Arthur Wilkinson, a young man from Kirtland, Ohio.

* Brigham Young, an early convert and a member of the Quorum of the Twelve Apostles.

Though too numerous to list here, there are many other actual people from the pages of history who are mentioned by name in the novel. Sidney Rigdon, Frederick G. Williams, John Boynton, Luke and Lyman Johnson, Isabelle Walton, Joseph and Mary Fielding, and many others mentioned in the book were real people who lived and participated in the events described in this work.

*Designates actual people from Church history.

The Benjamin Steed Family[†]

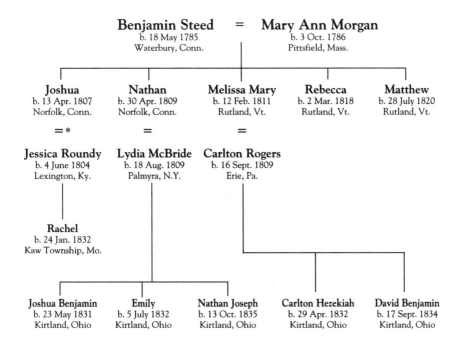

Benjamin Steed = **Mary Ann Morgan**
b. 18 May 1785   b. 3 Oct. 1786
Waterbury, Conn.   Pittsfield, Mass.

Joshua
b. 13 Apr. 1807
Norfolk, Conn.

Nathan
b. 30 Apr. 1809
Norfolk, Conn.

Melissa Mary
b. 12 Feb. 1811
Rutland, Vt.

Rebecca
b. 2 Mar. 1818
Rutland, Vt.

Matthew
b. 28 July 1820
Rutland, Vt.

= *

=

=

Jessica Roundy
b. 4 June 1804
Lexington, Ky.

Lydia McBride
b. 18 Aug. 1809
Palmyra, N.Y.

Carlton Rogers
b. 16 Sept. 1809
Erie, Pa.

Rachel
b. 24 Jan. 1832
Kaw Township, Mo.

Joshua Benjamin
b. 23 May 1831
Kirtland, Ohio

Emily
b. 5 July 1832
Kirtland, Ohio

Nathan Joseph
b. 13 Oct. 1835
Kirtland, Ohio

Carlton Hezekiah
b. 29 Apr. 1832
Kirtland, Ohio

David Benjamin
b. 17 Sept. 1834
Kirtland, Ohio

†Chart does not include deceased children
*Divorced Jan. 1833

Truth Will Prevail

Benjamin Steed was looking at his hands. He had them palms up, fingers bent over so he could examine his fingernails. He grunted softly in mild self-derision. These weren't the hands of a dirt farmer. Not anymore. Five years in Kirtland had smoothed and softened them. They were callused—he still chopped his own wood, dug Mary Ann's gardens, helped Nathan with the plowing now and then—but the hardness, the knotted muscles, the scabs and scars and blackened thumbnails were largely gone now.

He turned them over. For the first time he noticed an uneven brown spot on the back of his left hand. Absently he reached out and touched it with his fingertip. He also saw that the veins on the backs of his hands stood out more prominently now, like the furrows of a mole across a meadow. He hadn't noticed that before either.

Like my father's hands, before he died. Surprisingly, the thought did not depress him. Next month Benjamin would celebrate his fifty-first birthday. It was no surprise that he was showing signs of aging.

A movement brought his head up. The Prophet Joseph was passing the sacramental bread to the Quorum of the Twelve Apostles, who were seated on the stand on one side of the western pulpits. Sidney Rigdon and Frederick G. Williams, his two counselors in the First Presidency, were assisting. Benjamin watched as the plates with bread passed among those on the front row—Thomas B. Marsh, David W. Patten, Brigham Young, Heber C. Kimball.

The great room that occupied the main floor of the temple was filled to capacity. More than eight hundred Saints sat quietly and reverently, preparing themselves to receive the emblems of the Lord's Supper. As the First Presidency finished passing the sacrament to the Apostles, the Twelve arose to help pass it to the congregation. It was the Sabbath in Kirtland, the first Sunday in April in the year of our Lord, one thousand eight hundred and thirty-six. It was a bright, sunny afternoon. Spring was heavy in the air and poured fresh, cool air through the great Gothic-arched windows.

Benjamin's eyes dropped again to the spot on his hand. *Fifty-one years!* He marveled a little at the thought. He had been born in 1785, not even a full two years after the peace treaty was signed ending the revolutionary war. And now, here it was, more than a third of the way through the nineteenth century. That meant that, short of a miracle, two-thirds of his life was behind him. Possibly more. But he wasn't bothered by that. He was, in fact, quite content.

He turned. Frederick G. Williams was at the end of their pew, extending the plate of broken bread to Mary Ann. His wife reverently selected a piece of bread and placed it in her mouth. Her eyes closed momentarily, then she took the plate, turned, and offered it to Benjamin, who quietly took a piece of bread and put it in his mouth.

He took the plate, then held it out for Rebecca, who sat on the other side of him. He watched her hands, graceful and elegant, as she took the bread. To the family, this youngest daughter had always been "Becca." It suddenly occurred to Benjamin that of late he and Mary Ann had dropped the shorter form of the name and always called her by her full name. He smiled. *Rightly so*, he thought. At eighteen, she was fully a woman now—lovely, gentle, so much like her mother. So much like Isaac's Rebekah of the Bible must have been.

He watched as the plate moved on, realizing that along this row sat the primary reasons for his contentment. Next to Rebecca were Nathan and Lydia. Not surprisingly, they were holding hands and had to disengage to take the bread. That took his mind back six years. Lydia had been the pampered, only daughter of one of Palmyra's leading businessmen. Benjamin had been disgusted at the thought of his son marrying such a woman. "It ain't smart to put a thoroughbred and a mule in the same harness," he had grumbled. But he had been wrong. Dead wrong!

Beside Lydia sat Jessica Roundy Steed. Technically, Jessica was no longer related to the Steeds. Benjamin frowned. Thoughts of his oldest son still brought the same reaction—anger, frustration. Joshua had run away from Palmyra close to nine years earlier after a bitter confrontation between him and Benjamin. Then they learned he was married and living in Independence, Missouri. In the summer of 1831 Nathan had gone west with Brother Joseph to visit the land of Zion and look up his brother. What he found had rocked the family—a battered, pregnant wife and Joshua fled to Mexico Territory to escape the law.

By the time Nathan returned to Missouri with Zion's Camp in the summer of 1834, Jessica had a two-year-old daughter and a divorce paper from Joshua. She had come back to Kirtland with Nathan, and she and Rachel now lived in a small cabin just next door to Benjamin and Mary Ann's home. Here, as with Lydia, bonds had been forged now as strong as any blood ties.

The furrow in Benjamin's brow smoothed as he let his eyes move to the last of the family members sitting on the row. Matthew Steed would be sixteen in July. The little towheaded, rooster-tailed boy who had incessantly tagged after his father was gone now. The blond hair was gone—it was dark brown now and thick as a tangle of prairie grass; the boyish slimness was gone; the high voice was gone now too, given way to the deep richness of a man's voice. Matthew *was* a man now, straight and tall, full of fun and yet with a depth that was already causing older men to accept him with respect.

As he slipped the piece of bread into his mouth, he turned and saw his father watching him. There was a quick smile, like a flash of sunlight rippling off the waters of a pond.

Benjamin smiled back at him. He had learned, hadn't he? He hadn't repeated the mistakes he had made with Joshua. The relationship between him and Matthew had become a treasure of immeasurable worth.

The old Benjamin Steed had been all hard rock and thick logs. It had taken the Spirit a full six years to remodel the building into something more serviceable. But just a week ago, in this very room, during the temple dedicatory services, the Lord had whispered that he was pleased with the changes in Benjamin Steed. "Benjamin, my son," had come the still, small voice, "be still and know that I am God. I am well pleased with your desires and with your labors."

This was why today he could look at age spots on his hands, note the protruding veins, and still feel a great contentment. He reached out and took his wife's hand. She looked up in surprise; then her mouth softened as she saw the love in his eyes. He gave her a gentle pull, bringing her shoulder up firmly against his.

"What?" she mouthed.

He shrugged, knowing he couldn't tell her even if he wanted to.

"Hi."

Every person sitting in the Steed parlor turned in surprise.

Melissa gave a little wave. She had come in through the back door, and obviously no one had heard her entry.

Her mother spoke first. "Did you forget something?"

She shook her head quickly, momentarily flustered by the small stir her return was causing. "No. I got young Carl and little David asleep." She gave a little shrug. "Carl's working at the stable. He said he wouldn't mind if I came back and visited for a while."

"Wonderful, Melissa." Lydia slid closer to Nathan and patted the sofa next to her. "Come sit down. We're all just sittin' here being lazy."

Removing her shawl and tossing it across the table in the hallway, Melissa moved over to take the place offered. "Have you got your three to sleep too?" she asked Lydia.

Lydia laughed. "I doubt it. Matthew took them home. Supposedly he's getting them to bed, but . . ." She shook her head ruefully.

Benjamin sat in his favorite chair in the corner, a big wingback they had brought from Vermont to Palmyra, then to Kirtland. He shook his head. "You'll be lucky if the house still sits square on its foundation when you get home. When he's with them, Matthew is more kid than the grandkids."

Melissa laughed, then looked around. "Where's Jessica?"

"She and Rebecca are trying to get little Rachel to sleep," Mary Ann said. "I think she's coming down with something. Her head felt a little hot to me after dinner."

Nathan leaned back on the sofa, stretching out his legs to their full length. He was pleased Melissa had been able to come back. Sunday dinner at Grandma and Grandpa's house twice a month had become a family tradition. Following the afternoon worship services, they would all gather—sons, daughters, daughters-in-law, a son-in-law, and grandchildren. Fifteen of them in all. After a light supper, and after the dishes were done, they would gather in the parlor while the children played.

Melissa's husband, Carlton Rogers—or Carl, as everyone called him—always came and seemed to enjoy it. He was not a member of the Church, and when he was with them the family made a special effort to avoid topics of religion or any discussion of people Carl did not know. He would join in the conversation, seeming relaxed and comfortable. But invariably he was the first to suggest it was time to go.

Nathan frowned slightly as he watched his sister throw back her head and laugh at something Lydia was saying. When Melissa and Carl had first begun to court, the Rogers family had been neutral toward the Church. Didn't bother him none, Carl claimed, if Melissa was a Mormon. But in the last year or so Kirtland had seen a great influx of Latter-day Saints. Many came dirt-poor. It had thrown a burden on the community as well as the Church. Many of the locals had soured, blaming Joseph Smith and the Church for not doing more. Hezekiah Rogers, Carl's father, had become particularly bitter, and that had undoubtedly influenced his son. In the last month or two, Carl had started to dig in his heels whenever Melissa tried to participate in Church activities. She had missed the temple dedicatory services the previous week, something which nearly broke her heart. But he wouldn't budge. And today, being Easter Sunday, she had especially wanted to join the family at the worship services. He had insisted they attend church with his parents.

At that moment Melissa turned and caught Nathan's eye. She smiled quickly. She and Nathan were only two years apart, and there had always been a deep bond of affection between them. It made him ache a little inside when he saw the hurt in her eyes and the eagerness with which she sought opportunities such as this tonight.

She reached across Lydia and touched Nathan's arm. "Will you tell me about what happened in the temple today? I heard Mama and Lydia talking about it earlier."

But just then, from behind them, someone spoke. "Wait for me if you're going to talk about that."

Everyone turned. Rebecca was standing in the hallway.

Mary Ann leaned forward to see Rebecca more clearly. "How's Rachel?"

"Sleeping. I think she was just very tired. Jessica's coming."

"Good," Melissa said, moving over closer to Lydia. "Come

on, there's room for one more here. I was just asking Nathan to tell me about today."

Rebecca came and sat next to Melissa. Nathan watched his two sisters. There was seven years' difference in their ages. With marriage and two children, Melissa had put on some weight. Her face had filled out in contrast to Rebecca's more youthful slenderness. But the greater contrast was in their coloring— Melissa with the dark hair and brown eyes that always reminded Nathan of Joshua, and Rebecca, more fair of skin and with pale blue eyes.

Melissa turned back to Nathan. "Please tell me, Nathan," she urged. "I never get to hear much anymore."

Nathan looked to his father. "We were all there. Pa, why don't you tell her what happened?"

Benjamin frowned a little, but Nathan could tell he was pleased his son had deferred to him.

They all quieted, turning in anticipation to Benjamin, who was collecting his thoughts. Finally he leaned forward, hands on his knees. "Well, the services themselves were wonderful, but nothing unusual. But then"—he leaned back, letting his eyes rise to look at the ceiling—"when we were finished with the sacrament, Joseph asked that the curtains around the western pulpits be lowered."

Melissa looked a little surprised. "He lowered them while you were sitting there?"

Benjamin's head went up and down. "They completely enclose the pulpits. Once the curtains were down, Joseph and Oliver Cowdery retired behind them."

"We all sat waiting," Lydia said. "We sensed that something very important was going on, but we didn't know exactly what. They were behind the veil for what seemed the longest time."

"Finally, Joseph and Oliver came out." Benjamin's voice went suddenly soft. "The moment we saw them, we knew *something* had happened. Their faces seemed to glow, and they were very excited."

"So what was it?" Melissa asked eagerly.

For several moments no one answered. Those that had been there looked at each other, as though acknowledging that words could do little to convey what had happened. Then Mary Ann looked at her daughter. "It was the most marvelous thing. The Savior appeared."

Melissa's mouth opened slightly. She was staring at her mother. "The Savior?" she whispered.

Mary Ann went to speak, then couldn't. Benjamin stood and came over to sit by her. He took her hand, then turned to the others. "Joseph said he and Oliver bowed themselves in solemn and silent prayer. When they finished they stood, and that's when it happened." His voice dropped even lower. The awe had returned. "Joseph said the Savior was absolutely glorious to behold. He stood on the breastwork of the pulpits, and under his feet it was like there was pavement made of pure gold."

Rebecca couldn't hold it in any longer now either. She took Melissa's hand in both of hers. "Oh, I wish you could have been there, Melissa, to hear them tell about it. Joseph said the Master's eyes were like a flame of fire and that his face shone like the very sun itself."

"No, even more brightly than the sun," Lydia corrected her. "He said his face shone more brightly than the sun."

"Yes, that's right. Can you imagine it? And we were right there, just a few feet away."

Melissa's eyes were wide. "Did you hear him?"

"No," Rebecca replied. "The curtains are made of heavy canvas. But I think it was more than that; I think this was a vision from the Lord and could be heard only with spiritual ears. And remember, at this point, we didn't know what was happening."

Lydia jumped in again. "According to Joseph and Oliver, the Savior said that we should rejoice because he had come to accept the temple. He also said that as long as his people do not pollute his holy house, he will manifest himself unto us and appear to his servants from time to time." Tears suddenly welled up, and her voice caught. "The Savior of all the world, and we were *right there*."

Melissa's eyes were suddenly moist now too. "Oh," she whispered, "how I wish I could have been there!"

"That's not all," Nathan said slowly.

"It's not?"

"No. When the Savior was finished, the vision closed, but almost immediately thereafter another one opened." He had to stop. He was remembering the way Joseph and Oliver had looked when the curtains were lifted. "This time it was Moses who appeared to them."

That rocked Melissa back. "Moses? You mean the Moses of the Bible?"

"Yes," Nathan exclaimed. "He told Joseph he had been sent to give the keys of the gathering of Israel. Now they could begin the gathering of Israel from the four corners of the earth, including leading the ten tribes from the land of the north."

Benjamin smiled at Melissa's bewilderment. He understood her feelings well enough. They had all been dazed, and still were. And they had had several hours to digest the idea. "That's not all, either," he went on.

"There's more?" She was reeling.

Lydia, Rebecca, Mary Ann, Nathan—all were nodding at her, but they left it to Benjamin to tell.

"After Moses left, two more of the ancient prophets appeared to them. One called Elias appeared and committed to Joseph the dispensation of the gospel of Abraham. The other was the prophet Elijah."

"The same Elijah who was taken to heaven in a chariot of fire without tasting death," Rebecca inserted quickly.

"Do you remember the promise found in Malachi, the last book of the Old Testament?" Mary Ann asked eagerly. "Malachi said that before the great and dreadful day of the Lord would come, Elijah would return to the earth and turn the hearts of the fathers to the children and the hearts of the children to their fathers. He told Joseph and Oliver that his coming was a sign that the great and dreadful day was near."

Melissa sat back. "I can't believe it. And you were all right there." Her countenance fell. "And I was sitting listening to a preacher drone on and on about hell and the torments of the damned. I'll bet he didn't spend more than five minutes on the Resurrection."

Nathan stood up, moving over to the fireplace where he could look more easily on the group. "Do you know what today is? Besides Sunday, I mean."

"Easter," Lydia said.

"Yes, but something else too." When no one answered, he gave a little smile of triumph. "It's Passover season for the Jews. Jesus was crucified during Passover week, so Easter and Passover always come at the same time."

"Yes." Melissa was puzzled. "So?"

Nathan, eager now, rushed on. "The Jews have a custom, or a tradition, during Passover. They believe that when Elijah comes as Malachi promised, it will be during the feast of the Passover."

"Oh," Benjamin said, the light starting to dawn in his eyes.

"That's not all. Each family hopes Elijah will come to their home, so they always set a place at the table and leave an empty chair. It's called Elijah's chair."

Melissa still seemed puzzled, but beside her Rebecca was nodding excitedly. "So," she said, her voice rising, "Elijah came during Passover."

"Yes," Nathan finished, "but he came to the house of the Lord." He looked momentarily sheepish. "Sidney Rigdon told me all this, that's how I know."

Mary Ann looked at her son. "That's not the only significance of what happened today."

"It's not?" Benjamin said.

"No. It is Easter Sunday. This is the day Jesus rose from the tomb. This is the day he was resurrected. What more appropriate day for him to appear on earth again?"

Nathan felt an overwhelming rush of gratitude and awe. He looked around at his family. "I think we ought to kneel in prayer and thank God for what has happened today."

"Yes," Benjamin said, "an excellent suggestion. Nathan, will you lead us?"

He nodded and they got up, then knelt down at their places. A hush fell over the room as Nathan took a moment to collect his thoughts. Then in a low voice he began.

"Our Father who art in heaven, hallowed be thy name. On this very special day, we kneel together as a family to thank thee for what has transpired. We know that it was on this day many years ago that thy Beloved Son rose from the grave and broke the bands of death for us. Oh, how glorious was his life, and oh, how wondrous was his rising in the Resurrection! We thank thee from the deepest longings of our souls that thou didst so love the world that thou gavest him for us that we might be saved.

"We know that others in our family have preceded us in death—our sisters and our brother who were taken home to thee while still in their youth." He paused, sensing his mother's pain as she remembered the children she had lost. "Oh, how grateful we are to know that because of thine Only Begotten Son they shall live again and we shall see them in the flesh!"

He took a deep breath. "Dear Father, we are humbled to have been in thy holy house this day, when thy Beloved Son, in whom thou art well pleased, chose to return to earth and reaffirm to all the world that he does live! That he still reigns in power and glory over his church and kingdom!"

Suddenly Nathan found it difficult to speak. There was so much he wanted to say, to express—their gratitude that angels had again come to earth, that prophecy was being fulfilled, that God spoke to men again. But the thoughts of the resurrected Lord being there—just feet away—in all his majesty and glory, completely overwhelmed him.

"O God," he finally choked out, "how we thank thee! Oh, how we thank thee! And this prayer we give to thee in the name of our beloved Savior and Redeemer, amen."

Mmm, Mama, this pie is wonderful." Rebecca was finishing the last bite. There were instant murmurs of assent from the others.

"Thank you, Rebecca." Mary Ann was justly proud of her apple pie. It too had become part of their Sunday evening tradition. They would talk for a while; then, as the time drew closer for the ones who lived elsewhere to return to their homes, she would bring out the apple pie and large glasses of cold milk.

Jessica, finally satisfied that her young daughter was asleep, had joined them about a half hour earlier. She stood and began collecting the dishes. Melissa speared the last piece of her pie with her fork, made short work of it, then finished her glass of milk. As she handed the dishes to Jessica, she turned to her younger sister, who still sat by her on the sofa. "By the way, Miss Rebecca Steed, I want to hear more about this young man everyone is telling me about."

Rebecca started, then instantly color touched her cheeks.

She ducked her head as Nathan laughed aloud at her discomfort. For a moment she seemed twelve again and the shy little Becca they all had loved to tease. The dimple in her one cheek showed prominently now.

"Come on," Melissa urged. "Everyone in town is talking about what a handsome couple you make. Am I going to be the last to know?"

"There's nothing to tell," Rebecca murmured.

Benjamin snorted in derision. "Nothing besides the fact that we have an extra houseguest about half the time now."

Rebecca's head snapped up at the betrayal. "Papa, that's not true. He's only been here two or three times."

Now it was Mary Ann's turn to look incredulous. "How many times?"

Rebecca was blushing furiously now. "All right, maybe four or five times."

"Arthur . . . what's his name?" Melissa said, more gently now.

"Wilkinson."

"He's a nice boy," Lydia said. "We like him."

Nathan hooted. "Like him?" Lydia had had Rebecca and her beau to their house for dinner on three different occasions. Lydia was definitely playing matchmaker on this one.

Jessica had come back from taking the dishes to the kitchen and stood in the doorway. "I like him too," she said.

Nathan's eyes turned mischievous. "You *are* eighteen now, Rebecca. Until Arthur came along, Pa and me were thinking we'd have to go up to Cleveland or somewhere and hog-tie some young man and drag him home for you."

Lydia slapped his arm. "Nathan!"

Rebecca sniffed disdainfully at her brother. "Don't you have to go help Matthew put the kids to bed or build a fence or something?"

But Melissa didn't want to get thrown off course by Nathan's banter. "So," she said, leaning forward, "how serious is it?"

Rebecca shrugged.

"He's talking marriage," Mary Ann said softly, watching Rebecca closely.

Melissa clapped her hands. "Really?"

Rebecca finally looked up and met Melissa's eyes. "*He's talking marriage,*" she said slowly.

That took both Melissa and Lydia by surprise. Melissa, with her characteristic bluntness, blurted out, "But you're not?"

Rebecca was studying her hands carefully now. "I'm not sure."

"You're not sure!" Lydia cried in dismay. "But why not, Rebecca? Arthur is a fine young man."

Watching Rebecca carefully, Nathan had a quick flash of discernment. The time for teasing—and for pushing her on this—had passed. "Honey," he said, patting his wife's knee. "Rebecca's got to make up her own mind."

Lydia gave him a sharp look, but Melissa totally ignored his attempt to deflect the questions. "Why aren't you sure?" she bored in.

Rebecca glanced quickly at Lydia, then at Melissa. Then she turned to her mother. An unseen something passed between them, and Mary Ann gave an almost imperceptible nod. Rebecca turned back. There was a quiet determination in her eyes. "I'm not sure he's the right one."

Melissa's lips tightened. "It's because he's not a Mormon, isn't it?" She was not quite able to keep the stiffness out of her voice.

The question hung in the air. No one moved. Though she was frustrated by Carl's stubbornness on the subject of religion, Melissa was fiercely defensive of him. Nathan watched his little sister—not so little anymore—out of the corner of his eye. He knew what was going through Rebecca's mind. She didn't want to hurt Melissa, but the fact that Arthur was not a member was exactly what was troubling Rebecca. She had watched what was happening in Melissa's marriage, and it troubled her.

Surprisingly, it was Benjamin who finally spoke. He too had

been watching Rebecca closely. "I think Arthur is a fine young man. But if Rebecca hasn't made up her mind yet, let's not be pushing her on it."

Melissa nodded and forced a quick smile. She started to speak, then thought better of it and stood up. "Well, I'd better be getting home. Carl will think I'm staying for the night."

Lydia got to her feet quickly. "We'd better go too, Nathan, and see if Matthew has finally gotten the children to sleep."

Jessica was still standing in the doorway that led to the kitchen. She straightened. "Before you go there's something I need to say."

They all turned in surprise. There was a fleeting smile, then she gave a deprecating little laugh, looking at Melissa and Lydia. "Maybe you ought to sit down again."

As Lydia and Melissa sat back down, Lydia shot Nathan a questioning look. He shrugged. This had caught him by surprise as much as anyone. Nathan's mind flashed back to the first day he had seen Jessica. It had been in a little sod hut in Kaw Township, in Jackson County, Missouri. He had been shocked by her appearance: a left eye badly discolored, lower lip cracked and puffy, the whole side of her jaw swollen and dark—all the marks of Joshua's fury at her refusal to aid his scheme to cheat in a game of poker. But Nathan had been almost as surprised at her plainness. He hadn't consciously thought about it much; he just assumed Joshua would have chosen a handsome woman. And Jessica Roundy was not a handsome woman. She was *plain*— that had been the first word that came to Nathan's mind that day. Her hair was straight and cut square across the back at the neck. The slimness of her body was hidden beneath the folds of a heavy, homespun dress. Her eyes were unusually large and perhaps her best feature, but they had been so filled with sadness, they were almost haunting.

Now, as he watched her move across the room to stand where she could better see them all, Nathan marveled a little that he had once thought she was plain. *Handsome* was probably still not the best word for her, but somehow over the past five years she had become a lovely woman. She had an inner serenity that seemed to soften her features and fill her with grace. And she had grown very close to her adopted family.

But there was little serenity in her deportment now. Her hands were nearly fluttering as she faced them. She took a deep breath. Her shoulders lifted, then fell again as she expelled the air slowly. "I . . ." She shook her head, blinking rapidly.

Nathan stared. She was on the verge of tears! He had to fight not to outright gape at her. Nathan had seen her cry only once, when he had blessed her and promised her she would have children. Jessica just never showed emotion. Not even in the toughest of circumstances.

Mary Ann leaned forward. "What is it, Jessie?" she asked gently.

She took another deep breath, then her head came up. "I don't want you to take this wrong. You have been wonderful to me and Rachel."

Benjamin's head came up slowly. Nathan heard Lydia's intake of breath next to him. Melissa and Rebecca were both staring. "*Have been?*" Benjamin echoed.

Now it came out in a rush, her words tumbling over each other, those large dark eyes pleading for their understanding. "Ever since the temple dedication last week I've not been able to get it out of my mind. It just keeps coming back and coming back. I can hardly sleep at night for thinkin' about it."

"Thinkin' about what?" Lydia asked.

Jessica seemed not to hear. "I've tried to tell myself it's crazy. But it won't leave me be. Not until I made up my mind last night. Now I know it's right. I don't necessarily like it, but I *know* it's right."

"Know *what* is right?" Benjamin exploded. "What are you talkin' about, Jessie?"

Her chin came up. Her eyes were shining now, and she bit softly on her lower lip. "I'm talkin' about my decision to go back to Missouri."

That there's the Tybee Island lighthouse. Way off there."

Joshua Steed turned, looking in the direction the young man indicated. For a moment there was nothing in the thick darkness, then two or three miles to the right of the ship—the starboard side, Joshua reminded himself—he saw a thin beam of light swing slowly toward them. It flashed directly at them for a moment, then disappeared again.

"That means we're almost to the mouth of the river."

Joshua stifled an involuntary yawn. "So how much longer?"

The lad was not yet sixteen, maybe a year or two less. He spoke with a heavy British accent, as did most of the crew. "Savannah's another fifteen, maybe twenty miles upriver." He squinted at the eastern sky, where the first streaks of dawn were just starting to lighten the sky. It was going to be a beautiful April day along the Atlantic seaboard. "Three hours, maybe four. Be there by ten o'clock sure, mate."

"Good." Joshua stretched, working out the kinks in his body. In addition to getting back on solid ground again, he looked forward to sleeping in a man-size bed. Even the first-class cabins on the big packet ship were a full two handspans shorter than Joshua's six-foot height. He had not had a decent night's sleep since he had boarded four days earlier.

It had surprised Joshua a little when they sailed from New Orleans with him as the only passenger, but this was a British packet ship. Up until 1818, ships waited in port for a full load of cargo and passengers and generally refused to sail until good weather prevailed. Then one of the British lines had come up with the idea of the packet ships. Running on regular schedules, the packets sailed empty or full, good weather and bad. The service had become so popular that there were now several shipping lines regularly crisscrossing the Atlantic and hopping between the islands of the Caribbean.

Joshua moved away, threading his way between the barrels and crates lashed down to the deck. He went all the way back to the stern before he stopped. He had come here often during the voyage. It was his favorite spot. He liked to hear the soft hiss of the water slipping past the wooden hull and to watch the soft phosphorescence of the ship's wake in the darkness.

He reached in his coat pocket and took out a cigar. Without thinking, he got his knife out, cut off the end, and stuck the cigar in his mouth. There was nothing out here with which to light it, but he didn't really care. His mind was already focusing on the day ahead. He was a little surprised at the eagerness in him. He didn't know one thing about cotton, and yet before the week was out, if all went right, he would be purchasing a shipload of it, maybe more. He took the cigar from his mouth and laughed inwardly. If things turned out as planned, he could very likely end up a really wealthy man, and not just by Jackson County standards either. For a man who would turn twenty-nine in another week, that wasn't bad. Not bad at all.

He found the prospect exhilarating. He liked nice things. He liked the look in men's eyes when he passed by. He liked the power that accompanied wealth. Most of all, he liked knowing life had not beaten him. Considering that he had lost more than ninety percent of his freight business in a poker game nearly five years earlier, the fact that he was about to start negotiations for an entire shipload of Georgia cotton proved it without a doubt: Life had not beaten him. Jessica had not beaten him.

He jammed the cigar back in his mouth and chomped down hard on it. *Fool woman!* It still sent his blood boiling when he thought about how close he had come to taking the slick gambler from Pittsburgh for the whole pile of money on the table. Instead, his wife had brought him within a muskrat's whisker of losing everything he owned, everything he had worked for. All he had asked of her was to stand behind the bedroom door and signal him as to who had the better hand, Joshua or the Pittsburgh man. But she had walked away. If she had even let him know she was leaving . . . But she hadn't. And he had lost.

But he had brought his business back, inch by sweat-fought inch. Half of America was on the move. Independence was the trailhead for both the Oregon and the Santa Fe trails. The population along America's western frontier was burgeoning and needed increasing numbers of goods from the East. More and more the East was becoming a lucrative market for the wheat, corn, and furs of the West. And Joshua's natural aggressiveness and growing shrewdness gave him a larger and larger share of the wheels that kept the merchandise moving in both directions.

And for a time the freight business had kept him satisfied. He paid off his gambling debts, bought new stock and equipment—more than thirty wagons now had his name stenciled on their sides. But then the restlessness had started. Things took on a stultifying sameness—bale the furs, crate the goods, load the wagons, crack the whip over the teams, tote up the returns in the big ledger books. He began to crave something more, like a man satiated with food but still hungering for some elusive dish.

Frowning, he took the cigar out of his mouth and fished for

a fleck of tobacco that had stuck on the tip of his tongue. He knew it wasn't just business that brought him here. This last-minute decision to come to Savannah was just one more manifestation of the growing sense of discontent he had been feeling for the past couple of years.

Eighteen months ago he had opened a second stable and warehouse center in St. Louis. It prospered quickly, and soon he tired of it too. He had more and more money and less and less satisfaction. When four St. Louis businessmen approached him, he was ripe for listening. They were thinking of bringing a textile mill to St. Louis. The expanding West was paying a premium price for cloth goods exported from the East. It was time to break the tight monopoly on textiles held by the New England mills. They were looking for a partner. One with capital. One who could freight in the heavy machinery from Pittsburgh. Someone who could keep a supply of cotton coming up the Mississippi so that the machines wouldn't stay idle. Someone who could then get the finished cloth to widely scattered markets.

Joshua had agreed almost instantly.

He could have bought the cotton in New Orleans. That had been the original plan. But there had been a friendly poker game during the riverboat trip to that city. One of the cotton brokers let it slip that he got the best of his cotton from Savannah. At the mention of Savannah, another man burst into rapturous praise of the city's beauty and charm. He told of huge plantations with cotton fields stretching farther than a man could walk in half a day. That night Joshua sent off a quick letter to his partners. Two days later he was on a ship headed for Great Britain, with intermediate stops at Savannah, Georgia; Charleston, South Carolina; and New York City.

Joshua looked around. Sunrise was still a half hour away, but on either side of the ship, flat marshlands and tidal waterways were discernible now—Georgia on the left, South Carolina on the right. He straightened. It was time to get some breakfast and pack. Long before the sun reached its zenith, he would be in Savannah.

The ceiling was just a little lower than six feet high, and Joshua had to keep his head bent as he moved about. That was another thing he looked forward to with relish—more room. For a man used to crossing half a continent in an open wagon, even the best and biggest of the first-class cabins on the ship was cramped and terribly confining.

He finished cleaning up the breakfast he had cooked for himself over the small brass pot filled with hot coals, then he set about to do his packing. It felt funny, not having the constant rolling and pitching of the ship beneath his feet. Surprisingly, he had gotten his sea legs quickly and experienced no more than some temporary seasickness when they ran through a squall off the Florida Keys. Now it seemed strange to have the ship steady and level in the river's current.

He took down his clothes and folded them neatly on his bunk. Next came his toilet articles. He moved about the cabin, his eyes moving back and forth to make sure he didn't miss anything. Finally satisfied he had everything, he dropped to one knee by the side of his bunk. Below it was a purchase he had made in New Orleans, a large leather valise with three sturdy buckles.

He placed it on the fold-down table used for meals and started to undo the buckles. Slowly he lifted the top of the valise. For a long moment he just looked at the plain brown package in the case. He was filled with a curious mixture of emotions now. Part of him felt faintly disgusted. Joshua Steed was not a man given to impulse, and yet he had bought this on impulse. Another part of him was puzzled. Sentiment was not part of his disposition either, and yet even the sight of the package filled him with a strange sense of sadness, of longing for what now would not and could not ever be.

He reached down and lifted the package. Slowly he untied the string. He let it fall back into the valise, followed by the outer paper, then the rolls of soft cotton fabric that the saleswoman had used to pack it. When he was finished he set it down carefully on the table and stepped back.

The doll was made of the finest German porcelain. It was a young girl, about seventeen or eighteen. In one hand was a bouquet of flowers. She was studying them intently, her eyes showing pleasure, her mouth half smiling. Her other hand held a parasol, which lay on her shoulder. Counting the parasol, she stood nearly twelve inches high. Her face was exquisite. Dark black curls fell in abundance from beneath a pale blue bonnet. The hands were finely crafted with long, slender fingers. The dress was also pale blue and full length. It was crisscrossed with real satin ribbons. The flowers in the bouquet were tiny, some of the blossoms no larger than the tip of a horseshoe nail, and yet every petal was formed to perfection.

When he had seen it in the store window, he had stood there for nearly five minutes, transfixed. Twice the saleswoman came to the window and smiled her encouragement to him. Finally he went in. He had gasped at the price. Fifty-five dollars! For a doll! That was six months' wages for a working man. Then, going against every rational part of him, he bought it.

He crossed the room and pulled out a chair. He sat down, his eyes still on the doll but his thoughts turning back. At the store he had told himself he would give it to the daughter he had not seen since about five months after her birth. She would be four years old now. And he was surprised how often he thought of her lately. What did she look like? Did she have any of his features? On two different occasions Joshua had ferried across the river, waited until nightfall, then made his way to the settlement of the Mormons in the Missouri River bottoms. From the trees he had watched, hoping to catch even a glimpse of Rachel. Both times he had failed. Twice he had sent money over anonymously so that his daughter would not starve.

Even now the anger began to churn inside him again. Jessica had turned his daughter into a Mormon, and on top of that, she had taken her away. He felt cheated. Robbed. A man had a right to see his own child.

And then he shook his head. He knew there was blame on his part too. He still burned with shame when he thought about that terrible night when he had struck Jessica. Then struck her again and again. He had been mean-ugly drunk and out of his mind with fury at her for her betrayal of him. But those rationalizations weren't good enough. From the time he was a toddler at his mother's knee, he had been taught that no man worthy to be called a Steed ever struck a woman. Not in anger, not in fun.

He had tried to tell her that later, that he was shamed beyond measure, that down deep in the core of his being he had vowed that never again would liquor take control of him. But by then she had fled to the Mormons, and worse, she had become one of them. There was no reasoning with her, not from him, not from her father. Joe Smith and all the craziness he stood for had infected her so deeply that she refused to change. And so he had divorced her.

He stood and moved his chair over closer to the table and sat down again. He leaned forward, peering more closely at the doll's delicate loveliness. Along with the restlessness of the past two years had come something else. Joshua was finding that he had a growing tendency to be brutally honest with himself. He didn't always like the result, but he could no longer tolerate his old tendency to hide behind excuses of his own making. And he knew that that was what all these thoughts of Rachel were. Excuses.

He leaned back, closing his eyes, letting his mind go back. Back to the summer of 1827, back to Palmyra and the dry goods store on Main Street. He should have seen it from the first instant he had laid eyes on the doll. The girl was Lydia McBride. He opened his eyes again. It was, the girl was Lydia. Nine years had blurred his memory of her, but in his mind the face was Lydia's—so lovely that it drove out everything else from a man's thoughts. It was Lydia's slender hands and wistful smile, her slim body and dancing brown eyes. And the porcelain made the doll's likeness to Lydia all the more appropriate. For when all was said and done, that's how Lydia had been for him—beautiful beyond imagination but cold, stiff, aloof; smiling daintily, but not for Joshua Steed.

It was not love anymore that bothered him. He was past the infantile fantasizing about Lydia that had driven the wedge between him and Jessica. He knew now that he never had a chance with the Palymra beauty. Not from the very first day. He had even come to the point at which he could honestly admit to himself that Nathan was the better man for her. No, it was not love anymore that haunted him. It was something much more terrible than that.

For nearly the past two years Joshua had had a reoccurring nightmare. It was coming less frequently now, but it was always the same. It began with the image of Lydia's face. At first it was small, far away in the distance. He would feel a flash of joy and call out to her. Then the face would begin to approach him. It was always her face, no other part of her body. But it was not a face filled with happiness, or one that smiled like the doll. As the face loomed larger and larger, he could see that her mouth was twisted in shock, that the eyes were filled with horror and revulsion. As he watched, she would open her mouth in a soundless scream that seemed to go on and on and on.

For a long time Joshua had not known what the dream meant. Then one day it hit him with terrible clarity. Nathan Steed had come to Missouri with the Mormon army in the summer of 1834. Against all counsel, he had snuck across the Missouri River into Jackson County to look for the older brother he had not seen for almost seven years. Jackson County was still seething with anti-Mormon sentiment. Four men caught Nathan. When he claimed he was from New York and knew Joshua Steed, the men had brought him to Joshua.

Abruptly, Joshua stood. In quick, jerky motions, he took the cotton material and wrapped it around the doll again. He rewrapped the brown paper around her and tied up the string. He swung around, taking the clothes from the bed. He packed them in around the doll, covering any sight of the package. His toilet articles went in next, then the top of the valise went down and was buckled on tight. Only then did Joshua stop. He was breathing hard, trying to keep his thoughts focused on his packing.

But it didn't work. Never again would he be able to get that terrible memory from his mind. Nathan bound to a chair. Himself shocked to see the brother he hadn't seen for so long. They had talked that night, he and Nathan. Suddenly both were angry. Emotions exploded. Words were hurled like spears. Joshua had walked out. As he passed the man with the bullwhip he had said simply, "This man's lying to you. I've never seen him before."

Joshua knew that what he saw in the dream was Lydia's face at one precise instant in time. It was that instant when Nathan bared his back and Lydia saw him for the first time. The effects of a bullwhip on naked flesh are a sight that inspires horror and shock and revulsion.

Joshua had walked out on Nathan that night. He had not seen the whipping, never seen Nathan's back. Except in his mind. But that was enough. He knew Lydia's revulsion was not only for the scarred and battered flesh. It was for Joshua. It was for the man who had done this to a brother. And what was equally unsettling to him was that he knew if he ever saw his mother's face, or Melissa's or Rebecca's, they would be filled with the same horror. Their eyes, like Lydia's, would be filled with loathing and abhorrence. And that filled him with a sadness that was surprisingly sharp.

He picked up the valise, gave one last look around the cabin, then stepped out into the sunshine. He walked past the young sailor and an older crew member, barely nodding at their greeting. He walked to the bow of the ship, set the valise down, and stared upriver. Far off in the distance, on some green bluffs that lined the riverbank, he could see the outline of buildings. He looked a little closer. There were larger buildings along the river itself. They were in sight of Savannah.

—·—

Joshua sent the carriage driver on to the hotel with his bag. After four days of confinement, he wanted to walk. He wanted to see Savannah from the ground, not from a passing carriage. Now he was on River Street, the heart of Savannah's trade district. Several oceangoing ships were tied up along the wharves. Rows of four- and five-story cotton warehouses looked down on him. He let his eyes drop to the street. He had seen cobblestone walks in Palmyra and cobblestone streets in Cincinnati, but they were nothing like the large, round stones that were laid into the soil here. Some were twelve or more inches long. They looked like they had come from a streambed.

"Those are ballast rocks."

Joshua turned in surprise. "Pardon?"

A young boy was leaning up against the corner of the nearest warehouse. "Those are ballast rocks. Mostly from England, brought in the bottom of the ships to give them ballast. They dump them out here when they load the ships with cotton or rice for the return trip. So we make our streets out of them."

Joshua was a little taken aback. "You don't say."

The boy nodded wisely, then straightened and sauntered over to join him. Joshua guessed him to be eleven years old, maybe twelve. He was dressed in a cotton shirt, and knickers held up by suspenders. A hat, French beret style, was perched jauntily on his head. Bright brown eyes, wise beyond their years, peered up at Joshua. Suddenly the boy turned, pointing up at the warehouses. "We got a lot of wrought iron here too. Same thing. Iron is brought in as ballast." He shrugged matter-of-factly. "We got to do something with it."

Joshua suppressed a smile and let his eyes follow where the boy was pointing. He had already noted the wrought-iron balconies. They had caught his eye because iron railings and balconies out west were a luxury not yet affordable for even the most well-to-do.

He turned back. "And how is it you know all this stuff about ballast?"

The boy removed his hat, revealing a thick shock of deep-auburn-colored hair. He wiped his brow with his sleeve. Though it was still not nine o'clock, the day was already warm and humid. He put his hat back on. "I know everything there is to know about Savannah."

"I see," Joshua responded, keeping a straight face. The lad's impudence was startling, and yet Joshua liked it.

"You from out west?"

That startled Joshua. "Yes, how'd you guess?"

He shrugged again, and Joshua was beginning to recognize it as his trademark—enigmatic, nonchalant, brushing aside the inconsequential. "You talk like a Northerner, but you came in on a ship from New Orleans."

"Oh." His admiration for the boy's quickness moved up a notch. "I'm from a place called Independence, Missouri. Ever heard of it?"

He looked offended. "Of course. It's on the Missouri River."

An eyebrow lifted. This boy was just one surprise after another.

"That's close to Indian Territory." It wasn't phrased as a question.

"Yes," replied Joshua. "Twelve, fifteen miles maybe."

For the first time a boyishness crept into his voice. "Have you seen real Indians, then?"

Now it was Joshua's turn to be a little nonchalant. "Yep. See them all the time. Osage, Choctaw, Pawnee, Oglala Sioux."

Impressed, the boy sized Joshua up. He seemed to make up his mind. "Seems to me, a gentleman like you, being in Savannah for the first time, could use a boy like me, that knows all about the city, to show him around."

Joshua laughed right out loud. "I don't suppose this 'guide service' is free, is it?"

The chin came up, and there was a flash of defiance in his eyes. "I'll not be chargin' you anything."

For a moment Joshua felt guilty. Maybe he had misjudged the boy. But then an impish look played around the corner of the lad's eyes. "However, when we're done, if you think my services are worthy of some thanks, then . . ." He shrugged again, as if it mattered not in the least to him.

Delighted, Joshua clapped him on the shoulder. This boy had already lifted his spirits, and that was worth something to him. "Fair enough, lad. What's your name?"

"Will. William Donovan Mendenhall."

"Pleased to meet you, Will. My name is Joshua Steed." Curious, Joshua decided to do a little probing of his own. "You don't talk like a Southerner."

"My mama and my daddy were originally from Maryland. We've only been here about seven years."

"Oh."

"Come on, let's start with Factors' Walk."

"Factors' Walk?"

"Yes. Don't you know about cotton factors?"

Joshua's look was answer enough for him.

"A factor works with a plantation owner, gives him the cash he needs to raise a good crop, finds a market for it, makes sure he gets the best price."

"So he's kind of like a cotton broker."

Will nodded. "Yep. You here to buy cotton?"

"That's right."

"Then we'll have to find you a cotton factor."

———◆———

Lying on the southern bank of the Savannah River, just one block south of River Street, Factors' Walk was more like a tunnel than a street. On its northern side, the side closest to the river, the warehouses formed a solid wall of buildings three and four stories high. On the southern side a natural bluff rose sharply away from the riverbank. This bluff had been partly cut away and shored up with a sheer, twenty-foot-high wall of stone. The space between the wall of stone and the wall of buildings formed a deep, narrow channel running parallel for several blocks with River Street. But what made the narrow way most unusual was that all along the row of warehouses, at the second-story level, there was a continuous balcony with door-ways facing Factors' Walk. From each doorway a steel catwalk ran from the warehouses to the bluff, bridging the street below in a dozen places.

Joshua and Will were standing on the top of the bluff, near one of the catwalks. Will grunted softly. "Look," he said. "Now you'll see why they call it Factors' Walk." He pointed off to their left. About a hundred yards away, a wagon was turning off Bay Street. It had huge wheels and creaked under the load of several bales of raw cotton—each bale as big as a sofa and weighing nearly five hundred pounds.

As the driver turned the wagon into the narrowness of Factors' Walk, the clatter of the steel-rimmed wheels came reverberating down the passageway. Evidently the sound served as a signal, for almost immediately warehouse doors started opening everywhere. Men in suit coats or shirt sleeves stepped out of the buildings and walked onto the catwalks.

Directly across from them, a tall man with a pipe clamped hard in his teeth came out, blinking at the brightness of the sun. He was just putting on his long suit coat. He stopped for a moment, looking in the direction of the wagon, then buttoned his coat, puffed once on his pipe, and moved out onto the catwalk until he was directly over the street below.

"That's Mr. Richard Wesley," Will said in a hushed voice. "He's the best factor in all of Savannah."

The other men were also out in the middle of their catwalks now, leaning over the rails to peer at the load of cotton as the wagon passed beneath them. The wagon was nearly to where Joshua and Will stood. Joshua saw Wesley's eyes narrow for a moment as he scanned the bales. There was a slight flicker of one finger.

Will gave a little exclamation of excitement. "Did you see that?" he said. "That means Mr. Wesley wants that load."

"What if someone else wants it too?"

"If Mr. Wesley wants it, he'll get it."

The wagon rumbled on past them, then turned at a place

where there was a passageway to River Street beneath one of the warehouses. As Wesley and the others returned to their offices, Will straightened, not trying to hide his excitement. "Give that cotton a week or two and it will be on its way to England or Boston, I'll bet."

Joshua was nodding thoughtfully. "Or maybe St. Louis."

"Yeah," Will said, understanding immediately what Joshua had meant.

Joshua watched his young guide closely. Suddenly he made a shrewd guess. "You gonna be a cotton factor someday, Will?"

Will threw back his shoulders proudly. "Yes sirree! I'm gonna be one of the best. Just like Mr. Wesley."

"Good for you." Joshua was surprised at the warmth of his feelings for this boy. He straightened, taken with a sudden thought. "I think maybe I'll pay a call to Mr. Wesley tomorrow." He stopped, musing. "Savannah's a big city, though. I could use a guide to help me find my way back here again."

Will's head jerked up so fast that it was lucky he didn't pull a muscle. "Really?" he cried.

"Really," Joshua said soberly. "Now, come on. You've still got a bunch of city to show me."

Joshua and Will were sitting on a stone bench in Emmet Park near the end of Bay Street. Their seat commanded a wonderful overlook of the river, and Joshua watched for a moment as another packet ship nosed its way toward a berth. They were eating some roasted pecans Joshua had bought from a street vendor. Two squirrels edged their way closer, hoping for a handout. It felt good to Joshua to just sit. Will had walked him steadily for nearly two hours. "So that's why all the streets are so straight?" he asked.

Will nodded soberly. "James Oglethorpe laid out the whole city before they even started building houses."

"How long ago was that?"

"The year 1733."

Joshua marveled. "You learn all that in school?"

Will looked up mischievously. "Some. Mostly I read books."

"Why aren't you in school today?"

"Our teacher quit last week. With summer comin', we won't get another teacher until September."

"Oh." It was obvious to Joshua that Will wasn't emotionally shattered over the loss. "So what do you—"

A sharp call cut Joshua off. "William Donovan Mendenhall!"

Both of them turned their heads. Coming across the grass toward them was a woman in a full-length dress and matching bonnet. She had a young girl in tow, who was almost running in order to keep up with the woman's purposeful stride.

"Uh-oh!" Will muttered. He stood quickly, brushing off his shirt and squaring his shoulders.

Joshua stood too. "Your mother?" he said out of the side of his mouth.

"Uh huh." It was barely audible.

The skirt of the woman's dress was fully hooped and it snagged on a small bush, but if she noticed, she made no sign. Her eyes, flashing with anger, were pinned on the boy standing next to Joshua. She pulled up short, not even giving Joshua so much as a second look.

"William Mendenhall! Where in the world have you been for the past three hours?"

"I—"

"Didn't I tell you not to go farther than where I could call you? Didn't I?"

"Yes'm." Will was definitely cowed. There was little evidence in his manner of the impudent young man who had been guiding Joshua around the city.

She shook her head, clearly exasperated. "What am I going to do with you? You never mind my wishes anymore."

Joshua was glad she hadn't yet taken note of him. This allowed him a chance to study her as she spoke. There was no question about where Will got his auburn hair. Beneath the bonnet her hair was full and long. He could see that in the back it came down over her shoulders and disappeared beneath her light shawl. Her features were fine, her nose straight and well proportioned, her mouth full and nicely formed. But the most arresting feature was her eyes. They were large and remarkably green, like the crest of an ocean wave with the sun behind it.

"Mama, I just wanted—"

"No!" she burst out. "I don't want to hear any more of your excuses, Will. I've had enough of this. Do you hear me?"

Without realizing it, Joshua had removed his hat and now held it in his hand. "Ma'am, beggin' your pardon, but don't blame the boy. I'm afraid I'm the one at fault."

She stopped, as if startled by his presence. Her chin came up, bringing her face full into the sunlight. The emerald eyes were wide and curious as she appraised him slowly.

He smiled and stuck out one hand. "My name is Joshua Steed. I've just come off a ship from New Orleans." She made no move to take his hand, and he slowly let it drop again. "Young Will here was showing me around Savannah. I'm sorry if I kept him . . ."

Her lips compressed into a tight line and her eyes were blazing. Beside him, Will stiffened, and though he didn't understand why, Joshua realized he had just added significantly to Will's problems.

"Will, you didn't!" his mother cried. "Not again."

Will ducked his head.

"Give it back!" she said, her voice thin with anger.

"Mama, I didn't—"

She reached out and grabbed a shoulder and shook him firmly. "Give it back, Will!" She turned, and Joshua saw that her cheeks had colored with shame. "I'm very sorry, Mr.—?" She stopped, even more embarrassed that she had not gotten his name.

"Steed," he said. "Joshua Steed."

"I'm sorry, Mr. Steed. How much did my son take from you?"

Understanding dawned. Joshua wanted to smile. So this was not the first time Will had offered his guide services. But he didn't smile. He was aware that Will was looking up at him, anxiety clearly written in his eyes. "Beggin' your pardon, ma'am?"

"How much did Will charge you for"—her voice became heavy with sarcasm—"showing you around?"

For the first time the little girl spoke. She was a miniature of her mother, and when Joshua looked at her more directly, he could also see a strong resemblance to Will. "Will always asks men for money," she said primly, clearly enjoying her brother's discomfort.

"You hush, Olivia!" Will hissed.

His mother swung back around to him, but before she could speak, Joshua broke in. "Ma'am, this young man of yours did not ask me for any money, nor have I given him so much as a single penny."

Will's eyes widened for a moment, then there was instant relief. He looked at his mother in triumph.

"I won't have any more of—" She stopped, and her head came up again.

Joshua shook his head slowly, his eyes grave. "Not a penny."

She was clearly taken aback, and he was enchanted to watch as both surprise and gratitude played around the corners of her mouth.

"This is my first time to Savannah—to the South, for that matter—and I was in need of someone to show me around. Your son has been a perfect gentleman and of the greatest service to me. I would happily pay him, but to this point all he has allowed me to do is buy him some roasted pecans."

Will was fighting hard not to look smug. "That's right, Mama. I was just helping him out a little."

She stepped back, her eyes still not fully believing. "If you are sure, then . . ." She was clearly embarrassed at her earlier outburst.

"I am," Joshua said firmly. "But I apologize for not being more thoughtful of his time. I didn't mean to create worry for you."

"Mr. Steed is from Missouri, Mama," Will burst out. "He's come out to buy a shipload of cotton."

"Where's Missouri?" Olivia said, squinting up at him.

Joshua bent over and smiled at her. She was going to be as beautiful as her mother. "It's a very long way from here."

"It is I who must apologize, Mr. Steed," the woman said, finally holding out her hand. "Mrs. Caroline Mendenhall. I'm pleased to make your acquaintance."

Straightening, he took her hand briefly, then let it go. "No apology necessary."

"William has this habit of disappearing on me. But it was most rude of me to barge up like this without so much as a hello." She smiled, and brief as it was, it was dazzling. "Well, if you'll excuse us, we must be getting home. Come, Will. You have studies to do."

Will turned and stuck out his hand. "Thank you, Mr. Steed." It was said with great fervency.

Joshua shook the boy's hand. "Thank *you*, Will. I feel like I know more about Savannah than I know about Independence." He looked at Will's mother. "Your son is very bright. You should be proud of him."

"I am." She shook her head ruefully. "And believe it or not, I love him very much."

"That is obvious," he said gallantly. "It is a poor mother who lets a son roam free all day without worrying."

She curtsied slightly, pleased. "Thank you, Mr. Steed." She took Olivia's hand and motioned for Will. "I hope you have a pleasant stay in Savannah." She turned and they started away.

Joshua stared for a moment, suddenly realizing he was about to lose contact. Then he remembered something. "Will?"

They stopped, all half turning back toward him.

"Remember, you promised to take me to Mr. Wesley's office tomorrow."

His mother looked startled for a moment, then instantly was shaking her head at Will. "I'm sorry, Mr. Steed, but Will needs to spend some time with his studies. Our schoolteacher has left us, and he mustn't get behind."

Joshua was not about to be swayed from the only opportunity that lay at hand. He moved over to face her. "Mrs. Mendenhall, I don't know how things are here in the South, but where I come from, when a gentleman gives his word he's expected to keep it."

"It is no less so here," she said, the puzzlement evident in her eyes.

"Well, I gave my word as a gentleman that I would take Will with me tomorrow to see the man he tells me is the best cotton factor in Savannah. Now, I know I did that without askin' for your permission, and I apologize for that. But a man's word is his bond."

She cocked her head to one side slightly, examining his face closely. "I don't know how it is out west," she said, with just the faintest trace of a smile, "but here gentlemen don't take twelve-year-old boys with them to do their business."

He matched her expression. "Hmm," he mused. "In Missouri we take twelve-year-old boys and make them into men."

He could see she wanted to laugh, but she didn't. Her eyes told him that she accepted his besting of her.

"Oh, please, Mama," Will exclaimed, grabbing for her hand. "This could be my only chance to meet Mr. Wesley. Please, Mama, please!"

She looked down at her son, then back to Joshua. He raised his right hand. "I promise to bring him right home the moment we're through."

Her shoulders lifted and fell in a shrug of defeat. "All right."

Will nearly leaped into the air. He could not stop the grin from nearly splitting his face in two. "Thank you, Mama!"

"Yes, thank you," Joshua said to her. He turned to Will. "I'll meet you right here at nine tomorrow morning, then?"

"Yes, sir!" Will said. "I'll be here."

The Steed clan stood in front of the Newel K. Whitney store down in Kirtland Flats. A lone wagon sat on the roadside. It had been only four days since Jessica had stunned the family with the announcement that she was returning to Missouri. Now they had gathered to say good-bye.

Little four-year-old Rachel broke down first. Her lower lip started to tremble. The large blue eyes filled with tears. She spun around and buried her face in her mother's skirts. "I don't want to go, Mama," she sobbed. "I don't want to go."

That set Emily off. Emily was Lydia and Nathan's second child, and was just six months younger than Rachel. From the moment Nathan had brought Jessica and her daughter to Kirtland, Rachel and Emily had become more like sisters than cousins. Not that they looked a lot alike. Emily was going to be a miniature of Lydia. She had long, dark hair, thick and lustrous. Her huge eyes were of such a deep brown that sometimes they looked black. Her features were as finely shaped as her mother's. Rachel, on the other hand, had some of her mother's plainness. Her hair, dark brown and with a natural curl, was worn long. She was a solemn child, with grave blue eyes and a way of seeming preoccupied most of the time.

Jessica took her daughter's face in her hand. Her own lips were quivering too, and she blinked rapidly. "I know, Rachel," she soothed, "I know."

Mary Ann watched the interchange, feeling that her own heart was going to break. At her side, Benjamin was trying to be stern. "All right, now," he said gruffly, "we all made a promise we weren't going to make this any harder for Jessica than it already is."

He stepped forward and went down to one knee, touching his granddaughter's shoulder. At first Rachel just buried her head all the tighter against her mother's legs. Jessie straightened, smiling down at her. "Rachel, it's Grandpa."

Rachel swung around blindly and threw her arms around his neck. That was too much for Mary Ann, and she felt a great sob well up inside her. Her husband loved all of his grandchildren, but from the day she had arrived, Rachel had taken a special place in his heart. She was always tagging after him, one tiny hand in his, her lips puckering in concentration as she would help him with this task or that.

Matthew—tall and straight, and at almost sixteen, too much of a man to cry—looked away. He had become the big brother, almost the father, that Rachel had not had, and he had taken Jessica's announcement hard. Rachel's happy cry of "Uncle Matt, Uncle Matt" would be sorely missed around the Steed household.

Surprisingly, Carl Rogers had come with Melissa and their children. That meant his taking off work at the livery stable, something Carl rarely did. But Jessica had kept books at the stable for him, and so Carl had made an exception in this case. It was obvious that Jessica was touched. Carl and Melissa's two boys started to whimper now too—young Carl because he understood what was happening, little David because he saw the girls crying.

Joshua, Lydia and Nathan's oldest and about a month and a half short of his fifth birthday, was standing next to Mary Ann, trying very hard to be brave. He and his Aunt Jessica had developed a special relationship, and in the past month Jessica had started to unfold the mysteries of the alphabet for him. Mary Ann heard him sniff and saw him swallow quickly. She took his hand, no longer trying to stop her own tears from flowing.

Lydia evidently saw her son's reaction too, for she suddenly broke free from Nathan and ran to Jessica, throwing her arms around her. In a moment Mary Ann and Melissa and Rebecca were there too, all of them weeping and trying to hold each other and making promises about writing and never forgetting and maybe coming out to Missouri sometime.

From the wagon, Newel Knight watched soberly. The Knights were making the eight-hundred-mile journey back to Missouri and had agreed to take Jessica and her daughter along. Finally, Newel stepped forward. "I'm sorry, Brother Steed, but it's time to go."

———◆———

For a long time after the wagon had disappeared from sight, Benjamin and Mary Ann and Rebecca stood together in front of the store. Carl and Melissa had left immediately. Lydia and Nathan, along with Matthew, had taken the children home to try and get their minds on something other than Rachel's leaving.

Benjamin watched his wife and youngest daughter with a great feeling of tenderness. The two of them were standing together, eyes still red, not feeling a need to speak but only to be there for each other. Mary Ann had been just shy of eighteen when Benjamin had first met her and started courting her. Now Rebecca, at that same age, looked so much like Mary Ann had then, it made him feel as though no time had passed at all. And she had so much of Mary Ann's nature. He stepped up beside them. "They'll be all right. They're traveling with good people."

Mary Ann turned and managed a smile. "I know. It couldn't

have worked out any better." A group of Saints from Missouri, including most of the leaders, had come to Kirtland in the past few months to be present for the temple dedication. Now they were returning. Hyrum Smith had loaned the Knights a wagon, team, and driver to get them to the upper Ohio River, where they planned to take a steamer. The Knights had promised to take good care of Jessica and her daughter and see that they arrived safely in Missouri.

"I just worry," Rebecca said, "their being alone, without family, and all."

"Don't underestimate Jessica," Mary Ann said. "She is very strong."

Benjamin said a soft inward amen to that. When the Saints had been driven out of Jackson County, Jessica had fled into the night wearing nothing more than a nightdress, a shawl, and a thin pair of moccasins. She had carried Rachel, not yet two, in her arms for more than twenty miles. The prairie was covered with a thin sheet of sleet and ice. By dawn, she was leaving bloody footprints on the prairie. Yes, Jessica was strong.

Mary Ann took a deep breath, turned to look once more down the road where the wagon had disappeared, then slipped her arm through Benjamin's. "We're not doing Jessica and Rachel any good standing around here. Let's go home."

"Will we ever get to see Aunt Jessica and Rachel again?"

Lydia looked up at her older son, then let her sewing drop into her lap. He was sitting across the room from her. The picture book he had been looking through was closed. Now as he looked at her, his light blue eyes were clearly troubled. Her first impulse was to soothe him, cushion the hardness of the reality a little, but then she knew she couldn't do that. Not with young Joshua. He was so much the child at times, then in an instant could turn into a little five-year-old adult. Like now.

She shook her head slowly. "I don't know, Joshua. I hope so."

Emily looked up, the dark bangs around her forehead

bouncing slightly. She had a square of slate and a piece of soap-stone. She was laboriously drawing a stick family in front of a building. What was obviously a wagon and a horse were nearby. Just thirteen and a half months younger than Joshua, Emily had neither his maturity nor his basic seriousness. "I'll bet we do," she said matter-of-factly, always the optimist.

Joshua only saddened the more. "Emmy, you don't know how far Missouri is. It's a long, long ways. And it's dangerous."

She shrugged that aside. "Aunt Jessica said she will help Rachel write to me." As if that made everything perfectly all right.

Lydia smiled brightly at her children. "And she will, I'm sure, Emily." She looked at her eldest. "Joshua, you must make yourself stop worrying about them. They will be all right."

But she knew it sounded forced. Like her son, Lydia had this terrible dread that they might never see Jessica and Rachel again. But it was more than that. In addition to a difficult jour-ney, there was the stark reality of what awaited them once they arrived. The citizens of Clay County, who had kindly taken in the exiles from Jackson County two years earlier, were now say-ing that the Saints had overstayed their welcome. The leaders there had written to Joseph. Plans were being made to look for a haven elsewhere in the state, but for now, tension in Clay County was mounting. It wasn't a good time to go to Missouri.

There was a sound in the hall, and Lydia turned. Nathan had been putting six-month-old baby Nathan to bed. Evidently he had been able to hear part of the conversation, because he moved directly over to Joshua and dropped into a crouch, facing his son. "Your mother's right, Joshua. Aunt Jessica and Rachel aren't traveling alone. Besides the Knights, they'll also have the Lord with them."

There was a momentary look of surprise, then Joshua's lower lip shot out into a pout. He gave a stubborn shake of his head and looked away.

Nathan was a little startled. "What?"

There was no answer. Nor did the head come around.

"Come on," Nathan prodded gently. "What is it?"

"It was the Lord who took Aunt Jessie and Rachel away from us."

"Joshua!"

Nathan held up one hand toward Lydia. "No, Mother, in a way Joshua's right. Jessica said she felt a strong prompting to return to Missouri. So in that sense it was the Lord who took them away from us." He turned to his son again. "Do you think Heavenly Father did that because he wanted to hurt us?"

There were several seconds of silence, then a barely murmured, "No."

"I don't either. It does hurt. We're going to miss them a lot, but Heavenly Father always does what is best, even if sometimes it hurts others a little."

Emily had pushed her slate aside. She stood and came over to her father, putting one arm around his shoulder. "Can't Heav'nly Father make it so nobody hurts?"

Nathan sat down on the floor and took his daughter in his lap. "Come here, Joshua." He patted the floor next to him. As Joshua did so, Lydia's mouth softened into a smile. Her two children were looking up at their father, their eyes wide and trusting. She knew what was about to happen, and she felt a great upsurge of love and gratitude for this man who was her husband. This was something she had never had from her own father. He had always been there, had always loved her. But, in his mind, it was a woman's place to show affection, to hold and cuddle the children, talk to them, teach them. He had never been harsh or unkind, just aloof and distant. Nathan had given her a whole new perspective on what it meant to be a father.

"Joshua," Nathan was saying, "Emily has asked a very important question. Can Heavenly Father make it so no one hurts?"

The handsome little face twisted in deep thought. "I don't know."

"Did Jesus ever hurt?"

Emily nodded soberly. Joshua did the same. Lydia stood and set her sewing aside. She moved over and sat down next to them. She wanted to be part of this. "Could Heavenly Father have made it so Jesus didn't have to hurt?" she asked.

Emily nodded immediately. Joshua, more slowly, was shaking his head.

"Why not, Joshua?" Lydia asked softly.

"Because Jesus had to die for us."

"Do you think Heavenly Father *wanted* him to hurt?" Nathan asked.

"No," he finally said, again after some thought. "I don't think so."

"Then why did he let him suffer so much pain?"

Now Joshua understood. "To help us?"

Nathan reached out and touched his arm. "Exactly, Joshua. Sometimes doing what's best may cause some people to be hurt or be sad, but we have to trust Heavenly Father. He always knows what is best."

"Papa, do you think we'll ever get to see Aunt Jessica and Rachel again?"

Nathan took a deep breath, then let it out slowly as he considered that. "Yes, Joshua," he finally said. He saw his wife's eyebrows raise, but he went on more firmly. "I don't know when. I don't know how. But I have a feeling we'll get to see them again."

Joshua's large blue eyes appraised his father's for a moment. Then he seemed satisfied. "Good," was all he said.

Lydia watched her son's face closely, noting once again how strong the resemblance between him and his Uncle Joshua was becoming. Was this why the Lord had inspired Nathan to name him as he had? She had not seen Joshua Steed for over eight years now, but his image was still clear in her mind. And young Joshua had the same handsome features, the same dark hair, the same habit of jutting out his chin in stubborn defiance when someone was trying to make him do something he did not want to do.

She remembered with perfect clarity the day Nathan had taken their infant son in his arms to name and bless him. Beforehand they had both agreed they would call their firstborn Nathan Benjamin Steed, after his father and grandfather. Nathan had begun the blessing normally enough, but suddenly his voice had changed. And then he had stunned everyone, including himself. *"His name shall be Joshua Benjamin Steed."* Later, others had felt bad for Lydia. But she did not. At the very moment Nathan was speaking the words, Lydia had felt a thrill shoot through her. Like Nathan, she didn't fully understand why the Lord wanted their son called Joshua, but that he did was not a question in her mind.

Nathan stood up, swooping Emily up in his arms. "Come on, kids. We got you up early this morning. It's time for bed. Let's say our prayers."

He walked over to the large sofa and let Emily down gently, then knelt beside her. Lydia took young Joshua's hand and led him over, and they both knelt down too.

"Can I say the prayer tonight, Papa?" Emily asked.

He started to nod, but Lydia answered quickly. "I think we ought to let Papa say it tonight. Have him say a special prayer for Aunt Jessica and Rachel. And ask that Heavenly Father will keep our family strong."

Emily nodded immediately at that and dropped her head to her hands. Joshua followed suit. Lydia smiled at her husband as they took each other's hands, then bowed their heads as well.

———————•—•———————

Lydia leaned over the bed and pulled the blanket up under Emily's chin. She gave her a kiss on the cheek. "Good night, Emmy."

"Good night, Mama."

"Good night, Joshua."

"Good night, Mama."

She turned to Nathan and gave him a stern look. "Don't wake the baby."

He looked offended that she would even imply such a thing. She smiled as she left them. He always lingered for a few minutes after Lydia had kissed the children good night. Supposedly it was to talk softly to them until eyes became heavy and they drifted off to sleep, but as often as not, he would get them giggling or squealing in delight. No wonder they loved him so much.

Out in the hallway she stopped and leaned against the wall, suddenly feeling a great surge of happiness. What a good life! What a wonderful, rich life they had! Surprised at the depths of her feelings, she walked into the living room, went to the chair, and picked up her sewing again. But she just held it in her lap, not wanting to lessen the feelings that had welled up in her. She and Nathan had three healthy, lovely children who were the delight of her life. The love between them was deepening to the point that she found herself a little bit awed by it. Not many couples had what they enjoyed.

They were not rich, by any means, but compared to many of the Saints in Kirtland, they were doing well financially. The two farms Nathan was running for his father had produced their second bountiful crop. Lydia no longer substituted for William McLellin at the Kirtland School, but her experience in her father's store had prompted Newel Whitney to bring her in one day a week for a few hours to help out in his store. He paid in goods, and it proved to be a small but appreciated addition to their other income.

A knock at the door brought Lydia out of her thoughts.

Nathan was just coming out of the bedroom. "I'll get it."

"Brother Nathan. Good evening."

Nathan blocked her view of the door, but there was no mistaking that booming voice. It was Heber C. Kimball, one of the Twelve Apostles. That surprised her a little. Not that it was that late, but Heber ran a pottery business on the Painesville Road, some distance northeast of town. She stood and went to join Nathan.

"Well, hello, Brother Heber," Nathan said. "This is a pleasant surprise. Come in, come in." He stepped back, holding the door open.

"Good evening, Brother Heber."

"Good evening, Sister Lydia. It's good to see you again."

He swept off his hat, which showed his balding head, the hair in some disarray. Heber Kimball was the son of a blacksmith and had spent the first years of his life working in his father's shop and performing other tasks on the family farm. He was as strong as any two men, and built somewhat along the lines of a two-hundred-year-old oak tree. He often said he was the only man alive whose chest measurements were the same from side to side as they were front to back. But he was a pleasant man, quick to laugh, and always congenial, especially with women and children.

"Can I get you some bread and a glass of milk?"

He smiled broadly. "Thank you very much, Sister Steed, but I'm on an errand just now." He turned to Nathan. "I was wondering if you might help me, Brother Steed."

"Of course. What is it?"

"Normally I get Brigham to help me, but he's not available. Brother Joseph is away right now with President Williams. I stopped at Brother Sidney's house, but he has company. Then I thought of you." He looked at Lydia. "I hope you don't mind me coming this time of night."

"Not at all. What do you need?"

He sighed, turning back to Nathan. "Of late I've felt a great concern for Brother Parley Pratt."

Lydia felt a little start of surprise. As they had walked home from the Whitney store that morning, she and Nathan had somehow started talking about the Pratts. They had moved to Kirtland a few months ago from the town of New Portage, which was about fifty-five miles south of Kirtland. Word was that Parley, who was also one of the Twelve, felt the need to go on another mission but was totally destitute. His wife, Thankful, who had been stricken with consumption for the past six years, was quite ill.

"We have had some concern as well," Nathan was saying. "What would you like me to do?"

"I've been thinking that perhaps Parley could use a blessing," Brother Kimball said. "I need a good, faithful elder to assist me."

"Of course. Let me get my coat."

Nathan was back in a moment. He gave Lydia a quick kiss. "Don't wait up for me. I don't know how long we'll be."

"I'll be up. Take what time you need."

The two of them left, and Lydia watched them for a moment from the door. As she started to shut it, she heard footsteps behind her. She turned to see Joshua standing there in his nightshirt. She shut the door and walked to her son. "I'm sorry, Joshua, we didn't mean to wake you."

"I was awake."

"Papa is going with Brother Kimball to give Parley Pratt a blessing."

Joshua looked up. "What's the matter with Brother Pratt, Mama?"

"He's having a difficult time right now with his family."

"How come Sister Pratt always looks so sick?"

She gave him an appraising look. It was startling what children noticed sometimes. "She has consumption."

"Is that bad?"

Lydia sighed, thinking of times she had seen Thankful so weak that she could barely lift a hand from her bed. "Yes, Joshua, it's a disease in the lungs. It can be very bad."

"Is that why she can't have any children?"

Lydia nodded in surprise. Joshua's maturity continually amazed her. "Probably. They both so want a baby, but they just haven't been able to have one so far."

His eyes were solemn as he considered that. "Should we pray for them, Mama?"

Lydia's mouth dropped slightly, then she smiled warmly. "That's a wonderful idea, Joshua. Let's offer a prayer for the Pratts, and let's also pray that Brother Kimball and Papa will have the Spirit with them when they bless Brother Pratt." She bent down slightly, taking his face in both hands. "It makes me very happy that you would think of that, Joshua. Very happy."

Nathan was a little shocked at the appearance of Thankful Pratt. She had always been a frail person, thin, wan in complexion, ravaged by the consumption that would not leave her body. But now she looked especially weak. Her eyes were sunken and rimmed with dark circles. Her lips were pale and looked parched. Her hands trembled as she pulled at the front of her robe.

They had raised Parley and his wife from their bed, even though it was not yet eight o'clock in the evening. Parley had been stunned to open the door and find his brethren standing there. Nathan had to smile. There wasn't much that left Parley P. Pratt speechless. Thankful was equally glad to see them, but after asking a few questions about Lydia and Emma and Nathan's mother, she fell quiet, exhausted by the effort that speaking required.

Now, as he and his wife sat on the simple bench that served as their couch, Parley looked at Heber. "So what has brought about this pleasant surprise?" he asked.

Heber paused only for a moment. "Just an impression," he said simply. Then he leaned back. "So how are things, my friend?"

For a moment, Parley just looked at the two of them, his face troubled. Finally he shook his head. "Not good, Brother Heber, not good."

Heber just nodded, waiting.

"I have been deeply troubled of late. It is spring now, and many of the elders are preparing to leave on missions. I feel the urgings to do the same. After all, I do hold the holy calling of the apostleship. But things here are not well. Thankful has still not recovered from the strain of moving from Missouri. This past winter I went deeply into debt to purchase a lot and build this home so we would have a place to stay. As you know, my mother is here as well and must be cared for. So I know not what to do. Shall I go on a mission, leaving Thankful to the care of others? Shall I simply forget my debts, or shall I stay here in Kirtland and by my industry endeavor to earn sufficient money to care for my family and meet my other obligations?"

He passed a hand over his eyes. "This very night I became so troubled by the question that I retired to bed early. I was lying there pondering my future course at the very moment your knock came at the door." He gave them a grateful smile. "So you can see why I am so pleased at your coming."

"We are so grateful you would come," Thankful said quietly. "It is very good of you."

Heber stood. He looked to Nathan, who stood to join him. "We are here to give you a blessing, Brother Parley. That is what the Spirit whispers, and I am a firm believer in following what the Spirit tells us to do."

He took one of the simple chairs from the table and set it in the middle of the room. Parley rose slowly, smiling briefly at the two of them before sitting in it. Nathan and Heber moved around behind Parley, Heber standing directly behind him. He paused for a moment, his eyes hooded, then laid his hands on Parley's head. Nathan did the same.

"Brother Parley Parker Pratt," Heber began in a quiet voice, "in the name of the Lord Jesus Christ, and by the authority of the holy Melchizedek Priesthood which we hold, we lay our hands upon your head to give you a blessing."

He fell silent for several moments, and Nathan felt a little stir of excitement within him. He had once heard Joseph Smith say of Heber C. Kimball that here was a man in whom resided the gift of prophecy. Nathan had not witnessed that personally, but had heard others relate examples of it. Now it was a thrill to be standing beside him.

"Brother Parley"—Heber's voice was suddenly strong and sure—"I come at this time to give you a blessing as one of the Lord's chosen Apostles. And this blessing is not only for thee, but for thy good wife as well. The Spirit whispers that your wife shall be healed of her affliction from this very hour. She shall also conceive and bear you a son."

Nathan felt Parley stiffen beneath their hands. He also heard a soft gasp of amazement from Thankful. Parley and his wife had been married for ten years now and were childless. And Thankful's consumption had been declared to be incurable. This was electrifying.

Heber was continuing. "Thou shalt call his name Parley, after your own name. He shall be a chosen instrument in the hands of the Lord, to inherit the priesthood and walk in the steps of his father. He shall do a great work in ministering the word and teaching the children of men."

Heber paused again for a moment, and Nathan could hear Thankful crying quietly beside them. Then with great firmness Heber went on. "Arise, therefore, and go forth in the ministry, nothing doubting. Take no thoughts for your debts, nor the necessaries of life, for the Lord will supply you with abundant means for all things. Thou shalt go to Upper Canada, even to the city of Toronto, the capital, and there thou shalt find a people prepared for the fulness of the gospel. They shall receive thee, and thou shalt organize the Church among them, and it shall spread thence into the regions round about. Many shall be brought to the knowledge of the truth and shall be filled with joy because of your labors. And from the things growing out of this mission, shall the fulness of the gospel spread into England, and cause a great work to be done in that land."

Nathan was reeling. The promises were coming faster than he could comprehend them.

"You shall not only have means to deliver you from your present embarrassments," Heber went on, "but you shall yet have riches, silver and gold, till you will loath the counting thereof."

There was one last pause, then Heber's voice dropped, and he finished more slowly. "This blessing we pronounce upon you by the power of the holy priesthood and through the promptings of the Lord's Holy Spirit. And we do it in the name of our beloved Savior, Jesus Christ, amen."

Instantly Parley was on his feet, tears streaming down his

face. Thankful was up too, her cheeks stained as well. Husband and wife embraced, hugging each other tightly, not speaking. Then finally Parley pulled away and turned to Heber. He stuck out his hand. "Thank you, Brother Heber," he whispered huskily. "Thank you so much."

He looked at Nathan, then threw his arms around him. "Thank you, Brother Nathan. Thank you for coming."

———·—·———

Heber and Nathan walked slowly, both of them still fired by the thrill of what had happened. Heber had his hands behind his back, his head down. He was lost deeply in his thoughts.

"That was a marvelous blessing," Nathan finally said.

He could tell that Heber nodded, but the Apostle said nothing.

"I'm glad I was there to hear it."

For several moments Heber still said nothing. Then he stopped, turning to peer at Nathan. Nathan saw in the man's face the intensity that was so characteristic of Heber C. Kimball. He waited, sensing that Heber had something to say. But he was not prepared for what came next.

"You know why you are here, don't you?"

Nathan started a little. "Because you asked me."

Heber chuckled. "There are a lot of elders in Kirtland, Nathan. Why should I specifically feel impressed to seek you out?"

"I don't know. Why did you?"

For a long moment he just looked at Nathan. Then he laughed and clapped him on the shoulder. "Because you are to accompany Brother Parley on his mission to Canada."

Nathan went stiff as a rod. "What?"

"That's right. I will discuss it with Joseph tomorrow, make sure he confirms it, but I feel it strongly. Parley will be pleased to know he will have a traveling companion." He clasped his hands behind his back and started walking again.

For a moment Nathan stared after him, his mind racing.

Canada? What would Lydia say? What about the farms? But even as the thoughts tumbled wildly in his mind, he felt something else. He recognized it instantly. He had felt this deep inner peace before. *Yes,* he thought. *Canada. Of course.* He quickly fell into step beside the Apostle.

Heber gave him a sidewards glance. "And that is not all, Nathan."

"It's not?"

"No. I don't know how, but your going on this mission will prove to be a great blessing to your own family. You shall live to see it, and you shall rise up and thank the Lord you were privileged to be part of it."

He laughed softly at the look on Nathan's face. They had come back out to the main street that ran in front of the temple. Heber lived to the north, Nathan to the south. "And now, my friend, I must say good night. I am very weary and should like to reach home as quickly as possible." He stuck out his hand. "Thank you, Nathan. It was wonderful to have you with me."

And with that, he turned and walked off, not waiting for a response, leaving Nathan to stand there in the dark, filled with wonder and not a few questions to which he would have very much liked to have answers.

Factors' Walk, Savannah, Georgia

The office of Richard Wesley, Savannah's most preem-
inent cotton factor, was conservatively furnished, but everything about it spoke money and class. The chairs and sofa were
of fine leather, the pictures on the wall obviously more than the
common prints lesser folk bought. The moldings around the
doors and ceiling were thick and polished to a soft gleam. Even
the secretary's desk was as fine as anything Joshua had seen west
of St. Louis.

"Do you have an appointment, sir?" The secretary, a tall
thin man with a nose like a rooster's beak, peered at them over
half-cut horn-rimmed glasses.

Joshua shook his head. "I just arrived yesterday by ship. I am
from Missouri. I am looking to buy cotton. Mr. Wesley has been
highly recommended to me."

Out of the corner of his eye, Joshua saw that Will never
broke his expression, though he could sense that the boy was
nearly bursting with pride and excitement. He was dressed to

the nines with waistcoat, well-tailored breeches, and low-cut boots that showed some wear but which Joshua had noticed had been highly polished as though by a bootblack. His shirt was of cotton, neatly pressed and with a small black tie at the throat. He looked every inch the young businessman, and Joshua was strangely proud to have him with him.

The secretary frowned, his mouth pinching down into a tiny circle. "It is most unusual to come without an advance appointment."

Joshua smiled patiently. "When a man has come almost two thousand miles, it is most unusual if he has an advance appointment."

The secretary's eyes widened, not sure whether to take offense or not at such brashness. "I'll have to confer with Mr. Wesley. Who shall I tell him is calling?" His eyes darted to Will, then flitted back to Joshua.

"Mr. Joshua Steed, from Independence, Missouri. And my young associate here is Master William Donovan Mendenhall, originally from Maryland but most recently from Savannah, Georgia."

———◆———

Richard Wesley took the pipe out of his mouth and knocked out the ashes against the metal railing. When he spoke it was with the same deep Southern accent Joshua had found prevailed here along the coast of Georgia. "I shall call for you, suh, at the hotel at nine a.m. on Monday, two days after tomorrow."

They stood on the narrow metal catwalk that ran from his suite of offices across Factors' Walk to the bluff that bordered Bay Street. Joshua nodded. "I shall look forward to meeting Mr. and Mrs. Montague. I'm also looking forward to seeing my first cotton plantation."

"I'm sure you'll find it most impressive," Wesley said. "And if you find the cotton acceptable, as I have promised, then we shall draw up the papers, and you, suh, shall be loaded and on yo way back to St. Louis"—he pronounced it Lou-ee—"by the end of next week."

Joshua was pleased. "Very good. It's a pleasure doing business with a professional, Mr. Wesley."

"May I say the same to you, Mistuh Steed. I like a man who knows what he wants and is prepared to see that he gets it." Wesley turned to Will. "And I must say, young Mr. Mendenhall, yo knowledge of the cotton trade is very admirable for one of yo age."

Joshua thought Will would nearly pop every button on his tailored double-breasted waistcoat. "Thank you, sir."

Wesley leaned forward, his eyes narrowing slightly. "Wait a moment. Mendenhall. Mendenhall." He pulled at his lip. "Was yo fathuh Donovan Mendenhall, by chance?"

"Yes, sir, he was." Will had perceptibly straightened.

Joshua's head came up. *Was?*

"Ah," said Wesley thoughtfully, "that explains a great deal. Give my best to yo lovely mothuh. Mrs. Wesley asks about her often."

"I will, sir. Thank you kindly. And our best to Mrs. Wesley."

"Thank you."

Joshua was watching Will with new interest now. He had been most impressed with Mrs. Mendenhall yesterday, but because he had assumed she was married, he had not allowed himself to let his thoughts dwell on her.

Wesley was suddenly struck by an idea. He gave Joshua a quick, appraising look, then turned to the boy. "Say, if I remember correctly, yo mama and yo daddy were good friends with the Montagues."

"That's right," Will responded eagerly. "My daddy and Mr. Montague worked together for a time."

"I remember now." He pulled at his lower lip. "Tell you what. I'm gonna drop over and see yo mama and have y'all come out to the Montagues too."

Will couldn't believe his ears. "That would be wonderful, Mr. Wesley."

Joshua tried not to look too pleased. He could think of few things that would give him more pleasure than to spend a couple of days in proximity to Caroline Mendenhall.

"Don't y'all be sayin' anything, now," Wesley warned Will. "I don't want her thinkin' up no excuses. It's time she starts getting out again."

"No, sir, I won't, sir." There was no way Will was going to jeopardize what was developing.

Wesley turned to Joshua. "You won't mind, will you, Mistuh Steed? The Montagues have plenty of guest rooms."

Joshua nearly choked. "Not at all," he managed. "Not at all."

As Joshua and Will walked away, they moved quietly and sedately until a row of dogwood trees screened them from the view of Wesley's offices. Joshua turned his head to make sure they were no longer in view, then stopped and looked down at Will. "Well, Master Mendenhall," he grinned, "you've just been part of your first cotton deal. What do you think?"

Will's smile nearly split his face in two. "Great!" he said, all traces of the mature young gentleman gone. "Thank you so much for taking me, Mr. Steed. And to get to go out to the plantation—that's terrific!"

Joshua chuckled at his excitement, then he sobered a little. "Actually, I was glad I had you. When he started asking questions about whether I wanted Sea Island cotton or American Upland, I suddenly realized how little I knew."

Will was instantly serious. "Sea Island cotton was first grown off the southern Atlantic coast. It's kind of like Egyptian cotton. It has long, silky fibers and makes wonderful textiles. But it's very costly because it grows more slowly and the yields are smaller. But Upland cotton, now that—"

Joshua threw up his hands, laughing helplessly. "All right, all right. Where do you learn all this stuff?" Then he remembered their previous conversation. "From books, right?"

Will shook his head slowly, his eyes dropping. "My daddy taught me."

Suddenly Joshua understood. "Your father was a cotton factor?"

"Yes. Not a big one. He was still learning when he died. But he would have been as good as Mr. Wesley." The last was said with fierce intensity.

"What happened?" Joshua asked quietly.

Will was twisting a corner of his coat, staring down at it without really seeing it. "He got yellow fever."

"How long ago?"

"Two years next September."

Joshua fell silent, feeling the boy's grief, but also feeling his own heart skip a beat. In the South a widow was expected to stay in mourning for a year. Wesley's comment that it was time Will's mother start getting out indicated that enough time had passed. Feeling guilty for his soaring thoughts, he reached out and laid a hand on Will's shoulder. "Was your father planning to teach you to be a cotton factor too?"

Will nodded glumly. "He said when I turned eighteen we'd be partners." He dropped the part of his coat he was holding and smoothed it out, his face struggling to hide the pain. Then he started to walk again. Joshua watched him for a moment. He had been pleased to have his young friend with him. In fact, it had given him as much pleasure as anything Joshua could remember in a long time. And then on top of that, the boy had proven his worth. Not only had Joshua been pleased, he had been grateful. And that, he was happy to recognize, had nothing to do with his growing interest in Will's mother.

Joshua walked quickly to catch up with the boy. "I think you are going to make one fine cotton factor, Will Mendenhall."

He looked up, brightening. "Really?"

"Yes, really."

The ear-to-ear grin suddenly erupted again. "Thank you, Mr. Steed. Today has been the best day of my whole life."

Joshua took hold of Will's arm and turned him so that the boy was facing him. "My friends call me Joshua," he said soberly. "I'd like it if you called me Joshua, Will."

Will's shoulders came back proudly. "Really?"

"Yes, really." He clapped him on the shoulder. "Now, I'd better get you home for your studies"—he dropped into a deep drawl—"or yo mama will skin us both and hang us out to dry."

———•———

Arthur Wilkinson's eyes were gray, nearly the color of a winter sky. When he was angry they changed color, becoming like the underside of a heavy thunderhead. Also, his jaw would tighten, his mouth would draw into a slight pout, and a tiny cleft in the center of his chin would appear. He always looked a year or two younger than his twenty-one years, but the changes that anger caused in his appearance made him seem all the more boyish.

Rebecca Steed watched those changes in his face now, feeling a deep sadness that it had come to this. She was tempted to reach out and smooth the cleft with her fingertip as she had done so often before, but she forced herself to keep her hands folded in her lap.

"Rebecca, I love you. Doesn't that mean anything?"

"Of course it means something. You know that."

They were sitting on the grass behind the Kirtland Temple. It was a clear Sabbath afternoon, the air clean and cool, with no hint of the summer heat that would soon be coming. The sunlight filtered through half-formed new leaves on the beech tree above them, dappling their faces and arms and clothing with soft patterns of light and shadow. This was Rebecca's favorite spot in all of Kirtland, and she and Arthur often came here to talk.

"Do you love me?" he demanded.

For a moment she hesitated, considering all that those words implied, everything he would assume was included in their meaning. His eyes flashed even more darkly when she didn't immediately answer. But finally she nodded. "Yes, Arthur," she said softly, "I do." She did not try to hide the pain she was feeling.

He threw up his hands. "But if I don't read the Book of Mormon, then it's no deal. No marriage!" His words came out sharply, snappish.

"I never said that, and you know it."

"You asked me to read the Book of Mormon. I said I'm not interested, now you won't marry me."

"Do you really think I would use our love to blackmail you like that?"

His anger faltered in the face of her challenging gaze.

"Do you?" she demanded.

He finally shook his head, but it was clearly acquiescence under pressure.

"I hoped you would read the Book of Mormon because you wanted to. I hoped you would investigate the Church because you wanted to find out for yourself if it was true. I don't want you doing it for me, Arthur. I want you to do it for you."

"And because I'm not interested, now you won't marry me."

She looked away, saddened that this great gulf stood between them. And trying to tell herself they could make it work did nothing to lessen the anxiety she felt.

"Rebecca, I don't care what you believe. If you want to be a Mormon, that's fine with me. If you want to believe Joe Smith—"

"Joseph," she corrected him automatically.

"*Joseph* Smith," he said with an angry shake of his head. "If you want to believe Joseph Smith got a Bible from some angel, I don't care. So why can't you give me the same freedom? That's what's so exasperating about you Mormons. Everybody's got to believe like you do."

That made Rebecca's head come up sharply. "My brother-in-law is not a Mormon. We haven't kicked him out of the family yet. We even have him over for dinner. Right in my father's house."

"All right, I didn't mean it that—"

In her anger she rode right over him. "As you know, I keep house for the Bradfords. They're Methodists. I'm even tutoring their children a little. When the parents aren't around, I tie the children to their beds and read the Book of Mormon to them, but they haven't found out yet."

He threw up his hands. "All right, I'm sorry. That didn't

come out like I meant it to." He sighed deeply. "But if it doesn't bother you that they're Methodists, why is it so important to you that I be a Mormon?"

She shook her head. That was what frustrated her more than anything. He couldn't even begin to understand what she was trying to say. She took a breath, wanting to try again, wanting to make him see. She did love him. The thoughts of being his wife left her a little dizzy with joy. But there was also the other part of her. Her heart couldn't completely silence her head.

"Well?" he demanded.

"I clean house for the Methodist family, Arthur," she said, fighting to keep the impatience out of her voice. "They haven't asked me to live with them for the rest of my life. They haven't asked me to bear their children."

He shot forward. "Well, I have. That's all that matters. I love you, Rebecca, and I want to spend the rest of my life with you. Don't you understand that? I don't care if you are a Mormon."

She closed her eyes, the pain inside her so sharp that for a moment she couldn't breathe. It was like this every time. He would demand answers, and then when she gave them he would brush them aside without a moment's consideration. Just one week before, she had sat inside the building that loomed above them. And there the Savior had appeared. Just feet away from her. She had thrilled to that. She wanted to share her feelings with Arthur. But she couldn't. Not about what had happened a week ago. Not about many other things. She had come today, hoping against hope that this time they could break the impasse, that this time she could get through to him. She had also come with the determination that if they failed, there would not be a next time. It was too painful for the both of them.

"May I ask you a question?" she said, looking up to search his face.

"Of course."

"When our first child is old enough, I'm going to teach him

about Heavenly Father. I'm going to teach him about Jesus. But I'm also going to teach him that Joseph Smith is a prophet of God. I'm going to teach him that the Book of Mormon is scripture, just like the Bible. Will that bother you?"

Now it was Arthur who hesitated. She was sorely tempted to pounce on his momentary discomfiture, but she didn't want this to turn into a game of strike and counter-strike. Finally, he shook his head—a little begrudgingly, she thought. "I can live with it."

"And when our child is five or six and comes to you and says, 'Papa, do you believe Joseph Smith is a prophet?' what are you going to say to him?"

Arthur suddenly grinned. "You keep saying *him?*" he echoed. "So it's going to be a boy?"

The smile was more painful to her than his anger, for Rebecca loved how his whole countenance lightened when he smiled. She couldn't bear it, and stood quickly, turning away from him to gaze at the temple. She blinked hard, fighting the tears she felt welling up behind her eyelids.

He stood too and stepped to her, taking her gently by the shoulders. "Rebecca, I don't know all the answers. I guess I'll just say to him that I don't believe in all that, but you do, and if he wants to, that's fine."

"So at six, he must decide who is right, his father or his mother."

His fingers were suddenly digging into her arms. "I don't know, Rebecca!" he exploded. "I can't see the future. All I know is that I love you and you love me. Isn't that enough for now?"

She made no move to turn around. The moment had come. There was no escaping it. "No, Arthur," she whispered. "It is not."

He stepped back, jerking his hands away from her as though she had turned to fire.

"I'm sorry, Arthur," she went on, fighting the tremor in her voice. "But there is a future, and there are others in it besides you and me. I can't just ignore them."

She could hear his breathing behind her, and turned to face

him. His face was mottled and drawn back into an ugly mask. She recoiled a step at the fury she saw there. She reached out a hand, frightened at what she had done. "I'm sorry, Arthur. I don't want to hurt you. I do love you—"

"No!" He was raging now. "Don't you say it! Don't you dare say it." He started to back away from her, his hands up at waist height, clenching and unclenching, his eyes now like two smoldering coals.

"Please, Arthur, I . . ."

Suddenly the rage was gone and he was more rigid than the huge blocks of ice the men cut from Lake Erie in the dead of winter. "Well, that's fine. You and your Mormon church can burn in hell, as far as I'm concerned," he hissed.

His hands dropped to his sides. He spun on his heel and stalked away. As he reached the corner of the temple, he turned his head and spat on the stuccoed surface. He rounded the building without looking back.

Rebecca stared after him. Inside her there was a searing pain, but it was far too great to be contained by the hollowness there. With one terrible, wrenching sob, she dropped to her knees on the grass and buried her face in her hands.

———•———

Nathan set his knapsack down and knelt in front of his son. "You'll be the man of the house now, Joshua," he said gravely. "I expect you to help your mother with your sister and brother."

"I will, Papa."

Nathan reached out and took him by both shoulders, the pride evident on his face. "I know you will, son. " Suddenly he felt something catch in his throat. He reached out blindly, pulling both young Joshua and Emily to him, and buried his face against them.

Lydia had vowed she would not cry, at least not until later when she was alone, but that nearly did her in. She was holding six-month-old Nathan and turned away quickly, biting her lip. The baby reached up, trying to touch her face.

Finally, Benjamin spoke softly. "Nathan?"

He looked up. His father motioned with his head. "Parley's ready."

Looking in the direction his father was indicating, Nathan saw a figure standing alone about a half block up the street, a valise in one hand, a knapsack over his shoulder. He nodded. As usual, Parley was right on time.

Mary Ann stepped to Lydia and took the baby from her. Nathan had already made his good-byes with the rest of his family—a massive bear clasp from Matthew; desperate hugs from Melissa and Rebecca; a long, clinging one with a soft kiss on the cheek from his mother; a quick handshake with Melissa's husband; a longer, harder one with his father. Now he turned to his wife.

He gathered her into his arms with great tenderness. "Good-bye, my darling. I shall write you often."

"Good-bye, Nathan," she whispered. "May God be with you."

He kissed her long and tenderly, then stepped back and picked up his knapsack. He looked around at each one of them once more, and sighed and smiled at the same time. Then, with one last look at Lydia, he strode down the walk and out the gate.

They watched him as he joined Parley and they both turned and set off, moving north. It was only the eleventh of April, and Lake Erie was not yet open for shipping; so they would walk to Painesville and there catch a series of stagecoaches across Ohio and Pennsylvania to Buffalo, New York.

As they finally moved out of sight, the family turned back to face each other. Mary Ann looked to Melissa's husband. "Carl, thank you for coming to see Nathan off. I know this is a busy time at the livery stable. That was nice of you."

He shrugged it off, but seemed pleased at the compliment. Melissa turned to Matthew. "I suppose you'll be the next Steed to be leaving, off on your own mission somewhere."

"Him or Papa," Rebecca said.

Melissa's jaw dropped "You, Papa? You're going on a mission?"

He shrugged. "I haven't been asked yet." He sounded a little disappointed. "Actually, I'm beginning to wonder if Joseph thinks I am unworthy."

"You've been too busy working on the temple," Mary Ann said, jumping to his defense. "The Lord needed you there so you—" She stopped. Carl had made a soft sound of disgust and was shaking his head. "What, Carl?"

He looked quickly at Benjamin and shook his head again, more firmly now. "Nothing."

But Benjamin had caught the look too and wasn't about to let it pass. "No, Carl, say it. We've always been honest with each other."

Melissa was warning Carl with her eyes, but he was just stubborn enough to speak his mind, no matter what she thought. "That's right. Let's call you and Matthew both, then there won't be a single male left in the Steed family to care for the women and children."

"Carl!" Melissa said in dismay.

"No," Benjamin said, waving a hand at his daughter, "it's all right. I suppose it does look like that to you, Carl. But we feel pretty strongly about answering the call of the Lord."

"I don't think the Lord wants men to leave their families."

Though Carl had not spoken to her, or even looked in her direction, Lydia felt that she had to say something. After all, it was her husband who had just left. She looked at her brother-in-law. "Carl, I would like to say something," she said. Her voice was even and calm. "I will miss Nathan terribly, but there is nowhere I would rather have him right now. Nowhere."

He gave a short, derisive laugh. "Sorry, Lydia. I know you're trying to be brave, but I don't believe that."

Melissa's eyes flashed anger. "I don't think it's necessary that you be rude to Lydia, Carl," she said tightly.

"I'm not being rude. I'm being honest." His voice was getting snappish. "I know she thinks missionary work is important, but do you really believe Lydia would rather have Nathan gone than here?"

Lydia stepped around to face him more directly. "Why are you asking Melissa, Carl? Why don't you ask me?"

"Because I think you have convinced yourself to be the noble Mormon wife. I don't really think you are being honest with yourself."

"Carl—," Benjamin started.

"No," Lydia said, "I want to answer." She took a deep breath, her eyes steady and determined. "When Nathan came home the other night and told me Heber Kimball had called him to go to Canada, for a moment I was sick. I hate it when he's gone."

Carl started to respond to that, but she cut him off quickly. "But . . ." She paused for a moment to gather force. "But almost instantly there came into my mind and heart a feeling of peace, a feeling of great joy. I knew, Carl"—her voice dropped with a sudden intensity—"I *knew* the Lord wanted him to go. And so I say again, I will miss him terribly, the children will miss him terribly, but there is nowhere I would rather have my husband be at this moment than on the road to Canada."

"Well," Carl muttered stubbornly, "I think when a man's got a wife and kids, his place is with the family."

Rebecca was only one day past breaking off her relationship with Arthur Wilkinson. And a major reason for her doing so stemmed from watching what was happening between Carl and Melissa over religion. So, surprisingly—for gentle Rebecca—she took him on. "As I remember it," she said, "when the Savior said, 'Follow me,' to Peter, James, and John, he didn't add, 'unless, of course, you have a family. Then you're excused.'"

He swung around to her. "Peter, James, and John were Apostles. That's different."

"Parley P. Pratt is an Apostle," Lydia broke in.

He blew out his breath in an explosion of exasperation. "I'm sorry, there are no more Apostles today."

Rebecca was not about to be deflected. "In the Gospel of Matthew, Jesus said that if we love our family more than him, we are not worthy of him. Doesn't that suggest sometimes God asks us to put him first, even before our families?"

"Of course. We always love God more than anything. But he doesn't say anything about leaving your family time after time. This is the seventh or eighth time Nathan has left Lydia."

Before she could answer, Benjamin raised a hand. When he spoke, it was slowly and with kindness. There was no animosity, no irritation. "Carl, you're right. A man's family is very important. It is in God's sight too."

"Then why would you leave them?"

"May I ask you a question?"

Sensing a possible trap, Carl nodded warily.

"Last month you took a business trip to Cleveland. As I remember, you were gone for almost a week."

"Yes."

"So you left your family."

Now he saw it. He shook his head vigorously. "That's different. I had to purchase two new carriages. They're not sold here in Kirtland. Besides, I was only gone for a week, not two or three months."

"And what if you had to go somewhere else—let's say, to New York or Boston? Suppose it took you a month. There is no choice. If your business is going to survive, you've got to do it. Would you?"

"That's not a fair comparison. The livery stable is how I support my family. It's my livelihood, my work."

"Ah," Benjamin said sagely. "That's exactly the point. God has a work also. He has told us it is his *work* to bring to pass the immortality and eternal life of man. He calls on us to help him do that work. It would be wonderful if we could do that work without ever leaving Kirtland, but unfortunately we can't."

Carl's jaw was set. "It's not the same. One's your occupation, one is religion."

"I see," Benjamin said slowly. "So man's work is more important than God's work?"

Carl's mouth opened, then shut again. Melissa watched her husband closely, but said nothing. Mary Ann was looking up at Benjamin, her eyes filled with a little bit of amazement and a considerable amount of love. "And," she said very softly, not taking her eyes from his face, "if the Lord does decide it's time for Benjamin to labor somewhere besides here in Kirtland, I want you to know, Carl, I will miss him more fiercely than I can describe to you. But, like Lydia, I will truly say to you, there is nowhere else I would rather have this man be than where the Lord wants him."

———◆———

Joshua kept half turning his head so he could eye Caroline in the moonlight. He was enchanted. Her features were so finely shaped, the nose and mouth in perfect balance, the lips more soft than the velvet surface of a rose petal. He had not had a woman stir him like this since the spring of 1827 when he had fallen wildly in love with Lydia McBride.

Caroline caught him watching her and stopped in the middle of the path. She looked up at him. Her eyes were half in shadow, dark and lustrous and unreadable. "And just what are you thinking about so deeply, Mr. Steed?"

He wanted to laugh, toss off something clever and profoundly witty, but it was not part of his character, so he decided to answer her honestly. "Well," he began, "I was thinking two things."

She nodded primly. "Number one?"

"I was thinking that we have been out here with the Montagues for two days now, and this is the first time we have been alone together."

She laughed lightly. "I think Mr. and Mrs. Wesley felt it was time the situation be remedied."

He smiled. Richard Wesley, with some obvious nudging by his wife, had come forth with the suggestion that it was a lovely night for a walk. The Montagues had been startled, then jumped in enthusiastically, almost pushing Joshua and Caroline out of the door.

"And number two?"

He hesitated. "I was wondering how many days it will be

before it is proper to call you Caroline instead of Mrs. Mendenhall."

She cocked her head slightly, then turned and started to walk again. "I thought we had passed that point yesterday, but I didn't want to be forward."

He felt a little jolt of excitement. "Then Caroline it is."

"Yes, Joshua," she said with a winsome smile, "Caroline it is."

They strolled on for several moments, neither speaking. Without looking at her, he finally spoke. "And just what are *you* thinking about so deeply?"

Her head came up quickly, and he could see he had startled her. And more surprising, he saw she was blushing. She shook her head quickly.

"I see," he said with mock disappointment. "So the old saying 'Turnabout is fair play' doesn't apply here?"

She stopped again and looked at him searchingly. "All right," she murmured. The blush deepened and she had to look away. "I was thinking that you've asked me all kinds of questions about myself. You know a lot about me. I know hardly anything about you. What about your family? Are they in Missouri? Have you . . . ?" She couldn't get it out.

"Ever been married?" he said, trying to keep his voice casual, even though he had felt a sudden chill go through him.

She laughed quickly in embarrassment. "Yes."

Joshua fought down the turmoil. For the last four years things in the past haunted him, dogged his heels in spite of every attempt to put them behind him. Were they now to intrude upon him again when they could do him the most damage?

He realized she was looking up at him with a sudden concern. He forced a quick smile. "No, my family is not in Missouri. I'm originally from New York. My family is now in Ohio somewhere. I haven't seen them for several years."

"Oh." After a moment, she looked away, and he realized that her other question still hung in the air between them. But she was too much a lady to push him further. Once again she turned and started walking slowly. He watched her for a moment, torn with conflicting feelings: tell her everything; tell her nothing. He knew that neither of those was a workable option. Not if he wanted to have the relationship continue its favorable progress.

He moved quickly to her side and, after a moment, took her by the elbow. She slipped her arm easily through his. He took a quick breath and plunged in. "I was married once." He was choosing his words carefully. "About five years ago."

She looked up, and this time her smile was broad and filled with amusement. "Good," she said. "For a moment there I thought you were trying to work up enough nerve to tell me you are married now."

He laughed, more easily now. "No. I'm not married now. I . . . well, to be honest, I married on impulse one night. We had known each other for some time, but . . ." He pushed down a stab of guilt, glad that Jessica wasn't hearing this. "But there weren't a lot of single women in Independence at that time." He went on more quickly now, trying not to let his emotions reach his face. "It was never wonderful. After a couple of years, she joined a group of religious fanatics. I tried to talk some sense into her, but she . . . she ran off with them. I divorced her a short time later."

"Oh," Caroline said again, this time quietly, letting the information digest.

"Are you getting chilly?" he asked before she could ask anything further. They were approaching the big main house.

She nodded, pulling the shawl around her a little more tightly. "Just a bit."

He squeezed her arm and smiled. "Well, I'm sure everyone inside is dying to know if this walk could mark the beginning of a formal courtship."

She looked up. At the angle she was standing, the moonlight caught her face in full light. He could see that her eyes were filled with both amusement and questioning. "And what shall you tell them?"

He laughed easily, then instantly sobered. "I shall tell them that I do not know what the beautiful Caroline Mendenhall thinks, but as for Joshua Steed, he's hoping the answer is yes."

Her lips softened and parted slightly as she smiled up at him. At that moment he could not remember ever seeing anything more beautiful than her face. "I think you could tell them that Caroline Mendenhall was hoping the handsome Joshua Steed would say something exactly like what he just said."

Chapter Six

Parley Pratt stopped and turned back. For a long moment he stared at the courthouse whence they had just come. His heavy brows lowered until they almost touched. "I don't understand it, Nathan. The prophecy Brother Kimball pronounced upon my head back in Kirtland was so clear, so definite."

Nathan sighed. He was as despondent as his companion. He didn't have the answers.

" 'You shall go to Toronto,' " Parley quoted softly, " 'and you shall find a people prepared for the fulness of the gospel, and many shall come to the knowledge of the truth.' " He sighed. "If it hadn't been *so* definite."

Nathan nodded wearily. They had come with such high hopes. It had been a tedious and hard journey, taking just over a week, but their expectations were such that their spirits did not lag. They had stopped briefly at the mighty falls of Niagara, awed by the thunderous majesty of the torrent. By the time they crossed into Canada, spring had come in full force, and the roads were muddy and nearly impassable.

As they approached Hamilton on the western tip of Lake Ontario, cold, dirty, hungry, and exhausted, residents told them the steamer service between Hamilton and Toronto had just opened again. It would save them four or five hard days of traveling. Unfortunately, neither of them had enough money to purchase the two-dollar fare required. Undaunted, Parley pulled them off into a grove of trees, and they knelt in prayer and asked the Lord to help speed them on their journey. They rose and continued on. Barely had they entered Hamilton when a man accosted them on the street, saying he felt impressed they were in need of money. He slipped ten dollars into Parley's hand and a letter of introduction to one John Taylor, a resident of Toronto. Needless to say, their spirits had been buoyed up tremendously by that event.

But they had quickly been dashed again. The Taylors were kind enough, but offered them nothing more than a place to leave their baggage while they found a room. They had found lodging and the next morning set out to find a place to preach. That had been over eight hours ago now. They had visited more than a dozen ministers, asking if they might preach to their congregations or at least hold meetings in their church houses. They had been to the civic offices and sought permission to preach in the marketplaces. And they had been to the courthouse and asked for the use of that building. But word of the Mormons had already reached Toronto. The response had ranged from cool politeness to blunt rejection, and the bottom line was that no one was going to give them the opportunity to preach. It had been a long day. Nathan's feet hurt, his calves ached abominably, and he was tired of being treated as though they were anathema.

Parley finally spoke. "We had better return to the Taylors' and get our belongings as we promised."

"But what shall we do, Parley? After steamer passage and our board and room last night, we are out of funds. Where shall we stay?"

Parley pulled his coat closer around him. The sun was low in the sky, and the air was already losing its earlier warmth. "I do not know, Nathan. This is surely a rather unpromising beginning. What more can we do?"

Nathan had no answer for that either, and for several minutes they trudged on in silence. Suddenly Parley stopped. They were nearing a stand of pine trees where there were no houses. Nathan walked on for several steps before he realized that his companion had fallen behind him. He stopped and turned. "What?"

"We are being fools again, Brother Nathan."

Nathan laughed without mirth. "That wouldn't surprise me, Parley. That wouldn't surprise me at all."

Parley laughed now too, only with real enthusiasm. "Do you remember me ever talking about my promissory notes?"

Nathan shook his head. "I don't think so."

Parley got a faraway look in his eyes. "Around the beginning of 1830, Thankful and I started a list of what I called the Lord's promissory notes."

"What do you mean by a promissory note?"

His eyes half closed as he quoted softly. " 'Seek ye first the kingdom of God, and his righteousness; and all these things shall be added unto you.' 'Every one that hath forsaken houses, or brethren, or sisters, or father, or mother, or wife, or children, or lands, for my name's sake, shall receive an hundredfold, and shall inherit everlasting life.' "

Nathan was nodding. "Yes, I see what you mean."

"That's when we decided to sell our farm. It was while Thankful and I were coming east to 'collect' on those notes that I felt impressed to get off the canal boat in Newark. Within hours after that, I had the Book of Mormon in my hand." He looked directly at Nathan. "The Lord's promises are sure."

"I believe that too, Parley."

"Well, I have found others since then. In the Book of Mormon. In the Doctrine and Covenants. There's one in the Doctrine and Covenants that may apply to our circumstance right now."

"What is that?"

"I can't quote it exactly, but it was given by the Lord when some of the elders were returning from their missions. The Lord said something like this: 'Go forth and proclaim the gospel, and I will go before your face. I will be on your right hand and on your left, and mine angels shall be round about you to bear you up, and my Spirit shall be in your hearts.'"

Nathan was looking at his companion with open shame. "We haven't really trusted in him yet today, have we?"

Parley shook his head, then gestured toward the trees. "Shall we?"

They found a secluded spot, hidden from sight of the roadway. Parley smoothed a place for them with his foot, then they both dropped to their knees. He looked to Nathan. "Would you petition the Lord in our behalf?"

Nathan nodded, then bowed his head. But for a moment he did not close his eyes. He let his thoughts turn heavenward, trying to push down the frustrations and discouragement that filled him.

Then he started inwardly. *Today is April nineteenth.* The thought popped into his mind unbidden. He felt instant shame. Just a little over two weeks ago he had been sitting in the Kirtland Temple. Within a few feet of where he sat, the Savior had appeared to Joseph Smith and Oliver Cowdery. *The Savior! How quickly we forget!*

Moses had come too. "I give you the keys of the gathering of Israel," Moses had told Joseph and Oliver. Wasn't that the reason why he and Parley were here in Canada, to help restore scattered Israel? And now they were discouraged? They were questioning whether God could fulfill his word. The very blessing Heber C. Kimball had given Parley was a promissory note! In deep shame, Nathan closed his eyes, and began to pray.

———◆———

John Taylor was a very distinguished-looking man. He was nearly six feet tall and carried himself with an erectness that gave him a natural dignity. Born in England, he had not lost his distinct British accent. That, added to his tendency to speak with deliberation, always choosing his words carefully, gave him an air of nobility that was most impressive. Not yet thirty, he was dignified without being stiff, affable without being frivolous. Unfortunately, he had heard numerous unfavorable tales of Joseph Smith and the gold Bible.

So when the two young men from Ohio returned for their baggage, though he was a little disappointed they had been treated so shabbily, he still showed no inclination to help. His wife, Leonora, a lovely woman of considerable grace and charm, seemed more distressed by what had happened. Several glances passed between husband and wife as Parley related the experiences of the day, and Nathan sensed that she was ready to offer their home to the two missionaries. But her husband gave her no encouragement, and so she said nothing. He would treat the Mormons courteously, but he would not provide them a place from which they could carry on their work.

After hearing their report, Mr. Taylor took them into the back bedroom where they had left their belongings. As they came out, Mr. Taylor softened a little. He seemed a little chagrined at his intransigence. As they reentered the hallway, he again began questioning Parley about the ministers they had visited and their responses to the two Mormons.

Nathan went on down the hall a few steps to wait. He could tell that Parley was hoping this meant Mr. Taylor was changing his mind, but Nathan didn't believe it would happen. A gentleman through and through, John Taylor was simply trying to soften the blow a little.

A rap on the front door brought Nathan's attention away from the two men. He heard footsteps. Mrs. Taylor came from the kitchen to the entry hall. There was the sound of an opening door, then an exclamation of pleased surprise. Another woman's voice could be heard. Still half-focused on Parley and Mr. Taylor's conversation, Nathan also listened idly to the exchange between Mrs. Taylor and her visitor. Suddenly he leaned forward. Mrs. Taylor's voice was carrying clearly down the hall.

"Oh, Mrs. Walton, I am so glad to see you, particularly at this moment."

The other woman seemed surprised. "Why is that?"

"Because we have two gentlemen visiting with us from the United States. They say the Lord has sent them to this city to preach the gospel. They've spent the day applying in vain to the clergy and the various authorities for an opportunity to fill their mission. Now they are about to depart."

Nathan edged closer to the arched opening that led into the sitting room, feeling only partially guilty for trying to eavesdrop.

"These men may be men of God," Mrs. Taylor was continuing. "I feel sorry they have to leave."

"How remarkable!" said the unseen Mrs. Walton. "Now I understand the feelings and the spirit which brought me to your house at this time."

Nathan was waving at Parley behind his back. Parley evidently saw him, for the two men fell silent. Now the conversation going on in the next room carried clearly to them as well.

"What do you mean?" Mrs. Taylor asked.

"I have been busy doing the wash today. Bending over the tub all day had made me weary, so I felt as though I needed to take a walk. I decided to follow that feeling and thought I should visit my sister, on the other side of town. But as I passed your door, the Spirit bade me go in. I thought to myself, 'I shall, on my way back from my sister's house.' But then the Spirit spoke clearly. 'Go in now,' it said. So I did."

Nathan turned. Mr. Taylor and Parley had now moved up quietly to join him and were listening intently.

Mrs. Walton spoke again. "Now I understand why I am here, and I am thankful I have followed the promptings I received. You tell those men I am a widow, but I have a spare room and bed, and food aplenty. They shall have a home at my house, and two large rooms which they can use to preach in as they wish."

Nathan felt a hand on his shoulder and turned to see Parley smiling at him. Nathan reached up and gripped his arm, suddenly feeling overwhelmed.

"You tell those men," Mrs. Walton said clearly, "you tell them I will send my son John to pilot them to my house. In the meantime, I shall gather up my friends and relatives to hear them preach this very night. I feel, dear Mrs. Taylor, that you are exactly right. These are men of God, and the Lord has sent them to us with a message that will do us good."

———•———

True to her word, Mrs. Walton returned and immediately sent her son to escort the two missionaries to her home while she spread the word that there would be a meeting there later that evening. When Parley and Nathan arrived they were welcomed warmly. They were given one of her best rooms and an ample and most welcome supper.

Now the hour had arrived. They were seated around a large table. Mrs. Walton's parlor was nearly filled to overflowing. Mrs. Walton stood. The conversation died out immediately, and all turned to look at her. She smiled at the group, her eyes resting for a moment on each one. "Thank you all for coming. I am pleased to introduce to you Mr. Parley Pratt and Mr. Nathan Steed, from the United States. They have come to Canada to preach the gospel and have been looking for someone willing to hear their message."

She turned to Parley. "Mr. Pratt, there is a small group here in Toronto who have, for some years, been meeting together on a regular basis to search the scriptures. We have been anxiously looking for some providential event which would gather the sheep into one fold, build up the true church as in days of old, and prepare the humble followers of the Lamb, now scattered and divided, to receive their coming Lord when he shall descend to reign on the earth."

Parley nodded soberly. "That is most commendable, Mrs. Walton."

"As soon as Leonora Taylor spoke of you being there in her house, I felt assured, as by a strange and unaccountable presentiment, that you were messengers with important tidings on these subjects. I was constrained to invite you here. Now, here we are, and we anxiously await your words."

Parley stood slowly, then bowed slightly to their hostess. "Thank you, Mrs. Walton. I believe you will see that the presentiment of which you speak was none other than the influence of the Holy Spirit, and that you will be blessed for following its promptings."

As usual, Parley wasted no time in idle conversation but went right to the task at hand. In moments he briefly recounted the story of Joseph Smith and told of angelic messengers bringing back the priesthood and its keys to the earth again. He testified of ancient scripture being restored and the blessings of having additional volumes of God's word. No one spoke. Every eye was fixed upon him as he then told them that the Church of Jesus Christ had been restored to the earth again with the same organization and ordinances that were established when Christ was on the earth.

Parley stopped, letting his eyes scan the group. "I myself have been ordained an Apostle and commissioned to go forth among the peoples of the world, to minister the baptism of repentance for remission of sins in the name of Jesus Christ. Brother Steed and I are also commissioned to administer the gift of the Holy Ghost, to heal the sick, to comfort those who mourn, to bind up the brokenhearted, and to proclaim the acceptable year of the Lord."

Mrs. Walton was sitting right beside Parley. Now he turned so he could more easily face her, but still he did not look down at her. "My companion and I were directed to this city by the Spirit of the Lord, with a promise that we should find here a people prepared to receive the gospel. But when we came and were rejected by all parties, we were about to leave this city."

Now finally he looked down at Mrs. Walton. When she saw him looking at her with those piercing eyes, she looked away quickly, embarrassed by his attention. Now Parley's voice softened, and he spoke more slowly. "But then the Lord sent a widow, at the very moment we were preparing to depart, and thus my companion and I have been cared for like Elijah of old." He smiled gently. "And now, dear Sister Walton, I bless your house, and all your family and kindred in His name. Your sins shall be forgiven you. You shall understand and obey the gospel, and be filled with the Holy Ghost."

Her eyes were shining when she finally looked up at him. "Thank you," she whispered. Then immediately she turned to look at the circle of rapt listeners. One by one they began to nod. Satisfied, she turned back to Parley. "Well, Mr. Pratt, this is precisely the message we were waiting for. We believe your words and are desirous to be baptized."

Nathan caught himself as he realized his mouth had dropped open and he was gaping at Mrs. Walton. Again several heads around the table were bobbing up and down to signify their agreement. But that was nothing compared to the shock he received next. Parley smiled around at the group, but he was shaking his head. "It is your duty and privilege to be baptized. But wait a little while until we have the opportunity to teach the others with whom you are religiously affiliated, so that you may all partake of the blessing together."

———— • ————

The next morning was gray and overcast, the humidity putting a definite chill in the air even though it was the third week in April. They had stayed up well past midnight answering questions from the group Mrs. Walton had gathered, and Nathan and Parley showed signs of having had little sleep. But nothing could dampen the spirits of the two missionaries as they joined the Walton family for morning prayer and an excellent breakfast fare.

Nathan watched Mrs. Walton closely to see if she was feeling any disappointment over Parley's suggestion that she delay her baptism. But she greeted them with enthusiasm, and the moment grace had been said over the food, she turned to the two elders. "Mr. Pratt, Mr. Steed. Would you mind if I asked you a question?"

"Of course not," Parley boomed, spearing a thick piece of sausage onto his plate.

"Last night you spoke of your commission."

"Yes."

"You are both elders in the Church?"

Parley seemed reticent to take the lead this morning and looked to Nathan.

"Yes," Nathan said, "both Brother Pratt and I hold the office of elder in the Melchizedek Priesthood."

She nodded quickly, pressing on. "In the book of James it says, 'Is any sick among you? let him call for the elders of the church; and let them pray over him, anointing him with oil in the name of the Lord.' " She hesitated now, not wanting to appear to be too forward. "Last night Brother Pratt spoke of healing the sick. Is that part of your commission too?"

Nathan smiled. "You know your Bible well, Mrs. Walton. Yes, we believe that the authority given to us includes the privilege of laying hands on the sick."

John Walton, who was nearly sixteen, had been following the conversation closely. Now he spoke through a mouthful of scrambled eggs to his mother. "Are you thinking of Widow Compton, Ma?"

His mother nodded firmly, then turned back to her guests. "Would you consider visiting her this morning? She is a dear friend and in such need." She looked first to Nathan, then to Parley.

Parley set down his fork. "But of course. Tell us more about her."

"She is a woman who has met more than her share of tragedy. Her husband died of cholera about two years ago. She has four little children to support and was forced to resort to teaching school in order to care for them."

Nathan thought of some of the widows he had known, frontier farmers' wives who could barely read and write themselves. "She was fortunate to have enough learning to qualify as a teacher."

"Yes," Mrs. Walton agreed. "Except now even that is taken from her."

"She's gone blind!" little twelve-year-old Laura chimed in.

"Yes," John said, clucking his tongue. "She's totally blind."

———————•———————

When the raging inflammation struck both of Mrs. Compton's eyes at the same time, within days the pain was so intense and the swelling so complete that she was totally unable to see. No longer able to teach school, she and her children became public wards, cared for by the Methodist society as best their meager means would allow. The economic havoc the disability had wreaked on the family was evident the moment Laura turned the two missionaries in at the tiny house in a poorer section of Toronto. The yard was cluttered with discarded furniture and tools. The door hung loosely from rusty hinges. Dirty sheets and blankets hung at each of the windows. From inside came the faint sound of a young child screaming its lungs out. There was a deeper voice, the words not quite intelligible but seeming to direct someone to help the child.

Nathan looked at Parley, who merely shook his head slowly. If Laura Walton was shocked by the situation, she gave no sign of it. She walked right up to the door, banged twice on it sharply, then immediately opened it and stuck her head inside. "Mrs. Compton," she called cheerfully, "it's Laura Walton. My mother has asked me to bring someone to see you."

Nathan peered through the door, trying to see into the gloom of the house, but everything inside seemed perfectly black. With the opening of the door, the howling of the child was now loud and piercing.

"Charlene," a woman's voice shouted. There was a tired desperation to it now. "*Please* get your sister."

There was the sound of grumbling from the voice of a girl who Nathan guessed could not be much older than eight or ten, then footsteps. In a moment, the cry started to lessen, first to a fussy wail, then finally to a whimper.

Again the woman's voice spoke. "Tell me again? Laura Walton, is that you?"

"Yes, ma'am, Mrs. Compton. My mama asked me to bring two visitors to see you. Can we come in?"

There was a murmur of shock, perhaps even a hoarse no. Nathan leaned forward, straining to hear.

"They're men of God, Mrs. Compton," Laura said firmly. "They've come to see if they can help you."

Nathan gave Parley a sharp look. Oh, the faith of a child! Parley nodded soberly, and Nathan felt a little stir of uncertainty down in his stomach. What had Mrs. Walton gotten them into here?

There was another sound, and while Nathan again could not distinguish what it was, Laura took it as an invitation. She opened the door and stepped back. "There you go, Mr. Pratt, Mr. Steed. Please help her."

Once inside, they stood in the small entryway for a moment, letting their eyes adjust to the deep gloom. Gradually things came into focus. It was one room, with a small alcove off the far wall. There was very little furniture—a mattress with wadded up bedclothes in the corner; a sofa that was low to the floor, obviously so worn as to be no longer serviceable to anyone else; and a wooden table with a single chair. The woman sat on that chair, seemingly staring at them, her eyes a white slash in the darkness. With a start, Nathan realized she wore a white rag around her eyes.

The noise of the little child noisily sucking on her thumb drew his eye to one corner. The older sister was not as old as Nathan had guessed. Either that or she was very small for her age. She looked to be barely six. She was holding a little girl who probably was not two yet. Suddenly he realized two more children—both boys, one maybe three, one four or five—were staring at them from almost right beneath their feet. The floor was strewn with things Nathan couldn't identify. The table was likewise a clutter of nameless things. The odor in the room was strong, musty, almost fetid.

"Mrs. Compton," Parley said softly, starting across the room toward her, "my name is Parley P. Pratt. I'm from America. I have Mr. Nathan Steed as my companion. Your good friend, Mrs. Walton, asked us to come."

Nathan started to follow. His foot kicked something and sent it off clattering. A wooden cup. The boys started to giggle wildly.

"I'm sorry," Mrs. Compton said, too quickly, "I've been meaning to clean, I . . ." She let it die, seeming to realize how empty it sounded.

Parley was to her now and took her hand. "It's all right, Mrs. Compton. Mrs. Walton has told us all that has befallen you."

"Bless Isabelle Walton," the muffled voice said fervently. "She is a true Christian woman."

Closer now too, Nathan was shocked to see that she could be no more than thirty. The impression from across the room had been of a woman in her fifties. She was clad in a long nightgown, which even in the darkness he could see was soiled and worn. Nathan wondered how long it had been since she had been dressed. Her hair was matted and tangled. But suddenly he felt an overwhelming sense of love and compassion for this woman. Two years ago what had she been like? Happy, educated, safe, secure. Then a husband dies. Then inflammation strikes. Sight is taken from her. How quickly life can snatch happiness away!

He reached out and touched her arm. "We're here, Mrs. Compton. We want to help you."

There was a quick clamp on his hand and a desperate pressure from her fingers. "God bless you, sir."

"May we open the curtains a little, Mrs. Compton, to let in a little light?"

"No!" The fingernails dug into the back of Nathan's hand. "No," she said more softly, "even this much light brings me excruciating pain. I cannot bear the tiniest sliver of sunlight."

Parley straightened. He began to speak, softly and soothingly, but with quiet power. He told her of their call to come to Toronto, and of their coming to the Taylor home and then to the Widow Walton's. He told her of the previous night's meeting, and of Mrs. Walton's request that morning.

"We are ministers of Jesus Christ, Mrs. Compton. Do you believe me when I say that?"

There was a long pause. Even the youngest child seemed to sense that something different was happening. All four children watched the tableau in the middle of the room without a sound. "Yes," she finally said.

"Do you believe Jesus Christ has the power to heal you?"

There was another pause, then a muffled sob. "Yes."

Parley turned to Nathan and nodded. He took a small jar of oil from his pocket and handed it to Nathan, who stepped around behind the woman, took the stopper from the bottle, and gently poured one drop onto the crown of her head. Then, after handing the jar back to Parley, he reached out and laid his hands on the woman's head. "Mrs. Compton, in the name of Jesus Christ, and by the power of the Melchizedek Priesthood which I hold, I anoint your head with this oil that has been consecrated for the express purpose of healing the sick. And this I do to the end that you may be blessed of God. In the name of Jesus Christ, amen."

He lifted his hands. Parley placed his hands on the woman's head, and Nathan, feeling a great sense of awe coming over him, laid his hands on top of Parley's.

"Mrs. Emmaline Compton," Parley began, "by the power and authority given to me, and in the name of Jesus Christ, I seal this anointing upon your head. The Lord is mindful of you, Mrs. Compton. He is mindful of your sorrow and of your affliction. He is mindful of your needs."

There was the briefest pause, then Parley's voice rose in solemn majesty. "By the power of the Master who loves us all, I now say unto you, Mrs. Compton, that your eyes shall be well from this very hour. The Lord has looked down on you in mercy. Give him the glory, for it is his will that you shall see again. We say these things by the power of his authority and in his holy name, amen."

"Amen." Nathan dropped his hands to his sides.

The woman was openly crying now, and Nathan saw that

Parley had let one hand drop to rest upon her shoulder. Then suddenly she stopped. Her hands came up in front of her, as though she were looking at them, which was impossible because she still had the heavy bandage around her eyes. She stood up slowly, and both men stepped back. "The pain is gone," she whispered.

"What did you say?" Nathan asked, leaning forward to hear.

"The pain is gone!" One hand shot up to the back of her head and untwisted the strip of cloth. She let it fall from her face to the floor. "It's gone," she said again, turning first to look at Parley, then to Nathan.

"Mama?" One of the little boys had stood up. He sounded frightened.

In three steps she crossed the room to the front window. With one swipe of her hand the blankets came down. Though it was still gray and overcast outside, it was as though the room was flooded with sunlight. Laura Walton stood in the front yard, stunned at the sight of the woman at the window. Mrs. Compton waved, then without lowering her hand, began caressing the glass in tiny circular patterns.

Suddenly her shoulders began to shake and she buried her face in her hands. "I can see," she sobbed. "I can see."

The home of the Honorable Mr. William Patrick was in one of Toronto's finest neighborhoods. It was a large two-story home, set well back from the street. The white paint looked as new as yesterday, the dark green shutters as if they had been hung earlier in the day. The lawns were immaculately trimmed, the gardens profuse with shrubbery and flowers. It was a Sabbath afternoon in Upper Canada—the first Sabbath after Nathan and Parley's arrival—and the two missionaries were approaching the Patrick home with two newly found friends. Earlier that day they had gone to worship services with one of the men who had been coming to the meetings at Mrs. Walton's home. After the services, he had taken them up and introduced them to the preacher, who then invited them all home for dinner. During the meal, the minister told them about a group of people who met twice a week to study the Bible and see if they could find the truth. He said they were to meet that very afternoon and asked if Parley and Nathan wished to attend. Parley, with his usual aplomb, casually responded that yes, he thought that might be an enjoyable thing. Now as they saw the house where the meeting was to be held, Nathan was suitably impressed.

"My, my," he breathed. "What does this Mr. Patrick do for a living?"

The preacher gave the home an appraising look, then turned to the two missionaries. "Mr. Patrick holds an important office in the government. But he's a silver spoon. Born to money, he was. A real aristocrat. But he's a kind gentleman, a fine Christian."

"Then we care not what else he may be," Parley said magnanimously.

"Does your study group meet here all the time?" Nathan asked.

"No, but often. As you'll see, he has a room large enough for all of us to be together."

Nathan moved closer to Parley. "I feel like a bumpkin coming to the palace to see the king," he whispered.

Parley laughed softly, looking down at the plainness of their clothes. "Perhaps they'll put us in the servants' quarters." Then more earnestly he added, "I feel this is the reason we have come to Canada, Nathan. Let us go in and observe and see what shall develop."

As they moved up on the large front porch, the front door was standing open, so they went right in without waiting for someone to invite them. Nathan saw immediately that this was a house more finely furnished and tastefully decorated than anything that existed in Kirtland. As they walked down the short entry hall and into a large sitting room, Nathan felt more and more keenly that they were going to be misfits. Extra chairs and small benches had been brought in and there was seating for thirty or forty people. A well-dressed man was standing near a small cherry wood table on which lay several Bibles. He turned as they came into the room. "Welcome."

"Good afternoon, Brother Jackson," the preacher said. "May

I present two men who wish to join with us this evening. This is Mr. Parley Pratt and Mr. Nathan Steed."

As the man shook their hands, Nathan gave their companion a quick look, a little surprised that he did not say more about who they were and where they were from. But Mr. Jackson seemed not at all surprised at the thought of new guests. "Mr. Patrick is over with some of the others, but I'm sure he would bid you warm welcome." His hand reached out and touched a Bible. "We hope you find our little study group to be an uplifting experience. I don't know if you were told, but our purpose is to study the Bible and find out God's will for us." He glanced down at their empty hands. "Would you like a Bible? It's a rare night when we are not in the scriptures."

"Indeed," Parley said. "Thank you for your thoughtfulness."

They moved to four places near the back of the room. Nathan began to feel a little better as he watched the people come in. Some were obviously from the upper classes, but many were simply dressed and looked like farmers or laborers. Most carried Bibles, but some—like him and Parley—were given books by Mr. Jackson. Suddenly Nathan's head came up. "Look, there's Mr. and Mrs. Taylor." The couple they had first met when they came to Toronto was just coming into the room. "And the Widow Walton."

"But of course," their friend explained. "I thought you knew. They are part of our group as well."

The Taylors and Mrs. Walton spotted them. John Taylor raised one eyebrow, but smiled pleasantly and raised a hand in greeting. As they found their seats, the man who was obviously hosting the meeting moved to the front of the room. Mr. Jackson sat down. "The hour has arrived," Mr. Patrick said without preamble. "It is time to begin. We'll ask Mrs. Patrick to lead us in a hymn. Then Mr. Sharp will invoke the Lord's blessings and we shall begin."

As they sang the hymn, without accompaniment, Nathan felt his fears start to calm. There was a solemn but pleasant spirit about the group. They were obviously a God-fearing people, and he was impressed with their desire to study the scriptures and know what God would have them do. Like Parley, he had a strong feeling they had finally found their purpose in coming to Canada.

To his surprise, when the prayer was finished Mr. Patrick stood only briefly. "As you know, this is not a formal worship service, and we have no prepared sermons delivered. This is a study group. Anyone is at liberty to introduce a subject of his or her choosing for our discussion. We have invited the Spirit to be present. May we incline our hearts toward God so that it may be." And with that, he sat down.

For several moments no one spoke. Nathan gave Parley a sidelong look, half expecting him to seize such a ripe opportunity; but true to his word, Parley did not stir. Then, to Nathan's surprise, John Taylor did. For a moment Mr. Taylor looked around, seeing if there was anyone else who wished to speak. When it was obvious there was not, he stood. He already had his Bible open in the palm of one hand. He looked down at it for a moment, then up at the group.

"I should like to discuss a text from the eighth chapter of the book of Acts," he said in a measured and dignified voice. "It is the story of Philip and his ministry in Samaria."

Instantly there was a noticeable rustling sound as people opened their scriptures and began turning pages. Nathan quickly found the "Acts of the Apostles" and flipped over to the eighth chapter.

Taylor led them through it slowly, reading with great solemnity, his voice rising to emphasize certain points. Philip went to Samaria and there began a remarkable ministry, preaching Christ unto the people. And the people gave heed to him with one accord. Great spiritual power was shown. Unclean spirits were cast out, the sick healed, the lame made to walk. Many were baptized, but Philip could not give the gift of the Holy Ghost.

Now Taylor began to read more slowly, pausing to look around at the group after points he felt were important that they not miss. " 'Now when the apostles which were at Jerusalem heard that Samaria had received the word of God, they sent unto them Peter and John—' " He looked around. "Remember, now, that Peter and John are of the Twelve." Down went his eyes again. " '—who, when they were come down, prayed for them, that they might receive the Holy Ghost: (for as yet he was fallen upon none of them: only they were baptized in the name of the Lord Jesus). Then laid they their hands on them, and they received the Holy Ghost.' "

Mr. Taylor closed the book and let his eyes run across the upturned faces. No one stirred. There was not a sound in the room. "Where is our Philip?" he suddenly demanded.

There was a ripple of surprise.

He held up the Bible and waved it at them. "We have had the gospel of Jesus Christ preached to us. Do we believe?"

"We do!" someone murmured fervently. "Amen," said another.

He was very somber now. "So where is *our* receiving the word with joy and being baptized? The Samaritans were given spiritual gifts. Where are *our* spiritual gifts? Where are *our* Peter and John?"

Nathan had turned to Parley and was staring at him wide-eyed. Parley nodded thoughtfully, then turned back to watch John Taylor.

"Where are *our* Apostles? Who shall come and give *us* the gift of the Holy Ghost?"

Nathan wanted to leap to his feet, pound Parley on the back, and say, "Here is an Apostle of the Lord, right here in your midst." But Parley seemed unaffected. Twice more Nathan shot him querying looks, but the first time he just smiled and shook his head slightly. The second time he patted Nathan's knee, gently reminding him to be patient.

"In the New Testament, we find the Church as Jesus himself organized it," Taylor continued. Now his face was grave, his eyes troubled. "Are we not safe in looking to what the Church was like then as a model on which to base our own worship?"

"Hear, hear!" a man behind Nathan said loudly.

Encouraged by that response, John Taylor pointed at the Bible. "Yet look at the pattern we find, and where is its equal? We do not have the ordinances and the ministry as described here. It says that when the Samaritans believed and received the word with joy, then they were baptized. We, for the most part, were sprinkled in our infancy, but this was not baptism as we find it in the New Testament. And if it was, we neither believed in it nor rejoiced in it at the time, because we were infants.

"Again, looking to this as our pattern, it says Peter and John were commissioned as Apostles, and therefore they could administer the Holy Spirit by the laying on of hands, a gift of such supernal worth that Simon the Sorcerer tried to purchase it from them. Do we have men who hold such a commission? No. We have ministers commissioned by the King and Parliament of England, or by John Wesley and his successors, without any pretence of a word from the Lord or his angels to commission them."

Nathan felt a little lightheaded. Was it just him? It was as if he or Parley had written out the things that John Taylor was saying in order to set the group up to hear their message. He saw Mrs. Walton watching them. She was smiling broadly. He looked at Parley and saw the wonder in his eyes too.

"And here is a third thing in the pattern that I find troubling," Taylor said, jabbing at his Bible with one finger. "The Samaritans had spiritual gifts. It says that unclean spirits were cast out, that the sick were healed. And this is a pattern not just in this chapter but throughout the New Testament. Before his ascension, Jesus said, 'These signs shall follow them that believe—in my name you shall cast out devils, and heal the sick, and speak in tongues.' And this is exactly what we find in the Bible. Peter and John healed a man lame from his mother's womb. On the day of Pentecost, the Apostles all spoke in tongues. They cast out evil spirits, healed those who were infirm. And that is not all. Everywhere in the New Testament they enjoyed the ministering of angels. Peter was delivered from prison by an angel. The women at the tomb were greeted by angels. When Jesus ascended to heaven from the Mount of Olives, two angels were standing by."

He stopped and looked around, a little out of breath, his gaze full of challenge. "Where are our angels? Where are our spiritual gifts, my good friends?"

He waited, but no one spoke or moved. "I'll tell you where. Nowhere. We have none. We claim none! And so I ask again, If we in our churches today vary in every respect from the pattern and model given here in this book"—he held up the Bible and shook it at them—"then how can we, or any Christian church, be considered the Church of Christ? We do not have even a shadow of anything according to this pattern. We cannot boast of even an approach to a base resemblance or counterfeit."

His voice dropped, and he looked suddenly weary. "What say ye to this, my brethren and sisters? This is what I would propose be the topic of our discussion." He paused for one more moment, then sat down.

The silence lasted for only a moment, then the group erupted in a babble of voices. Mr. Patrick stood again. The noise gradually died once more. "My friends, our good brother Mr. John Taylor has raised some very thoughtful and thought-provoking questions. Let us discuss them in a proper fashion. Raise your hand if you wish to speak."

Instantly a woman's hand went up. "I agree with Brother Taylor," she said when Patrick nodded in her direction, "but those principles of which he speaks are lost. It is pointless to look for them again, for they are gone."

The man beside her, probably her husband, Nathan surmised, shook his head. "If God gave them to his people once, he can do so again. I think as a group we need to pray earnestly to God, ask that the heavens be opened again and men commissioned by a new revelation."

Nathan started to raise his hand, but Parley reached out quickly and caught his arm. He shook his head slightly. Nathan was baffled. Never had he seen Parley so reticent, especially when the opportunity was so ripe.

The discussion went on for nearly an hour. There were many insights given, but the group could come to no agreement. At that point, one of the men who had been at the meetings at Mrs. Walton's house raised his hand. Mr. Patrick nodded at him.

"Mr. Chairman, we have a stranger from the States in our midst. A Mr. Pratt. Perhaps he would like to speak to the subject under discussion."

At last! Nathan could have jumped up and kissed the man on both cheeks.

"I was not aware of any strangers among us," Patrick said quickly, "but he is at liberty to make such remarks as he chooses, as are all in our group." He looked around. "Mr. Pratt?"

Parley rose slowly. Every eye in the room turned toward him. Some of those who had been present at the meetings held in the Walton home were nodding their approval. But once again, Parley Pratt totally sidestepped what Nathan expected.

"Mr. Chairman, thank you for that kind invitation. I am indeed a stranger from America, as is my companion, Mr. Steed. But we are not strangers to the great principles that have been under consideration here. I am prepared to speak on the subject at hand, but I feel the afternoon has been well spent, and all have been edified. Perhaps it would be best if we waited until another time."

Mr. Patrick nodded. He looked pleased that this American was considerate enough of the time not to push himself forward. "We shall be meeting again this evening, Mr. Pratt. Would that be sufficient time for you to prepare?"

"It would indeed, sir," Parley boomed cheerfully. "I would consider it a privilege."

"Then let us pray now and adjourn until seven p.m. this evening." He bowed his head, and all in the room followed suit. "O Lord," he said with great solemnity, "we have neither Apostles, visions, angels, revelations, gifts, tongues, ordinances, nor a Christian ministry. We acknowledge that we are destitute of everything like the pattern of the true Church, as laid down in thy holy word. And we pray thee to send whom thou wilt to help us. Amen."

Solemn amens echoed throughout the room, and then as people stood and began to break up the meeting, Nathan turned to Parley, who was grinning like a little boy. "I told you, Nathan," he crowed softly. "You just have to be patient."

It was Tuesday evening, the twenty-sixth of April, and the fourth time in the past three days that Nathan and Parley had come to Mr. Patrick's commodious home. With each meeting the numbers had grown, and now as the time for this latest meeting to begin approached, there was not even room to stand. Some had spilled out into the other rooms, and Parley was going to have to speak loudly so all could hear.

At their second meeting on Sunday evening, Mr. Patrick had immediately turned the time over to Parley when the hymn and prayer were finished. And for the next two to three hours, Nathan sat and marveled. He had never seen Parley preach to nonmembers in this kind of a formal setting, and it was amazing to watch him. He picked up the discussion exactly where John Taylor's questions earlier that day had left off. Parley boldly stated that the New Testament did indeed provide a pattern of what Christ's church should look like, and then he had proceeded to lay out five principles or characteristics found in the New Testament Church—namely, an inspired priesthood and apostleship, the need for faith, the ordinances of salvation, the presence of spiritual gifts, and the need for a reformation of life.

Nathan was amazed at Parley's mastery of the scriptures. He led the group through passage after passage which illustrated the points he was making. It was obvious that the group was most impressed with what he had to say. But after more than two hours, Parley said there was more he would like to say but that the time was growing late. Instantly someone called for another meeting. Mr. Patrick suggested one for the following evening, a motion which was unanimously sustained by the group.

That next meeting had been held last night. This time Parley focused on prophecy, starting with Moses and continuing through to John's revelation. Nathan felt like a child at the feet of a university instructor. He thought he knew the Bible well, but he realized he had much to learn as Parley laid out a chain of references which showed there would be a great restoration in the last days in preparation for the second coming of Christ. Again, Parley spoke for more than two hours. As they passed the hour of nine, Parley again apologized, much to Nathan's growing amusement. There was still more to be said, he suggested, but the hour was late and perhaps it was best to continue in another meeting. Once again a meeting was called for the following evening. And so they had come again this night.

At the close of the invocation, Mr. Patrick once again turned the time over to the preacher from the United States. Parley rose slowly this time, and Nathan sensed that at last he was ready for the summation. The previous two nights were only preparation. "My dear brothers and sisters," he began, "it has been a most enjoyable labor to sit with you these past few days and discuss the Lord's holy word."

He turned to where John Taylor and his wife sat. "How grateful I am to Brother Taylor's most thoughtful challenge to us all. As you will recollect, he asked us why we do not find in the Christian churches today the things which were evident in Philip's day. 'Where is our Philip?' he cried. 'Where are our Apostles to bring us the gift of the Holy Ghost?'

"We have labored long in holy writ these past two evenings to show, first, that Christ's church is the pattern we must follow and, second, that the holy prophets from the time of Moses to the end of the New Testament have foretold of a time when God's church would once again be restored to the earth.

"Brother Taylor asked about angelic ministrations. He asked about spiritual gifts. He asked about a commission from heaven by which men are authorized to preach the holy word and administer the ordinances to men. No one doubts the sincerity of the preachers and ministers of the various faiths. They are good men. Men who for the most part seek to do God's will. But remember, the Apostle Paul himself declared it in the book of Hebrews. 'No man taketh this honour,' meaning the priesthood authority, 'unto himself, but he that is called of God, as was Aaron.'"

He paused, letting his eyes move from face to face. No one moved, for, like Nathan, they seemed to sense something of significance was coming.

"Well," he said soberly, "my companion and I have come to Toronto for this very purpose. We have been sent by God, no doubt because of your faith in seeking his will and studying his word. And we are here to bear witness to you that the heavens have not been sealed. We are here to bear witness that God still speaks to his children, just as he did in days of old. We are here to bear witness unto you that his holy priesthood has been restored to the earth once again, not through any act of man or government, but through the ministering of angels.

"The authority to baptize which Philip held was restored to earth when John the Baptist, even he who baptized the Savior in the river Jordan, came to earth as a resurrected being."

A ripple of interest and shock swept through the group.

"That's right," Parley cried. "And that glorious angel, sent from God above, laid his hands on the heads of two young men alongside the banks of the Susquehanna River and said, 'Upon you my fellow servants, in the name of Messiah, I confer the Priesthood of Aaron.' And just a short time after that, Peter, James, and John, who held the holy apostleship anciently, returned to earth and restored the priesthood of Melchizedek to the earth once again."

"When was this?" a man cried from one side of the room. "I've never heard of such a thing."

"This happened in the spring of 1829," Parley said. "And you have not heard of it, because as yet the messengers are few and the field so broad. But that is why we are here."

Mr. Patrick was looking at Parley closely now, and Nathan saw that there was open concern on his face. But if Parley saw it, he gave no heed.

"Nor is that all," he went on. "God restored this priesthood authority to a young man by the name of Joseph Smith and then directed him to use that authority to organize the Church of Jesus Christ on the earth once again."

At the mention of Joseph Smith's name, a murmur went through the group. But Parley, filled with emotion, rushed on. "And I am here to testify to you that that church fits the pattern laid down in the New Testament. It does have the authority. There are once again Twelve Apostles. In it are found the ordinance of baptism and the power to give the gift of the Holy Ghost."

He turned to John Taylor now, who seemed mesmerized by the power of Parley's testimony. "And I testify to you that the spiritual gifts are found again on the earth. The gift of tongues, the gift of healing, the power to preach in God's name and bring people into the kingdom. Angelic ministration is once again a reality. In fact, it was through an angel that new scripture has come forth. A resurrected being by the name of Moroni returned to the earth and visited the Prophet Joseph Smith, and told him of gold plates hidden in a nearby hill."

Suddenly Mr. Patrick was on his feet, his mouth working. Parley was still looking at the Taylors, and didn't see him for a moment. His voice was at the peak of a crescendo now. "Joseph Smith translated that book, which is called the Book of Mormon, by the gift and power of God. It is another witness of the Lord and Savior. It bears a powerful testimony of Christ's reality and—"

"Enough!" Patrick roared.

Parley turned in surprise, as did all the others. Patrick's face was red and his jaw set. "You are a Mormon."

"I am indeed, sir."

"I object to the line of preaching you are taking, Mr. Pratt. This has been nothing more than a ruse to get us to listen to the false preachings of Mormonism."

Instantly, pandemonium erupted. Several cried out in support of Mr. Patrick, turning and shaking their fists at Nathan and Parley. But there was an equally vigorous cry of protest at Patrick's remarks. For several minutes the room was a tangle of heated debate and earnest conversations. Finally, shouting until he got their attention, Mr. Patrick took control again.

"I am sorry," he said flatly. "I know it was I who invited Mr. Pratt to speak to us, but I cannot feel good about opening my house to such falsehoods any further. Mr. Pratt and Mr. Steed are no longer welcome here."

"Out with them," cried a man near the front.

"Let them speak!" shouted another. "They speak the truth."

Suddenly John Taylor was up and on his feet. The group quieted as he looked at their host. "I honor that decision as your right and privilege, Mr. Patrick. And we thank you for being a most generous host." He turned and looked around the group. His voice rose with fervency. "We are here, ostensibly in search of truth. Hitherto we have fully investigated other creeds and doctrines and proven them false. Why should we fear to investigate Mormonism? This gentleman, Mr. Pratt, has brought to us many doctrines that correspond with our own views. We have endured a great deal and made many sacrifices for our religious convictions. We have prayed to God to send us a messenger, if He has a true church on earth. Mr. Pratt and his companion have come to us under circumstances that are peculiar. And there is one thing that commends them to our consideration— they have come amongst us without purse or scrip, as the ancient Apostles traveled. And none of us are able to refute Mr. Pratt's doctrine by scripture or logic."

As Nathan looked on in amazement, Mr. Taylor continued: "I desire to investigate Mr. Pratt's doctrines and claims to authority, and shall be glad if some of my friends will unite with me in this investigation. But if no one will unite with me, be assured I shall make the investigation alone. If I find his religion true, I shall accept it, no matter what the consequences may be; and if false, then I shall expose it." And with that, he sat down.

The widowed Mrs. Walton was up instantly, looking at John Taylor and then around at the rest of the group. "I believe Mr. Pratt has preached the truth to us these past three nights. Most of you, by now, have heard of the miraculous healing of my good friend, Mrs. Emmaline Compton, who was totally blind. That healing was done by the power and authority which Mr. Pratt holds. Can we deny that he is a representative from God? I think we can come to no other conclusion but that the Lord has answered our prayers and sent us his servants so we may find what we have been looking for."

She turned to Nathan and Parley, ignoring both the angry mutters and the murmurs of assent. "Therefore, while my house is not nearly as large and fine as Mr. Patrick's, I hereby say to those who wish to continue this study, we shall be meeting at my home each evening at seven p.m. All are welcome."

Newel Knight and his wife, Lydia, along with Jessica and her daughter, arrived in Clay County, Missouri, on Sunday, the fifteenth of May. The following Sabbath, a meeting was called for all the Saints in the area. Unlike the study group in Toronto, Canada, this group did not meet in a palatial home filled with the fine furnishings. Their meeting place was a grove of cotton-wood trees along the Missouri River bottoms across the river from Jackson County. There were few who were well dressed and born to wealth. Most of their clothes showed signs of con-siderable wear. Many, and not always just the children, were barefoot. Yet, like the seekers of truth in Canada, they met to determine a course of action that would keep them in harmony with God's will.

There were nearly two hundred of them gathered in the shade of the great cottonwood trees a mile or so out of the town of Liberty, and Jessica Roundy Steed and her four-year-old daughter, Rachel, were among that number. As she looked around, Jessica knew she had done the right thing. Here were the people she knew and loved. It had been hard leaving the

Steeds—one of the hardest things she had ever done—but now she felt at peace. This was where she belonged.

John Corrill, counselor to Bishop Edward Partridge, pulled away from a small group of men and walked to the front of the assembly. The group immediately fell quiet.

"Brothers and sisters," he said, "we've gathered here today to discuss our future. As you know, Bishop Partridge and W. W. Phelps have returned from their scouting expedition up north. We're anxious to hear their report. We'll ask Father Morley to ask the Lord's blessing to be upon us in this meeting, then we'll immediately turn the time over to Brother Partridge and Brother Phelps."

Isaac Morley, who was the other counselor in the bishopric, gave an eloquent but simple prayer, and Jessica had to smile to herself. Father Morley was not known for giving short prayers. That said a lot about how anxious he was to hear what the two brethren had to say.

When the prayer was finished, Edward Partridge came forward. Every eye turned and followed him as he walked to the front of the group. Brother Phelps remained where he was near the back of the group.

"Who's that, Mama?" Rachel whispered.

"You know Bishop Partridge, honey. He was in Kirtland for a time. He's the bishop here in Missouri."

"What's a bishop, Mama?"

"Shhh," Jessica smiled. Rachel's little-girl voice carried clearly, and several people had turned to smile at her. "A bishop is called of God to help us take care of our temporal needs."

"Our what?"

"Shhh. I'll tell you later."

As Bishop Partridge reached the front of the group, he smiled easily as he let his eyes sweep across the gathering. Then the smile faded away and he became quite somber. "Brothers and sisters." It was almost a sigh. "As you know, the good citizens of Clay County were kind enough to take us in when we were driven from our homes in Jackson County. They have given us shelter, allowed us to live on their land, in many cases provided food, jobs, and other necessities. At the time we promised them our stay in Clay County would be brief. It has been more than two years since we came. They have been patient. But more and more they are asking when we shall keep our promise."

A hand came up in the back, and Bishop Partridge stopped. He nodded in the man's direction.

"Bishop, is there no hope that we can ever return to Zion?"

"Ever?" The bishop's eyes filled with a sad wistfulness. "There is still hope, Brother Carter. The Lord has said Zion has not been moved out of her place. But he also said we must wait a little season for the redemption of Zion. But we can't wait any longer to decide what to do. More of our people are coming all the time. The people of Clay County are becoming alarmed. We do not wish a recurrence of the depredations we experienced south of the river in Jackson County. The citizens have assured us that if we commit to remove hence, they shall protect us from further violence."

"But where shall we go?" one of the sisters in the back cried. Instantly a ripple of murmuring swept through the crowd.

John Corrill stirred, looking a little irritated. "That is what Brother Phelps and Bishop Partridge are here to speak with us about. Let them speak."

As the noise settled down, Bishop Partridge continued. "As you know, since Brother Phelps and I returned from Kirtland we have ridden north to the area that is called 'Far West.' "

Far West was the name the Missourians gave to the northwestern areas of the state that were as yet largely unsettled. Jessica found herself nodding. That would be one solution. Go where no one else had laid claim to the land. Since her arrival, she had learned that the brethren had already started purchasing some land up in that area.

"And what did you find?" It was the same sister who had cried out from the back.

"I'd like Brother Phelps to answer that." He was motioning for W. W. Phelps to come forward. As he did so, Jessica noted that Rachel's eyes were beginning to droop. Smiling down at her, she took her gently by the shoulders and pushed her down into her lap.

"I'm all right, Mama," she said sleepily. "I'm not tired."

"I know, dear. Just rest your eyes for a minute." Gratefully she complied with her mother's wishes. Almost instantly her body relaxed, and she began to breathe more deeply.

Brother Phelps was at Bishop Partridge's side now. Because both of his given names—William Wines—started with W, many of the Saints called Brother Phelps, "W. W." He was a thin man, a little above average height. His high cheekbones and narrow chin gave his face almost a gaunt look. That impression was heightened by a Vandyke beard and mustache and heavy eyebrows. He was one of the most literate men in the Church. He had been a newspaper editor in Canandaigua, New York, a few miles south of Palmyra, at the time Parley P. Pratt brought him a Book of Mormon. Almost immediately after his conversion, the Lord had called him to go to Missouri and establish a newspaper and a printing office. Nearly a dozen hymns in the new hymnal published the previous year under the direction of Emma Smith had been written by W. W. Phelps. Jessica especially loved his "Redeemer of Israel" and "The Spirit of God Like a Fire Is Burning," the latter having been written for the dedication of the Kirtland Temple.

Brother Phelps cleared his throat. "Well, we didn't find all we had hoped for. However . . ." He paused for effect.

Isaac Morley shook his head in good-humored exasperation. "Come on, W. W.," he said. "Don't keep us in suspense."

He gave Brother Morley a quick glance, half-irritated that he would not let him build the expectations a little, then chuckled good-naturedly. "All right, all right." He looked at the group. "As expected, the Far West is mostly prairie with tall grass and gently rolling hills. Nearly every skirt of timber from here to the Iowa Territory has someone on it."

There was a collective sigh of disappointment. While a few small plots of prairie were being cultivated on the Great Plains, people did not yet believe that settlements could be established unless there was a nearby creek or river and plenty of trees for buildings and firewood. So this was disappointing news.

Again Phelps paused, but seeing the look on Isaac Morley's face, he hurried on. "But please note I only said *nearly* every place." He smiled broadly. "We have located an area up on Shoal Creek, in northern Ray County. Some of you remember Jacob Haun. He went up last season and built a gristmill there. Well, there are some possibilities west of there. There are two creeks in the area and very few settlers there now. We plan further scouting expeditions, but we believe there are places with definite promise."

That brought several murmurs of approval.

Brother Phelps looked across the group. "We have recommended to the presidency that we purchase sixteen hundred acres and begin looking for more as quickly as possible."

"Yes!" someone called. "Hear, hear!" said another. "Amen," cried a third.

Rachel stirred on Jessica's lap, her eyes fluttering open. "What is it, Mama?"

Brushing the dark hair back away from the little girl's eyes, Jessica shushed her gently. "It's all right, Rachel," she whispered happily. "I think we have found a home."

———•———

Nathan was unbuttoning his shirt as Parley finished washing his face at the basin of water and turned around. As Parley groped for a towel, Nathan spoke his thoughts. "It's been quite an exciting month, Parley."

Parley peeked at him for a moment over the towel. "A month, Nathan? Tomorrow is May twenty-third. That will be five weeks to the day since we arrived in Toronto."

"Five weeks . . . yes, I guess it has been that long. I can't believe it. The time has flown by so swiftly."

"But you are right about one thing, Nathan. It has been exciting. Most exciting."

"That first night at Mrs. Walton's house, when she asked to be baptized and you said no—I was dumbfounded. Now we've baptized virtually every person who was there that night. And the work now spreads to the surrounding areas."

"Ah, don't forget to mention the Taylors."

Nathan laughed softly. "Yes, the Taylors." His mind went back swiftly. "He was so cool toward us at first. Then that first night at Mr. Patrick's house, can you believe it? 'Where is our Peter?' he cried. 'Where is our John?' he asked. And you just sat there! I thought I'd bust."

Parley hung the towel on the rack, nodding thoughtfully. "The Spirit whispered patience."

Nathan hung up his shirt and sat down on the bed and began taking off his boots. "It probably whispered that to me too, but I was too impatient to listen."

"Well, Brother Taylor gave my sermon that night, outlining what Christ's church ought to be like. You could tell they've been studying the Bible diligently for two years."

Nathan nodded and tossed one boot in the corner, then started tugging on the other one. "I wish Heber was here."

Parley was moving toward the bed. He stopped, his face wistful. "Wouldn't that be wonderful? He would have loved to witness the fulfillment of his inspired prophecy. And inspired it was." He moved to his bedside and dropped to his knees. "Shall we pray, Brother Nathan? I think we have much for which to be grateful."

Chapter Eight

Can you give me five minutes, Joshua? I need to get this manifest out to the ship's captain. He wants to push off within the hour."

"Of course. I'm in no hurry."

As Richard Wesley nodded his thanks and left, Joshua turned to the window that opened to the south, giving him a view of the city across Factors' Walk and Bay Street beyond it. He pulled a face. *That's exactly the problem. I'm in no hurry.*

He reached in the inside pocket of his coat and withdrew the letter. He took it from the envelope and opened it slowly. It was dated May fourth, but it had just arrived at the hotel the previous evening, so it had taken nineteen days to reach him from St. Louis. He didn't read it again. He already knew too well the words on the paper. His partners had reached the last stages of construction on the textile mill. The big water-driven looms were to arrive from New England by steamboat the third or fourth week of May. Joshua shook his head. That was now!

They could already be there. It would take two more weeks to assemble the looms and get the mill completely functioning, and then they would be ready for the cotton. How were arrangements coming? They were concerned that they hadn't heard from him. They were not panicked, but he could sense they were getting very nervous. His letter to them would be there by now. That would help, but it wasn't letters that kept the looms going.

He swore softly as he folded the letter and returned it to his pocket. He had twenty-five wagonloads of cotton sitting directly below his feet in Richard Wesley's warehouse. Twenty-five! That represented an out-of-pocket investment of nearly eight thousand dollars. By now it should have been sitting on the docks of St. Louis. Instead it still sat in Savannah, taking up floor space and costing Joshua three dollars a day for storage fees.

He thought for a moment. It had been April fifteenth, the day after their return from the Montagues' plantation, that he and Richard Wesley and Abner Montague had signed the papers for the purchase of Montague cotton. Today was the twenty-third of May. That meant he had been paying storage fees for over a month now. He gave a soft snort of disgust. He might just as well have walked to the edge of the wharf and thrown the money into the muddy waters of the Savannah River. And all because of this obsession he had over this widow with the bewitching eyes, who toyed with him like a cat playing with a beetle.

Joshua turned around and walked to Wesley's liquor cabinet and splashed some bourbon in a small decanter. He started to put the bottle down; then, frowning, poured that much again into the glass. He walked to the large side chair beside the desk and dropped heavily into it. As he sipped the fiery liquid, he thought back on the previous six weeks. He had enjoyed them as much as any time he could remember. And that was not just due to Caroline. He had come to love Savannah with its neatly laid-out squares and streets. And Wesley had introduced him into his social circles, and so now, twice a week, Joshua joined a group of eight or ten of the city's well-to-do men who gathered in a private club on Bull Street. There they drank fine Irish whiskey, smoked Cuban cigars, and played some high-stakes poker.

Joshua smiled at that. These genteel Southern businessmen didn't know what high-stakes poker was. Playing seven-card stud with Wilson Everett, and putting your whole life's work on the line—now, that was high-stakes poker.

Quickly he took a deep swallow of the liquor, focusing on the burning sensation as it went down his throat. He didn't want to be thinking about that night anymore.

As he felt the warmth of the liquor begin to spread through his stomach, he leaned back and half closed his eyes. On the other hand, as painful as the memory was, it was interesting to ponder the outcome of that night's events. Ultimately they had led to his divorcing Jessica; and if he and Jessica hadn't divorced, would he be here now? Would he be in partnership with wealthy men in St. Louis, or would he still be mule-skinning dried cod and New England broadcloth across the Santa Fe Trail? He smiled to himself. And would he be courting the person who most of these Georgian gentlemen agreed was Savannah's most beautiful and eligible woman?

But that was exactly what was frustrating him. In the South a courtship was like a fine business deal. It was not to be rushed. It went half step by maddening half step. Caroline was attracted to him. He knew that. He could see it in her eyes, feel it in the warmth of her welcome when he came to call. Two weeks ago he had paused at the door as he prepared to leave. He had not asked. He just took her in his arms and kissed her. There was no question about her response. It was warm, eager, almost hungry. But then three or four more days went by before he could even see her again.

He longed for the frontier simplicity of Independence. There, when you thought it was time, you asked the question, got a preacher, got it done. Here, courtship was an elaborate and silly game. But it was more than that. Wesley and his wife, Margaret, kept hinting that Caroline could not be rushed right now. There were things of a "troublin' nature" she had to work out. Of course, Southern gentility kept them from saying more than that. "Just be patient. She's not trying to be difficult. You must give her time."

And so he waited. With his St. Louis partners in a stew, with eight thousand dollars' worth of cotton sitting in a warehouse, with a freight business running practically on its own without him, he sat and waited.

The door opened and Richard Wesley came back into his office. "It's done," he said. "Sorry for making you wait." He moved behind his desk and sat down. Immediately he opened a leather box and fished out his pipe. He took some tobacco, tamped it in carefully, then withdrew a match from a package that sat next to the pipe box. He leaned down and drew the match across the base of the chair. It flared into life, and he touched it to the end of his pipe, puffing heartily until it was glowing.

"Margaret asked me to be sure you and Caroline are planning on dinner this evening."

Joshua nodded.

"Good. Seven o'clock."

"Yes. By the way," Joshua said, watching as Wesley blew out the match, "don't forget you promised to send ten cases of those matches with me."

Wesley laughed. "Of course. You can probably make more profit on those than you can with the cotton."

Joshua gave him an answering chuckle. That was probably true, but he had no intention of selling them. The strike-anywhere match, invented in France just a few years before, was becoming popular along the East Coast, but they were still too expensive on the frontier to be more than a novelty. Joshua found them a wonderful convenience and would keep them for himself.

Joshua stood and set the decanter back on the cabinet. He

thought of the letter in his pocket. It was time to stop playing little boy and to get on with what he had come for. "The ship from England is due on Thursday?"

"Yes. It will be here two days, then leave for New O'leans." He was watching Joshua narrowly through the clouds of smoke. "The next packet ship after that isn't due in until the middle of June."

Joshua stood abruptly. "I can't wait that long. I want my cotton loaded this week. Can you arrange that?"

"Can do." The cotton factor set his pipe in an ashtray and leaned back, putting his hands behind his head. "You're sure?"

Joshua's breath came out in an explosion of disgust. "Yes. I've waited too long already. I've got a business to run."

* * *

An hour later, Joshua was in the warehouse below the offices of Richard Wesley. He was counting the exact number of bales of cotton he had purchased and would be loading on the *American Colony* when it arrived from New York later in the week. He turned to the black man who served as Wesley's warehouse foreman. "I count one hundred ninety-eight bales, Samuel."

It was a hot day outside and the warehouse was stifling. They had the big doors that faced River Street thrown open, but it made little difference. They were both sweating heavily, and with its sheen of sweat, Samuel's face looked like oiled ebony. "Yessuh, Mistuh Steed. That's what I got." He picked up a sheaf of papers from a small table, leafed through them until he found the one he was looking for, then showed Joshua the figure at the bottom. "That's what it says here you bought from Mistuh Montague. One hundred and ninety-eight. 'Xactly the same."

"Good." He clapped him on the shoulders. Joshua liked this big man with the ready grin and quick, intelligent eyes. "Well, Sam, give me a few more days and you can have this space back."

Samuel's face fell a little. "We gonna miss you, Mistuh Steed. It's been a real pleasure havin' you here in Savannah. Y'all gonna be comin' back?"

Joshua didn't answer. He turned and looked around, feeling the frustration rising up again. "I don't know, Sam. Not—"

All of a sudden he started. A figure was walking briskly by the doors, moving west along River Street. Her head was turned, watching the ship pulled up to the wharf and the men swarming over it; but there was no mistaking the profile nor the green hat with its ostrich feather and large bow, the hat he had bought for her at one of Savannah's finest millinery shops.

"Caroline?"

But she was past the door, not hearing him for the noise along the docks. He started after her, then realized what state he was in. He turned quickly to where Samuel kept a towel hanging from a peg on one of the thick wooden pillars. "Get my coat for me, will you, Samuel?"

He wiped his face and brow quickly, then turned to where Samuel was holding his coat for him. The foreman was smiling broadly. "That Miz Mendenhall. She be one fine woman."

Joshua laughed. "Yes, she is." He smoothed back his hair and beard, then thrust his arms into his coat and buttoned it quickly. "Tell Mr. Wesley I'll be back to sign those shipping orders."

Not waiting for an answer, he hurried outside, blinking in the dazzling sunlight of midday. For a moment he thought he had lost her. River Street was always a busy place, with sailors, dockworkers, teamsters, merchants, and planters milling about. But few of the people along River Street were women. He shaded his eyes, squinting against the brightness. Then he had her. She was several buildings up the street, moving briskly, ignoring the interest she was generating as she passed.

Joshua started after her, walking swiftly, tempted to call out, but wanting to surprise her. Ahead of him, she suddenly stopped beneath one of the signs that hung out over the warehouses. She started as if to go in, then stopped again. Even from a distance he could see her indecision. Curious, Joshua slowed his step.

She was standing beneath the sign that read, "Berrett and Boswell, Merchants, Cotton Factors." She seemed hesitant, almost reluctant. Twice she started forward, then stopped again. Joshua could sense the tension in her. He stopped, moving closer to the buildings so she wouldn't notice him. Finally, she took a deep breath, squared her shoulders, and went inside.

For several minutes Joshua stood there, debating with himself. Wesley would be waiting for him. But he wanted to see her—as always! But more than that, he was puzzled. Ladies of Savannah did not favor strolling along River Street. Not that Caroline had been strolling. Whatever it was that had brought her here, it was obvious it was not going to be pleasant.

Making up his mind, he moved across the street to where one of the large cotton wagons was standing. He moved around behind it, leaving himself a clear view of the door where Caroline had entered. He took out a cigar, fished out one of Wesley's matches, lit the cigar with the match, then settled down to wait.

———◦—◦———

Mr. Jeremiah Boswell's eyes always reminded Caroline of a cat's. They were wide, seemingly filled with nothing but lazy curiosity, but there was always a faint sense of something sinister lurking behind them.

"But Miz Mendenhall," he was saying, "we have been more than patient. It will have been two years in September."

She looked at him coldly. "I quite well remember when my husband died, Mr. Boswell."

"Now, Miz Mendenhall." Theodore Berrett was always the soothing one. He never raised his voice. He always had a sincere, caring smile that had no more substance than a coat of varnish. As Caroline looked at the smooth face, the waxed mustache, the fluttering fingers, in her mind she corrected her impression of him. Not soothing, she thought. Oozing. Mr. Berrett was always the oozing one.

The two men looked at each other. They must have known it wasn't going to be easy. Or pleasant. But that had never deterred them before.

"Donovan signed papers—," Boswell started, but Caroline swung on him with such loathing that he stopped.

Someday, heaven willing, she would learn what these men had done to her husband to get him to sign away his interests in the business, his one-third ownership in an upriver plantation, his sizeable investment in one of the ships owned by these two men. And the house. She felt the dizziness sweep over her for a moment. Somehow they had even gotten the house Donovan had built for her and the children, the house on which she had lavished so much time and effort.

"We have been more than patient," Berrett started, more cautiously now. "There was really no legal obligation on our part to let you stay in the house this long."

"Nor to provide you with the monthly annuity," Boswell rumbled.

Her head shot up, and she had to fight to keep the panic out of her eyes. In all the battles, all the bitter words, the monthly income—supposedly her share from her husband's investments—had never been questioned before.

"Please understand," Berrett drawled with obvious satisfaction, "we are not about to put a poor unfortunate woman and her two children into the street. But that house is far too commodious for a family of three. We have found a place for you down on Abercorn Street, near Taylor Street. It's near Calhoun Square. Very adequate."

Caroline turned slowly to Boswell, the sudden fear giving way to fury. "And how many children do your sister and her husband have?" Caroline demanded of Boswell.

The eyes hooded over quickly, and she could tell she had struck the mark. No one was supposed to know Boswell's plans for the Mendenhalls' house. Not yet. His sister had one girl, a five-year-old. It was rumored she also had three cats and a surly dog. Boswell was giving the house to her.

Boswell's lip curled in open contempt. "We told you right at the outset we would give you two years to make other arrangements. Obviously you have made no effort to find other accommodations."

Berrett seemed distressed at his partner's directness. "Now, now, let's not get angry with one another here. That will solve nothing." He turned to Caroline, wringing his hands. "We don't wish to turn this into an ugly fight, Miz Mendenhall, but we have been more than patient."

She stood, close to tears, but only because there was nothing that could sufficiently convey the contempt she felt for these two men. "Well," she said, her voice trembling with anger, "an ugly fight is just exactly what you will get if you try to evict me from my home."

Boswell shot to his feet. He leaned over his desk, his eyes crackling with anger. "We would welcome that, ma'am. We have total confidence in the legality of our position."

Mr. Berrett was up too now, dancing around her like a hit bird. "Oh, Miz Mendenhall," he chirped, "you must not let yo emotions govern yo actions in this regard. We are most anxious to be fair. Most anxious."

Suddenly his eyes took on a hard shrewdness, and for an instant he much more closely resembled his partner. "If you should reconsider, we would put the deed to the new home in yo name with no restrictions. And we might even be persuaded to guarantee the monthly annuity, so yo mind could be put at rest over that matter once and for all."

"Of course," Boswell cut in, really enjoying himself now, "you would have to sign papers declaring you have no further interest in Berrett and Boswell."

"Berrett, Boswell, and Mendenhall," she said icily. Then she turned to Berrett. "When my husband first met me, Mr. Berrett, I was helping my mother run a dress shop in one of the less acceptable sections of Baltimore. He spent over eleven years and a considerable part of his inherited fortune trying to make me into a lady. Well, it didn't take, Mr. Berrett. So you take your house on Abercorn Street and your guaranteed pension and you stuff them into that rat hole that serves as your twisted little mind."

She turned and smiled sweetly at Boswell. "And you, Mr. Boswell, we'll see you in court. Then we'll see who is the better street fighter."

She spun around and walked out of their office. As she went through the outer office she saw that the male secretary's eyes were wide with shock, and she realized he had probably heard every word. She flashed him one of her most radiant smiles. "Good day, Mr. Barber."

She went down the narrow stairs, her head high. But when she reached the little alcove at the bottom of the stairs, out of their sight and out of their hearing, suddenly her shoulders sagged and her head dropped. She fought the shuddering sensation that was building within her and the tears that burned her cheeks. She stood there for almost a minute, helplessly caught between fear, rage, and a powerful sense of hopelessness.

Above her, there was a soft sound. She looked up in panic, brushing frantically at the corners of her eyes. Not waiting to see what or who it was, she plunged out the door and into the street.

———•———

Joshua crossed River Street quickly, angling so he came up right behind Caroline. He really had to stride out, for she was walking very swiftly, the heels of her shoes making a staccato rattle on the boardwalk. Grinning, he reached out and touched her shoulder. "Caroline?"

She whirled, slashing at his hand, knocking it violently away.

The fury he saw in her face was more shocking than her blow. "Whoa!" he cried, raising both hands in front of him. "I didn't mean to frighten"—his voice trailed off as he saw the swollen, puffy eyes—"you."

She blinked twice. "Joshua?"

"Caroline, what's the matter? What happened?"

She fell back a step. "I thought you were—" There was a quick, angry shake of her head. "I'm sorry. You startled me." She looked away. "What are you doing here?"

"I was at Mr. Wesley's. I saw you go past the warehouse."

Her head jerked back around. "You followed me?"

Now it was he who fell back a step in the face of her reaction. "I . . . I came out in time to see you going into the offices of Berrett and Boswell." It sounded so lame. "I wanted to see you, so I waited across the street."

That seemed to satisfy her. She obviously wasn't pleased, but at least it seemed to defuse the anger. She turned and started up the street again, but walking more slowly now. He quickly fell into step.

She looked up at him, started to speak, saw two men approaching them, and waited until they passed. Then she spoke. "I'm sorry, Joshua. I didn't mean to snap at you."

He took her by the arm, motioning with his head across the street toward the river. She started to resist, but when he gently persisted, she gave in and let him steer her over to the low wall that lined the riverbank wherever there was a gap between the wharves. As they got there he let go of her arm. Instead of turning to face him, she moved right up to the wall, staring down into the muddy water moving slowly past them.

Joshua watched her for a moment, then took a deep breath. "Caroline, what happened in there?"

She didn't turn, didn't move.

"Look, I don't want to pry. I just want to help."

There were some pebbles on the top of the wall. She picked them up and began to drop them slowly into the water. She seemed mesmerized by the soft plop, plop, and by the ripples that moved slowly downstream away from them.

Joshua watched her, struck once again by the fineness of her features, the soft line of her lips. Half bent over as she was, the slimness of her waist was emphasized. And the position of her head let the sunlight catch the rich darkness of her hair, filled with an auburn sheen that turned it into burnished copper. If she was mesmerized by the falling pebbles, Joshua was mesmerized by the sight of her. This was a woman of uncommon loveliness, and Joshua never tired of watching her.

Suddenly she straightened. "I was sixteen when Donovan first came to the little dress shop my mother owned." She hadn't turned around. She just gazed out across the river, her eyes not focusing on anything.

Joshua stepped closer, listening intently. She was speaking barely above a murmur.

"He was the handsomest man I had ever laid eyes on." There was a deep sigh. "He was charming and funny and rich. It's no wonder I loved him." She finally turned and looked up at Joshua. "I loved my husband a great deal."

He nodded, but before he could think of an appropriate response, she went on. "He was charming and funny and rich"— she took a breath, her eyes turning bitter—"and he was a fool. The biggest, most naive fool ever to land on the docks of Savannah."

Joshua's face exhibited shock, but she seemed oblivious to him now, even though she was looking right at him.

"I don't want to stop loving him," she cried softly. Her fists were clenched now, the fingernails digging into the palms. "But I am so angry with him! Why did he do this to us?"

"What?" Joshua asked, struck to the core by the anguish he saw on her face. "What did he do, Caroline?"

She stiffened, her eyes widening a little as her mind registered that she was not alone.

"Caroline, I want to help."

She shook her head quickly, not meeting his eyes.

He reached out and took both of her hands. "Caroline, I—"

She pulled free, fighting the trembling in her lower lip. "I would like to be alone."

She saw the instant hurt in his eyes. "Please, Joshua. This has nothing to do with you. I just need to pull myself together. I'll be better by tonight for the dinner." She managed a wan smile. "I promise."

He stepped back, trying to be manly about it. "All right."

On an impulse she went up on tiptoes and kissed him on the cheek. "Thank you," she whispered. Her eyes were shining again. "Really, I'll be better by tonight."

———◆———

Richard Wesley's home was built in the beautiful English Regency style. It was two stories high with an attic above that. But most impressive was the large front porch with four stately columns supporting it. Two matching staircases swept in gentle curves up to the main entrance. The first time Joshua had come here with Caroline, she had told him, with a sense of reverential awe, that the home had been designed and built by William Jay. He had nodded and tried to look impressed. Since then he had learned that Jay had been a brilliant young architect from England who had built some of Savannah's finest homes during the previous two decades. To live in one of them was now a considerable mark of distinction. It said something that Richard Wesley, only five or six years older than Joshua, should now own one of them.

As Joshua helped Caroline from the carriage, he looked up at the imposing entrance. There was nothing like this in Independence. St. Louis was starting to have its own upper class and to get some beautiful homes, but Independence was not even five years out of the log cabin and sod hut stage yet. Someday, if this cotton deal proved to be what he hoped for . . .

Caroline slipped her hand through his arm. "It is a beautiful home, isn't it?"

"Yes, it is. But then so is yours, Caroline. You have a lovely home."

She looked away quickly. "Thank you," she murmured.

He kicked himself mentally. Earlier she had promised him that she would have herself pulled together by this evening, and she had kept that promise. There had been no trace of this afternoon's mental turmoil. On the short ride over to the Wesleys' she had been cheerful and witty, and seemed to be genuinely happy to be with him. Once or twice he sensed that her geniality might be a trifle forced, but he didn't care. Now, however, he had triggered the somberness again.

But as quickly as it came, it passed. "Come on," she laughed, "I'm hungry, and Margaret's cook is one of the finest in Savannah."

"I know," Joshua grinned back at her. "If you'll remember, I ate far more than I should have last time. Richard had to sell one of his ships to cover the costs."

She poked at him. "There's no way to make Sally happier than to have a second helping of her cooking."

One of the maids answered the door even before they had reached for the knocker. "Evenin', Miz Caroline. Evenin', Mistuh Steed."

"Good evening, Mary."

She took the knitted shawl from Caroline's shoulder. "I'll tell Miz Wesley y'all have arrived."

"Thank you, Mary."

As the servant walked down the hallway, Caroline stepped across the entryway to stand in front of a table that was up against the one wall. It was made of beautifully carved black walnut. A large mirror in a gilded frame hung above it. Caroline turned to face it, reaching up one hand to fluff at the hair around her ears.

Joshua watched her reflection with open admiration. She wore a gown of deep green that looked like silk. She had chosen not to wear a hat, which had surprised him. But the effect of the deep forest green with her red hair was stunning. Her complexion was flawless, and she wore little makeup. That was something Joshua had especially come to appreciate. He had learned, much to his distaste, that many of the women of the South wore heavy makeup to hide the scars left by smallpox. The makeup was wax based, and during the winter, according to Caroline, special tilt-top tables were set in front of the fireplaces to shield the ladies from the heat so that their makeup didn't run. Gratefully, Caroline had been spared the need for such artifices.

She looked up and caught his eye. "You look especially lovely tonight," he said.

She smiled at him in the mirror, then curtsied slightly. "Why, thank yuh, Mistuh Steed," she said, imitating the heavy drawl of the South. She stepped back away from the table and looked down. The table was of an unusual design. Just a few inches above the level of the floor there was another mirror, set back between the table legs and running the full length of the table so as to be almost up against the wall. This is what Caroline was looking at. She turned slowly, letting the full skirt float freely just barely off the floor while she watched it carefully.

Suddenly, understanding dawned on Joshua. "Is that what that's for?"

"What?"

"The mirror down there."

She laughed. "Of course. Why do you think they call this a petticoat table?"

He hadn't known they did. He had only noticed a similar table in the entry hall of almost every Savannah house he had been in, including Caroline's.

She dropped back into her accent. "Why, suh, it would be simply too, too embarrassin' if a lady were to be found with her petticoats showin'."

At that moment Margaret Wesley appeared at the head of the stairs. "There you are," she cried. "Welcome to our home."

———— •◆• ————

There were just the four of them. The Wesleys had three children, but Joshua had learned that the children of genteel Southern families always ate in a separate part of the house with the mammy. Even the best loved children were not allowed to eat at formal dinners until they were in their mid to late teens and had proven their maturity.

The dining room was large, the table big enough to sit fifteen or sixteen people around it when all the leaves were inserted. It was on the second floor. And that was another thing

Joshua vowed he would remember. The first floor of the houses in the city picked up the sounds and smells of the streets, so the main living quarters were always on the second floor.

As they finished their dessert, he looked around. There were many things he wanted to imbed in his memory so that when he built a home in Independence he could furnish it in a similar manner. The bull's-eye mirror was one example. Round in shape and with a curved surface, it was mounted on one wall a little higher than the height of a man. It allowed the hostess to sit at her end of the table and monitor how each guest was doing in terms of food service. There were sconces on the candles and lamps—metal reflectors with polished surfaces to reflect the light back into the room instead of diffusing it all around. Joshua determined that in his future home there would also be a "Sheraton" like the one that stood in Caroline's bedroom. Will had proudly shown that to him one day when his mother was out. It was a cleverly crafted cabinet which provided all the conveniences for personal hygiene right in the bedroom. The top lifted to reveal a mirror. The upper drawers were lined with zinc so as to hold water for washing. The bottom compartment was large enough to hold the "necessary," a large chamber pot made of porcelain. He had really chuckled at that, but had to admit it had distinct advantages over the rickety, drafty out-houses that stood behind most homes in Missouri. Especially in winter.

As he watched the servants clear away the service, he admitted to himself that he knew full well what all his mental note taking was about. There was an imaginary house starting to take shape in his mind, and he knew whom it was for. The promise of such a home could be enough to convince her to come with him to Missouri. If he did it right.

"Well," Wesley said, pushing his chair back, "Joshua and I will retire to the gentlemen's study for a glass of sherry and a good cigar. Ladies, if you'll excuse us."

Joshua stood too. Normally this was a custom he did not prefer, this leaving women together to do lady talk while the men gathered off by themselves. He even found it irritating that in some homes, especially on the larger plantations, the gentlemen's study had a door specifically designed to be too narrow to allow ladies with their wide-hooped and many-petticoated skirts to pass through. But tonight he didn't mind. He had some things he wanted to discuss with Mr. Richard Wesley.

He waited only long enough for Wesley to shut the door and get the cigar box down. Joshua took a cigar, but just held it in his hand. He watched as his friend got out a match and struck it. "Tell me about Berrett and Boswell," he said.

Wesley jerked around, nearly burning himself. He recovered, touched the flame to the end of his cigar, and puffed it into life. "What about them?" he said, eyeing Joshua narrowly through the smoke.

"Come on, Richard," Joshua snapped. "You know how I feel about Caroline. This is my business now." He told him quickly of the experience he had had that day.

Wesley let out his breath slowly, the sigh showing a deep weariness. "I had heard they were about to make another move. I had hoped it wasn't true."

"So, I want to know the full story."

For several moments Richard looked at him, then finally he nodded. He reached over and stubbed out the cigar in an ashtray. "All right. Sit down. This may take a while."

Chapter Nine

Joshua Steed stopped for a moment on the sidewalk outside the entrance to the offices of Berrett and Boswell, merchants and cotton factors. He looked up at the sign that hung from a wrought-iron holder bolted to the brick wall of the warehouse. There was no evidence that the sign had ever read, "Berrett, Boswell, and Mendenhall." Not that it surprised him. From what he had learned in the past two days, Mr. Berrett and Mr. Boswell would not stoop to something as crude as simply painting over a name. Squeezing a man's fortune from between his fingers, driving him into virtual bondage, legally robbing any vestiges of the estate from his widow and children—now, that was a different matter entirely. But crudity was certainly not the style of Mr. Jeremiah Boswell and Mr. Theodore Berrett.

Joshua took a breath. He knew full well that these two were masters at playing their game. Three different lawyers had convinced him that Caroline stood not one chance of breaking the contracts signed by her late husband and witnessed by men of impeccable credentials. One by one, Donovan Mendenhall had signed away his assets, thinking that the guarantees he was promised in return justified the risks he was taking. And one by one, he had lost it all. Will Mendenhall believed with all the faith of his twelve-year-old heart that his father had died of yellow fever. There was no doubt in Joshua's mind that the dreaded disease had been the ball that killed him; but he also knew now that by that time, Donovan Mendenhall had been a totally shattered man.

Angrily he jerked the door open and took the stairs two at a time.

"I assure you, Mistuh Steed, everything is in perfect legal order. We understand Miz Mendenhall's discontentment, but—"

"Look, Berrett," Joshua cut in sharply, "let's get a couple of things straight. I run a freight business in Missouri. I know when there's something in the corral you don't want to step in. Putting a handkerchief over it doesn't make it stink any less."

Theodore Berrett was shocked by Joshua's bluntness, but Jeremiah Boswell didn't move or react in any way. He was watching Joshua closely, his eyes hooded and unreadable. Joshua noted it with no surprise. Everyone had said that Boswell was the shark you had to watch.

"Why don't you just say what you've come to say," Boswell said evenly.

Joshua nodded. "Fair enough." He took a cigar from an inside coat pocket, then a small knife from his vest pocket. He began to trim off the end slowly and deliberately. He stuck the cigar in his mouth, took a match from the box on the desk without waiting to be asked, and lit it up. Only when it was glowing and the air around his head was filled with smoke did he continue.

"I know what your legal standing is. I've checked that out carefully."

"Then surely you know we are in a very strong position to—"

Boswell shot his partner a withering look, and Berrett clamped his mouth shut.

Joshua never took his eyes from Boswell. "I also know that, legally or not, you two robbed Donovan Mendenhall just as surely as if you put a gun to his head."

A faint smile played around Boswell's mouth, but his eyes were, if possible, even colder than before. "In Savannah, Mistuh Steed, if it's legal, then it isn't robbery."

"Well," Joshua said, taking another long puff on his cigar, then blowing it at the ceiling, "that's just it, Boswell. I'm not here to play by Savannah's rules. Out west we speak a different kind of language."

"How quaint."

Joshua laughed shortly. The man was good. Pure ice. This was not going to be easy, but that would make it all the more enjoyable. He stood and walked to the window that looked down on River Street and the docks. It was a warm day outside, and the window was open. The sounds of the street floated up to them clearly. Across the street, a ship was tied up at the docks. Men were wheeling bales of cotton up the gangplank and disappearing into the holds. He didn't have to look at the name on the bow. He knew it was owned one hundred percent by the two men who sat behind him now.

"Cotton," he mused, "now, there's a flammable cargo for you."

Berrett shot out of his chair as though someone had touched his posterior with the tip of Joshua's cigar. "Are you suggesting—" His eyes popped out in near apoplexy. "How dare you threaten us!"

Joshua turned around. "Why, Mr. Berrett, I do think your emotions have gotten the best of you."

Boswell had risen now too. He leaned forward, resting his hands on the desk. "Get out, Steed, or I'll send for the constable."

Joshua returned to his chair and sat down. "My, my, aren't we testy today?" He smiled pleasantly. "You mustn't think—"

A sharp cry from outside cut him off. "Fire! Fire on deck!" Before it even had time to register, the cry was picked up by other voices and pandemonium erupted outside.

Boswell went pale, then kicked his chair aside and leaped to the window. Berrett was beside him in an instant. Joshua got up and strolled back to join them. Across the street, men were running from every direction toward the ship. Some had grabbed buckets and were passing them up to eager hands reaching down. A small column of black smoke was rising from the deck near the main mast. Joshua watched as several buckets of water were hurled at the base of the pillar of smoke. In a moment, it was over. Cries of relief went up. By the time Boswell and Berrett were certain that their ship was no longer in danger, Joshua had returned to his chair again.

He noted with satisfaction that Boswell's icy veneer had been shaken. He had suspected it would be. At least twice in recent memory Savannah had been devastated by fires, the last one burning for three or four days and destroying large portions of the city. Savannahans were deeply paranoid about fire.

He looked past them toward the window again as they turned to face him. "Lucky thing it didn't happen at night, and down in the hold. Before you know it, a whole ship could be lost."

"Theodore," Boswell said between pinched lips, "go fetch a constable."

Joshua was rolling the cigar back and forth between his fingers. He raised his eyes in mock horror. "Surely you can't think I had anything to do with that. Why, you would have to testify that I was right here with you during the whole time. How could I be responsible for something clear across the street?"

"We'll see about that, Mistuh Steed." He waved angrily at his partner.

Joshua chuckled softly. "Why, Mr. Boswell, I believe it was you who said that in Savannah if something is legal, it isn't robbery. Might I suggest that in Savannah if something isn't provable, it isn't arson." His voice went suddenly flat and hard.

"Especially if the men making the accusation are held in contempt by respectable officers of the law and all gentlemen of integrity."

For several seconds, Boswell just stood there, the eyes almost black in their fury, his hands clenching and unclenching. Berrett was too shaken to remain standing. He collapsed into a chair and began mopping at his forehead.

Finally, Boswell walked back behind his desk and retrieved his chair. He sat down slowly, his eyes never leaving Joshua's. "What do you want?"

Joshua felt a tiny leap of exultation. The man was far from down, but at least Joshua had his attention. "You're paying Mrs. Mendenhall a stipend of about two thousand dollars per year. The home in which she lives is worth about twenty thousand dollars."

"That house already belongs to us," Berrett cried. "Donovan Mendenhall gave us title to it."

"It will take a long and costly court battle to have her evicted."

Boswell nearly snorted outright in disgust. "We can afford it. Mrs. Mendenhall cannot."

Joshua nodded thoughtfully. "Assuming, of course, you don't have any costly fires."

Berrett's mouth dropped open. "Blackmail and extortion are against the law in Georgia, young man!" He was nearly screaming at Joshua. "You'll spend the rest of yo life in prison."

Joshua ignored him. He spread out his free hand, looked at his fingernails closely, then finally looked up at Boswell. "There is a simpler solution."

Boswell's eyes were little more than narrow slits now, but Joshua could see something new in them. Respect. "I'm listening," he said.

"A twenty-five-thousand-dollar, one-time settlement."

Berrett shot right out of his chair, spluttering, his eyes like a startled possum's. "*What?*"

"Shut up, Theodore," Boswell said quietly.

"But . . ."

Boswell whirled on him. "Shut up!" Without waiting to see his partner's reaction, he turned back to face Joshua. "Go on, Mistuh Steed."

———•———

"Will, would you and Olivia go downstairs and play? I have some important business to discuss with your mother."

Caroline whirled around in surprise, but Joshua was not looking at her. He was watching her son steadily.

"Yes, sir."

Olivia's lower lip shot out in that pouty look which she had so mastered. "I want to stay. I don't want to go downstairs."

Caroline felt a touch of irritation at Joshua's request. He was so assured of himself, so completely confident. "I have not kept secrets from my children, Joshua," she said. "I don't mind if they stay."

Will's eyes darted back and forth between his mother and Joshua. Joshua merely smiled at him. That was enough for Will. He straightened his shoulders and took his sister's hand. "Come on, Olivia."

"But I don't want to go."

"Come on," he said more forcefully, starting to pull on her.

Caroline was caught. One part of her was peeved at Joshua for ordering her children around in her own house. Yet she was also deeply grateful that after almost two years a man had come into Will's life who commanded the same respect and adoration he had for his father. "Olivia," she finally said, "go with Will. Joshua and I will only be a few minutes."

Knowing when she had lost, Olivia sniffed, pulled loose from her brother's grasp, and marched out on her own.

"Thanks, Will," Joshua said softly. Will gave him a little wave, then pulled the door shut behind him.

Caroline decided she did not want to quarrel with him. It had been a pleasant dinner, and Joshua was wonderful with the children. They really enjoyed his company. She smiled wryly to herself. As if their mother didn't. "My, my," she teased, "this must be terribly important."

But Joshua did not smile. He took her by the arm. "I think you'd better sit down."

She laughed, tossing her head so her hair bounced on her shoulders. "I feel like a little girl who's about to be spanked by her father." But she let him steer her to a chair and sit her down.

He pulled up a chair to face her, but to her surprise he didn't sit down. Rather he began pacing in front of her. Slowly the humor in her died. She had never seen him quite this serious before. "What is it, Joshua?"

He stopped, his eyes earnest and dark beneath the furrowed eyebrows. "Caroline, I . . ." He stopped and came to his chair. He turned it around so the back was to her, then sat down facing her. It was as though he wanted the chair as a shield between them if things did not go well.

She was completely sober now too. "What is it, Joshua?" she asked again.

"I . . ." He let out his breath in disgust. "Caroline, I'm not a man who's good with words. I'm not one of your polished Southern gentlemen."

She smiled warmly at him. No, he definitely wasn't that. But that was part of what made him so attractive. "I know what you are, Joshua. You don't have to apologize for that."

Her words seemed not to sink in. He was obviously struggling. "I don't know how to say this, so I'll just lay out what has to be said and let the chips fall where they may."

"Fair enough."

He took a quick breath. "I know about Boswell and Berrett and what they did to your husband."

Caroline's mouth dropped open. If he had reached out and kicked her, she couldn't have been more stunned.

"I know it all," he went on, the words pouring out now. He told her about what he'd done since he had seen her go to their offices. He told her about his investigations and about hiring lawyers to check and double-check the contracts. By the time he finally stopped, his hands were clenched on the back of his chair, and she could see the beads of perspiration on his forehead. But that did nothing to lessen the anger she felt.

"What right do you have to pry into my affairs?" she asked coldly.

He didn't dodge her anger. "None. But I did it anyway. Because I don't want to see you lose everything."

"I can handle my own problems," she snapped.

"Caroline, I have as much admiration for you and your capabilities as for any woman I have ever known, but you are going to lose. Even the best lawyers in the city are saying that. You will lose this house. And you will probably lose your pension."

She jumped up, turning her back on him. She didn't want him to see the fear on her face. She had lived with that thought now for over a week, the dread like some great knot inside her.

"Those two are jackals, Caroline," he said softly, standing now too, but not coming to her. "You fight them, they'll tear you apart."

"I'll manage," she shot back at him.

"No, you won't," he snapped angrily. "You don't know how to deal with men like that."

She whirled, her eyes blazing. "And I suppose you do."

He reached in his coat pocket and withdrew some folded papers. "Will you sit for just another minute or two and listen to me? Then I'll leave. If you wish, I won't come back."

"I—"

"Please, Caroline. This will only take a minute."

Breathing hard, she finally nodded and returned to her seat. He took a deep breath, then let it out slowly, painfully. "What I have here is an offer from Boswell and Berrett. They want to buy you out once and for all."

Her eyes narrowed suspiciously. "For how much?"

"They are willing to pay you twenty-five thousand dollars in gold."

"What?" She shot to her feet. "My husband invested twice that amount in their company. This house is worth almost that much alone." She was near tears, but this time they were tears of anger. "You call this helping me?" she asked incredulously.

"Sit down and listen for a minute!" he roared.

She rocked back, shocked by the anger in him.

"Please, Caroline," he said more softly. "Just one more minute."

She sat down slowly, her lips tight. "All right, Joshua, I'm listening."

He put the papers back inside his coat. "I don't know how they did it, or what they held over your husband's head, but the contracts he signed are legal and binding. They're foolproof. Your lawyer has already told you that. I've had the best lawyers in town tell me the same thing. You fight them on this and you're going to lose."

He leaned forward, his eyes boring into hers. "Do you hear me, Caroline? You're going to lose."

"I haven't lost yet," she said stubbornly.

He threw up his hands. "Come on, Caroline! You're not one of those plantation girls with a face full of makeup and a head full of cottonseed. Wake up. You think just because you don't want something bad to happen, that makes it go away?"

She finally dropped her gaze. He was right, but it hurt like fury to have to admit it. The very thought of the triumph in Mr. Boswell's little pig eyes galled her more deeply than she could express.

"They'll let you take all the furniture."

"How gracious of them," she said bitterly.

He ignored that. "There are two conditions."

She didn't look up. For the first time, a bleakness came into Joshua's voice. "You will have to sign papers renouncing all claims to the business."

Her head came up. "Only that?" she sneered. "What else?"

He took a deep breath. He couldn't meet her eyes. "Having you around is an embarrassment to them. You will have to agree to leave Savannah."

For a moment her eyes widened, then instantly they turned dark. "*Now*, is that all, Mr. Steed?" she said, the words coming out clipped and hard-edged.

He nodded.

She stood slowly now, the fury in her giving her an icy calm. "Well, thank you for all you've done, Mr. Steed. But you go back and you tell your two friends I shall see them rot in hell before I give in to them."

He moved a step closer to her, facing her anger. "Well spoken, Caroline," he said softly. "And when you're out of your home, with no money and no food, you cut that pride of yours into strips and fry it up and see how long it feeds your children."

She flinched as though he had struck her.

He stepped forward and took her by the shoulders. "Look, Caroline, I don't blame you for not wanting to see those two pieces of cow dung win this. *But they are going to win!* If I wasn't absolutely sure of that, I wouldn't have gone to see them. If you stay and fight, they'll strip you cleaner than bleached buffalo bones on the prairie. This way, at least, you come out with something. This is a small fortune."

For a long moment she stood there, looking up into his eyes. She felt the anger calm a little. But only a little. "You really think I ought to do this?" she asked in disbelief.

"Yes."

"Leave Savannah?"

"They'll drive you out one way or the other."

She looked away, her eyes taking in the room around them. She loved this house. Donovan had let her pick out the furnishings from the finest stores in the north. This was her home. "And where would I go?" she whispered.

Joshua dropped his hands from her shoulders and stepped back. His eyes were wide and filled with uncertainty. Surprised, she looked at him more closely. "What, Joshua?"

"How about Missouri?" he asked softly.

There was a sharp intake of breath, and her head snapped up. For what seemed like an eternity, they both stood frozen, eyes locked together, then finally she shook her head. "You have an incredible sense of timing."

There was a small tic around the corner of his mouth, but

other than that his face remained impassive. "I told you, elegance is not my long suit."

He took the papers from his coat again and handed them to her. "There's the offer. All it requires is your signature."

She took the papers slowly, her eyes never leaving his face. She felt as though she had been in the sun too long. The room seemed to be whirling around her.

"I've got a shipload of cotton to get to St. Louis. It leaves in three days. I wish there was more time, but I've already stayed here over a month longer than I should have."

Three days!

He shook his head, not looking at her, half talking to himself now. "This is crazy." Suddenly he looked up. "If you say no, I'll understand." He gave a short, explosive laugh. "It was an insane idea." He pointed at the papers in her hand. "But the offer is not, Caroline. Don't throw it away without giving it careful thought."

He shrugged, looking suddenly helpless and vulnerable. "Well, I'm sorry for spoiling a lovely evening." He turned and moved swiftly to the door.

"Joshua . . . "

He stopped.

"I . . . I don't know what to say."

"Don't say anything. I'm at the hotel. If you don't come, I'll assume that's your answer." He opened the door, then stopped again. This time he did not turn around, and she had to step forward to hear him. "I'm not Donovan Mendenhall, Caroline, but I'll try and be a good husband to you and a good father to your children." Then he turned and was gone.

It was ten o'clock the following morning when there was a soft knock on Joshua's hotel room door. In an instant he was up. He grabbed his coat and put it on quickly, then went to the door, not daring to hope.

"Good morning, Joshua." She looked drawn and very tired.

For a moment he felt his pulse quicken, but instantly he pushed it aside. Sometime during the long night, he had decided Caroline would come to see him either way. She had too much class to answer him by simply staying away. He smiled briefly. "Good morning, Caroline."

Her green eyes were wide, filled with anxiety. "Can we walk?"

"Of course."

As he pulled the door shut and turned to join her, she produced the contract from Boswell and Berrett. He stopped.

"You didn't tell me about the clause that has to do with you."

"I didn't want you to think that I made the offer of—" He caught himself. "The offer to go to Missouri because I was after your money. I didn't want them to think that either."

"Do you think *I* would have thought that of you?"

He shrugged. "I wanted to be sure. That money is yours. I don't want it coming between us. This way, there is no way I can get it."

"It wasn't necessary. But thank you for leaving no doubts."

He nodded, and took her elbow as they started down the stairs. She didn't speak again until they were out of the hotel and walking slowly along Bay Street.

"You know how to ruin a woman's sleep, don't you?"

He smiled ruefully. "Oh, I slept like a baby."

"It serves you right." She smiled for the first time that morning.

He didn't answer, and they walked on in silence again for almost another block. Without looking up at him, she spoke again. "You can't delay leaving?"

He shook his head. "The next ship won't be here until mid-June. My partners need the cotton a lot sooner than that. They're already frantic."

"Will you be coming back to Savannah again?"

He looked at her closely. He had thought about that question constantly for the past six weeks. "Originally, I didn't plan to."

"But?"

"But what?"

She dug at him with an elbow. "I thought I heard a 'but' in your voice."

He nodded. "I guess if there was something here besides another load of cotton, I might consider it."

She stopped. They were under one of the dogwood trees which lined the street. The sunlight filtered through the leaves, making gentle patterns on her face and hair as she looked up at him, her eyes troubled and yet filled with a softness that arrested him.

"I'm not sure that I love you, Joshua."

That caught him totally by surprise.

"I do find you attractive, but we've had so little time together."

He was staring at her, not believing what her words were implying. "But you're considering it?" he said, almost wanting to shout it.

"Considering what?" she asked innocently.

He grabbed her and almost shook her. "If you're considering marriage to me, I'll come back whenever you say."

Slowly the smile on her lips died, and he felt his heart sink. She turned and looked across the street to Factors' Walk and the river beyond. "I love this place," she said softly.

"I know," he said.

She straightened, as if suddenly making up her mind. "I hate long good-byes, Joshua."

He blinked in surprise. What was that supposed to mean?

Slowly she smiled, but there were tears in her eyes too. "If I'm leaving, let it be now."

He leaned forward, peering into her face. "Do you mean . . . ?"

She lifted the papers she held in one hand and unfolded them. Carefully she turned to the last page. Her signature was written neatly across the bottom. She closed them again and looked up at him. "One of the conditions, as you'll remember, is that I leave Savannah."

He swept her up, swinging her around, still not daring to believe what he was hearing. "Do you really mean it? You'll come with me to Missouri?"

Now she gave him the full radiance of her smile. "Yes, Joshua, I will come with you to Missouri. Will you come home with me now? I'd like you there when I tell the children."

To say that Emma Smith was large with child was to understate her condition. There were some who were predicting she would give birth to a second set of twins, but Frederick G. Williams, who was not only Second Counselor to Joseph in the First Presidency but also the Smith family physician, said no.

But twins or no, Lydia could see that Emma was miserable. Between the heavy awkwardness and the June heat, she looked exhausted. "Come sit here by the open window, Emma," she said. "There's a little bit of a breeze."

Mary Ann was up immediately and to the window. "Here, we can open this even more."

"Thank you, Lydia. Thank you, Mother Steed."

Lydia noted that Mother Smith watched her daughter-in-law closely as she changed places, moving slowly and awkwardly. Emma was due, and everyone was anxious for her welfare.

No wonder, Lydia thought. Emma had had six previous children—four of her own and two adopted. And of those six, only two were still alive. Her firstborn had died on the same day he was born. That had been back in Harmony, Pennsylvania, when Joseph was first starting on the translation of the Book of Mormon. The next two—twins—lived only three hours. When another sister Saint had died giving birth to twins the following day, the husband had offered them to Emma to compensate for her loss. One of those, the boy, was lost in a tragic set of circumstances less than a year later. On the night a mob broke into the home where Joseph and Emma were staying, Joseph was dragged outside and tarred and feathered. The door to the house was left open to the cold night air. Already seriously ill with the measles, the boy succumbed to the exposure and died five days later.

Finally, on her third pregnancy, Emma had given birth to a child that lived. Little Joseph—actually, Joseph Smith the Third—was not yet four, and was the absolute pride of his father's eye. It was about time. Emma had suffered enough tragedy.

Lydia looked around the room and suddenly realized there was hardly a sister there who had not faced tragedy of one kind or another. There were about a dozen women. They had come to the home of Benjamin and Mary Ann Steed to mend the clothing given in a collection for the poor the previous Sabbath. They were visiting quietly, laughing from time to time, enjoying the opportunity of sisterhood and friendship while they worked steadily.

Lydia had lost a baby in a miscarriage that nearly killed her as well, so she knew keenly what feelings could be generated by such a loss. But she was far from being alone. Joseph's mother, Mother Smith, had lost two babies—her firstborn, who died at birth, and then Ephraim, who lived only eleven days. She had also lost Joseph's older brother, Alvin, in the prime of his manhood. And what of Mary Ann, her own mother-in-law? Her firstborn had died within an hour of birth, three other children had been stillborn, and another had been lost to pneumonia when he was four. Five out of ten children dead.

And then she thought of Mary Ann's Joshua, not dead, but

as lost as though he were. The thought struck her hard. *Death is not the only sorrow, is it?* There was a sharp pain inside her breast, sharp enough to make her gasp, as she thought of her own parents. Since she and Nathan had left Palmyra that final time and come back to Kirtland, there had been no answer to her letters, no response to her pleadings. No, she thought. There were other ways in which loved ones could be taken.

Intrigued by the thought, Lydia let her mending fall to her lap as her eyes moved from sister to sister. There was Rebecca— dear, sweet, lovely Rebecca. Lydia wanted to weep every time she thought of Arthur Wilkinson and his perfidy. Since Rebecca had said she would not marry him, he had spread ugly and vicious rumors about her. It had become so bad that if she went unaccompanied through the main part of town, she was subject to the most vulgar humiliation from some of Kirtland's lower male element.

Her eyes stopped on Eliza Snow. She was sitting with Jerusha Smith, Hyrum's wife, and Thankful Pratt. Her hands fairly flew as she stitched a patch over a hole in the knee of a pair of boy's trousers. On the surface, Eliza Snow seemed to have everything going for her. She had been baptized a little over a year ago, in April 1835, and then in the fall had moved to Kirtland from Mantua, a small town about thirty miles south of Kirtland. She boarded with Joseph and Emma and helped tutor Julia—the surviving twin—and little Joseph. She also ran a school for girls. Eliza was a woman of unusual gifts. She was an expert in needlework. She was such a master at making straw hats and bonnets that her work was in great demand. By the time she was in her early twenties, her poetry had become so well known that she was asked through the press to compose a requiem for John Adams and Thomas Jefferson when both of those famous men died on Independence Day in 1826.

And yet Lydia couldn't help but wonder. Eliza Snow was now into her early thirties. She was still single and had no one courting her. Did visions of a marriage-less future haunt her?

Would she ever be privileged to carry a child of her own instead of teaching everyone else's?

"Lydia!"

Her head came up in surprise as she realized that that was the second time Mary Ann had spoken to her.

"My goodness, child, where were your thoughts?"

She smiled quickly, a little flustered. "I—"

"I'll bet they were in Canada," Rebecca teased.

Lydia laughed lightly. "Normally, Rebecca, you would be right. But not this time." For a moment she thought about trying to explain it all, then decided against it.

"I've got the corn bread ready," Mary Ann said. "Can you and Rebecca help me?"

"Of course." But as the three of them started for the kitchen, the front door to the home burst open. It was young Joshua. His hair was tousled, his shirt pulled half out of his pants, one suspender half off his shoulders. He looked in at the room of women in dismay. "Mama, Mama!" he called.

Lydia stepped from around Mary Ann. "Here I am, Joshua," she said in alarm. "What is it?"

He spun around and darted to her, throwing his arms around her legs. "Papa's back! Papa's back!"

———◆———

"Papa, Papa!"

Nathan was still half a block from his father's house when he heard the cry. He moved forward swiftly, then dropped to one knee, setting aside his knapsack. Little Emily was running toward him as fast as her little legs could pump up and down. Her pigtails were bouncing wildly back and forth. Behind her, young Joshua was hurrying as quickly as he could. But he was holding eight-month-old Nathan, and that was a load for a boy of five, even one as husky and strong as Joshua was.

Emily nearly bowled her father over as she hurtled into his arms. "Papa, Papa, Papa," she kept shouting over and over. He swept her up, swinging her around until her legs were sailing out nearly horizontally, and she started to squeal with delight. Finally he stopped, staggering a little as the dizziness hit him. He hugged her to his chest, feeling the hot burning behind his eyes. "How's my Emily?" he whispered huskily.

"I'm fine, Papa. I'm glad you're home."

Parley watched the reunion with pleasure for a moment, then spoke to Nathan. "I'll be going on home, Nathan. Give my best to Sister Lydia."

Young Joshua looked up at him. "Sister Pratt's at Grandpa's house, Brother Pratt."

"Is that so? Then that's where I shall go."

As Parley walked swiftly away, Joshua turned to his father, still puffing hard from his burden. "Here's little Nathan, Papa."

"No!" he said, taking the baby and holding him up high. "This can't be *my* Nathan."

"Yes, it is," Emily said matter-of-factly. "He's just grown since you left."

Nathan held his youngest son away from him, laughing. "Why, so it is, Emmy. So it is."

The baby's eyes were wide as he stared into the face of the man who had snatched him up. Suddenly his lower lip jutted out and he began to whimper.

"It's all right, Nathan," Joshua said quickly. "It's Papa. It's Papa."

It didn't help. He started to wail. "Hey, little man," Nathan cooed, "it's all right." He tried to bounce him, then pulled him close to comfort him. His namesake would have none of it. Little Nathan reared back, howling in earnest now.

"Take your brother, Joshua."

Nathan whirled around. Lydia was coming toward him down the walk. In an instant Nathan handed the baby to Joshua. He turned and in two steps threw his arms around his wife, nearly crushing her in his grasp. She was laughing and crying all at the same time. "I can't believe it, Nathan. I didn't think you would . . . Oh, Nathan, I'm so glad you're home!"

"It is good to be home." He tipped her head back and kissed her hard.

Little Nathan watched them, curious enough now to stop crying. Emily moved forward to stand next to her father, content to let her mother have her time too. Joshua just kept grinning and grinning.

Finally Lydia stepped back. "Come on. Your mother is anxious to see you. Rebecca has gone to fetch your father."

Lydia took the baby from young Joshua, who then proudly picked up Nathan's knapsack. They started back toward his father's house. As they turned in at the gate, Nathan looked up. The door opened. It was Parley. He stepped out onto the front porch, bringing a woman with him. Immediately, other women began filing out to stand around them. There was Emma, heavy with child. Mother Smith. Elizabeth Whitney. He stopped, aware now of the air of expectation that hung over the group. Suddenly Nathan stared more closely at the woman standing at Parley's side. "Thankful?" he blurted. "Is that you?"

"Yes." She laughed, a burst of pure joy. "Yes, Nathan. It is me."

He just gaped at her, not believing his eyes. It had been just a little more than two months since he had stood in Parley's house with Heber C. Kimball, talking with Thankful Pratt. Thankful had been a gaunt, wasted shell of a woman. She barely weighed a hundred pounds. The bones in her face protruded sharply, and that, along with skin that was yellowish gray and eyes rimmed by huge dark circles, left her looking almost ghostly. Violent coughing spells would rack the fragile body to the point that it made Nathan ache just to listen to her. But now . . .

Parley stepped back, holding her at arm's length. "Can you believe it, Nathan? Look at her!"

Nathan *was* looking at her. And he couldn't believe it. The change was stunning. She had gained fifteen pounds, maybe twenty. Her face had filled out, and the dark shadows were completely gone. Her cheeks glowed with healthy color, and her eyes, always so dull and listless before, were vibrant and sparkling. With a start, Nathan realized Thankful Pratt was a lovely woman, something that had not occurred to him before.

Lydia wiped at her eyes with the back of her hand. Several other women were crying as well. Nathan stepped forward and took Sister Pratt's hand. He started to speak, then swallowed hard. "This is a most wonderful surprise, Thankful," he finally managed shakily. "Does Brother Kimball know?"

She nodded her head, tears trickling down her cheeks now. "He's in the East on a mission now, but he came to say good-bye before he left."

Nathan turned to Parley and opened his mouth to speak, but this time he couldn't get it out. Parley just nodded, his lower lip trembling. Then he opened his arms, gathered his wife into them, buried his face against her shoulder, and began to sob uncontrollably.

———— ·•· ————

Mary Ann came into the kitchen. "That's good enough, you two. The rest can wait until morning."

"All right!" Matthew wadded up his dish towel and threw it at a rack of pegs. Incredibly, it hit the wall just above it, slid down, and caught over two of the wooden pegs. It wasn't neat, but it stayed. Rebecca, wiping her hands on her apron, shook her head in mild disgust. Only Matthew . . .

He grinned at her mischievously. "Bet you can't do that, Becca."

"Bet I'm not going to try," she retorted.

Mary Ann tried to look stern. "You're just lucky it didn't hit the floor, young man."

Matthew looked offended that she would suggest something so unthinkable. As he walked by her, he leaned down and gave her a quick peck on the cheek. "Hello, Mother."

She swatted at him affectionately, still a little shocked that her "baby," nearly sixteen years old, now towered a good four inches above her. As Rebecca came up, she slipped her arm through her mother's. "You didn't let Nathan begin without us, did you?"

Mary Ann shook her head. "No. They're waiting now. We want you and Matthew to hear this as well."

—————•————

Mary Ann slipped her hand into Benjamin's. He looked at her, the pride as evident in his eyes as it must have been in hers. She nodded, pretty sure she knew what he was thinking. It felt so good! The scriptures said that a fulness of joy was not possible until the body and the spirit had been inseparably joined in the resurrection. But if the joy ever became any more intense than what she was feeling now, she decided, then the Lord was simply going to have to increase her capacity to endure it.

Nathan had spent the afternoon with his own family, so at supper they had decided it was the adults' turn. Matthew had nearly split the buttons on his suspenders when his father casually mentioned that Nathan and Lydia should get one of the neighbor girls to watch the children. Matthew was old enough now to be with the family.

Not surprisingly, Carl Rogers had declined the invitation to join them—he had too much to do at the livery stable—but he had not balked at all at Melissa's getting a sitter for the children and coming to be with her family.

And so they had gathered in the parlor. Nathan had written one letter from Toronto not long after he and Parley arrived there, and Lydia had read it to the entire family. But that mattered not; they made him start right at the beginning and recount it all.

"So the Taylors were baptized after all?" Lydia exclaimed. "It sounds like a lot went on after you wrote your letter."

"That's for sure," Nathan said. "I would have written more letters, but we were really busy. When I finally did get a chance to sit down and write another letter, I chose not to mail it, since we decided to come home so soon."

"That was a surprise to us, Nathan," Benjamin spoke up. "We didn't expect you for some time yet."

"Ben!" Mary Ann gave him a sharp look.

"Well," he grumbled, "I'm not suggesting it was wrong. I'm just surprised they're back so early."

Nathan took no offense. "Well, we had run out of printed materials—copies of the Book of Mormon and other literature—and also, Parley had pressing matters to attend to here relating to his personal finances. Fortunately, as we left, many people gave us money. Some of it was to buy books to bring back to them, but some of it was just as a gift to us. I gave it all to Parley." His eyes hooded a little as he remembered the touching scenes of the night before their departure. "It was several hundred dollars."

Benjamin whistled softly. He knew how badly Parley needed financial help.

"What about that widow lady?" Matthew said. "Tell us what happened to her."

"You mean Widow Walton, who took us into her home? She and all her family were baptized."

"No, the other one," Matthew said. "I don't remember her name. The blind lady."

Nathan's face fell. "Oh, yes, the Widow Compton." He shook his head slowly, the corners of his mouth pulling down as he remembered.

Mary Ann was surprised at his reaction. "Surely she was converted."

"No, and that is a sad tale to relate."

"After a miracle like that, she wasn't baptized?" Rebecca said, her voice registering her disbelief.

Nathan took a breath and began again. "The moment she was healed, everything began to change for her. Many people knew of her affliction, of course, and so her healing made quite a stir in the area. People came from all over the city and countryside to see her. So many people wanted to know all the particulars of the miracle that she finally came to Parley and me and asked what to do. Parley was adamant about it. 'Just tell them God has healed you, and give him the glory,' he advised.

"But that wasn't enough for people. They continually teased her for more detail. They pressed her to know more about the men who had done this for her. 'What did they do to you?' they would ask. 'They laid their hands on my head in the name of Jesus Christ and commanded my eyes to be made whole,' she would reply, 'and it was instantly done.' 'Well, then give God the glory, for these men are followers of Joseph Smith, the false prophet. They are impostors.' She in turn would reply, 'Whether they are impostors or no, I cannot tell. But this much I can tell. I was blind, but now I see. Can impostors open the eyes of the blind? Are you asking all of these questions because you wish to become their disciples?' "

Nathan gave a soft hoot of disgust. "That really infuriated them. 'We are disciples of John Wesley,' they would say. 'We belong to the Christian church.' They continually wearied her with their badgering."

"But surely she did not falter," Mary Ann cried, "not after such a remarkable experience."

Nathan looked at his mother. "Toward the end, they took a new tack with her. 'Ah,' they would say, wagging their heads, 'we see how it is with you. You are determined to forsake the Christian church for the sake of these weak impostors—the Mormons. Well, farewell. But remember, you will have no more support from our society, no more encouragement of any kind. You shall not even be allowed to teach school anymore. Then how will you live?' "

He sighed deeply, the only sound in the silence of the room. "You have to remember that her husband had died. When she went blind, the Methodist society had cared for her. So that threat really hit her hard. After weeks of having contention and lying and railings heaped upon her head, the poor mother began to weaken. I'm sad to report that soon afterwards, she stopped coming to our meetings." He looked at his hands. "We saw her no more."

"How tragic," Mary Ann breathed. "How utterly tragic."

He nodded, then brightened after a moment. "But oh, how the work has progressed! Those who did believe began to introduce us to friends and relatives. Brother Taylor, for example—and this was before his baptism—took us out to an acquaintance of his, a Mr. Joseph Fielding, who lived with two of his sisters on a farm about nine miles outside the city. The Fieldings are also from England, like the Taylors. There are lots of people from Great Britain in the area."

He began to chuckle. "These two sisters, both intelligent and amiable women, turned and ran from the house when they saw us coming."

"But why?" Matthew blurted out.

"Because we were Mormons," Nathan laughed, "and they did not want to give any countenance to Mormonism."

"What did you do?" Benjamin asked.

"We convinced their brother to come to the meeting which had been called for the evening. He fetched his sisters back, they served us a good supper, then came to hear us preach that night."

Rebecca clapped her hands. "And you baptized them?"

"Yes," Nathan said with great satisfaction. "The people in the area drank in truth like water. We baptized the Fieldings and several other families. In fact, we organized a branch there. There are more than thirty members there now." His mouth drooped for a moment. "I'm really going to miss the people of Canada."

Lydia's eyes widened in surprise. "Do you mean you're not going back?"

He looked offended. "Do you think you can stand to have me home?"

"Don't tease me, Nathan," she cried. "Parley said he is returning very soon. I just assumed you'd have to go with him."

"Parley is returning. But now that Thankful has made such a remarkable recovery, he plans to take her with him." He grinned at his wife, who was staring at him in wondrous disbelief. "I guess he thinks she's a more amiable companion than I am."

Tears had sprung to her eyes. "That's wonderful news, Nathan."

"Ah, but you didn't answer my question—do you really think you can stand having me home?"

Her eyes were shining as she smiled back at him. "It's got its drawbacks, but I'd like to try."

He pulled her against his shoulder, holding her tight. "I think it's time I spent some time with my wife and children."

———————————

It was past midnight, but Nathan and Lydia still were awake. Some of it was Lydia catching him up on all that had happened in his absence. Some of it was Nathan sharing more of the details of the last two months. Mostly it was just that they rejoiced in being reunited at last, and they did not want it to end quite yet. But Lydia could sense that Nathan was on the verge of sleep. She snuggled up in the crook of his elbow, her very favorite way of being close to him. "Nathan?"

"Hmm?"

She smiled. He was going.

"There is one part of Brother Kimball's prophecies you haven't mentioned."

"What?"

"Heber made you a promise too. Remember?"

He turned his head so he faced her in the dark. "Yes, I do."

"He said this mission to Canada would be a great blessing to your family too and that you would live to see the fulfillment of that as well."

"That's right."

"Well?"

He grinned at her in the dark. "Well, what?"

She poked him with her knee. "Well, do you know what he means?"

The smile faded. "No, Lydia. I don't. I have wondered about

it a great deal, but so far, I haven't the slightest idea what he meant."

"So far, everything Heber said that night has been correct."

"That's right. A few things have yet to be fulfilled, though. Like the part about Thankful being able to give Parley a son."

"I'll bet now that her health is better, she can become a mother."

"I think so too."

"So you think that he was right about our family too."

"Of course."

For several moments she thought about that. "I wonder what it could mean," she finally murmured.

There was no answer, and in a moment she knew she had lost him to sleep. Carefully she extracted herself from his arm. She went up on one elbow, then leaned down and kissed him gently on the cheek. "Welcome home, my darling Nathan," she whispered. "I missed you."

Brother Ben, would you mind if I drew upon your wisdom a little as we ride along?"

Surprised, Benjamin Steed immediately shook his head. "Of course not. But I'm not sure how much wisdom I have to offer you, Joseph. I much prefer to listen to you."

Joseph laughed, and then responded with his characteristic honesty. "I shall serve as your advisor in spiritual matters, Benjamin. But I need your advice in things that are more temporal."

They were headed south on Chillicothe Road, now called Smith Road by many of the Saints. Joseph Smith, Sr., and three of his sons—Joseph, Jr., Hyrum, and William—all lived along it. They were just passing the old Stannard stone quarry from which the blocks for the temple had been cut. It was a hot day in mid-July, and the team of horses that pulled the wagon were plodding along with their heads down. Joseph seemed in no hurry and did not push them to move faster. Ostensibly, they were going about five miles south of town to pick up a load of green lumber and take it back to the lumber kiln for drying. But Benjamin suddenly realized that this was not the real reason why Joseph had asked him to accompany him.

"I'm flattered that you would consider me in that light, Joseph. If I can help, I'll be glad to."

"I need you to be honest with me, Ben."

"I shall," Benjamin answered without hesitation. "Ask what you will. I hope I can help."

Joseph leaned back, cocking one arm to rest it on the back of the wagon seat. His face, usually open and filled with cheerfulness, now took on a more somber cast. "Do you remember the revelation in which the Lord said that if we humbled ourselves and were diligent and exercised the prayer of faith, he would soften the hearts of those to whom we were in debt and send the means for our deliverance?"

"Yes, I remember that."

"Do you doubt the Lord, Ben?"

That really caught him off guard. "No, I don't think I do."

"Nor do I," Joseph said slowly. "When the Lord promises, he fulfills."

"I agree."

Again Joseph seemed lost in his own thoughts, and Benjamin wasn't sure the Prophet had heard him. "You know why I've called the meeting with the brethren for Thursday, don't you?"

Several of the brethren had speculated about it, but Benjamin had a pretty good idea already. "To talk about our financial situation?"

"Yes. I don't have to tell you, Benjamin, we are in serious trouble. The Church is deeply in debt. I mean *deeply* in debt, Benjamin." He exhaled slowly, shaking his head. "Did you know we still have more than thirteen thousand dollars' worth of unpaid notes on the temple?"

Benjamin drew in his breath quickly. "Thirteen thousand?" he echoed.

Joseph sighed with great pain. "Yes, and that is not pleasing to the Lord, Benjamin. It is his house. If we do not pay those notes, we could lose it."

"Surely no!"

"Surely yes," Joseph shot back. "Do you think the Lord is pleased to think his house stands in jeopardy?"

"No wonder you're burdened down, Joseph."

The Prophet looked out across a stretch of fine farmland, his eyes brooding. "And the Church in Zion is no better off than we are. They have run up a deficit of more than six thousand dollars buying land in northern Missouri."

Benjamin whistled softly. A total of nearly twenty thousand dollars!

Now Joseph turned to him, his face pained. "So I ask you again, Ben. The Lord promised that if we were humble and diligent and exercised the prayer of faith, he would send means to us for deliverance from our debts. Yet here we are, more than two years later, and still deeply in debt. If the Lord fulfills his promises, then what would you conclude, Brother Steed?"

Benjamin was staring at the horses' feet, listening to the soft clop-clop of their hooves on the road. "That we have not met the Lord's conditions."

"Aye," Joseph said wearily. "I see no other conclusion."

They rode on in silence for several minutes. Finally, Joseph spoke again. "I have given this a great deal of thought, Brother Ben, and here are some of my conclusions."

"I'd like to hear them."

"Part of our problem has to do with the gathering. The Lord commanded us to gather to Ohio, but he said it was to be done in order. He said the branches of the Church were to gather their moneys and send them with their people so that land could be purchased and all things could be done in the proper order. How often is that happening?"

There was only one answer to that. "About one time in ten."

"That's right. Generally the rich stay back while the poor come with nothing to their names except a belly full of hunger and a cart full of children. The contributions cannot keep up with it. Here's something else the Lord warned us about." He began to quote softly. " 'Wo unto you rich men, that will not give your substance to the poor, for your riches will canker your souls! And wo unto you poor men, whose bellies are not satisfied, and whose hands are not stayed from laying hold upon other men's goods, whose eyes are full of greediness, and who will not labor with their own hands!' "

Joseph sighed, then finally looked at his companion. "Ah, Ben, is it any wonder the Lord has not fulfilled his promise to us?"

"So what do you propose, Joseph?"

Joseph forced a laugh. "That's what I have been praying about."

"And?"

"Well, something has been much on my mind of late."

"What?"

"To start a bank."

One eyebrow shot up, but immediately Benjamin began to nod thoughtfully.

Joseph went on eagerly. "We could sell stock, use the money to capitalize the bank. Then we would have our own financial institution. All the interest we are paying to others would be saved. Our own people could borrow from us, and we could use that interest earned to pay off our debts and also to help meet the needs of the poor."

"That would help with the cash problem as well," Benjamin threw in. "Almost everything we are doing now is on credit. That's one of the reasons prices are rising so fast. We need capital. We need cash money." A thought struck him. "Would you print your own bank notes?"

"I don't know. I think so." Joseph laid a hand on his arm. "That's why I need the counsel of wise men like you, Ben. Then I want to take the idea to the Lord for his final approval."

"I like the idea, Joseph. Let me think on it. I think it has real merit. Anything else?"

The blue eyes clouded, and when Joseph spoke, it sent a quick chill through Benjamin's soul. "We lost the privilege of laying the foundations of Zion, Brother Ben, because the Lord will not be mocked. He warned us that we had to be pure in heart. But we were filled with petty jealousies, covetousness, contentions." He looked down at his hands. The palms were open, as if in supplication. Then he looked at Benjamin. "And if we are not careful, the Lord may have to chasten us again. And I, for one, do not look forward to that in the least bit, Benjamin. Not in the least bit."

———————

There was a soft knock on the door. Elizabeth Ann Whitney, wife of Bishop Newel Whitney, arose and went to the door. The chatter among the dozen or so women in the room instantly stopped. Sister Whitney opened the door, smiling, then stepped back. "How glad we are that you could come!"

She moved back, and three women stepped into the house. The first was tiny Mother Smith, still as full of fire and spunk at sixty-one as many women half her age. Next came Emma. In her arms she carried a small bundle wrapped in a white blanket. Behind her was Eliza Snow, who was living with Joseph and Emma.

In one moment the women were around Emma. Soft oohs and aahs came out in a chorus. Smiling, her dark eyes filled with unabashed joy, Emma pulled back the blanket.

"Oh, would you look at that!"

"He's darling, Emma. Just darling."

"I think he's got Joseph's nose and mouth."

"I can see a little of Mother Smith in him too, can't you?"

Joseph's mother beamed at that, nodding as though she had seen the same thing herself.

Mary Ann Steed looked into Emma's face. "So he's almost a month now?"

Mother Smith answered for Emma. "He was born on the twentieth of June. So he'll be a month one week from today."

Mary Ann reached out and touched Emma's arm. Her eyes suddenly filled with tears. "We are so happy for you, Emma."

Emma turned. "Thank you," she whispered. "I almost can't believe it. He's so perfect."

Sister Whitney interrupted them. "I believe our food is ready. Shall we eat?"

———•———

Mary Ann gazed down into the tiny round face. One eye was fluttering slightly, as though little Frederick Granger Williams Smith were dreaming some unknown thoughts of the heaven whence he had so recently come. Mary Ann reached out and touched the eyelid very gently with the tip of her finger. It steadied. There was a soft sigh, and then he seemed to settle even deeper into sleep.

She settled back on the sofa, glad she had waited to be last to hold the baby. Now he was sleeping and she would have him for the longest amount of time. She looked across the room to where Melissa, her older daughter, sat. She and Thirza Cahoon, wife of Reynolds Cahoon, were crocheting a lace tablecloth for the sacrament table in the temple. Melissa had the ball of yarn propped on the roundness of her belly. Mary Ann's mouth softened at the sight of her. Two more months and there would be a new baby in the Steed family too. She looked forward to that eagerly. The last one born—Lydia's little Nathan Joseph—was now nine months old and pulling himself up to everything around the house. Cute as they were at that stage, there was nothing quite like having a newborn.

Lydia was sitting next to Mary Ann. She leaned over, her eyes tender as she looked down at Joseph and Emma's newborn son. "Isn't he adorable?"

Mother Smith was sitting in a rocking chair next to the sofa. She chuckled softly. "He's not a whole lot bigger than his name, is he?"

From across the room, Emma laughed. She and Joseph had decided to call the baby after Frederick G. Williams, Emma's doctor and Joseph's Second Counselor in the First Presidency. "Father Smith says we should just call him 'F. G. W. S.' for short."

Sister Cahoon looked up. "Can you imagine calling him and my son to dinner at the same time?"

Melissa gave her a puzzled look. "What is your son's name?"

Eliza Snow, sitting two chairs away, lowered the needlepoint piece she was working on. "You mean you haven't heard that story?" she asked.

"Oh, tell her, Thirza," Elizabeth Ann Whitney spoke up. "This is delightful."

"All right." She looked at Melissa. "A few months ago I had a little boy. Reynolds and I couldn't seem to settle on a name for him. Even after four or five days we hadn't come up with something that was satisfying to the both of us. Well, one afternoon my husband looked out of the window and saw the Prophet Joseph passing by. On impulse, he hurried to the door and called after him. 'Brother Joseph,' he said, 'how would you like to come in and give my son a blessing?' Joseph, of course, immediately agreed to do so and came into our home. Then, as Reynolds handed him the baby, he suggested that since we hadn't been able to settle on a name, perhaps Joseph could name him as well."

Melissa was nodding. "And?"

"And so Joseph named him . . ." She paused for effect. "Mahonri Moriancumer Cahoon."

Melissa blinked. "Mah . . . Mah–what?"

Eliza Snow clapped her hands in delight. "Mahonri Moriancumer."

"Oh my goodness," Melissa managed.

Thirza Cahoon laughed. "That's what I thought too."

Lydia leaned forward. "It's quite an unusual name, but tell Melissa what Joseph said about it."

"Yes," Elizabeth Ann said, "that's the most interesting part."

Sister Cahoon turned back to Melissa. "Do you recollect that in the Book of Mormon there is one prophet who was never called by his own name? His brother was named Jared, but all they ever called this man was—"

"The brother of Jared," Melissa finished for her.

"That's right." She was nodding. "Well, Joseph said it had been revealed to him that Mahonri Moriancumer was the name of the brother of Jared. And so he named our son Mahonri Moriancumer."

"Really?" Melissa said, suitably impressed.

"Isn't that just like Brother Joseph?" Sister Cahoon said. "Even in little, day-to-day things, the Spirit whispers to him. While I joke about it a little, we're very proud it was through our son that we came to know the actual name of this great prophet."

"It is a noble name," Mary Ann spoke up. "The brother of Jared was a man of great faith and righteousness."

Emma and Brigham Young's wife, Mary Ann Young, were in the process of hackling flax, combing out the long fibers and letting the tow, or short fibers, pile up on the floor at their feet. Sister Young turned to Eliza Snow. "Speaking of brothers, Eliza, I understand your brother Lorenzo was finally baptized."

"Yes," Eliza said, "yes, he was. On the third of June."

"Good for him," Mary Ann said. "He is such a handsome and fine young man."

"Yes, but so stubborn. I've been trying to get him to make up his mind to be baptized for the longest time now."

Mother Smith leaned forward, putting on a face of mock amazement. "Of course, he's the only one in the Snow family who is strong-minded."

They all laughed at that. Eliza had first met Joseph Smith shortly after his arrival in Ohio early in 1831, but she had not joined the Church until 1835. She wanted to "prove all things" before doing anything as important as being baptized.

Emma spoke up. "Joseph says he is an unusual young man and that the Lord has great things in mind for him."

"Well," Mother Smith said, "then he shall have to be strong. Especially now."

That took Mary Ann aback a little. Careful so as not to wake the baby, she half turned. "Why do you say that, Mother Smith? Why especially now?"

"Well," she answered, "after such an outpouring of the Spirit as we have seen in the last few months, you know that Satan cannot be pleased. He will redouble his efforts to destroy the Church now."

"It's already starting," Eliza intoned, her face grave. "Look what's happening among the people."

Many nodded in vigorous agreement with that. Sewing was laid in laps, knitting needles paused, the combing of the flax slowed as several began to talk at once. In a lull, Jerusha Smith, wife of Joseph's brother Hyrum, spoke up. "Can you believe the price of food right now? Six cents a pound for pork. Four for beef. Flour is seven dollars a barrel!"

Vilate Kimball, wife of Heber C. Kimball, chimed in. "I went to buy some butter the other day. Twenty-five cents a pound! I couldn't believe it."

Mother Smith was shaking her head. "The prices are shocking, but I'm far more concerned about the fact that we seem to be moving further away from the Spirit. There's so much contention, it seems. The poor are angry because they feel that no one helps them. Those with more of the world's goods are upset because there are so many poor who won't work. It seems like everyone is becoming more critical of everyone else." She frowned slightly. "But there are some good things happening too."

Thirza Cahoon had started to crochet again. She stopped. "Like what?"

"Well, for one thing, look how many of our families have other families staying with them. And often they are receiving nothing for rent."

"That's true," Lydia said.

"I hear stories all the time about people helping others," Mary Ann said quickly.

Mother Smith looked around at the women. "There are many things that should cause us concern. But there are also many good things to be grateful and happy about. We must not dwell only on the bad."

The conversation moved on to other topics, but Mary Ann

didn't join in. As the sisters droned on, Mary Ann suddenly made a vow to herself. She herself had made one or two comments about how this person or that person was acting, or about how someone was handling things. It was an easy thing to do. But beginning this very day she was going to watch her tongue closely. Mother Smith was right. A spirit of contention and faultfinding was not good. She, for one, would try to stop contributing to the problem.

"Brethren, we have to face the facts, no matter how unpleasant they may be." Hyrum Smith looked around at the group of priesthood holders assembled in an upper room of the temple. "We are facing a crisis of immense proportions, and unless we find some solutions, the very growth of the kingdom shall be hampered."

There were close to fifty brethren present, and everyone seemed a little on edge. Hyrum's comments did little to soothe them. He had laid it all out for them—the debts on the temple, the costs incurred by the Church in Missouri, the continuing drain on their resources for care of the poor. By the time he finished, a deep sense of gloom had settled over the group.

Martin Harris and Oliver Cowdery were sitting on the row of benches second from the front. Martin stood slowly. Hyrum nodded, acknowledging him. "I know we have problems," Martin began, "but all is not bleak. I say that in some ways we are doing better financially now than we ever have. We're in a building boom. From dawn to dusk our streets rattle with the sound of wagons filled with lumber, brick, and stone. New buildings are going up everywhere."

Oliver Cowdery got up now too, his eyes on Joseph. "We would be fools to say all is well here. But on the other hand, we are making significant progress, Joseph. The Church is beginning to establish itself. We now operate several of our own businesses. We have a brickyard, an ashery, a tannery, our own shoe shop, a steam sawmill, and a lumber kiln. We have a school, a print shop, and this beautiful temple. It's one of the largest buildings in Ohio."

"That's true, Oliver," Joseph said, "and we also still owe thirteen thousand dollars on it."

Brigham raised his hand again.

"Brother Brigham."

"We must write to the branches and tell them to stop sending people to Kirtland unless they have a minimum amount of money and have the means for making a living."

Martin Harris, who had sat back down, now shot to his feet again, giving Brigham a hard look. "That's easy for you to say, Brother Young. You're here now. How would you have liked it if back in '33 we told you to stay in New York?"

"I came with nothing, that's true," Brigham said testily, "but I was not dependent on the Church. I worked hard."

Several nodded in agreement. Brigham was a skilled carpenter and glazier. Many of the finer homes in Kirtland and the surrounding area sported exquisite fireplace mantels or cantilevered staircases, thanks to Brigham Young. He had also directed most of the finish carpentry work in the temple.

"Well," Martin grumbled, "I say we have to accept these souls, poor or not."

Brigham's eyes narrowed a little, but before he could speak, someone behind them said, just barely loud enough to be heard, "Brother Harris, your concern for these poor souls wouldn't have anything to do with the fact that you own several building lots you're trying to sell, would it?"

Martin whirled, his eyes blazing. "Who said that? Who dares to question my integrity?"

Luke Johnson and his younger brother Lyman, both in the Quorum of the Twelve, were on their feet now too, staring at the men behind them. Several eyes dropped; others met their gaze with open challenge. Hyrum stepped forward. "All right, brethren," he said calmly, "let's keep our emotions in check. We're not here to fight with one another. We're here looking for solutions."

Ben finally had had enough. He raised his hand, then stood even as Joseph turned to him. The room immediately quieted, showing the respect in which he was held. "Brother Steed," Joseph said.

"Martin and Oliver are right. We are in prosperous times, but that prosperity is hollow." Martin stirred, but Benjamin went on quickly. "That doesn't mean it is not real, just that it is hollow."

"Hollow? What's that supposed to mean?" Luke Johnson demanded.

Benjamin let his eyes sweep around the room. "It means it has no real economic base beneath it. We're living on credit. Some of us in this room have become so-called wealthy men of late." He smiled grimly. "But it is only on paper. Unless we get something—land, hard money, some real industry—behind all this credit we're using, we are just dithering about the problem."

"You're the only one dithering at the moment," Lyman Johnson said with half a sneer.

Benjamin swung around angrily, but Joseph was up instantly. His eyes were sorrowful, and when he spoke his voice was filled with gravity. "Brethren," he began, "some of you in this room were with me on Zion's Camp. Have we so soon forgotten those lessons? Have we so soon forgotten how the Lord chastened us when we fell to bickering and contention?"

Heads dropped and eyes looked away quickly as he looked from man to man. "We lost fourteen to cholera!" He passed a hand over his eyes. "Fourteen good people. God warned us if we did not become one, if we did not show more Christian charity for one another, we would have no protection from the scourge when it fell upon us. Is that what it will take again? Do you not remember that God has commanded us to be one, or we cannot be his?"

The challenge hung heavy in the air. The silence became so total that Benjamin noticed for the first time the sound of the leaves rustling outside the window. No one looked at Joseph now. Every head was down.

Joseph moved back to stand by his chair. His voice dropped again, now to little more than a whisper. "Brethren, the Lord has said that he is bound when we do what he says, but if we don't, we have no promise. He has promised us deliverance if we will but live his principles. But we are not living those principles. And if we do not repent we shall see the judgments of God in our lives again." He sat down. After a moment, Frederick G. Williams raised a hand. Hyrum nodded for him to speak.

He looked to Joseph. "Brother Joseph, I think you need to tell them about Brother Burgess. That could be the solution to this financial crisis."

Joseph was impassive for a moment, considering his counselor's suggestion, then finally he nodded. "I think you're right, Brother Frederick." He stood again to face the group. "Something happened yesterday that may prove to be the answer to our prayers. We're not sure yet, but it may prove to be."

That caught everyone's attention, and even the most volatile remained quiet to hear what was coming.

Joseph let his eyes sweep over them all. "Some of you know Brother Burgess, who recently came to us. Well, Brother Burgess has brought us some exciting news. As a boy he grew up in Salem, Massachusetts. As you may know, Salem is an important seaport a short distance north of Boston. Brother Burgess says he knows of a house in Salem where years ago a large treasure was buried in the cellar."

Benjamin's head came up sharply. *Buried treasure?* His eyes leaped to Joseph's face, but Joseph was watching Brother Williams.

Williams continued. "Brother Burgess says he is the only man alive who knows where the treasure is hidden."

"How much is it?" someone called out.

Joseph smiled for the first time. "He isn't sure. It's been a long time since it was put there. But it's a large treasure. Enough to solve our problems once and for all."

Joseph! Joseph! Benjamin couldn't believe the sharpness of his disappointment. *Surely not buried treasure.* He spoke, his voice filled with scorn. "And what percent of the total does Brother Burgess get?"

"Pa!" Nathan whispered in dismay.

"Well," Benjamin said to his son, not caring that Joseph could hear, "that's a fair question."

Joseph nodded. "Yes, it is, Benjamin." There was a soft note of rebuke in his voice. "Brother Burgess is asking for no part of it. He is willing to meet us in Salem and help us locate the treasure. If we find it, everything goes to the Church."

Brother Williams faced Benjamin. "Maybe the Lord's hand is in this. After all, it was building his house that got us partly into this debt in the first place. Maybe he will bless us now for it."

"And maybe my crop of peas will produce pansies."

Hyrum, still standing by Joseph, sighed. "Maybe it is a wild-goose chase, Brother Steed, but we would like to go to New York City and talk to some creditors anyway. Salem is not that much farther."

Nathan gave his father a sidelong look, not wanting to offend him but clearly troubled by his sudden negative turn. "Joseph, I think it would be foolish not to see if what Brother Burgess is saying is true. It could be such a simple solution. It could be the answer to our prayers."

"There are no simple solutions to this!" Benjamin shot back, giving his son a hard look.

"I think we have to try," Joseph said quietly.

"Amen," two or three called out.

Benjamin started a retort, but when he saw Joseph watching him steadily, he pushed it back down and just shook his head slowly. *Buried treasure?* He couldn't believe it.

By the time they came out of the temple, it was into that time of twilight when the sky was gray-violet and the forms of the trees and the buildings were becoming muted and soft.

"Benjamin, may we speak with you a moment?"

Benjamin turned. Martin Harris was with three members of the Quorum of the Twelve—Luke and Lyman Johnson and John Boynton. Warren Parrish was also with them. Parrish was serving as Joseph's personal secretary, but recently he had started to display a critical attitude about some things Joseph was doing.

Nathan touched his father's arm. "I'd better get on home and help Lydia get the children to bed."

"All right." Benjamin watched for a moment as his son strode off, then turned and walked to the group. He didn't like Parrish at all, and he found the Johnson brothers and Boynton a little too emotional for his tastes. They evidently sensed his hesitation, for they chose to let Martin speak for them.

Martin took his arm and turned him away from the temple, where the last of the brethren were still exiting. "Well, what did you think of the meeting?" he asked abruptly.

Benjamin hesitated, not sure yet what was on Martin's agenda.

Martin didn't wait for an answer. "What do you think about Joseph going to Salem?"

"I thought I made myself quite clear on that matter. I think it's an exercise in foolishness."

"I agree," Martin said darkly. "I don't know what has gotten into Joseph lately."

Benjamin looked at his old friend more closely. "Joseph is worried. Can you blame him? Twenty thousand dollars' worth of debt. That's a lot to worry about."

"Then why doesn't he let those of us who *can* help do something about it instead of chasing off after buried treasure?" The others were nodding now, but still kept their peace.

"Before I say what I'm going to say," Martin went on, lowering his voice, "let me make one thing clear, Ben. No one is questioning Joseph's spiritual leadership. We all know he has been chosen by the Lord."

"Yes," Benjamin said warily.

"But when it comes to financial matters . . ." He shook his head.

"What?" Ben asked. "When it comes to financial matters, what?"

Martin shoved his hands deep into his coat pockets. It was full cut and well tailored. Martin Harris was prospering, and it showed in the way he dressed. "Joseph was called by God to restore the gospel and the Church to the earth. His job is to build up the kingdom."

Parrish finally spoke. "A prophet is a prophet. That doesn't make him a financial genius."

Martin's hand shot out and grasped Benjamin's arm. "His strengths lie in spiritual things, Ben, not temporal things."

Ben felt a flash of irritation. At them. At himself for making them think he might be one of them. "Seems to me he hasn't done too badly so far. Sure, we're in debt, but most of that has come from building the temple."

Martin hooted softly. "Do you think the Lord's inspiring him to go look for buried treasure?"

Ben opened his mouth to speak, then shut it again.

"Neither do I," Martin hissed. "That's what I mean. Joseph needs to stick to the spiritual things. Let some of us with better business sense take charge of the other side. You're one of those, Benjamin."

Benjamin didn't answer. He felt a great sense of loyalty to Joseph, but he had been shaken by Joseph's determination to follow after this Burgess fellow. It was pure foolishness, in Benjamin's mind.

Martin seemed to sense he had pushed far enough. "Let's wait and see what happens. If Joseph comes home from Salem with a wagon full of treasure, I'll be the first one to say I was wrong. But if not . . ."

He let it hang there a moment, then nodded at the others. They murmured their farewells and walked away, leaving Benjamin alone with his thoughts.

Arriving in Independence, Missouri

Τhe prairie north of the Missouri River rolled in gently undulating swells for about as far as the eye could see in any direction. Occasionally it would flatten out for some distance, but only from the highest knolls could you see very far. There were no trees, except along the occasional stream bed; mostly this land was an oceanic expanse of waving green grass and clumps of wildflowers.

It bothered people from the East, this mind-bending openness, but Jessica loved it. Though she had to admit that the forestlands of Ohio had their own beauty, they were more confining than she liked. Her father had brought her to Missouri from Kentucky in 1826. So in many ways this felt like home to her.

As she crested a small rise, the darker line of trees and shrubbery that lined Shoal Creek greeted her eyes. She stopped, letting her knapsack drop off her shoulder. She squinted against the afternoon haze. Quickly she identified the gentle bend in the stream that signalled the location of the settlement of Haun's Mill. Though there were no telltale columns of smoke—in this mid-July heat there would be no fires except for cooking the evening meal—she quickly found the squat dark shapes of the cabins and the larger block shape of the blacksmith's shop.

She stood motionless, enjoying the moment of pause. Without conscious thought, she began to wiggle her toes, liking the feel of the powdery, hot dust of the wagon track on her bare feet. She had shoes in her knapsack, but they were far too costly to wear out on long empty roads where there was not another person to be seen for hours at a time.

Jessica looked up at the sky and smiled. She was pleased with herself. Immensely pleased. It would give her great satisfaction to return to the settlement and report on her success. Everyone—including Sister Lewis, with whom she was staying—had tried to dissuade Jessica from setting out to find families that needed a tutor for their children. Even the few scattered settlers in this part of northern Missouri knew about the Mormons. They were resentful of their coming and suspicious of their motives. But after two rather sharp encounters, Jessica decided to acknowledge right up front who she was and get to the point of her coming. "Good morning, sir (or ma'am)," she would say. "My name is Jessica Steed, from the new Mormon settlement over on Shoal Creek." And then before they could react, "I'm going to be coming through here twice a month, teaching reading, writing, and arithmetic to children."

Her instincts had been right. Though these families lived in the most simple—sometimes the most wretched—of conditions, they wanted something better for their children. Upon her solemn promise that there would be no talk of religion, the deal was struck. She had gotten commitments from ten families, usually clustered in groups of two or three cabins. It meant she would be gone four days at a time, twice a month, boarding overnight with the families on a rotating basis, leaving Rachel with neighbors and friends. It would involve a circuit of about sixteen miles, all told. On the even months she would walk it.

On the odd months she would borrow a wagon from the Lewises and collect her "payment." There was very little cash money in these parts, so her salary would be paid in trade—chickens, wheat, corn, perhaps a small hog; whatever she and the particular family settled on as fair payment.

Now she knew why she had felt so compelled to return to Missouri. Jessica Roundy Steed—saloon keeper's daughter, divorced wife of a mule-skinning teamster, uneducated illiterate who had taught herself how to read and write and do figures—was now a teacher. No, she corrected herself. Not just a teacher. A *paid* teacher! She threw back her head, wanting to laugh right out loud. But of course that was something Jessica rarely did, and so she just smiled up at the greatness of the blue sky. Finally, she hoisted the canvas sack again and started off, walking with long, sure strides.

Caroline Mendenhall Steed had steeled herself for this moment for seven weeks now, but nothing could have prepared her for what she saw as their carriage moved down the main street of Independence.

Savannah, Georgia, had been laid out with straight streets and pleasant squares and parks placed strategically throughout the city. Independence, Missouri, had been laid out by mountain men and teamsters following buffalo and deer trails. Savannah was street after street of well-designed, neatly built, well-cared-for brick homes. The businesses had attractive, neatly lettered signs, often done with gold-leaf paint. Independence was raw bawdiness. There was no order to the structures that they were passing, just a random tangle of sod huts, tin shanties, Indian tepees, canvas tents, packing-crate lean-tos, and log cabins, with only an occasional frame home. And the businesses, if that was what they were, carried hand-lettered signs at best and barely legible scrawls at worst.

She felt her heart drop. *What have I done?*

"Joshua! Joshua! Is that a real Indian?" Will, in the backseat behind his mother, nearly jumped out of the carriage in his eagerness to point at an approaching figure.

The man was tall and dressed in buckskin shirt, pants, and moccasins. His hair was black as fireplace soot and pulled back in a braid. He turned his head slowly and eyed the passing carriage. His eyes were dark and hooded, the expression impassive and unreadable. Caroline felt a little shiver go up and down her back.

"Yes, Will," Joshua said with a chuckle, "that's a real Indian. Osage tribe, I would guess. Maybe Choctaw."

"Really?" Olivia breathed.

"Really," Joshua said. "Indian Territory is just a few miles west of here. Some of them come into town from time to time."

Olivia dug her fists into her eyes, and leaned forward so as to see better. She had fallen asleep on her mother's shoulder during the hour-long carriage ride from Westport, the river landing located a few miles up the Missouri River from Independence. Will's cry had brought her up with a jerk, and now she looked out on this strange new world, eyes wider than the sand dollars they used to find on the beach when they went down to the ocean.

Suddenly Caroline was aware that Joshua was watching her closely out of the corner of his eye. The grin he had given Will a moment before had faded. His eyes were anxious. He was waiting for her response. She managed a quick smile and reached across and touched his arm. She knew he was hoping for more than that, but she also knew if she spoke now, even to say something halfway encouraging, her voice would give her away.

It had taken them over a month and a half to come from Savannah. They were married the night before Joshua's shipload of cotton left for New Orleans with them and the children on board ship. They had stayed three days in New Orleans while he arranged riverboat passage for them and the cotton. That had been exciting. The wharves along the riverfront stretched on forever, the hundreds of oceangoing vessels making a veritable forest with their masts and rigging. And then there were the dozens of great paddle-wheel riverboats, nuzzled up to their berths like a litter of pigs snuggling up to their mother's belly.

She had been pleasantly surprised at St. Louis. It was definitely not Savannah, but it was a growing, bustling city with row after row of businesses along the river and some very adequate shops on its main streets. They had stayed there for about a month while Joshua worked with his partners to get the mill up and running. They had stayed long enough to see the first bolts of cloth come out of the great looms they had shipped in from New England.

But once they left St. Louis and started up the Missouri River, it quickly became evident they were leaving civilization behind. And the vastness of the prairie both surprised and bothered her. As the great riverboat chugged its way slowly upstream, Joshua seemed to sense her growing despondency. And the closer they got to Independence, the more nervous he became. Yesterday he had been worse than a raccoon in a shed full of hound dogs. She had tried her best to put on a brave face, but she had never been one to gush enthusiastically when she didn't really feel that way. Now she could tell he was openly worried as he waited for her to say something. She felt a rush of relief when her son burst out again.

"Look!"

"Look at what?" Joshua said, turning to see where Will was looking.

"Is that your wagon?"

A big Conestoga wagon, its canvas top stretched high and tight over metal hoops, was just passing them on the left. Six massive draft horses trotted slowly, their harnessing jingling, their hooves flipping little chunks of dirt into the air. The driver raised a hand as he saw who was in the carriage. "Welcome home, Mr. Steed." He tipped his hat toward Caroline, trying not to stare. "Congratulations."

Joshua acknowledged that with a nod, then turned to Will. "Yes, it is. So are the next two."

Caroline lifted her eyes and saw two more wagons coming, both identical to the first. Then, as the second team passed them, she saw what had triggered Will's cry. Along the side of the wagon box was neatly stenciled "Joshua Steed, Freight and Portage." She turned to look at Joshua, this time wanting him to see she was impressed.

He smiled, trying to be casual about it all, but he was obviously pleased. "They're on their way to Westport. They'll get our stuff."

"But how did they know we're here? We are just now arriving."

"Remember the man I spoke to briefly when we came off the boat?"

She thought for a moment. "Not really."

He laughed. "Well, that's Mr. Cornwell, my yard foreman. He's met every boat for the last ten days just to be sure he didn't miss us. He's the one who brought the carriage. He rode on ahead to let them know we were coming."

"Oh." They were into the main part of Independence now, and Caroline noted with some satisfaction that here things looked a little better. Some of the storefronts were actually presentable, one or two even sporting window displays. She also noted that there was a high proportion of saloons for a town of its size.

"Welcome back, Mr. Steed." Two ladies were on the sidewalk in front of a dress shop. They gawked at Caroline with unabashed curiosity.

"Afternoon, Mrs. Johns. Afternoon, Miss Charity."

Now Caroline became aware that they were causing no small stir as they passed. Men stopped to wave and call out. Women pointed when they thought she was looking the other way. Word of the arrival of Joshua Steed's new bride had definitely preceded them.

Will thrust his head between his mother and stepfather. "And you have twenty wagons like that?" he said with suitable awe.

"Actually, I have about thirty wagons. But no, they're not all like that. Conestogas are very expensive. I have to buy them in Pennsylvania and have them brought out. And those horses. They're called Conestogas too. They run about a hundred dollars a head."

"A hundred dollars!" Will echoed. Caroline genuinely smiled at Joshua now.

He smiled back at her, then looked down at Will. "Do you know what we're gonna do once we get your mother settled?"

"What?"

Joshua looked at Caroline. The nervousness was gone from him now. Without taking his eyes off her he answered Will's question. "We're gonna paint a new sign on the side of every one of my wagons. Know what it's gonna say?"

Will was fairly dancing in his seat. "What?"

"From now on, every wagon I own is going to say 'Joshua Steed *and Son*.' "

"Yea!" Will said, punching the air. "Can I learn to drive one?"

Joshua looked appropriately grave. "You ever hear of a partner in a freight business who couldn't drive a team by himself?"

Caroline watched her son nearly explode with joy, and suddenly she felt a lump in her throat. Independence was going to take some getting used to—a whole lot of getting used to!—but Caroline Mendenhall's children had a father again. And they both adored him. That could make up for a lot of Savannah in her heart. At that moment, she made up her mind about something she had been debating now for over a week.

She reached out and laid her hand on Joshua's knee. "You may want to wait a little bit before you change those signs."

"Mama!" Will exploded, not believing she would betray him like that.

But Caroline ignored Will and just kept looking at Joshua, who was looking puzzled. "You may want it to read, 'Joshua Steed and *Sons*.' " She gave soft emphasis to the plural.

For a moment he stared at her, then he jerked on the reins,

stopping the team and carriage right in the middle of the main street of Independence. "Do you mean that?" he said in half a whisper.

"I think so," she laughed, deeply pleased with his reaction. "It's still too early to know for sure. Once we're settled, maybe we can find a doctor."

"A doctor!" he exploded. "I have a doctor. Not just some horse doctor either. One from the East. I brought him here my-self." He reached out and took both of her hands. "I can't be-lieve it."

"What's the matter, Mama?" Olivia cried in alarm. To an eight-year-old, any talk of a doctor was alarming. "Are you sick?"

Will punched his sister on the arm gently. He was grinning like a kid who had just discovered a tree trunk full of honey-combs and no bees in sight. "No, Olivia," he beamed, "Mama isn't sick."

Eight hundred miles to the east, in a grove of maple and hickory trees about a mile east of Kirtland, Rebecca and Matthew Steed were enjoying a brief respite from the summer's heat. Off to the west the first clouds of what would develop into an afternoon thunderstorm were just beginning to build. The air was heavy and still, laden with enough humidity to bring beads of perspiration to Matthew's brow even in the coolness of the deep shade.

Just beyond the trees lay fifteen acres of chest-high corn. It was one of three farms owned by Benjamin Steed. Normally, Matthew's brother Nathan took care of this plot and the one just beyond the next woodlot, but Nathan and Benjamin had gone with Joseph and Sidney Rigdon to visit some branches of the Church in the adjoining counties. So Matthew took over in their absence. Rebecca had brought him out some fresh bread and honey and a crock jar of cold milk. They had lunched to-gether, and now Matthew dawdled, postponing the time when he had to go back out into the heat of the sun.

He was stretched out on the matting of leaves, his hands behind his head, his straw hat pulled down over his eyes. Becca surveyed his lankiness, noting how long his legs had become. He had outgrown her somewhere around his fourteenth birthday, almost two years ago. Now he towered a good half a foot above her five feet four inches, and he was still growing. She also noted that all traces of the little-boy softness were gone. He did a man's work now, and it showed in the lean hardness of his torso and the muscular lines of his upper arms and shoulders. His face was deeply tanned, the hair on his arms bleached almost bone white against the darkness of his skin. Though his hair still had a touch of blond, it had darkened considerably and was now more of a light brown, like Nathan's.

He turned his head and pushed the hat back slightly with his thumb and looked at her steadily, his blue eyes wide and innocent. She smiled at him with genuine affection. They were only a little more than two years apart in age, and being the youngest children in the family, they had been friends for each other since the time Matthew could walk. She reached out with her foot and nudged him slightly. "A penny for your thoughts."

"I was thinking of Jessica and Rachel."

Rebecca sobered. "I think of them often too. I miss little Rachel."

"Me too." Matthew laughed softly. "But I don't think any of us miss her as much as Grandpa does."

"No," she agreed, "no one could miss her that much."

Matthew sat up, reaching out to a nearby elderberry bush. He broke off a small branch and began to methodically strip off the leaves, shredding them neatly as he did so. His face had grown thoughtful. Finally he looked at his sister. "Do you think Jessica still has hopes that she and Joshua will someday get back together?"

Rebecca shook her head.

"You don't? Why not?"

"Because she doesn't, that's why." She couldn't tell him about the conversation she and Jessica had about this very subject just before Jessica's departure from Kirtland.

"How can you be so sure?"

"Because I'm sure," Rebecca said flatly. "They won't get back together. Not ever. Not after what he did to her."

Matthew flipped the branch away. "What *did* Joshua do to her? All I ever hear are all these dark hints."

Rebecca shrugged. "You'll have to ask her. She asked me not to say."

"Come on, Becca," Matthew pleaded, sounding suddenly more like her little brother. "I won't tell anyone."

She gave him a long look. "It's no worse than what he did to Nathan."

That brought his head up with a jerk. "What did he do to Nathan?"

The thought brought pain to Rebecca's face. "You've seen his back."

Matthew's mouth dropped open. "Joshua did that?" he whispered. "Nathan told me he was caught by some Missouri mobbers."

"He was. But Joshua was there. He could have stopped it."

For a long moment Matthew let that sink in. Then in a mixture of awe and horror he went on. "No wonder Mama won't talk about it."

"And no wonder Papa won't even say his name."

They both fell silent for a moment, busy with their own thoughts. Finally Matthew spoke again. "Becca, I . . ." He dropped his head, still watching her out of the corner of his eye, afraid she would laugh at him, or worse, rebuke him. His hands were suddenly fidgeting, plucking at the dead leaves around him.

"What?"

He was searching her eyes, clearly wanting to finish what he had started, but then he lost his nerve. "Nothin'."

"What, Matthew?"

He shook his head. He decided to change the subject. "I saw Arthur the other day."

Now it was Rebecca who was taken aback. Her mouth tightened.

"He was at the harness shop when I went to see Melissa and Carl." Matthew waited for a response, but there was none. However, he saw that her hands, which had been folded in her lap, were now twisting slowly.

The blue in Matthew's eyes darkened perceptibly. "I waited for him up the street."

She whirled. "You what?" Then a look of alarm crossed her face. "What did you do?"

Matthew smiled slowly, but it was only a surface smile. Behind it his eyes were hard and the muscles along his jaw were tight.

"Matthew! What did you do?"

Slowly his face relaxed, and the smile became a genuine Matthew-grin. "I was real polite and all that, but I told him if I heard any more about him spreading those stories about you, I was going to improve on what the Lord had chosen to give him for a face."

For a second Rebecca looked horrified, then suddenly she started to giggle. "You didn't!"

Relieved at her reaction, he chuckled. "I did. I told him I could give him eyes to match the color of his boots."

The giggles burst out into peals of laughter.

Matthew was enjoying himself now. "Or lips big enough to kiss a cow."

"Stop it!" she cried, holding her sides. "You didn't really, did you?"

He sobered a little. "Well, not the lips."

She caught her breath, wiping at the corners of her eyes. "Matthew, what were you thinking of? Arthur is a good two or three inches taller than you and outweighs you by at least twenty-five or thirty pounds."

He shrugged as if offended. "Remember back in Vermont how Mr. Anderson's little terrier would take on some of them big ol' hunting dogs in town? His lip would curl back. He'd start toward them, all stiff-legged, the hair on his back bristlin' up like a porcupine's."

She was nodding, smiling with the memory. "And nine times out of ten those big dogs would turn tail and run."

"That's right. And that's what Arthur Wilkinson did. Remember, dear sister, it ain't how big the dog is that matters; it's how big what's *in* the dog that counts."

Still smiling, but now with her eyes moist, she reached out and laid a hand on his arm. "Thank you, Matthew."

"Well," he said, "it made me mad when he started saying those things about you. They were mean and vicious things."

"It doesn't matter."

"Well, it does to me."

She gazed at him for a moment. "Thank you, my little terrier."

He lay back down and pulled the hat over his eyes again, embarrassed by her emotion. She watched him for a moment, still sensing a certain tension in him. "Was that what you were going to talk to me about?"

His eyes opened and he searched her face.

"Come on. Please tell me."

For several moments he lay there, chewing on his lower lip, his hands on his stomach, the fingers drumming slowly on his shirt. Finally, he turned his head, knocking the hat back so she could see his face clearly. "Promise you won't laugh?"

The corners of her mouth softened. "Of course I won't laugh."

He took a deep breath. Let it out slowly. Took another. Then he plunged. "Becca, I want to go to Missouri."

———•———

Will and Olivia went racing through the house, exploring the rooms at breakneck speed. Joshua stood in the living room, half smiling as he listened to their excited squeals and cries to come see this or come see that. Caroline, who had dropped into one of the big overstuffed chairs in the main room of the big two-story frame house—one of the nicest in Independence— watched the ceiling, her ears following the progress of her offspring as they explored the bedrooms upstairs.

Will came to the head of the stairs and stuck his head down low enough to see them. "Which room is mine?" he called.

"The one on the end," Joshua answered. "The big one at the head of the stairs is your mother's and mine. The one next to that is Olivia's."

"Yippee!" came the cry from behind Will, and off they went. In a moment the squeak of the bed could be heard as Olivia tested the mettle of her new accommodations.

Joshua turned to Caroline. "Is that all right?"

"Of course. I'm glad they're so excited."

His head bobbed once, but his eyes were sober. "I wish their mother were more so."

She was instantly up and walked to him, the contrition clearly written on her face. "I'm just very tired, Joshua. It's been a hard trip."

"I know." His eyes said, *I also know that's not the only reason.*

She slipped her arm through his. "This is a lovely home. It will be more than adequate for our needs."

There was a quick, impatient shake of his head. "Only until I can build you one of your own. And believe me, it is going to be the finest home in all of Jackson County." He snorted at his own shortsightedness. "No, it's going to be the best house west of St. Louis."

Her eyes widened at that. This was the first he had said anything about building a house for her. "I don't expect that."

"Well, I do," he said shortly. "You're gonna have a home every bit as big and beautiful as that home you had in Savannah."

She stepped around to face him squarely, searching his eyes. "Is that what you think? That I'm disappointed in this house?"

"I . . . no, but . . ." He shrugged, and turned when there was a noise above them.

She reached up and touched his face, turning his head back to her. "But what, Joshua?"

He didn't answer.

"Joshua, this house is fine. I mean it. I don't want you—"

He was shaking his head.

"It is!" she said more forcefully. "I mean it."

"No. I won't have you living here. I'm sorry we have to come here for now. But as soon as possible, we're putting you in your own home."

Suddenly she understood. She laughed, touched by his concern. "You think I'm bothered by the fact that your first wife lived here? Is that it?"

He pulled away from her and walked to the window.

"That *is* it, isn't it?" She went to him and slipped her arms around his waist, laying her head against the broadness of his back. "Thank you for even thinking of it, Joshua, but that doesn't bother me. Not in the least."

"I won't have you living here," he said shortly. "Not permanently."

She stepped back, a little baffled by the strength of his feelings about the matter. Before she could speak, Will came thundering down the stairs, his younger sister right behind him. "Is that your barn out back, Joshua?"

"*Our* barn," Joshua corrected.

"Can we go see it?" Olivia asked, her eyes like two great green lamps shining out from her face.

"Sure."

"Be careful," Caroline called after them as they raced for the back door. Then she laughed hopelessly. "They are having so much fun."

He nodded, and she saw that the tension in his face had softened a little. "Thank you, Joshua."

"For what?" he asked in surprise.

"For caring for my children. For treating them with respect. They adore you, you know."

She was surprised when he looked away. "I've always wanted children. And you have two of the finest."

She watched him for a moment, aware of how little she knew this man she had married. He stood motionless, still looking toward the back door. "Will you tell me about her, Joshua?" Caroline asked softly.

He jerked around. "Who?"

"You know who. Your first wife. I don't even know her name."

He shook his head in one quick violent motion.

"That's your response every time I ask you. I know you don't want me to be hurt, but not knowing anything about her isn't the answer. You know about my husband."

He turned his head away from her.

Other times when she had asked, she had run into the same wall. Now it was time to break through it. "Please, Joshua," she pleaded. "Tell me about her, then I'll not ask again."

He started to shake his head again, but caught himself. His eyes had a faraway look in them, one of bitterness and anger. But at least he had not cut her off. She took that as at least some sign of agreement. "You said before that you married quickly. Was she young?"

He shrugged. "A little older than me."

"What was her name?"

"Jessica. People usually called her Jessie."

"Was she pretty?"

He gave her a sharp look, then his eyes looked disinterested. "Not particularly. Not anything like you."

It was meant as a compliment, but somehow it cut Caroline. He had answered the question so quickly, almost callously. That was a side of him she had not seen before. She knew very little about this Jessica, but suddenly she felt sorry for her.

"I'll go out and see how the kids are doing."

She reached out and touched his arm. "You said she left you because of religion?"

His breath exploded outward in a burst of genuine anger. "Yes. She became one of them Mormons!" he spat.

"A what?"

"A Mormon!"

She looked a little bewildered. "I'm sorry, Joshua, I don't know what that is."

"It's a . . ." He groped for an adequate word. "A church. A

religion. But a bad one. An evil one. The people are crazy. Talkin' all the time about angels and revelations. Tryin' to make everybody believe like they do. Sayin' we're all goin' to hell 'ceptin' them."

Caroline stood motionless, a little aghast at the bitterness he was showing. "Are they around here?" she finally managed.

"Not anymore!" he said with angry satisfaction. "We drove them out at the point of a gun. They'd better not be comin' back."

A chill ran up her back. "What happened to your wife? Was she driven out too?"

He swung around, his mouth tight. "You asked your questions, Caroline, and I answered them. Now, there'll be no more talk about the Mormons or about the woman who left me to become one of them."

He turned and stalked to the back door. He paused only for a moment. "I'm going to take the children up to the freight yard to show them around. I know you're tired. Why don't you rest for a while."

Without waiting for a response, he went out, shutting the door sharply behind him.

———•———

Mary Ann was crying softly. Rebecca was wiping at the corners of her own eyes with a small handkerchief. Matthew got up from his chair and went over to sit beside his mother on the sofa. He put one arm around her awkwardly. "Mama, it's not that I'm not happy here. I just—"

She reached up and took his hand. "I know, Matthew. I know."

"I just feel like I need to be in Zion. I worry about Jessica and Rachel so, but it's more than that. I just can't get it out of my mind."

"I know," she said again, trying to smile through her tears. "I've known for two weeks now."

He reared back, his eyes widening. "You have?"

Rebecca was as surprised as Matthew. "You have, Mama?"

She nodded. "I told your father over a week ago, didn't I, Benjamin?"

Matthew's father was standing in one corner of the room. His head bobbed up and down once. It was clear this wasn't easy for him either.

"But how?" Matthew began. He shook his head. "How could you have known? I hadn't said a word to anyone until I told Becca this afternoon."

Mary Ann sniffed back the tears, and pulled his arm off her shoulder so she could take his hand in both of hers. "I think the Lord knew I needed some preparation for this."

Matthew leaned forward eagerly. "Really?"

Benjamin sighed, looking first toward his wife, then back to Matthew. "Your mother and I have been talking. We are very concerned about Jessica and Rachel being out there alone."

Rebecca nodded vigorously at that. "Matthew and I were talking about that very thing today."

"I think maybe it's time for Nathan and me to go to Missouri and make sure she's all right. Get her established. We could leave in September, as soon as we get the crops in." His shoulders lifted and fell. "If you still want to go, then—"

Matthew shot to his feet, his face ecstatic. "Of course I will!"

His father stepped across the room to face him, now very solemn. "There is one condition, Matthew."

"What?"

"You must give us the most solemn promise."

"I will. I will. What is it?"

"Under no circumstances—none!—are you to ever try to see your brother in Independence."

That nearly bowled Matthew over, but immediately he nodded, now as sober as his father. "I understand, Pa."

"And you must never go into Jackson County. No matter how good your reasons. Not ever."

"I won't, Pa."

"Swear it!"

Matthew hesitated only a moment. "I swear it, Pa."

Mary Ann stood slowly and opened her arms. Suddenly there was a terrible catch in Matthew's throat, and his chest felt as if it were collapsing inward. He stepped into her arms, and encircled her with his. "I'm sorry, Mama. I'm going to miss you all terribly."

"Don't talk about it," Mary Ann whispered hoarsely. "Just don't talk about it. I've still got my baby boy for another two months."

That must be it, Pa."

Nathan and Benjamin turned to where Matthew was pointing. To the west of them, across the seemingly limitless spread of dry prairie grass, there was a prominent knoll, the highest in the area. Against the backlight of the late afternoon sun, they could make out the dark outlines of several tents and the shape of a wagon. The wagon tracks they had been following since they had struck Shoal Creek and turned west led straight up the gentle rise toward where the tents were.

Nathan nodded. "I think you're right, Matthew. That must be Far West."

Benjamin let his eyes sweep across the breadth of the horizon. He turned to Nathan. "Remember that article in that Eastern newspaper I showed you? About that fellow, name of McCormick?"

Nathan looked blank.

"The one that invented that wheat harvester a couple of years ago?"

"Oh, yeah." He still looked puzzled that his father would remember that right at the moment.

"Know what he said about his reaper? Said that now that the great flatlands of America were opening up to wheat farming, we had to have a machine to help us. Get spaces this big and you can't get enough men to cut the wheat down by hand. They say a man and a good team of horses can cut twenty, maybe thirty acres in a day with one of those machines."

Matthew's eyes widened. "Really?"

Benjamin nodded, turning back to the land around them. "Imagine what a man could do out here. Put this all in wheat, get a couple of them reapers." He turned to Nathan. "That's the future, Nathan. Think about it."

Nathan smiled with a ruefulness that betrayed his weariness. "I will, Pa, soon as we find a place to sit down and get off these feet."

Benjamin laughed. "You're right. And here I am standing around jawing. Let's get on up there and find this daughter-in-law of mine."

Nathan pulled his coat tighter around him and fell in behind his father and younger brother. It was the sixth day of October, and earlier in the day the temperature hadn't been too unpleasant, but now that the sun was low in the sky, the air had taken on a definite chill. By nightfall there would be frost. He lowered his head and plodded on.

———————

To say that the city of Far West was beginning to take shape would have been to overstate the case. There were only five permanent structures, all of them simple log and sod huts. There were several dozen tents of varying quality. Some were worn thin; some were torn to the point that they offered little more than a minimal privacy. Here and there, Nathan noticed, families had camped as best they could around their wagons. Children huddled around small fires, and there were simple bedrolls laid out on the prairie.

Their welcome was hardly a warm one. Heads lifted and people stared at the three men as they walked by. The expressions ranged from the openly curious stares of the children to the nervous, darting glances of the women. The men were sullen and suspicious. Nathan didn't blame them. He had been in Missouri with Zion's Camp. He knew what it meant when strangers appeared. Were they friendly newcomers or Missouri wildcats out looking for trouble? He kept smiling and nodding to the people as they passed, but expected no more than the response they were receiving.

Suddenly he stopped. Matthew and their father stopped alongside him. Nathan was gazing at a lean-to made from hazel brush and propped up against the side of a wagon. Crouching down in front of a small fire, nursing it with small twigs and buffalo chips, was a tall, slender figure. Beside him, half in profile, was a woman heavy with child.

Nathan strode forward. "Newel?" he called. "Newel Knight?"

The man straightened and turned. For a moment his face was blank, then it exploded into a broad smile. "Nathan? Benjamin?" In three great steps he was to them, sweeping Nathan up in a crushing bear hug.

———————•◆•———————

"When is the baby due, Sister Knight?"

Newel and his visitors were seated on the ground around the fire. Newel's little son had gone off to play with some of the other children. Lydia Knight was in the wagon box above them, half propped up on a quilt stretched over some sacks of grain. She looked very tired as she answered Nathan. "A little less than two months now."

"I hope all goes well."

"Thank you."

"So tell me," Newel said eagerly, "how are Joseph and Emma?"

Nathan shook his head. "Actually we haven't seen Joseph since late July. He and Hyrum and Sidney and Oliver all went to New York City, then on to Salem, Massachusetts."

"Salem?" he said, a little surprised. "Why there?"

Benjamin snorted in disgust. "Some fool claimed to know where there was a chest of buried treasure."

"Hmm. Did they find it?"

"Of course not. Once they got there this man who claimed to know 'right where it was' walked around the city with a dazed look on his face muttering, 'My goodness, this place has really changed since I was last here.' "

"Pa," Matthew broke in, "you know that's not what Joseph's letter said."

"Well," Benjamin retorted, "he said Burgess couldn't even find the right house, let alone the treasure chest."

Nathan was watching his father. This had turned out to be a real sore spot with him. There were several others in Kirtland, including some of the leading brethren, who were sharply critical of Joseph on this matter. Nathan decided to change the subject. "Emma had a little boy in June."

"Oh, good," Sister Knight said. "And everything is all right?"

"Yes. They named him after President Williams."

"Yes," Sister Knight said, "I remember Emma said that was what Joseph wanted to do."

"And guess what else," Nathan said, suddenly remembering. "Thankful Pratt is with child."

"No!" Both husband and wife blurted it out together.

He told them quickly of Heber C. Kimball's blessing and of the wonderful surprise they had when they returned from Canada and found Thankful cured. A week before Benjamin and his two sons left Kirtland, the Steeds had received a letter from Toronto announcing Parley and Thankful's news that she was expecting. Newel's wife clapped her hands. "That is wonderful news. I'll bet she is so happy."

"Parley too," Benjamin agreed.

They fell silent for a moment as the Knights considered that news. Nathan turned and surveyed the scene that surrounded them. The sun had gone down, leaving the prairie in soft shadows. The air was cold enough that their breath was visible. "It looks like you've found yourself a lovely place here," he finally said.

Newel looked surprised for a moment. "We're just up here looking for possible sites for homes, since my relatives are all planning to move here. I don't know if Lydia and I will be able to move when the rest of them do, but we're hoping to get up here sometime next year."

Benjamin was looking at the rows of tents. "Oh. By then this will be a full-blown city. When we came through Clay County looking for you, it looked like half the population was packing up getting ready to move."

"Yep. Tempers in Clay County were on the rise again, and some were threatening to drive us out of there. I know Lydia's time is near, but I didn't want to leave her there alone while I was up here locating some places to build. You know, I guess, that the Saints agreed to move up here. The state has created a six-mile buffer zone between us and the non-Mormons." He swung an arm, catching the scattered tents and wagons in his sweep. "And we're gonna fill this place up with Mormons. There are more coming in from Kirtland and the East all the time."

Matthew turned to the east, letting his eyes follow the line of trees that marked Shoal Creek's meandering path. "This settlement called Haun's Mill, how far is it from here?"

"About twelve miles." The news from Newel that Jessica and Rachel were not in Far West but in Haun's Mill had come as a bitter disappointment to them all, but especially to Matthew. If they had known, they could have just as easily gone straight there. The road up from Clay County reached Shoal Creek about midway between Far West and Haun's Mill. Had they turned east, they would have been with Jessica and Rachel by now.

Newel's wife sat up. "They've had some fevernager in the settlement."

Nathan felt a quick lurch of concern. "Very much?"

Newel was grim. "Quite a bit. Someone said Jessica is down with it too."

Lydia Knight frowned. "I had a real bout of it a few weeks ago."

Benjamin's eyes were grave. "How bad is Jessica?"

Their host shrugged. "Reports are pretty sketchy at this point. It's the shakes, no doubt about it."

Nathan looked at his father as he spoke to Newel. "We didn't think we'd need it this late in the year, but we brought some quinine, just in case."

"Good," Newel said. "They'll be glad to hear that."

Matthew looked at his father, the concern clearly written on his face. Benjamin nodded somberly. "We'll leave at first light."

Malaria got its name from the Italian word meaning "bad air." Like the dreaded yellow fever, it had probably been carried north from the West Indies in the bloodstreams of slaves and slave traders, sailors and merchants. These innocent walking carriers of death simply had to come into contact with the right species of mosquito to provide incubation and transmission of the disease across much of America.

At that point, of course, medicine had not yet learned the role of the mosquito in the spread of malaria. It was widely held in early America that disease came from an imbalance of the "humors," or the basic body elements. The settlers were perceptive enough to see a correlation between the occurrence of the disease and what they called "sickly country"—areas with enough wetlands to provide the breeding ground for mosquitos. Unfortunately this described most of the country penetrated by settlers up until the Civil War. But people thought "the shakes"—or "fevernager" or "ague" (pronounced ay-gyoo) as it was usually called—was caused by the bad air that came from the decay of vegetable matter around swampy areas. This bad air, or "malaria," set the body's functions in imbalance.

But whatever the cause, malaria was commonplace through-out the first half of the nineteenth century. In its most virulent form, death would come in an agonizing alternation between raging fever and violent chills and shaking. In its milder forms, it could be tolerated, but often left the victim susceptible to other ailments. Ague was so commonplace that it was accepted as a natural part of life. One Missourian, when asked if he had become acclimatized to the area—meaning, had he become im-mune to malaria—replied, "I've been here twenty-five years, and bless my soul if I haven't gone through twenty-five separate and distinct 'earthquakes' in that time." Many a large family ex-pected the chills on a daily basis. One child would have it one day, another the next. Usually a cup of sassafras tea and a dose of quinine kept it manageable, and people accepted it as part of the mortal experience.

The problem was, no one in Haun's Mill had any quinine. The drug was extracted from a South American tree, and while it was widely available along the Eastern Seaboard, it was much less so—and terribly more expensive—along the frontiers of America. Among the little body of Saints who had settled with Jacob Haun on Shoal Creek, what quinine had been available had been thoroughly exhausted by summer's end. So for more than a fortnight now, Jessica had fought the fevernager without help.

Now she was exhausted. Sister Mary Beth Lewis sat on the edge of her bed. It had been the Lewises who had first taken Jes-sica in when she came stumbling into Kaw Township back in the summer of 1831, battered and dazed from Joshua's beating. When she returned to Missouri, Jessica found that Joshua Lewis had died. Sister Lewis offered her room and board in return for her help with her family of small children. It was Mary Beth Lewis who had cared for Jessica throughout her long siege of the ague.

Now Sister Lewis was sponging her skin with a wet rag. The flesh was hot to the touch. Jessica's eyes fluttered open. "Rachel?"

Sister Lewis reached out and took her hand. "It's all right, Jessie. Rachel's out playing."

For a moment, it didn't register, then finally she turned. Her face was gray, the eyes sunken and listless, the skin drawn tight across her cheekbones. "Is she—" She had to stop for a breath. "Is she all right?"

"Yes, yes." Sister Lewis patted Jessica's arm. "She hasn't had the shakes for almost five days now."

Jessica nodded weakly, then suddenly moaned and tried to rise. Sister Lewis tossed the rag into the basin of water and grabbed her shoulders. "What are you doing? You can't get up."

"The children. School. I've got to go."

Mary Beth Lewis was a small woman, but there was no lack of determination in her. She gently pushed the weak and struggling Jessica back down to the pillow. "If you do, it'll be on a slab."

"They'll be wonderin' what happened to me." She gave up and stopped fighting it. "I can't lose this chance, Mary Beth. If I don't go, they'll find someone else."

"In this country?" She gave a short, mirthless laugh. "Who they gonna find?" When that didn't take the anxiety from Jessica's eyes, she went on with a more soothing tone. "Some of the brethren have spread the word about you being sick as best they can. Those families will understand. You can't be teachin' school with the shakes."

For several seconds Jessica stared up at the woman who was not much older than she was and who had been so kind to her. Suddenly she turned her head toward the wall. "It was all a mistake, wasn't it?"

Mary Beth leaned forward. "What?"

"I should never have left Ohio."

"Nonsense! Now, don't you be takin' on like that. You're just feelin' poorly and that makes your heart feel poorly too."

"No." Jessica turned her head back. Her eyes were filled with tears, a rare thing for Jessica Steed. "I thought it was the Lord calling me back here. But look at me. No husband. A child to care for. At least there I had family."

"You got family here," Sister Lewis said, looking a little hurt.

"I know that," Jessica said quickly. "You have been wonderful to us. But—" She had to stop, exhausted by having spoken that many words.

"But nothing," Sister Lewis said firmly. "I won't have you talkin' like this. You said the Lord called you here. You said you knew that sure as anything. So, here is where you're going to stay. As soon as you're over this, you'll feel better about it. You'll see."

Jessica just shook her head, closing her eyes. That squeezed the tears out and they started to trickle down the sides of her face. Mary Beth Lewis reached out and wiped them softly with her two thumbs. "You will, Jessie. I promise. Just try and sleep some more now."

About an hour later, Jessica awoke. She had fallen into a deep sleep, and only gradually did she realize that someone was gently shaking her shoulder. She opened her eyes, aware that the chills were gone and she was being consumed with the fever again. Mary Beth stood directly above her, smiling down at her.

"Jessie?"

She tried to shake off the lethargy, come up out of the depths, but it was a struggle.

"Jessie, there's someone here to see you."

Jessica Roundy Steed had never been much concerned about personal appearance, but almost immediately her hand lifted up to touch her hair. It was matted and greasy. More than a week had gone by since she had been out of bed. "No, Mary Beth," she started, her voice half a croak, but Mary Beth just smiled the wider and stepped back.

"Hello, Jessie."

She turned, blinking against the light coming through the doorway. There was a large figure there, blocking some of it, but she couldn't see any features. Nevertheless her heart leaped at the familiar voice. The figure stepped into the room, and another figure, not as broad but equally tall, took its place.

"Hello, Jessica."

"Nathan?"

Suddenly they were at her side, both men kneeling at her bed, reaching out for her hands. She stared up at them, barely comprehending. "Benjamin?"

"Yes, Jessie." Benjamin's voice suddenly caught and he shook his head quickly. "We're here, Jessie. We're here."

She was still too dazed to believe what her eyes were seeing. She reached up and touched Nathan's face. "Is it really you?" she whispered.

He couldn't answer, just nodded, swallowing hard twice, gripping her hand tightly.

Tears sprang to her eyes, and this time there was no effort to fight them back. For a long moment, they sat that way, none of them speaking, Jessica and Mary Beth crying freely, the two men struggling to get control of their emotions.

Finally, she pulled her hand back and brushed at the tears. "Rachel?"

"We saw her," Benjamin said. He laughed huskily. "I'll bet she's grown a foot since you left."

She nodded, then had to stifle another sob that rose in her throat. "I can't believe it," she cried. "I just can't believe it."

Benjamin stood slowly. "We brought someone else."

She looked around. "Not Mary Ann?"

He shook his head. "We thought you might need a man around the house, someone to take care of you and Rachel."

She was baffled. Then a third man stepped into the room. Rachel was at his side, holding his hand. "Hi, Jessica."

She came up on one elbow, her head jutting forward. "Matthew, is that you?"

"Yep!" He stepped forward, grinning widely. "It's me." Then in a rush he was to the bed and putting his arms around her shoulders.

"I can't believe it. I can't believe it." She just kept saying it over and over as she hugged Matthew tightly to her.

Nathan, smiling now too, swung his knapsack around. "We brought you some medicine."

Her eyes turned to him, puzzled.

"Quinine. For the ague."

Matthew stood, stepping back. Jessica was shaking her head. Now it was the men who looked bewildered.

She smiled, through the tears, through the weakness, through the fever. "You three are the only medicine I need," she said softly.

———•———

Clinton Roundy reached under the counter and retrieved a bottle of whiskey, then turned for a glass from the shelf behind him.

Joshua held up one hand. "I'll just have a beer tonight, Clint."

Roundy set the bottle down slowly, eyeing Joshua curiously. Then he shrugged, got two mugs, and stepped to the large cask of beer mounted on a stand. He drew two full mugs, stood for a moment while the heads foamed over the sides of the glasses and onto the towel folded below the spigot, then turned his head. "Jack, watch the counter for me." The man at the far end of the bar looked up and nodded. Roundy came back to Joshua. "Come on. There's a table in the corner there."

When they were seated, Roundy left his beer untouched and watched Joshua steadily as he downed half of his in three great gulps. Finally, Joshua set the drink down. "What?" he said.

Roundy considered that for a moment before he spoke. "I was beginning to think that this new wife of yours had told you not to have anything to do with me."

Joshua's eyes widened a little. "Caroline? Don't be ridiculous. Why would she do that?"

"Because I'm Jessica's father."

He laughed shortly, without mirth. "Caroline's not that way. She don't brood on what's been."

"Then why you building her that fancy house south of town?"

"Because I want to," Joshua snapped. "As if it's your business."

Roundy waved a hand. "All right, all right. Ain't no need to get testy about it. I was just wonderin'."

"I get testy when there's things being said that aren't true."

Roundy backed down a little, but he was still smarting enough not to surrender completely. "Well, you been back near on three months now. I'll bet I ain't seen you more than two or three times in that whole time. We pass on the street and you nod politely and grunt and hurry on." He took a quick sip of his beer. "I thought maybe you was gettin' too good for old friends and former business partners anymore."

Joshua picked up his beer again, watching his ex-father-in-law over the top of the glass. He drank, then wiped his mouth and beard with the back of his hand. The defensiveness was gone now. "It's been real busy since I got back, Clint. Being gone for over three months really left the business here needin' lots of attention. Then I've got this cotton deal goin' in St. Louis. I've been down there twice, and once on to New Orleans to meet my cotton factor from Savannah." He took another drink. "I don't abandon old friends. And I consider you more than a former business partner. I consider you an old friend. That's why I came in tonight."

"Good." Roundy was satisfied.

The brief tension was gone as they drank silently for several minutes. Then Roundy looked up. "What does the doctor say about the baby?"

Now Joshua positively beamed. "He says Caroline is a strong, healthy woman. He says the baby should be comin' along about mid to late March."

"That's good, Joshua. I'm happy for you." His eyes got a far-away look in them. "I've always wondered, had Jessica been able to carry a child earlier on, if things would have been different."

Joshua instantly bristled. "Carryin' a child or not carryin' a child had nothin' to do with what happened. When she went off and joined Joe Smith and his gang, that was it." But almost immediately his jawline softened a little and his eyes became more thoughtful. "But you're right. Not being able to have children those couple of years didn't help none."

Roundy nodded, a little wary now about saying the wrong thing and setting him off again.

"She's four," Joshua said softly. "Rachel is four now."

"I know," Roundy murmured. "I was wonderin' about her the other day. Wonderin' if her hair's still as dark and curly as it was."

"And those big blue eyes."

Roundy took a drink of beer. "I ain't the world's greatest grandpa, but it would be nice to be able to see your only grandchild now and again."

The steel was instantly back in Joshua's eye. "That's what galls me the most. That and knowing Jessica will turn her into a Mormon."

Roundy changed the subject quickly. "Those other two young'uns, your wife's—they're a couple of fine children too. Cornwell says that boy is about as quick as anyone he's ever taught."

Mollified, Joshua smiled. "Yes. Will is a whip. Someday I'll tell you about the first day I met him." His eyes softened around the corners. "Hadn't been for his spunkiness, I'd have never met Caroline."

"And the girl," Roundy went on, relieved to be back on safe ground, "she's gonna end up lookin' just like her mother. A real beauty."

"Yes."

The owner of Independence's two most prosperous saloons finished his beer and set the mug down carefully. Without looking up, he spoke softly. "I wish things could've worked out between you and Jessica," he said. "But it didn't. And what's done is done. I'm real happy for you now, Joshua. You've done yourself proud."

"Thank you." He watched the older man, his face devoid of any emotion. Finally, he pushed his beer aside and leaned back on his chair. "You ever hear from Jessica?" he asked casually. "I assume she's still with my family in Ohio."

That startled Roundy. "You mean you ain't . . . ? That's right. You were gone when she came back."

The chair legs crashed back to the floor.

"Yes, she's back. She wrote me a short letter when she arrived in Liberty."

"She's in Liberty? Just across the river?"

Roundy shook his head. "Not anymore. As you've probably heard, the Mormons are leavin' Clay County. Headed north."

"Good riddance," Joshua spat. He was relieved. Liberty was much too close. "They think that moving up there is gonna solve their problems. Well, they're wrong."

Roundy felt a little irritation at his friend's hardheadedness. "Let them go—long as they're out of our hair."

"They make trouble everywhere they go," Joshua said bitterly. "I saw a bunch of them just outside of St. Louis. Saddest lookin' bunch of misfits you ever saw. Moon-eyed and spouting scripture. I wanted to take out my pistol and fire it into the air. Spook them back to wherever they're comin' from."

Roundy sighed, sorry that he had told Joshua about Jessica. He stood, collecting the mugs. "Appreciate you takin' time to stop by, Joshua."

Joshua looked up, a little surprised. He had been far away. "What?"

"I've got to get back to work. Thanks for stoppin' by."

Standing now, Joshua reached out. Roundy transferred the mugs to his other hand and took Joshua's. "I didn't mean to make you think there was feelin's between us, Clint. I'll do better now that winter's comin' on."

"Good."

Roundy tried to pull his hand free, but Joshua held on. His eyes were staring past him again. "Clint?"

"Yes?"

"You mark my words. We're gonna have to do something about the Mormons."

The tone in his voice gave Roundy a little chill. He didn't answer.

"Until they're driven clear out of the state of Missouri, there ain't gonna be no rest for us. None."

He dropped his hand, and Roundy stepped back quickly.

"You mark my words, Clint," he muttered again. His eyes had narrowed, the pupils becoming darkened pinpoints against his face. "You mark my words."

When Joshua arrived home, to his surprise Caroline was still up. She was propped up in the bed with the lantern still burning. Not that it was that late. It wasn't even nine o'clock yet. But she was usually up early in the mornings, fighting the sickness in her stomach, and so she went to bed by eight o'clock, or eight-thirty at the latest.

"Hi," he said as he took off his coat. "I thought you'd be asleep."

"No, not tonight." She smiled and reached down to her lap and retrieved something. She held it up, waving it slightly. He looked more closely. It was a brown envelope, letter size. He stopped, the coat half on one shoulder. "What's that?"

"Mrs. Austin, down at the post office, she brought it by the house."

He finished removing his coat, moving more slowly now.

"It must be from your family. In Ohio. It says Mrs. Benjamin Steed here on the envelope." She held it out for him. He didn't turn, just hung up his coat in the wardrobe.

Her voice registered a note of disappointment. "Is your father named Benjamin?"

He turned and began unbuttoning his shirt. "Yes."

"So it *is* from your family." She was puzzled now by his sudden coolness. "Do you want me to open it for you?"

In three strides he was across the room and snatched it from her. "No."

"Joshua!" It was a cry of dismay.

He didn't look at her. He lifted the envelope and tore it slowly and neatly in half, then in half again. He walked to the table where the lantern sat, dropped the shredded paper into the wastebasket that sat beside it, then reached out to the knob that controlled the wick. In a moment the room was plunged into darkness.

When he finished undressing, he climbed into bed and pulled the sheet up over his shoulders. He could feel her stiffness as he lay beside her. For three or four minutes, neither spoke. Then she stirred, half turning to face him.

"Joshua?" she began.

"Don't, Caroline!" he said curtly. "Don't even start it."

For a moment she lay there, rigid, hurt, bewildered. He said nothing more. Finally, she turned over again, putting her back to him, increasing the distance between them.

For a long time after her breathing gradually softened and became deep and steady, Joshua stared up at the ceiling in the darkness. Alternately he cursed fate for bringing this back into his life again; he cursed his ex-wife, who had come back to Missouri and who wouldn't let the past lie dead; and most of all, he cursed himself for continually letting his emotions slam down a wall between him and this woman whom he had come to love more than he thought it was possible for him to love anyone.

Even though Nathan and Benjamin were still away in Missouri, Mary Ann invited Lydia and her children and Melissa and Carl and their children for Sunday dinner as was the tradition. This Sunday, to everyone's surprise, including Melissa's, Carl had not insisted they leave immediately after the meal was finished. Rebecca had taken the children upstairs to read them a story. Caleb John Rogers, Melissa and Carl's newborn son, not quite a month old, was asleep in a bassinet in the next room. As usual, Mary Ann brought out the pie, and they sat around the table talking.

Lydia Steed had always liked Carlton Rogers, though he often left her exasperated. His red hair and prominent freckles gave him a bit of a little-boy look, which could not be dispelled by the fact that he was twenty-seven years old and starting to visibly benefit from Melissa's excellent cooking. He had a quick humor, and an easy way with people, probably the result of working with the public in his father's stable since he was a young child. But he could also be stubborn and bullheaded. He was like an English bulldog: once he sank his teeth into an idea, you couldn't pry it from him with pick, ax, or shovel.

Now he was throwing gibes about the Mormon poor and how they were taxing Kirtland's resources. But Lydia had never been known for being a weak-minded person either, and though she sensed that Carl was deliberately baiting her, she didn't hesitate to pick up his challenge. She smiled sweetly, but there was the tiniest bit of bite to her voice. "We're doing more for the poor than any other church is doing."

He looked incredulous. "The vast majority of those people are Mormons. Why should it be our obligation to take care of them?"

She feigned surprise. "I thought the Bible said something about Christians caring for the poor. I don't remember that it specified any particular religious denomination."

"Ha!" It came out as a puff of derision. "You can't care for your own, so you expect us to solve your problem."

"It's not a sin to be poor, Carl. Other than that, what is it that you find so offensive about us?" She spoke in a half-teasing tone, baiting him back a little.

To her surprise, he went very quiet, and his face lengthened noticeably. "Do you want me to be honest?"

"Of course," Lydia replied.

He looked at Mary Ann, then away.

Mary Ann smiled encouragement to her son-in-law. "You can speak your mind freely, Carl. I think we're up to it."

"All right." He took in a breath, then released it slowly. Finally, he turned back to Lydia, and in that moment she realized this was the reason why Carl had stayed. The other comments were only prelude. Lydia had fallen right into his setup.

Melissa was watching him closely now, her eyes worried. She too sensed that a turning point in the conversation had just been passed, but she wasn't sure why or what it was.

"All right, Carl," Lydia said evenly. "What is it that you find so bothersome about us Mormons?"

His chin came up. The eyes were steady and challenging. "I think your church tears families apart."

It would have been difficult to tell who was the more surprised by his accusation. Mary Ann's eyes widened. Lydia's mouth dropped open slightly. From Melissa there was a soft intake of breath.

"Well," he said, half defensively. "You said you wanted to know." He glanced at his wife, then away quickly. "Melissa's going to think I'm just talking about her and me. But we're only one example. Everywhere you look, your religion is drivin' wedges between people."

"*Everywhere?*" Lydia said, making no attempt to hide her skepticism. "Isn't that a little strong?"

"All right, not everywhere. Not everyone. But I can sure give you plenty of examples."

"Name one," Lydia demanded.

"Martin Harris."

Lydia shot a look at her mother-in-law. Lucy Harris had been so incensed over Martin's support of Joseph, they had separated shortly after the Church was organized. They had never divorced, and Martin had come to Kirtland to live, leaving Lucy in New York. But he had sent her money up until a few months ago when he received word that Lucy had passed away.

"There were serious problems in that marriage long before Joseph Smith ever came along," Mary Ann said.

Carl brushed that aside. It was obvious that he had kept these thoughts pent up inside him for a long time. "All right. You want honesty? What about your own family?"

"Carl!"

He didn't look at his wife, just went on doggedly. "Well, can you deny it? Look what Mormonism has done to you. Look at Joshua and Benjamin. A son run away from home, a father who won't even speak his name. Then there's Joshua and Jessica. Jessica became a Mormon and the marriage ended in divorce." His voice dropped. He was looking at Lydia. "Or what about you and your own parents?"

No one spoke. There was too much pain with every example he had given. Lydia's hand had come up to the lace collar at her throat and was picking at it with quick, fluttering movements. Carl's face softened as he saw her pain, but his eyes were filled with determination. "I'm sorry, Lydia, but it's true. Your own parents won't even speak your name in their house. I'm not saying you were wrong to leave them, I'm just saying this church of yours seems to break up families."

Lydia finally looked up. "What Nathan and I have found together is worth more to me than what I lost with my family." She looked down, then her head came up again in challenge. He had spoken his mind, now she'd speak hers. "I just wish you and Melissa had what we have."

Melissa stirred, wanting to stop what was happening, but Carl went on quickly before she could speak. "That's right," he said bitterly. "If you're both Mormon, everything is wonderful. But if not . . ." He gave a little exclamation of disgust. "Look what happened to Rebecca and Arthur Wilkinson."

"And thank the Lord for that," Lydia retorted tartly. "We've come to see that Arthur Wilkinson is not quite the nice young man he seemed to be."

Carl threw up his hands in exasperation. "Only because he was so frustrated."

"Only because he was a scoundrel," Lydia said hotly.

"Like you and Melissa are frustrated, Carl?" Mary Ann said quietly, stepping into the conversation.

Carl shot Melissa a quick look before nodding. "Yes. I'll be honest, Mother Steed. I don't like what Mormonism is doing to my family."

She sighed wearily. "I understand. I understand the situation, and I understand the pain that it brings."

Carl turned to his wife, and suddenly there was a pleading look in his eyes. "It's the only thing between us that ain't right, Melissa. I love you, and I love our children, but I don't care one whit for Mormonism, because it keeps coming between us. All the time. Like some great wall we can't move."

"I've not pushed you to believe as I do, Carl," Melissa said in a voice barely above a whisper.

"I know. And I'm grateful for that. But you can't deny it's come between us. Can you?"

She only hesitated for a moment, then dropped her head. "No."

Mary Ann felt her heart ache for the anguish in Melissa's eyes. "May I try to respond to your concerns, Carl?"

Carl turned back to his mother-in-law. "Yes."

"And may I be as honest as you have been?"

"I would be disappointed if you weren't."

"Lydia spoke of the relationship between her and Nathan. I'd like to speak of my relationship with Benjamin." The corners of her mouth softened with the memory of long-ago times. "I've loved Benjamin Steed since the day I first saw him. He's always been a good man. A decent man. But he was also one of the most stubborn men I know. Hardheaded as a piece of granite. You met him not long before he joined the Church, so you've never really known him except as a Latter-day Saint. But I can tell you this—the gospel has changed him, Carl, changed him in ways that I never dreamed were possible."

Tears suddenly welled up, as much to her surprise as to the others'. "He is so gentle, so much more patient now. The gospel's changed him. And if—" She had to stop for a moment. When she finally went on, her voice was strained with emotion. "And if the Benjamin Steed I'm married to now had been the Benjamin Steed who went looking for Joshua that night nine years ago, I think . . ." Her shoulders lifted. "I *know* things would have turned out very differently than they did."

Her voice cleared and strengthened. "That's what the gospel of Jesus Christ has done for our family, Carl. And I pray constantly that you and Melissa can someday find what Benjamin and I, and Lydia and Nathan, now have."

"That's all well and good," he said quietly, still stubbornly trying to make his point, "but what I don't understand is why you think everyone has to join the Mormon church to unite the family. Benjamin becomes a Mormon, now you're happy. Lydia and Nathan both join the Church, now they're filled with bliss. Arthur Wilkinson refuses to accept Mormonism, so break it off; he and Rebecca can't be happy."

"Carl—," Lydia started, but he shook his head quickly.

"No, let me finish. I'm not Mormon, but I love Melissa. I love our sons. I belong to a Christian church. I try to follow Christ. Why should I be the one to join your church so Melissa and I can unite our family? Why doesn't Melissa renounce Mormonism and become a Methodist with me? That would eliminate the conflict too."

He sat back, relieved to have finally gotten it out. For a moment, no one spoke. Melissa was staring at her empty plate, toying with the fork. Any desire on Lydia's part to strike back, to best him in a conversational game, was now gone. She watched him with sad eyes, wishing she could make him understand, but not knowing what more to say.

He laughed scornfully. "Well, I see no one has an answer to that."

Mary Ann took a deep breath. "I have an answer, Carl." She appraised him with a steady, calm look. "But it may not be what you want to hear."

"I'm listening."

"You're right. You and Melissa do need to be unified on the question of religion in your marriage. For your sake and for the children's."

His face reflected his surprise. He had expected defensiveness, a quick lecture on the fact that the Mormon church was the only true church on the face of the earth. He had been prepared to answer that with a contemptuous retort. He didn't know what to say to this.

"So I have a suggestion," Mary Ann said.

Carl looked suspicious. "What?"

"Why don't you and Melissa start this very night? Kneel down at your bedside together, and tell the Lord that you desire to be united in your religious views, that you both want to belong to the same church, so that your present religious differences will not be a dividing force in your family. That is a good desire. So ask the Lord for his help. Ask him which church you should both join—yours or Melissa's or maybe another. And tell him that you are willing to abide by his answer. Continue your petition every night until the Lord gives you both an answer. Fair enough?"

He looked quickly at Melissa. "And what if the Lord says for Melissa to become a Methodist?"

"Then I'll do it," she said without hesitation.

Now Lydia leaned forward. "And what if the Lord says for you to become a Mormon?"

The question hung in the air. He didn't look at her. He didn't look at Mary Ann. Finally he turned to his wife. "I don't know. I don't know if I can pray about it. I'll have to think about it."

Lydia held Emily's hand tightly as they walked down the path that led from the bluffs down into what everyone called Kirtland Flats. Below them, still about three hundred yards away, the meandering of the river, marked by a dark line of trees and brush, cut across the snowy landscape. Near the junction of four of Geauga County's main roads stood the Newel K. Whitney store. It was flanked on both sides by homes—one his own, and the other Orson Hyde's, who was a member of the Quorum of the Twelve Apostles. All three buildings were nearly lost against the whiteness, since they were painted white and their roofs were snow covered. The two-story Johnson inn, across the street from the store, was made of local brick and was a bright red gash against the whiteness. All four buildings had lazy columns of smoke rising from their chimneys.

It had started raining lightly just at dusk the night before, then turned to snow during the night. It was less than an inch deep, but the wet base had frozen, and the pathway was slick enough underneath Lydia's feet to make for treacherous footing.

Twice Emily's feet nearly went out from under her and Lydia had to pull her back up again.

On the path, two sets of footprints, a man's and a woman's, and a set of narrow wheel tracks were the only marks in the new snow. It was early enough in the day that most of Kirtland's population were still in their homes, but obviously someone was out before Lydia and her daughter. As they rounded a slight curve in the path and cleared a row of low-lying bushes, Lydia saw a man and a woman ahead of them about half a block. The man was pushing a baby's pram. He was tall, broad shouldered. He wore no hat, and his hair was light brown, combed high and back from his forehead. The woman had a small woolen bonnet on, but it did not completely cover the mass of dark ringlets that bounced lightly as she walked.

Lydia tightened her grip on Emily's hand. "Come, Emily. Let's hurry a little. That's Brother Joseph and Sister Emma. Let's catch up to them."

Joseph must have heard them, for he stopped and turned around. Immediately a broad smile filled his face. "Sister Lydia," he called, "you're out bright and early."

Emma turned too, her eyes lighting with recognition. "Hello, Lydia."

"Hello, Brother Joseph. Hello, Emma." She came up to join them, pulling off her woolen mittens to shake hands with them.

Joseph went down on one knee, peering up beneath Emily's winter bonnet. "And who have we here?" He reared back, feigning wondrous surprise. "Why, I do believe it is the lovely Miss Emily Steed."

Emily's dark eyes danced with pleasure. "Yes, it is, Brother Joseph."

"Well, bless my soul. And aren't you getting to look more like your mother with every passing day?"

Emily curtsied slightly. "I hope so, thank you."

That won her a laugh from all three adults. Joseph fished inside the pocket of his vest and found a small coin. He handed it to her. "I understand Brother Whitney has some new licorice candy. Why don't you run along before it's all gone. We'll be along shortly."

"Yes, sir!" Emily said, her eyes wide. "Is it all right, Mama?"

"Yes, dear. We'll be there in a few minutes. Tell Mr. Whitney we're coming, or he'll wonder what you're doing out all by yourself."

With a perfunctory nod she was gone, her little feet making hardly any sound in the snow. Joseph watched her for a moment, then turned to Lydia. "She really is getting to be quite the little beauty. You and Nathan will have to watch her when she gets to be sixteen or seventeen. She'll have every eligible man in the county after her."

Lydia laughed with obvious pleasure. "You know the little Carter boy?"

"Yes."

"He and Emily are good friends. The other day I caught her standing before the mirror, looking at herself in a new dress. 'Oh,' she said, 'Daniel is going to just love me in this.' " She laughed and shook her head. "That's at a little over four years. I can imagine what it will be like when she's sixteen."

"Where are little Joshua and Nathan?" Emma asked.

"Rebecca's watching them. I had to get some things from the store. I tried to talk Emily into staying too, but she wouldn't hear of it." She took a step forward and bent down to look into the pram. There was a bundle of blankets there, but nothing else showing. Emma reached down and pulled back the top layer. Frederick G. Williams Smith was sleeping, his round little cheeks touched with pink from the cold.

"He is so precious, Emma," Lydia said. "And big. For four months old, he's really a husky young man."

"He's going to have his father's build, I predict," Joseph said proudly.

Emma tucked the blanket back around the baby's face, then they started walking again slowly, Joseph pushing the pram. He looked at Lydia. "Any word from Nathan and Benjamin?"

"Yes, we got a letter last week. They found Jessica and

Rachel up north in a small settlement there. They said they were going to try and build a small cabin for her and Rachel with a small shed out back for Matthew. They said it would take about a week, then they're going to start back."

"Matthew's doing a good thing," Joseph said. "Jessica needs a man there to help her."

"I know. Mother Steed misses him fiercely, of course, but we all feel so much better knowing Jessica and Rachel won't be alone, especially with winter coming on."

"When was the letter dated?"

"October eighth, I think."

"So they could be home soon."

"Yes. Mother Steed thinks toward the end of the week perhaps. They are going to take the steamers most of the way, so it shouldn't take them nearly as long to get back."

"Wonderful." Joseph seemed really pleased. "We are going to have a meeting next week, on the second of November. We'll be drawing up the articles for the Kirtland Safety Society."

"The Kirtland Safety Society?"

"Yes, our bank," Emma explained.

"Oh."

Joseph stopped in order to free his hands from the pram. Lydia had to smile at that. He always loved to punctuate what he was saying. "We are really excited about this, Sister Lydia. Our financial problems are too complex for simple solutions. But this bank should help immensely. That's why I need Benjamin here. And Nathan too, of course. All the brethren are coming. But I especially need Ben's talents and his good judgment."

"Well, I'm certainly hoping they make it by the first of the month."

They were approaching the crossroads now and passing by the hotel. Two men came out of the side door to the inn. They were bundled up against the cold, collars pulled up around their necks and half hiding their faces. One had a pipe in his hand.

They were laughing loudly, as if one had just told a joke. They did not particularly look like very fine gentlemen. Joseph had been about to speak, but the sight of the two men made him hold off.

As the men came out to the road, they came face-to-face with Lydia and the Smiths. The man with the pipe slowed his step, leaning forward to peer more closely at Joseph.

"Good mornin' to you," Joseph said pleasantly.

"Joe Smith, ain't it?" the man boomed.

"Yes. And who might you be?"

The man guffawed, slapping his companion on the shoulder and pulling him to a stop. "You know who this is?"

The other man made a long face and shook his head slowly. Then he couldn't hold it any longer and burst out laughing as well. "Why, isn't this the Joe Smith who goes out lookin' for buried treasure?" He stepped directly in front of Joseph and Emma so as to block their way, leering at Emma.

Lydia saw Emma tense. She felt her own heart suddenly start to race a little too, suddenly glad she had sent Emily on ahead. Joseph took Emma's arm with one hand and moved forward, steering the pram so that the first man had to step out of the way quickly or be struck. "Hey!" he cried angrily. "Watch where you're going."

"I was watching," Joseph said mildly, without bothering to turn around.

The second man stepped aside as the women brushed passed him. He cackled wildly. "You ladies going down to help ol' Joe here dig up that chest of treasure?"

"Come on, Garth," the first man cried, slapping at his companion. "You know there ain't no treasure here in Kirtland. Only in Salem, Mass." That was followed by another burst of laughter. It was a raw sound, like that made by dragging something metal over a washboard.

Joseph's step slowed, and his mouth pulled into a tight line, but Emma quickly slipped her arm through his and kept him moving. They were past the two men now and did not turn around to give them the satisfaction of a response. But the men hadn't moved on. They got in a final shot. "Watch out for them pirates, Joe. They might not like you taking all their hidden gold."

Again the cackling laughter rang out across the snow.

"Joseph," Emma said quietly, "pay them no mind."

His shoulders lifted and fell. Finally he nodded, but he remained stiff and tight-lipped as they crossed the street and entered the Newel Whitney store.

"Brother Joseph?" Lydia said.

He turned to her. They were on the porch of the store now. Joseph had the baby in his arms while Emma finished the last of her purchases inside. Emily was a few steps away, drawing patterns in the snow with her boots.

"You can't let what those men said bother you. You went to Salem with good intentions. So what, if it didn't work out? If you hadn't gone, you would always wonder."

He smiled, the blue eyes showing his gratitude. "I know."

"So pay them no mind. They are crude men. What do they know about the things of God?"

That brought his head up, and his eyes narrowed thoughtfully. "It's funny you should say that."

Lydia was puzzled. "Why?"

"What do *I* know about the things of God?"

Flabbergasted, Lydia could only stare at him.

He laughed, a deep pleasant sound in his chest. "Oh, I didn't mean it that way." He sobered. "You know, Sister Lydia, about a year ago—in fact, it was a year ago next month—a man came to visit Kirtland. He was from the East. Someone introduced me to him. When he heard my name he was surprised. He stared at me for a moment, then remarked that I was nothing but a man."

"What did he think you were?" she asked in surprise.

"Well, he had supposed that a man who communed with

God should look different. I'm not sure what he had in mind." He began to walk slowly back and forth, rocking the baby gently in his arms. "Some people seem to forget what the Apostle James said, that the prophet Elijah was a man subject to like passions as we are, even though he had such power with God that, in answer to his prayers, the Lord shut the heavens so that it did not rain."

Lydia wasn't quite sure where this was leading, or how to respond.

Now the inner hurt was evident on his face. "It's not just the nonmembers who are being critical about the fact that I found nothing in Salem. You've heard the complaints, I'm sure."

Now she understood, at least in part, what was bothering him. "I know, Joseph," she said softly. "But you can't listen to them either."

If he heard, he made no sign. He had turned and was gazing up toward the bluffs, where the temple and the main part of Kirtland were. "I'm sure Benjamin has some of the same feelings too. He tried to talk me out of it. Several times. From the beginning he said it was foolishness."

"Benjamin is Benjamin," Lydia said quickly. "You know how practical minded he is. He'll get over it."

He sighed. "I hope so. Some of the others aren't getting over it. They can't seem to let it be. Martin. Warren Parrish. Even some of the Twelve."

"Well, there are others that don't believe you were wrong. Not for a minute."

He looked grateful for a moment, then grew thoughtful again. "That's what the Lord said too, you know."

"What?"

"That it was folly."

"He did?" That really caught her by surprise.

"Yes. While we were in Salem, I received a revelation." He gave a self-deprecating little laugh. "It was most interesting how the Lord stated it. The revelation started out something like this. 'I, the Lord your God, am not displeased with your coming on this journey, notwithstanding your follies.' "

He paused, shaking his head slowly. "Think about that. We had been foolish, but he was not *displeased* with us. That suggests he was not really pleased with us either."

"I don't understand."

"Well, I'm not sure I do fully yet either. But I think the Lord was saying that he knew our hearts were right. He knew we hadn't come there simply for our own personal gain. Also, there were other things he wanted us to do. He said that he had other treasures for us in the city. I assume by that he meant the people. And so he was not displeased."

He gave her a long, searching look. "I had really prayed about this matter, Lydia. It was one of those times when I thought this might be the Lord's answer. But I was wrong."

Again he laughed, more at himself than at the situation. "That's what I meant when I said I may not always understand the Lord's ways either. In the revelation he reminded me that he too cares about our debts, that he too is concerned about the welfare of Zion. He seemed to be saying to me, 'I know you've prayed about it. I know you've come here to try and find some money to solve your problems. But you're trusting in the wisdom of man. Why have you forgotten me? Don't you think I care about those debts? Don't you think I care about Zion?' " He stopped for a moment, then more quietly concluded. "It is an important lesson, even for a prophet."

"I see," Lydia said, touched now by Joseph's honesty and self-examination. "We all do that, don't we? Trust in our own wisdom."

"Yes, we do." The baby stirred in its blanket, and so Joseph put him up on one shoulder and began to pat his back softly.

Behind them the door of the store opened and Emma came out, carrying a bag filled with her purchases. "Sorry, Joseph. Newel couldn't find the one kind of thread that I needed."

"We're fine. Sister Lydia and I have been having a good talk." He swung the baby down and stepped to where they had left the pram on the far end of the porch. "Come on, little fellow. Let's go home."

———•———

All the way back up the hill, Lydia was deep in thought about what Joseph had said. Finally she turned to Joseph. "I have a question. It's related to what you were saying."

"All right."

"Sometimes that's happened to me. I pray and pray and pray for something, but there doesn't seem to be any answer. So I'm left to wonder. Is it because I'm not faithful enough to hear the Lord? Or is it because he chooses not to answer me?"

He smiled, somewhat sadly. "I have asked myself that very question on more than one occasion. Especially after the Salem experience."

"And what answer did Brother Joseph find to that question?" Lydia said, laughing lightly.

" 'It is not meet that I should command in all things,' " he quoted softly, " 'for he that is compelled in all things, the same is a slothful and not a wise servant: wherefore he receiveth no reward.' "

Lydia was nodding. That was from the revelation Joseph had received shortly after he had arrived in the land of Zion back in 1831.

"And 'men should be anxiously engaged in a good cause,' " Emma continued for him, " 'and do many things of their own free will, and bring to pass much righteousness.' "

Lydia's face was wrinkled in thought. "So sometimes the Lord just wants us to act, without waiting to be told everything?"

"Yes," said Joseph. "And that may be another reason why the Lord was not displeased with us. We went to Salem without waiting to be told exactly what to do to get out of debt. So even though we may have been a little shortsighted, he let us go, then used it as an opportunity to teach us an important lesson."

"I see," Lydia responded, her thoughts tumbling now with

interesting new insights. Then she had a completely new thought. "Brother Joseph, there may be another reason for the whole Salem experience."

"Oh, and what might that be?"

"A test."

"Oh, it was definitely a test."

"Not for you. For us."

His eyes narrowed thoughtfully. "Explain."

She took a deep breath, still letting the thoughts fall into position. "Let's say Brother Burgess had been able to find the treasure and you had come back with a chest full of gold. Everyone would have hailed you as a prophet."

Emma started, giving Lydia a strange look. "But when Joseph didn't," she said slowly, "when he came back empty-handed, even some of the leaders began to doubt. They've started to criticize."

Lydia nodded, feeling a little chill. Her father-in-law was one of those who were doing that criticizing. And she knew that Martin Harris and others were just waiting for Benjamin Steed to return home so they could bring him into the growing circle of critics.

"A test for us?" Joseph mused. "That is a most interesting thought, Lydia. I should like to ponder more on it."

The first day of January, 1837, dawned cold and wet and dreary over the town of Preston, England. The heavy fog which had rolled in off the Irish Sea during the night had lifted and become a steady drizzle. By afternoon the temperature had dropped, and the rain became half mixed with sleet. It was miserable weather to be out in, but the few people hurrying about gave it little thought. This was a typical winter's day in the county of Lancashire. They expected no better.

Derek and Peter Ingalls hurried along under the gray overcast. Their shoes, wooden clogs worn with no stockings, made a sharp rattling sound against the cobblestones. Young Peter, twelve years of age, was shivering violently. He wore a ragged shawl over his narrow shoulders, but the wetness had penetrated through that and the thin coat beneath. Derek, about six and a half years his senior, wore only a thick woolen shirt. He was likewise wet and chilled, but he had grown used to the cold long before this and gave it little thought.

There was no mistaking that the two were brothers. Though Derek was more heavily built—something enhanced by four years of shoveling coal in the boiler rooms—and Peter was thin as a wafer, their features were similar. Both had thick black hair that kept falling into their eyes. Both had the same deep blue eyes, straight nose, and full mouth that, when they smiled, changed the whole countenance. Peter smiled a lot still. Derek's smiles came with increasing rarity.

They were passing one of Preston's several churches. The windows glowed yellow with lamplight, and through the thin curtains they could see the shadows of the worshippers sitting in the pews next to the windows. The sound of voices singing a hymn floated softly in the air.

Peter stopped, his eyes fastened on the church. This particular year, New Year's Day happened to be the Sabbath also. Special worship services were being held throughout the country in celebration.

"Come on, Peter," Derek said, "we've got to get home or we're going to freeze to death."

Reluctantly, Peter fell into step again beside Derek, but his head turned and he looked longingly back at the church. "Couldn't we wait long enough to see them come out?"

Derek shook his head firmly. He understood what was going on in Peter's young mind. He had once done the same thing himself. There was something mesmerizing about watching the congregations of the upper and middle classes as they came out of church. The women were the most arresting, with their long, full dresses of exquisite colors and material. Their beautiful faces were half-hidden beneath carefully coiffured hair and matching bonnets. But the men were not far behind them in dress and demeanor—long coats, vests with golden watch chains or jeweled fobs, high brimmed top hats of beaver skin or silk.

They would brush by the thinly clad, sometimes half-naked throngs of beggars, ignoring the pitiful cries and the clutching hands as the men helped their wives into the shiny carriages pulled by matching teams of horses. Then they would canter off to their cottages or castles to eat leg of mutton and plates full of steaming vegetables and dishes of English trifle. After dinner they would sit before blazing fires, the men smoking fine cigars and sipping brandy. Then they would retire to their wide beds with mattresses full of goose feathers, covered by fine down comforters.

It was exciting to watch such people, but Derek had learned long ago that it made the harsh realities of their own situation all the more unbearable. Where Derek and Peter were headed now there would be no fire, no well-laid table—cold coffee or tea and moldy bread, if they were lucky—no wardrobes filled with warm clothes. They lived in a cellar beneath a cottage which two other families shared. It was dark, cold, and damp, half-filled with coal, and home to three or four rabbits and several pigeons kept by the families above them. Two other men, older and hardened drinkers, shared the cellar with them.

The house was one of hundreds in the poorest section of the town, all made of the same red brick, stretching away for blocks in dreary sameness. The scene was identical to that found in a thousand other towns and villages throughout England's industrial belt. These were the working-class neighborhoods, inhabited by the illiterate and wretchedly poor factory workers who kept the flax and textile mills and other industries running. The homes were usually two-story, consisting of one or two rooms— each never larger than nine by twelve feet—and a kitchen. Open trenches in the alleys behind them carried raw sewage down to the rivers or the sea. In summer, the refuse thrown into the streets became fly infested and unbearably rank.

There were two beds in the cellar where the Ingalls brothers lived, both simple boxes made of unfinished lumber, with corded ropes for springs. The mattresses were straw filled and lumpy as a toad's back. And filthy. It was common to wake in the morning with fiery red welts from bedbugs. There were no pillows, and only a thinly worn blanket for a covering. Derek and Peter shared one of the beds. The two men shared the other.

It wasn't much, their little cellar, but Derek knew they were very lucky. The usual ratio was more like three to four persons per bed, requiring children either to sleep in shifts or on the floor. And here they were all males. Usually a whole family—husband, wife, single young women and maturing young men, little children, infants—would all have to share the same room, which was filled with beds, leaving only a small space in the center for all to dress or undress.

Peter had no clear memory of that kind of crowding, that utter lack of privacy. Just before his sixth birthday, cholera had swept across western England from Liverpool, probably brought from China or Japan on some ship. Wherever it had come from, it decimated the Ingalls family—father, mother, three older brothers, a married sister—and many other families. When it was over, twelve-year-old Derek Ingalls had been left to care for his only surviving sibling.

He grasped Peter's arm and gave it a gentle tug. "Come on, Peter," he said, his voice softening. "We need to get home."

Peter's voice trailed off. Derek looked up from the piece of slate that was on the bed between them. The flickering light of the stub of a candle played across the smoothness of Peter's cheeks and the fineness of his mouth. It also threw deep shadows across his eyes, but not enough that Derek couldn't see that they were getting heavy.

"Come on, Peter. Ten more words, then we can stop."

"I'm tired, Derek."

"I know. We're almost done."

It was ironic. For almost seven years now, Derek had fought against all the odds in order to care for his brother. He had begged and stolen and scavenged food. Twice he had fled from the town in which they were living when nosey government women came around asking about two orphan boys. He had finally come to Preston and clawed his way into a job at one of the mills. They had started out living in the streets. Through

Derek's sheer tenacity, they had moved from there to a wooden packing crate, then to a corner of a floor in a filthy tenement house, and finally to this cellar.

And now Peter was repaying it all by teaching his older brother how to read and write.

Three years previously the shameless exploitation of children by the factory and mine owners had finally reached the point where Parliament had acted. The Factory Act of 1833 was passed. The new law prohibited children under the age of nine from being employed in anything except the silk mills. Children under eighteen were limited to sixty-nine hours per week—shifts of twelve hours per day, with three hours less on Saturdays. Unfortunately, Derek was nineteen and was no longer protected by these limits.

But most important, the new law said that mill owners could employ children ages nine to thirteen only if those children could produce a "school certificate." This was an attempt to cure the widespread illiteracy among the poor. Many factories established schools of their own in order to comply. Peter attended the factory school for two hours each morning before moving into the mill to work an eight-hour shift. He was bright and inquisitive and learned quickly. And so, even though they were both exhausted at the end of the day, Peter was teaching Derek what he was learning each day.

"My eyes hurt, Derek," Peter moaned.

Derek sighed, then reached over and took the slate. He slid it under the bed. "All right. We'll do some more tomorrow night."

"Thank you." Peter immediately slithered down and pulled the blanket around him. Even though his clothes were still damp from their being outside, there was no thought of undressing. The cellar would be in the forties before the night was over, and one blanket was not sufficient.

Derek stood, pinched out the candle, then slipped off his wooden clogs. He set them at the foot of the bed, then looked over to the other bed. Their two roommates were still out, probably at the pub spending what tiny pittance they made on some kind of grog. Derek shook his head. He understood the desire to dull the senses. Many were the days when he longed to do the same. But alcoholism had become the bane of England's working-class poor, and many men spent more on liquor than they did on rent. That was not a challenge for Derek. Every penny dropped in the pubs meant one less penny he could put away in the leather pouch he had carefully hidden in the coal pile.

He crawled into bed beside his brother. Sliding beneath the blanket, he moved across the rough mattress and reached for Peter's shoulder. Immediately Peter moved over against him and they curled up together, spoon fashion. Out of necessity, they always slept that way throughout the winter months.

After several minutes, Peter turned his head. "Derek?"

"Eh?"

"Are we gonna go to hell?"

"What?" Derek started to laugh. Peter's question had caught him completely by surprise. "Why do you ask a fool question like that?"

There was silence for a moment, then in a troubled voice Peter went on. "Jenny said her mother's preacher said that people who don't go to church on Sunday are gonna go to hell." Jenny Pottsworth was an eleven-year-old who worked with Peter in the cutting department at the factory.

Derek snorted in derision. "It was also Mrs. Pottsworth's clergyman who said that what we need is another good war to kill off two or three million of the working-class people and solve our population problems."

"What is hell like?"

Sobering, Derek rubbed a hand along Peter's shoulder. He could tell he was really troubled. "It's nothin' you have to be worryin' about. God ain't going to send you to hell, Peter. You're too good. I mean that."

Peter thought about that and seemed pleased. But then a moment later he asked another question, and Derek knew he hadn't really satisfied him. "Why don't we ever go to church, Derek?"

For a moment Derek was tempted to snap out a glib answer, something cute and clever and funny, something to take Peter's mind off this troublesome subject. But then he changed his mind. Peter would be thirteen in May. Before too long he would be a man. He was already doing a man's work.

Peter turned. "Why don't we, Derek? I don't want to go to hell."

"I know," Derek nodded. After a moment, in a low voice, he went on. "One time, I made the mistake of going in one of those churches like we saw today. I wanted to see what it was like inside."

"What happened?"

"The preacher drove me out. Told me to go to a working-man's church."

"Did you?"

"Yes. For a few times."

"And?"

He let out his breath. "I don't know. I had lots of questions about God. I tried to ask the preacher, and he got angry with me."

"What kinds of questions?"

"Is God really there? If he is, how come things are so different for people? How come some people get to live in castles or big mansions while others live in a place like this? How come, when we're already so poor, God takes Mama and Papa and the rest of our family away from us?"

"I've wondered that too," Peter said. His voice sounded both frightened for having such thoughts and relieved that he was not alone in them.

"Know what I decided?"

"What?"

"If there is a hell and you and me end up there, it can't be much worse than old Mr. Morris's textile factory."

"At least it would be warm."

Derek laughed aloud. Every now and then, Peter's humor surprised him.

"Yeah. That can't be all bad, then, can it?"

They lay there together for several moments, each focusing on his own thoughts. Then Peter spoke again. "Derek?"

"What?"

"Do you believe there is a God?"

He let the question hang for a moment, then nodded. "Yeah, I guess."

"Me too, Derek."

"But . . ." He hesitated a moment, debating whether to share thoughts that to this point he had never talked about with another living soul.

"But what, Derek?"

"If there is a God, I don't think he cares too much about people like us. We're too poor, Peter. There's too many of us. I think he's too busy running the world and the universe to spend much time worryin' about two nobody people like us."

"Oh." It was a word laden with disappointment.

Derek pulled Peter's thin, cold body closer to him. Now there was almost a fierceness to his voice. "That's why we got to help each other. That's why you've got to teach me to read, Peter. We're on our own, and we've got to help each other get along."

"Do you know what this is all about, Benjamin?"

He shook his head as he pulled on his coat. "When the boy came last night, all he said was that Joseph had called an urgent meeting of those involved with the new bank for eight o'clock this morning."

Mary Ann reached up to the coatrack and got his scarf. "Melissa said she thought she saw Oliver Cowdery yesterday."

He turned around in surprise. "Really? Where?"

"She was walking down past the temple after worship services. He was nearly a block away, so she wasn't positive it was him. But she thought so."

"Hmm. That could be it. If Oliver's back from Philadelphia, that means he's got the printing plates."

"But has Elder Hyde returned from Columbus yet?"

Benjamin shook his head. "I don't think so, and that could be a bad sign."

"Surely the legislature will grant us a charter."

Benjamin took the scarf and wrapped it around his neck. He withdrew some gloves from the pockets in his coat and began to put them on. "If I was sure of that, I'd feel a lot better. Right now the hard-money Democrats pretty well control the state legislature, and I hear they're turning down applications for bank charters at every hand."

"What will Joseph do if they don't grant it?"

"I don't know. It's been the number one thing on his mind since Nathan and I returned home. I know he has high hopes for the bank." He leaned over and kissed her. "I don't know how soon I'll be home."

"Good-bye. I'll be anxious to hear."

When Benjamin arrived in the upper assembly room of the temple, the meeting had not begun. He was surprised and pleased to see that not only Oliver Cowdery but also Orson Hyde had returned, and both were now huddled in conference with Joseph and Sidney. Benjamin shook hands with several of the brethren, then turned toward one corner. Brigham Young, Heber C. Kimball, and Willard Richards were standing around the stove, rubbing their hands together.

Benjamin moved over and laid a hand on Willard Richards's shoulder. "Brother Richards, you don't look any the worse for wear."

He laughed and nodded. "Except that I am still trying to thaw out this block of ice that used to be my body."

Brigham was likewise chuckling. "I feel perfectly fine." He grinned mischievously. "At least from the waist up."

Benjamin laughed too, then shook hands with Brigham and Heber. Two nights before this, on New Year's Eve, a small group had gathered at the Chagrin River, not far from Brigham's house. It had been bitterly cold. Benjamin had helped Brigham and Heber chop a large hole in the ice, then watched as Brigham waded in, followed by Willard Richards, who was then baptized. It still gave Benjamin the shivers just to think about it.

Willard Richards was not a tall man, and the best word to describe his overall appearance would have been *rotund*. He was portly in build, and his face was round, almost cherubic. Though he was afflicted with a serious case of reoccurring palsy, he was always of a cheerful disposition and temperament, and Benjamin had come to like him very quickly. He was a cousin of Brigham Young's. While in Massachusetts he had become intensely interested in the Church when he came across a Book of Mormon, opened it at random, and read the prophet Lehi's words: "Adam fell, that men might be; and men are, that they might have joy. . . ." Pondering what he read, he exclaimed, "That book is either of God or of the devil, for no man wrote it." He had arrived in Kirtland in October, seeking out his cousin and determined to fully investigate the latter-day work. And that investigation had culminated in his baptism two days before.

"Brethren, let's begin."

They turned. Joseph was standing at the head of the table at the west end of the assembly room. Immediately the buzz of conversation died, and the men in the room found places on the benches or assembled chairs.

"We'll ask Brother Zebedee Coltrin to open with prayer, then we shall begin."

As the meeting proceeded, Benjamin learned that, by coincidence, Oliver Cowdery and Orson Hyde had both returned on the same day. Oliver brought from Philadelphia the plates for printing the bank notes, as well as a thick sheaf of bills in one-, two-, and three-dollar denominations. But Orson Hyde's mission had been far less successful. The state had refused to grant the Kirtland Safety Society a banking charter. Elder Hyde was quite put out, feeling that anti-Mormon sentiment had carried the decision against them. Benjamin believed that might have been a factor, but was also aware that the political climate in Ohio was not favorable to new banks at the present.

The resulting consternation of the brethren was obvious, and justifiably so. Benjamin and Nathan had arrived back in Kirtland just two days prior to the meeting on November second, where articles for the new Kirtland Safety Society were drawn up and approved. Joseph was elected treasurer and Sidney Rigdon president. By then, stock in the society was already being sold. By the end of the year, between forty and fifty thousand shares had been sold and nearly fifteen thousand dollars in subscriptions raised, with more shares being sold all the time.

Though the face value of the stock was supposedly fifty dollars per share, most of the purchase price was put up in subscriptions. In actual cash paid out, the shares sold for an average of about twenty-six cents per share. Two hundred investors had contributed. Benjamin, still somewhat skeptical after Joseph's treasure-hunting trip to Salem, had been impressed with the careful thought that had gone into organizing the venture. He put in over three hundred dollars in gold and silver, and put up two of his three farms as collateral. All in all, he purchased nearly a thousand shares, which made him one of the biggest investors.

There was considerable excitement among both members and nonmembers to think that Kirtland would have its own bank now. Communities of no greater consequence than Kirtland—Ashtabula, Warren, Ravenna—now had their own banks. It was time for Kirtland to move forward onto a more solid economic base.

After hearing the reports, Sidney Rigdon stood. "Brethren, the news from the state capital is discouraging. We know that, but all is not lost."

"What are we going to do?" Warren Parrish, secretary to the Safety Society, cried out from the back.

Parrish's voice was sharp and filled with a critical spirit. Since his return from Missouri, Benjamin had twice met with

what he had come to call the "Parrish group." Sharply critical of
Joseph's handling of affairs, the men who came to the group's
gatherings, including three members of the Quorum of the
Twelve, never seemed to have any constructive suggestions,
only their railings against Joseph. And so Benjamin had stopped
attending. He still had serious misgivings about what was happening, but Joseph was trying. And these men didn't want to
give him credit for even that.

"If you will be quiet long enough for me to speak, Brother
Parrish," Sidney said, with some asperity, "I'll try to answer that
question."

"Hear, hear," Benjamin murmured. That won him a sharp
look from Parrish and from the Johnson brothers, who were sitting next to him.

"Brother Joseph and I spent some time with our legal counsel last night after we heard the news from Brother Hyde. It is
not all bad." He paused, letting his eyes sweep over the room.
"As you know, in Ohio there are several banks operating without official charters from the state. The state is winking at these
institutions, because they are providing important and needed
services for their communities."

"Are these the anti-banks we keep hearing about?" Hyrum
Smith asked.

"Yes. They call themselves that to show they don't have
legal status as banks. But they sell stock, issue bank notes, offer
loans, and do all the other things that banks do."

"Isn't that against the law?"

Benjamin turned, but he hadn't recognized the voice and
couldn't see who had spoken.

"Yes," answered Sidney. As the murmurs started to rise, he
then added with a smile, "And no."

"What's that supposed to mean?" Luke Johnson cried.

"As you know, Oliver has obtained plates for printing our
own bank notes, on the assumption that the state would grant
us the charter. Those plates have been obtained at considerable
expense. Also, we have now sold about sixty percent of the

stock in the Kirtland Safety Society and have raised considerable capital. If we simply quit now, not only will we be out the money for the plates, but we will have lost the momentum that we have going for us. So—"

Joseph finished for him. "We think we have a solution."

"We're listening," Heber C. Kimball said.

Sidney smiled in appreciation, then took another breath. "Our lawyer says there is an Ohio law, passed in 1816, that prohibits the issue and circulation of unauthorized bank notes. But he says new statutes were passed in 1824 which supersede the old provisions. These new statutes are much more liberal. They impose no penalties for moving ahead without a charter."

Warren Parrish spoke up again, only now there was a definite interest showing on his face. "So you are saying we just go ahead?"

"Yes. We are proposing that we now change our organization from that of a formal banking institution to a joint-stock company with note-issuing powers. In other words, we become an anti-bank, like others have done."

"What about the notes we already have printed?" Brigham asked. "And the plates? Are we going to have to start again with new ones?"

"Brother Cowdery," Sidney said. "Would you like to respond to that?"

Oliver stood. He looked weary. He had come the more than four hundred miles from Philadelphia without an overnight stop, sleeping on the stagecoaches as best he could. "Brethren, it won't work in every case, but we have a proposal for a name that will allow us to use the notes we already have printed and also the plates we had prepared."

"What is it?" Warren Parrish spoke with an obvious note of respect, something unusual for him.

Sidney stepped forward to stand next to Oliver. "Our suggestion is that we change the name of our organization from the Kirtland Safety Society Bank to the Kirtland Safety Society *Anti*-Banking Company."

"Well, what do you think, Benjamin?" Joseph looked worn and tired too. He had caught Benjamin's eye as the meeting broke up and motioned for him to stay. Now only he and Hyrum and Benjamin were left in the room.

Benjamin let the question sink in for several moments. Finally he nodded. "Under the circumstances, you're doing the best you can, Joseph."

Joseph smiled. He knew Ben too well. "But?"

Benjamin again hesitated, trying to choose his words carefully. "Money is a strange thing, Joseph. When you think about it, it is a very strange thing indeed."

"How so?"

"Well, it has no value of its own, only what we give it. Especially paper money." He laughed, shortly and without mirth. "Take a bank note, for example. It is simply a piece of paper on which we write that it is worth so much. But in order to make it worth that much, you have to convince people that it really *is* worth that much."

"Yes," Hyrum broke in, "but you do that by backing it up with hard money—specie—gold and silver. That way people know they can come in at any time and get full value for it."

"That's right," Benjamin said. "But if you don't have those kinds of hard-money reserves, the value of the paper falls."

"We have about fifteen thousand dollars in hard-money reserves."

"And how much in bank-note value will you circulate?"

Joseph sighed. Obviously he had thought this through too. "More than that, of course. But every bank does that. They have only a portion of their assets in cash reserves."

"Exactly to the point. And that works fine." He paused for effect. "As long as people have confidence in your bank."

Joseph laughed. "Are you trying to cheer me up?"

Benjamin smiled. "I'm not trying to be the doomsayer, Joseph. You've started out on firm footing. But I do have a worry."

"Which is?" Hyrum asked.

"Much of the capital this company holds is in land and other property."

"Land is bad?" Hyrum said skeptically.

"No, land is good. But land is not liquid. You can't take it to a merchant and use it to buy potatoes. You can't carry it in your saddlebags. You can't hand it out in little pieces to redeem currency." He let that sink in, then made his point. "We are vulnerable in two ways, Joseph. Number one, we are undercapitalized. Number two, we have too little cash reserves."

Hyrum looked glum. "The very thing you and I were discussing last night, Joseph."

"Yes," Joseph responded, equally grave. "It may interest you to know, Benjamin, that I have already worried a great deal about this very issue. I have prayed mightily on the matter. The Lord has whispered to me that if we but follow some principles of honesty and frugality, we shall succeed." Then he laughed, that light, cheerful sound that was so characteristic of Joseph. "But I know that you can't use prayers to redeem currency either, so in recent weeks I have applied for and secured a loan from the Bank of Geauga. Hyrum and I shall go and finalize the closing of that loan this afternoon. Then we should be able to add some more to our cash reserves and also pay off some of our creditors."

Benjamin was impressed. Any amount would help tremendously. But Joseph was already heavily in debt. If anything happened, he was taking a tremendous personal risk.

"I'm also going to ask Brigham Young and Willard Richards to go east and sell stock in the company throughout the branches of the Church."

Benjamin sighed, watching the troubled look he saw in Joseph's eyes. He didn't want to say this, but someone had to. He took a breath. "There is one other possible problem."

Joseph chuckled, though his eyes still were worried. "Only one?"

"You have many enemies, Joseph. A dedicated one—and a

shrewd one—could use the bank to embarrass you greatly."

"How?" Hyrum demanded. He was suddenly defensive for his brother.

"If the real trading value of the bank notes falls very much, a person could buy large numbers of them up very cheaply, then come to the bank and demand full face-value payment. That could put you in a fine pickle."

Joseph whistled softly. "A wonderful understatement, Brother Benjamin."

Benjamin forced a smile, feeling a twist in his own stomach. Thoughts of Joseph running off to Salem flitted through his mind. He wished it had never happened. It was the one thing that kept nibbling at his confidence in Joseph's wisdom.

Benjamin took a breath. "I've purchased around a thousand shares in the Safety Society. I've done that because I believe it's right. I believe *you* believe it's right, and I trust you, Joseph. If we don't make a go of it, I may become one of those the Kirtland 'poor laws' are out to get."

Joseph's eyes showed that he was clearly troubled. Hyrum watched him for a moment, then said softly. "Joseph is planning to sell some of his property. With that and the loan we are getting today, it looks like he'll be making one of the largest investments in the Safety Society."

Benjamin's eyes widened.

"That's right," Hyrum nodded. "I think there's only one other person with a larger investment. If we don't make a go of this, Joseph stands to be one of the biggest losers of all."

Joseph managed a wan smile at his brother, then it slowly faded. "Brethren, if we don't make a go of this, money is going to be the very least of our worries."

Caroline looked up in surprise from her sewing as the front door opened. William stood there, hands at his side, his head down.

"Will?"

Suddenly his shoulders lifted and fell, there was a stifled sob, and he started across the room to her in stumbling steps.

Instantly she was on her feet, feeling the awkward heaviness of the baby pull at her stomach. She opened her arms and Will rushed into them. Now the sobs came in great racking shudders, tearing at his body. She clung to him, dumbfounded. He would turn thirteen in March. There were not many thirteen-year-olds more self-confident and self-reliant than William Donovan Mendenhall. She had not seen him cry once since the death of his father more than two years ago now.

Gradually the trembling began to subside and Will got control of himself. He stepped back from his mother and wiped quickly at the corners of his eyes. Caroline gasped softly and one hand shot out to grab Will's chin. She turned his face. In the doorway, his back had been to the light and she had not seen his face clearly. There was a smear of blood beneath his nose, and one cheek had an ugly abrasion. The shirt he had put on clean this morning was soiled on one side, and she saw that the knees of his trousers were brown with the dirt of the schoolyard.

She let go of his chin. His head dropped immediately, and he tensed for her reaction. Fighting against every motherly instinct that was tugging at her, she bit back the words. She reached out and laid a hand on his shoulder. "Why don't you go wash up," she murmured, "then we'll talk about it."

———•———

Joshua looked up in surprise. Caroline was still adjusting to her first real winter in several years, and she didn't like to be out in the cold. With the baby now due in about two months, she also found it uncomfortable to walk very far. And she definitely did not like the freight yard with its smell of oxen and horses and sweating men. So when he came out of the stable leading a team of horses and saw her standing there outside the office door, it took him aback a little. He handed the tether to his yard foreman and went to her.

"This is a surprise," he said. He reached out and touched her arm.

She was huddled against the cold air, holding herself tightly against the chill. She smiled faintly. "I thought it would be."

"Let's go inside."

She shook her head. "I need to talk with you, Joshua."

His face fell a little. "Right now?"

She nodded, the smile completely gone.

"Look, just go inside for a few minutes. Cornwell and I have got to get this team hitched up. There's a load of lumber—"

"Will was sent home from school today."

That stopped him. "He was?"

"Yes. He'd been fighting."

He grinned. "Did he win?" She just watched him steadily, and the grin slowly faded. "Who was he fighting with?"

There was a quick, impatient shake of her head. "That doesn't matter. He was fighting over you."

His mouth opened, then shut again. He couldn't remember when her eyes had been quite so grave. The emerald green had gone almost gray now. He turned to Cornwell, who stood waiting with the horses. "You'd better go ahead. Get Bart to help you."

Without waiting for an answer, Joshua turned, took her arm, and steered her toward the street. Once out of the yard, he turned south, away from the center of town. "All right," he finally said. "I'm listenin'."

But Caroline didn't answer. They walked on for nearly a block until they came to the framework of the large two-story house that stood near the outskirts of the town. Finally she stopped. This was the home Joshua was building for her. There was no question about it, it was going to be the finest that Independence had yet seen.

She just kept staring at the house, still not speaking. He felt a stirring of alarm. He had never seen her quite like this. "Caroline, I'm listenin'," he said again.

She looked down at the ground. "For your own reasons, you've chosen not to tell me anything about your first marriage."

His head came up sharply.

"But it's no longer just between you and me, Joshua."

———◆———

Joshua stood for a moment in the doorway of the barn, letting his eyes adjust to the dim light, then he stepped inside. "Will?"

The milk cow in one of the stalls looked up. Her large brown eyes watched him with curiosity for a moment, her mouth rotating slowly as she chewed her cud. Beyond her, Joshua's horse swished his tail, then again. But other than that, there was no sound, no movement.

He walked in farther and raised his voice. "Will, are you in here?"

Above him, in the loft, something stirred. Joshua turned, walked to the ladder, and climbed it slowly, his mind going four or five times faster than his feet.

Will was in the far corner, half lying, half sitting back against a pile of dried meadow hay. Joshua noted that the loft window was slightly ajar—which meant that Will had seen him coming.

"Hi."

The head did not raise.

"Mind if I sit down?"

There was an almost imperceptible shake of the head. Joshua moved over and sat down, putting his back up against one of the beams that supported the roof. He picked up a long stem of prairie grass and began to chew on it slowly. Will raised his eyes without lifting his head; then when he saw Joshua was watching him, he looked down again quickly—but not quickly enough that Joshua missed the look of betrayal that filled the brown eyes.

Joshua smiled sadly as an image flashed in his mind. It was of an impudent young lad standing on the cobblestone streets of Savannah, knickers held up with suspenders, a French beret perched jauntily on his head. "I know everything there is to know about Savannah," he had said with a boyish swagger. From almost the first moment they had met, something had clicked between Joshua Steed and William Mendenhall. Over the past nine months, that bond had deepened into something that meant a great deal to Joshua. He was surprised now how badly it hurt to see the disappointment on Will's face. And what hurt even worse, he wasn't sure he could say anything that would make it go away.

"Can we talk about it?"

Again there was no answer, but one shoulder lifted in a brief shrug.

Joshua tossed the stem of grass aside. "Look, Will, I'm not

very good at guessing. Why don't you just ask whatever questions you've got tumblin' around in your head?" He blew out his breath. "I'll try and answer them as honestly as I can."

The silence stretched on for well over a minute. Twice Joshua thought about trying again, saying something else, but something told him to give it time. So he waited. Finally, Will shifted his weight. He brought his knees up, hugged his arms around them, then rested his chin on top of them. He was no longer staring at the floor, but neither did he look at Joshua. He was staring at a knothole in one of the boards of the barn wall.

"Is it true?" he finally murmured.

"Your mother said your friends told you a lot of things," Joshua responded after a moment.

Will's voice was low and still carried hurt. "They weren't tryin' to be mean to me. They were braggin' on you. They said you were one of the bravest men in Jackson County. When they told me what you did, I said they were lyin', that my step-pa wouldn't do those kinds of things."

"And that's when you fought?"

He nodded quickly.

"So, ask your questions."

"Did you really beat your wife up?"

Joshua winced. When Caroline had chosen a word to describe what the boys said about him and Jessica, it had been *hit*. He had hit his wife. *Beat* was a much more brutal word. But he forced a nod. "Yes, Will, I did."

The brown eyes, nearly black in the dimness of the light in the barn, seemed to be trying to drill the knothole out of its board.

"You ever seen a drunk, Will?"

There was faint disdain at the inanity of the question. "Of course."

"I mean someone who is really drunk? Out-of-his-head drunk?"

"Yes. My buddy, John Watkins, and I used to sneak down to the saloon and watch the men come out sometimes."

"Well, liquor is a poor excuse for anything, Will, but it's the only one I have. Jessica—my first wife—and I had a lot of hate building up between us. It seemed like everythin' we did just fanned that hate all the hotter. One night, she did something that really made me angry. Now, as I look back on it, I guess I can't say as I blame her, but that night I was furious with her. Instead of lettin' it burn out, I went to the saloon and got mean, out-of-my-head drunk. Then I went lookin' for her."

He shook his head. "If there was a kind God anywhere in this world, he'd let us go back and undo some of the stupid things we do, Will. But that isn't part of life, it seems."

For the first time, Will was looking at Joshua, watching him closely, eyes wide and vulnerable. Joshua met his gaze. "Words are cheap," he said softly. "But right now, Will, there's nothing else to offer you. All I can say is that I'm deep-down shamed at what I did—enough that I made myself two promises." He shook his head angrily. "No, more than promises, solemn vows."

"What are they?"

"First, I vowed that I'll never let whiskey take me over again. Not ever. It's a terrible master, Will. I know that now." He paused, then added. "That's been almost five and a half years ago now, Will. I haven't been drunk since. Not one time."

Will's wide eyes blinked once, then again, and Joshua sensed at least some acceptance of that. He took a quick breath and went on. "Two, I've vowed I'll never, ever, lift my hand against a woman again. It was a cowardly thing, and I'll carry the shame of it to the grave."

He stopped, wanting to see if Will would respond. He didn't. Instead he looked away again. "Other questions?" Joshua finally asked.

Will turned. "Why do you hate Mormons so much?"

Joshua's lips tightened. "Because they're bad people, Will. Evil people."

"What did they do?"

"They—" Joshua stopped. "Well, it's not so much what they do, but what they are."

Will looked faintly disgusted at that.

Joshua felt an urgent need to help him understand. "They came in here trying to change everybody, claimed all of us Missourians were going to have to leave so they could build up a perfect society. They're high-and-mighty, filled with all kinds of ideas that are rubbish."

"Mama says it's not good to hate people simply because they're different."

Joshua nearly flashed out with a quick retort, but caught himself. "Your mama's right. I don't hate Mormons just because they're different. They've done bad things. That's why we drove them out of the county. Sometimes a man has to take a stand against bad things."

Will seemed lost in his own thoughts. "When we moved to Savannah, lots of people warned us to stay away from Negro people. They said they were bad. Couldn't be trusted. They called them 'niggers' and all kinds of stuff. Mama said it's not right to judge people like that. There were two black boys down on Factors' Walk who were my good friends. I didn't think they were niggers."

Joshua smiled, his eyes softening. "Your mama is a very good woman, William. A strong woman. You listen to her."

Will nodded. He unclasped his hands from around his legs and stretched. Joshua sensed a softening but knew the crisis hadn't passed yet. "Do you have other questions you want to ask me, Will?"

He looked away.

"Go on, Will. We can't let this be hanging between us."

He took a breath. Finally he turned and looked Joshua full in the face. The look in his eyes wrenched Joshua like nothing he had ever felt before.

"My friends said you drove your wife and your baby out of their house. They said it was a cold night and you drove them out with whips. Made them walk all night across the prairie. They said some people died."

Joshua closed his eyes, leaning forward, his head down. The

words had brought back memories that knifed through him with terrible pain.

"Is it true?" Will asked.

After a long time, Joshua looked up. "Sometimes, Will . . ." His shoulders lifted and fell. "Sometimes we start things that we can't control. I . . . we, a bunch of us, had been fighting the Mormons. There was a battle out near the Big Blue River. Two of my men were shot and killed. One of the Mormons was killed. Several on both sides were wounded.

"Emotions were very high. My men wanted revenge. And I'll be honest. I did too. It was like we were on the verge of an explosion. We decided to drive the Mormons out so no more trouble could happen."

His voice became distant, far away, as if he had moved back into the past again. "I was leading a group of about a hundred men out to the Mormon settlement. It was night. I knew that Jessica . . . actually she was not really my wife by then; we had been divorced. But anyway, I knew that Jessica and our little girl were there. Jessica's father was with me. I sent him on ahead. Told him to warn her to get out fast. But I couldn't hold the men back. They broke loose and went riding in, shooting and hollering and sending everybody running."

He shook his head, and his voice dropped to little more than a whisper. "Turned out it was mostly women and children. The men had gone off somewhere." There was a long pause. "It wasn't a great night for bravery."

Will's eyes were wide. "Did you whip them?"

He looked up, a little surprised, as though he had forgotten Will was there. Then he shook his head firmly. "No. I didn't whip anybody that night. Will, once things calmed down some, I turned around and went home."

For a long time they sat there, Joshua waiting, occasionally watching Will's face for some clue as to his feelings, letting him think about all he had heard. Finally, Joshua stood up. "I'm sorry you think less of me, Will. That hurts a lot. A real lot. But I understand. All I can say is that those things happened a long time ago. I'm sorry now. But like I said, you can't go back and undo things you did, no matter how much you want to."

Will's face was unreadable as he considered Joshua's words. "You ready to come in now?" Joshua asked softly after a moment. "Or do you want to stay out here for a little longer?"

Will dropped his head again. "I think I'll stay."

Joshua nodded. "I'll tell your mother where you are." He flashed a weak grin. "Probably beats goin' back to school anyway, right?"

"Yeah." Will didn't smile.

Joshua moved slowly across the loft to the ladder. He started down, but stopped after two or three rungs. "Will?"

The boy's head came up.

"I . . ." Suddenly Joshua's tongue was thick and heavy. Will was looking at him curiously. "I . . . I just wanted you to know that I think of you as if . . . well, it's like you are actually my own son."

Flustered now, he rushed on. "I know you loved your real pa, and all that. And I'd never want to take that away from you, but . . ." He shook his head. This was worse than taking a ten-mule team down the side of a muddy riverbank. "One of the things I wish for most in this life is that, someday, you'll feel like you can . . . like maybe you could call me your pa, too." He shook his head, giving it up. "I'd be right proud if you ever did, Will. Right proud."

With that he plunged down the ladder and walked swiftly out of the barn.

Dinner was a painful experience. Caroline spoke pleasantly to the children, but didn't even so much as look at Joshua. Will answered when asked a question directly, but spoke in monosyllables and monotones. Olivia seemed puzzled, but even at nine years of age, she was aware that this was not the time for her usual chatter and, for the most part, ate quietly and kept shooting sidelong glances at her brother.

Joshua had wanted to talk with his wife when he came back into the house, to tell her how it had gone with Will, but she had been at the table, preparing dinner. She had heard him come up behind her—there was no question of that—but she did not turn around or acknowledge his presence, and he had finally left and gone back to the freight yard.

After the dishes were done, Caroline read to the two children for almost an hour, twice as long as she usually did, while Joshua stayed bent over the books from the business, pretending to concentrate. The sun went down, and as twilight came the room darkened to the point that it became difficult to see. "Would you like me to light a lamp?" he finally asked.

Caroline stood, pulling Olivia up to stand beside her. "Not for us. We're going upstairs. I'm going to tell the children stories for a time."

There was not a murmur of protest from either Will or Olivia, something unheard of when it was still not even seven o'clock. They seemed glad to escape his presence as they trooped up the stairs.

For a long moment Joshua stared at the empty stairwell, his emotions churning. He expected hurt. He expected anger. But this? He shoved his chair back with a jerk. This was how Jessica had been. Withdrawing into her shell. Fighting back by not fighting. Was that what it had come to again? And what would tomorrow bring? The bitter invective? Words hurled like lances? He felt sick and angry and hurt and frustrated all at once. Only now did he realize how much those battles had drained him.

And that had been with Jessica. He knew now he had loved Jessica Roundy. In his own limited way. But Caroline! The pain tore at him. Caroline consumed him. The one thing he wanted most was to make her happy, to see her smile, to hear her laugh, and know it was because of him.

And now there was no laughter, no smiles, not even angry words. He could cope with those. Try and reason with her. At least be talking. But this ice-block approach . . . He blew out his breath in a quick explosion of disgust. The anger was starting to win out inside him now. He swore softly to himself. He *had* changed. He was shamed by the past, and he had vowed it would not be repeated. Didn't that count for anything? She wouldn't even listen to him, wouldn't even give him a chance to try to explain.

He stood abruptly, slamming the ledger book shut. Well, he wasn't going to sit here moping like a kicked hound dog, waiting for her to throw him a condescending glance. He started for the coatrack, making up his mind. He'd see hell freeze over before he stood still for another round of this.

Suddenly the longing for whiskey was as sharp as a stab in the side with a forked stick. He stopped, as though struck. His mind was already in the saloon. Go to Clinton Roundy's and get a bottle of whiskey! Let that fix things.

He looked at his hands. They were visibly shaking. He stared at them. It had been over five years since he had gone to the bottle to escape. Five years!

He turned and walked slowly in the half darkness back to the chair and dropped into it heavily. He sat back, staring at nothing, waiting for the darkness to envelop him.

———————◆———————

It was past nine o'clock when Caroline came down the stairs. After the children had finally gone to sleep, she had gone into the bedroom where she and Joshua slept. For a long time she lay there on the bed, wondering if he would come up. She knew she had hurt him terribly, and for a time she had fought feelings of gladness. She wanted revenge. Longed for it. The hurt he had dealt her was so deep, so vast, that she wanted a price exacted in return. But then the more rational part of Caroline's mind finally began to speak. It was a whisper at first, but it wouldn't go away. It had taken almost an hour for her to sort through the thoughts, decide what to say, then rehearse it over and over in her mind, playing off against his every possible answer.

Now she came softly down the stairs. She was only half-surprised that the house was dark. Upstairs she had listened carefully and had heard no sound. Now there was a momentary stab of fear that he had slipped out without her hearing, but then she saw the darkness of his shape by the table where she had left him.

She stopped on the last stair. She saw his head come up. Her pulse quickened. Now that the moment had arrived, she nearly lost her courage. But she knew that if she turned around now, a knot in the line would be tied that might never be undone.

"Joshua?"

He straightened.

She sighed softly, feeling the pain rising up again. "The women in town have tried to tell me all about the past. I want you to know I haven't listened. I won't listen. I won't learn what happened between you and Jessica from gossip, from some petty little person eager to dump trash onto my doorstep."

She could feel his eyes on her in the darkness. "But I keep asking myself," she said, her voice barely more than a whisper now, "are there two Joshua Steeds?"

A great sadness began to overwhelm her, and she fought the choked feeling that was starting in her chest. "Most of the time I see this man I met in Savannah. He's handsome, charming, wonderful with my children." There was a long pause, then more quietly, "I was even finding myself starting to love him, down deep, in a way I didn't think was going to be possible again."

She heard his soft intake of breath, but she hurried on, afraid if she stopped now it would not ever come out. "But from time to time, that Joshua suddenly disappears. He goes behind this great wall. I call to him, but there's no answer. And then I—" She bit her lip. This was far more difficult than it had been when she was doing it in her mind. "And then I see another man. Just a shadow. It's someone I've never met. Someone I'm not sure I ever want to meet."

She sat down on the step, suddenly finding that standing required too much effort. She hugged her legs, staring across the room at the dark shape. "I can't make you tell me what's back there, Joshua. You can show me all of it or part of it. I won't know if you're being completely honest with me or not. But I know this—if there is ever to be anything between us besides sharing the same bed and raising our children, you are going to have to take me behind that wall and show me there's nothing there to be frightened of. Because right now, I am very frightened."

For several long moments she sat there. There was no movement, no sound. Shaking her head, feeling the burning behind her eyes, she stood abruptly, turned, and ran up the stairs.

Caroline's first awareness was that it was still dark outside the window. And yet she sensed it was morning. Perhaps five o'clock or even six. She turned over lazily, not wanting to come up out of the deep sleep she had been lost in. Through the haze, she remembered the fitful hours she had spent before she finally slipped into the depths. Then suddenly she remembered what had happened before she came upstairs to bed, and lifted her head. The bed beside her was empty. She fell back. The disappointment was so sharp she could taste it.

She rose up slightly again, trying to hear if he had simply gotten up without waking her. Early mornings were not Caroline's thing, and often he would be up and dressed and downstairs working on this project or that before she finally rose. But there was no sound now. The house was silent.

And then as she lay back down, her heart jumped. There was a shape at the other window, blotting out half of the faint light coming in from outside. She sat up with a jerk. "Joshua?"

He was already turned, watching her. "I didn't mean to frighten you."

She let her breath out, feeling her pulse pounding. "How long have you been there?"

There was a long pause; then, "Most of the night."

"Why didn't you come to bed?" And then, even as she said it, she realized what a foolish question it was. She slid over a little and patted the bed beside her. "Come sit with me."

There was a moment's hesitation, then he came over and sat down. She reached out in the darkness and found his hand. He took a quick breath, then let it out again. She felt the tension in him, but at the same time she also felt in herself a great burst of elation. She squeezed his hand. "I'm listening, Joshua."

He began slowly. Surprisingly, he didn't start with Jessica. He started with his family. And gradually it all came out. Sometimes it was in a rush of words, punctuated with anger and disgust. Sometimes he stammered, his voice heavy with shame. Much of the time he spoke quietly, without outward emotion.

He didn't say much about the specifics of his family—his brothers and sisters and so on. That was not his purpose. But the other all came out—the relationship between a stubborn father and a proud, rebellious son; the terrible rainy night when he had come within a hair's breadth of killing his father; the flight into oblivion; working the great keelboats up and down the Ohio; coming to Independence and starting the freight business; Jessica; the poker games.

It took more out of Caroline than she had expected. When he talked about his obsession with Lydia McBride, she was surprised at how sharply the jealousy rose inside her. She felt strangely proud of her own ability to bear children when he spoke of Jessica's miscarriages and what they had done to their marriage. And she felt herself recoil in horror as he told of those final days with Jessica.

He spared himself no details. He made no attempt to soften his role in what happened. She had asked to see it all, that he hold nothing back. Evidently in the night hours he had decided to give her what she asked for. But many of the things he told her about filled her with revulsion and a great sense of abhorrence. It was all she could do to stop from jerking her hand away and screaming at him to get away from her, to stay back and never touch her again.

But then something else began to stir in her. Joshua was not a warm and emotional man. He was a very private person, locking up his feelings behind stoic masculinity. As he talked on, however, she began to feel the depths of his pain, the power of his remorse, what it had cost him to tell her all of this. And she was strangely touched.

He stopped. The room was filled with the heaviness of the silence. She didn't want to respond, not now. She wanted time to think, to choose her words with great care. But she knew he was waiting. He had laid himself bare, left himself terribly vulnerable. Now he needed to know if it had been for nothing. When she didn't say anything for a moment, he started to withdraw his hand. She held on, locking her fingers around his tightly.

He took another breath, then very slowly he finally turned to her. "Caroline, I can't go back and change the past. I'd have done it a thousand times if that was possible."

"I know," she said softly.

"If you—" He took a quick breath. "If you decide you can't live with what I've done, I'll understand."

That required an answer, and she was at a loss for words. Could she live with those horrible images in her mind? Would they rise up to haunt her every time he reached out and touched her? She pulled his hand to her and took it with both of hers now. "Joshua," she began, slowly, realizing how important these next few moments could be for them. "I am glad that you have told me. I will be honest with you. What you have done fills me with horror. It's like we have been talking about another man, a man called Joshua Steed whom I've never met, never seen."

"And whom you won't see ever again," he said with great fervency.

She nodded. "I want to believe that. I want to believe that very badly. If I couldn't . . ." She didn't finish.

She took a deep breath, then let it out in a long, soft sigh. "I don't know if I can ever put these terrible images from my mind,

Joshua. I don't know if I can promise you that nothing will change in our relationship." He started to speak, but she went on quickly. "But now it's out and we can deal with it. And that is less terrifying than not knowing, not having you fully."

She pulled him down to lie beside her. "You must be exhausted."

He nodded, not looking at her. She could feel his body, through the covers, still rigid and filled with tension. She reached out and laid one hand on his face, then gently turned it until he was looking at her. "Thank you for coming up, Joshua. I was afraid I had lost, that you weren't ever going to tell me."

One hand came up and he laid it over hers, keeping it on his face. "Caroline, I have . . ." This still wasn't easy for him. "I love you and the children."

"I know," she said. And then it hit her with sudden clarity. That was true! There was no question about that. She knew that Joshua Steed loved her more deeply and cared for her more deeply than Donovan Mendenhall had, and that had been a great deal. And Joshua loved her children intensely. She felt a great sense of wonder and gratitude. And a sudden hope.

"If I ever lose you," he started, his voice deep and husky, "I—"

She moved her hand down across his face, putting her fingers over his lips and stopping him. "You're not going to lose me," she whispered. She took his hands and brought them over to her stomach, let him feel the roundness beneath the covers. "This child needs a father." Her voice caught. "I want that father to be you."

Preston, England

A textile factory going at full steam was an awesome sight to the uninitiated—and a terrible assault on unprotected ears. The noise began at the gates, where huge high-wheeled wagons pulled by teams of six horses or mules came in a steady stream from Liverpool, thirty miles to the south. There the cotton had been off-loaded from the fleets of packet ships shuttling back and forth across the Atlantic. These wagons made the very ground tremble, and the clattering racket of the iron-rimmed tires on cobblestone filled Preston's main street with mind-numbing noise from first light to dark.

Inside the carding sheds, machines screeched and moaned like demented spirits. First, huge rollers covered with iron teeth drew the tangled fibers into straight, even rows. Then another machine began to roll the fibers over and over one another to form "slivers," loose ropes of cotton yarn. From there they went to the "spinning mules," hundreds of them, spitting out continuous lines of threads, as many as sixty-four at a time.

But it was in the long, low building that housed nearly two dozen of the great steam-driven power looms where the noise was so thunderous that it vibrated the skull and made it nearly impossible to speak. Even in the building next to it, where the boilers that fired the steam engines were housed, the noise of the looms was as real and as palpable as a living presence.

For the most part it was women who tended the weaving machines. As a boy, Derek hadn't understood why so many of the women who worked in the factories always spoke loudly. They seemed to be screaming at everybody, even when they were just making idle conversation. He no longer wondered why. They stood at the machines from seven a.m. to seven p.m., battered by the incessant roaring, from whose noise they were relieved for only an hour, their dinner break, plus two brief stops—one midmorning and one midafternoon—to clean the machines and gulp down some tepid water, or perhaps some cold coffee, before the machines started rolling again.

Three great boilers provided the steam for the power looms. Derek Ingalls had moved into the boiler room from the unloading sheds at the age of fifteen. When he had first started, he had been one of the lads who "lapped" the cotton—laid it out in bundles of similar-size fibers—when the bales were first opened. Now he shoveled coal to feed the insatiable bellies of the boilers. He worked without a shirt, and his upper torso—wet with perspiration from the heat and the labor—almost glowed in the dancing firelight. There were three shovelers. Derek was the youngest and the toughest. Four years of shoveling for ten to twelve hours per day had turned his developing body into something hard and muscular.

The man working alongside Derek tapped his shoulder. He was pointing toward the door. Surprised, Derek turned. His surprise was even greater when he saw Peter standing there, motioning to him frantically. He turned, threw the shovel-load of coal into the gaping mouth of the boiler, then stuck his shovel into the coal pile.

The foreman was on him like a hawk on a straggler pigeon. "Eh, mate, where do ya think yer goin'?"

Derek hesitated for a moment. England's unemployment was so horrendous that there were a dozen men for every job available. Often new men were so desperate for work that they would accept a lower wage, so the owners looked for the slightest letdown or misstep as an excuse to fire a person. Derek pointed to the door. "It's my little brother, sir."

The foreman looked, then nodded. He had a son a year younger than Peter who also worked in the cutting room. The boys were not close, but friendly. "All right," he muttered, "but make it snappy."

Peter stepped outside when he saw Derek was coming. Derek didn't even wait for the door to close. "What is it, Peter? What's the matter?"

His brother clutched at his arm. "Mr. Morris is here, Derek."

"The owner?"

"Yes, the young one. The son. The lady who runs the front desk fainted. They've taken her to hospital."

"So?"

His grip tightened on Derek's arm. "Mr. Morris is fumin'. He needs someone who can read the orders. Says he needs 'em today."

Derek was staring at his brother. "You can read."

"He don't want no kid, Derek," Peter exclaimed in disgust. "He wants a bloomin' adult. Go there. Tell him you can read."

"But I can't read."

"You can!" Peter shouted up into his face. "You're getting better all the time."

"I . . . I'm still learnin', Peter."

Peter slugged him on the shoulder. "It's three schillings more a month, Derek. Three schillings!"

Derek straightened, his mind racing.

"Do it, Derek, do it!"

He gulped hard. "All right."

Peter started away. "I've got to get back. I snuck away. Don't tell him how you knew."

He nodded, half-numb. This was crazy. He could lose everything.

No! It exploded fiercely in his mind. *I won't pass this up! I won't.*

In a moment he was back inside and to the foreman. He took a breath. He was taking a terrible risk. If Morris and the foreman ever got together . . . He swept his hat off. "They want me up front."

"What?" the foreman roared.

"Mr. Morris is here."

The foreman looked startled for a moment, glancing nervously at the door. "Old Man Morris?"

"No, his son."

"And what does he want you for?"

Derek shrugged, trying to look appropriately perplexed.

"All right, but you get your behinder right back here. What am I supposed to do for a shoveler in the meantime?"

Derek didn't wait to hear what the foreman's muttered answer to his own question would be. He grabbed his shirt and in an instant was out of the door.

Alexander Morris looked nothing like his father. He was nearing fifty and had gone quickly to corpulence. His father, the old man who had founded the factory and made it into one of the largest in Lancashire, was still, at seventy-two, lean as a buggy whip and tougher than a blacksmith's anvil. But though the younger Morris looked nothing like him, as he glared balefully at Derek it was obvious there had been some inheritance of the old man's genes.

"You can read?"

"Yes, sir." It was all Derek could do not to stammer.

"How old are you?"

"Nineteen, sir."

"Comin' up or already there?"

"I was nineteen last October, sir."

The narrow little eyes ran up and down Derek's clothes, black with coal dust. "You're in the boilers now."

"Yes, sir. Four years as a shoveler."

Morris swung around, grabbed a large ledger book and shoved it in front of Derek with a faint sneer. His thick forefinger jabbed at a line of writing. "Read this."

Derek leaned over, conscious of a roaring in his ears. For a moment he thought he was going to faint. He squinted a little. Thankfully, the cursive was not too elaborate. " 'Robert T. Little, Esquire. 71 High Street, Putney, London.' " He straightened, sure that the quaver in his voice would betray him.

Morris sat back, still scowling, but more interested now. "You know your numbers too?"

"Yes, sir." Fortunately, Derek had found numbers much less complex to grasp than the alphabet.

Morris stood up abruptly. "What's your name?"

"Derek Ingalls, sir."

"You got another set of clothes?"

"Yes, sir. At home, sir."

There was a trace of amusement. "I'll give you two weeks. If you don't work out, you're out of both jobs. Fair enough?"

"*Yes, sir.*"

"All right. You've got thirty minutes to get home and be back here in something that doesn't stink of sweat and coal dust. I'll send word to the boiler room to find a replacement."

It was all Derek could do to just walk out of the office and down the path without breaking into a run. But the moment he rounded the corner he gave a whoop and headed for the cutting building. He didn't have to go in. Peter's face was pressed against the end window, his eyes round as two china plates.

Derek stopped. He was grinning from ear to ear. He nodded, then punched his fist into the air. There was a moment's expression of disbelief, then a faint cry came through the glass. "All right!" Peter shouted. "You did it! You did it!"

"Mr. Steed?"

Joshua swung around sharply. Doctor Hathaway was at the doorway. He was wiping his hands on a towel. In three great strides Joshua was to him. Olivia and Will were not two steps behind him.

Hathaway smiled. "You can go in."

"Is she all right?"

"Yes. She did very well."

"And the baby?"

His smile broadened even further. Had it been any other day, Joshua would have been struck with the oddness of Hathaway's mood. In his proper, Bostonian ways, he rarely smiled, and when he did it was usually a thin, tight-lipped expression that came out as more of a grimace. But there was no mistaking it now. The man Joshua Steed had found practicing medicine in St. Louis and brought to Independence so he could specifically help Jessica Steed carry a child; the man who had been greatly frustrated when that same Jessica Steed had refused to see him after she miscarried—that man was now immensely pleased. "I'll let Mrs. Steed tell you that," he said.

He looked down at the children. "You let your father have a few minutes with your mother first, then you can go in."

Caroline looked up as Joshua slipped into the bedroom. Against the pillow, she looked drawn, washed out. Her eyes were filled with weariness, but a soft smile instantly lit her face. He went to her quickly and took her free hand. "Are you all right?" he asked, half whispering.

She nodded.

His eyes moved to the small bundle cuddled inside the crook of her other arm. She reached over and pulled the blanket carefully down. A tiny round face appeared. The eyes were closed, the nose a button stuck between fat, round cheeks, the mouth small and half-puckered. The head still looked a little squashed from the trauma of birth. Caroline pulled the blanket back further. Now he could see a shock of dark hair, thick as a rug but fine as goose down, still wet from the baby's birth.

"It's a girl, Joshua."

He dropped to one knee so he could get a closer look. "Really?" he breathed.

"Are you disappointed?"

He instantly frowned at her. "Why would I be? It's our baby. Boy or girl. It's our baby."

She smiled, deeply pleased.

He reached out with one finger, his face filled with wonder. "I can't believe it. Look at all that hair."

Caroline laughed. "Not only that, look at the color." She turned a little, moving the baby more into the light.

Joshua leaned over to peer more closely. At first glance it looked black with the wetness, but then he saw it, and he smiled broadly. "It's red," he exclaimed.

"Yes, much more than mine. She's going to have my mother's hair."

"That's wonderful. Our own little carrot top." He reached out, half gingerly, half in eagerness. Caroline lifted her to his hands. He straightened, holding the baby out at arm's length and looking at her in awe.

"Well," Caroline said after a moment, "now that we know it's a girl, we have to settle on a name."

"I already have."

Her eyes widened a little. "But the other day you said you weren't sure."

"I wasn't. Now I am."

Her look chided him a little. "What if I don't like it?"

"You will."

She laughed. "All right, if you're so sure, let's hear it."

"Savannah."

That startled her. They had discussed several girls' names—Elizabeth, Margaret, Belinda—but not once had that possibility come up.

He brought the baby back down and tucked her into one

arm, then began to rock her gently, still looking down into her face. "Savannah Steed. What more appropriate name could there be?" His voice went suddenly tight. "It's where everything important to me started."

Tears sprang to Caroline's eyes. It touched her more deeply than she could say that he was responding in this way.

He looked up, saw that she was crying. He met her gaze steadily. "Is that all right with you, then?"

She swallowed, smiling through the tears. "I think Savannah sounds absolutely perfect, Joshua."

He came back to her, handed her the baby. "Hold her for a minute. There's something I need to get."

"All right." A little puzzled, she took the baby and watched him as he knelt down beside the bed. He reached underneath and pulled out his valise, the one he had taken to Savannah. He looked up at her, his eyes grave, then quickly undid the buckles. She heard the rattling of paper. Finally he stood. In his hands was the porcelain doll he had purchased in New Orleans.

Her eyes widened as he held it out for her to see. "Joshua," she breathed, "what an exquisite thing!"

He glanced down at it, then smiled slowly. "It's for her, Caroline. I bought it in New Orleans, when I was on my way to Savannah. Thank you. Thank you for giving me this beautiful daughter."

"Do you think it's a boy?" Lydia asked.

Thankful Pratt nodded. "I know it is."

Rebecca, standing on the opposite side of the bed, cocked her head to one side, looking a little surprised. The doctors were estimating that Parley's wife was still two weeks from delivery.

Mary Ann saw the look and spoke up. "Remember? Brother Heber's blessing upon Parley?"

Rebecca's head bobbed. "Oh, yes. I forgot."

"Yes," Thankful said. "Brother Kimball promised Parley that

I would conceive and bear him a son and that he should be named after his father."

"That was a remarkable blessing," Lydia said. "You were so sick back then, and ten years without child. Now look at you."

Thankful laid her head back on the bed. They were standing around her in the small bedroom of the home in which the Pratts lived. Parley was off at a meeting with some of the brethren, and Mary Ann, Rebecca, and Lydia had brought her some chicken broth and some warm biscuits. Thankful's recovery from a six-year bout with "incurable" consumption had left her healthy and filled with energy. When she had accompanied Parley back to Canada the previous June, she had seemed like an entirely different woman than the frail wraith they had known. She was fairly tall and quite slender, though now she was heavy with child. But evidently the reserves of strength were thin, for the pregnancy seemed to have drained much of them. The strain of her and Parley's return from Toronto the week before had also taken its toll. She looked fragile and weary. That was partly what had triggered the women's visit.

Lydia smiled at her friend. "Maybe this boy of yours will grow up and be one of the missionaries who take the gospel to England, like Brother Kimball promised would happen."

To Mary Ann's surprise, Thankful's countenance fell. "Perhaps, but I shall not be here to witness it."

All three of the Steed women looked up in dismay. Lydia was the first to give voice to their shock. "Thankful, whatever on earth makes you say that? Of course you'll be here."

She shook her head, but now the sadness was mixed with a strange look of joy. "It's all right, Lydia. Everything is all right."

Mary Ann reached out and took one hand. "It's natural to worry at this point, especially with your first baby. But everything will be fine, Thankful. You'll see. We'll be praying for you."

Thankful turned to Mary Ann, her eyes wide and glistening. "You are sweet to say that." Her eyes moved to Lydia and then to Rebecca. "This shall be the other difficult thing for me. I shall miss you all terribly."

"Thankful," Lydia said, quite sternly now, "you must stop speaking in this manner."

Again the head dropped back against the bed pillow. She sighed deeply, but once more Mary Ann was struck with the fact that while there was sorrow, there was also a radiant joy that filled Thankful's face. "I must tell you something," she finally said. "Then perhaps you will understand."

She reached out both of her hands, taking Mary Ann's hand with one, and Lydia's with the other. She smiled at Rebecca, apologizing with her eyes that she could not touch her as well. Then her eyes left her three friends. She was looking at a spot somewhere behind Mary Ann, but her eyes were not focusing on anything in the room.

"It was only a few days ago now. I was sitting in the other room just at midday." Her voice dropped to an awestruck whisper. "Suddenly I was overwhelmed. I felt like I was immersed in a pillar of fire. It was all around me, and filled the room with light. I should have been frightened, I suppose, but instead I was filled with great joy. While I sat and marveled at what was happening, the Spirit whispered in my mind, saying, 'Thou art baptized with fire and the Holy Ghost.' "

"Really?" Rebecca breathed when she stopped. "How wonderful!"

Thankful nodded, barely hearing. She was lost completely now in her recollections of the experience. "The Spirit then intimated to me that I should have the privilege of departing from this world of sorrow and pain." Finally she looked at them, and her eyes were wide and luminous. "I am to be allowed to go to the paradise of rest as soon as I have fulfilled the prophecy in regard to my son."

Mary Ann, Lydia, Rebecca—they were all staring, so totally taken aback that they were left without words.

Thankful went on more slowly now. "The experience was

repeated the following day at exactly the same time and in exactly the same way."

"I . . ." Lydia's voice betrayed her, and she had to look away.

Thankful squeezed Lydia's hand and Mary Ann's firmly. "Do not be saddened. I am not. Oh, it grieves me to think of leaving my dearest Parley"—she pulled one hand free and rubbed her stomach—"and to think that I shall not be here to raise my son. But I have been filled with the most wonderful sense of peace and joy. I cannot describe it to you. I long to be gone. I count the days as though I were a hireling counting the remaining days of my servitude, or a prisoner the days until I am set free."

Lydia dropped her head and began to cry softly. Mary Ann was weeping too. Rebecca seemed to be in shock.

"Weep not, my dear sisters," Thankful said in a clear, steady voice. "We shall be apart for only a short time. Be faithful, so that we may greet each other again in the holy resurrection."

———————

In the early morning hours of March twenty-fifth, 1837, Thankful Halsey Pratt gave birth to an infant son. He was named Parley Pratt after his father. After the baby was cleaned and dressed, he was brought to Thankful. She embraced him tenderly for a short time, then passed away quietly about three hours after his birth. She was buried in the cemetery across the street from the Kirtland Temple, not far from Joseph and Emma Smith's infant twins, who had died at birth.

For a short time, the economic woes that were plaguing Kirtland were forgotten as the Saints turned out by the hundreds to weep and mourn the death of one of their sisters.

———————

As the wagon moved slowly toward the main square of Far West, Matthew Steed stared in open-eyed wonder. It had been six months since he and his father and Nathan had made their way up the gentle slope to the site of the new city and spent the night on the ground around Newel Knight's camp fire. He had been back to Far West only one time since then. Shortly after Christmas he had brought Jessica and little Rachel over to join in the brief celebration held by the Saints when they learned that the state had organized two new counties in northern Missouri.

There had been more people and more structures then than there had been in October, but not so many that it was surprising. Now he could scarcely believe his eyes. There were still tents and lean-tos aplenty, as there had been in October, but there were also dozens of permanent structures—log cabins, log and sod huts, even an occasional frame structure here and there. New buildings were under way everywhere he looked, and wagons filled with cut and uncut lumber rumbled past them almost continually. With a quick eye, Matthew counted, estimating what he couldn't see from what he could. He guessed there were close to a hundred buildings either finished or under construction, including, as near as he could tell, six or eight stores or places of business.

The city was on the highest spot of land in the vicinity, and the prairie—boundless and in the full blush of spring—spread out green and lush in every direction the eye turned. To the north, about half a mile, the lighter green of the prairie was bisected by the darker line of trees, just now coming into full leaf, that ran beside Shoal Creek. About the same distance south of town, another tree line marked Goose Creek. Both streams flowed east, Goose Creek joining Shoal east of town, then together continued on past the bend where Jacob Haun had chosen to place his settlement and eventually into the Grand River.

A soft breeze was blowing, moving the knee-high grass in slow undulations. Spring wildflowers were in evidence everywhere, and if one stopped for a moment, the soft drone of bees could be heard. Off to their right, a meadowlark was adding his cheerful song to the sounds of hammer and saw that were everywhere present.

Jessica leaned back in the wagon seat. She closed her eyes and tipped her face up so as to catch the sun fully. Her long hair fell behind her, bouncing lightly with the movement of the wagon. Matthew glanced at her quickly, and felt a quick rush of satisfaction. He had been shocked when they first saw Jessica last fall. The ague had taken such a toll that he had barely recognized her. She had lost considerable weight, and her dress hung on her bony shoulders like rags on a scarecrow. But most frightening were her eyes. They were like the ends of two burned-out sticks, charred and lifeless from a long-dead fire.

Now she had filled out again. Her cheeks were full and glowing with color. The gauntness was gone, and her eyes shone with health and life. More important, the coming of the three Steed men had worked miracles with her spirits as well. Using money Benjamin brought, they purchased five acres of government land for $1.25 per acre; built a cabin; bought a small wagon, a mule, a metal plow, and other basic tools; and purchased sufficient wheat and corn seed to plant their acreage. Jessica's teaching brought in a little cash money and enough food to see them through until Matthew could get a crop in. In one swoop, she had become much better off than many of the other Saints in Missouri.

Matthew's satisfaction came from knowing that his coming had been a major factor in that change. Though she loved the Lewis family, living in a small cabin with someone else's growing children had been more demanding on her and Rachel than she had expected. To have her own home again, no matter how simple, with beds for both her and her daughter, had buoyed her up. And when she had to be gone teaching, she knew that her daughter was in not only capable but also loving hands. Five now, and priding herself on becoming a young lady, Rachel was delighted to have her uncle tend her; her feelings for Matthew hovered somewhere between total adoration and complete infatuation.

Matthew turned to look at his niece in the back of the wagon. He smiled. Her head was jerking back and forth, her sky blue eyes neither wide enough nor quick enough to catch sight of every fascinating thing there was to see. For a five-year-old, a trip to Far West was like a journey across the ocean to a new world.

Jessica stirred, but didn't open her eyes. "They said the meetings would be at the new schoolhouse."

"Yes," Matthew answered. "We should be there in a few minutes."

———————

The sun was low, half-hidden by a scattering of fluffy cumulus clouds. Long shafts of light spread out from beneath the clouds like spokes in some vast, golden wagon wheel. In another half hour, Jessica realized, there was going to be a very spectacular sunset. She smiled slightly. How she loved the prairie! It had so many moods, so many faces, all of them clean and edifying and majestic.

Though they had received half a dozen invitations to stay with various families, she and Matthew had decided to camp out—she and Rachel in the wagon, Matthew underneath with his bedroll. During this time of year, the days were delightful, the nights cool and pleasant. Now she was glad they had made that choice, for she did not feel like making small talk or putting on a face for people.

"Look, Mama. Look what Uncle Matthew made for me."

Jessica turned to her daughter. She was holding out what had been, earlier that day, a stout length of tree limb, nine inches long and about three inches thick. Matthew had taken it from the small stack of wood that was feeding their cooking fire. Today was the sixth of April, 1837, and they had come to Far West to join the Saints in celebrating the seventh anniversary of the organization of the Church. The meetings had ended at about four o'clock. They had returned and had supper. Since that time, Matthew had sat on a short stump of a log and whittled away furiously at the tree limb with his pocketknife.

"My goodness," Jessica exclaimed. She took the wooden figure from her daughter, peering at it closely. It was the figure of a girl, a child. Her feet and legs were together, her hands tight at her side as if she were standing at attention. Jessica turned it so she could see the face more closely. There was no mistaking it. The features were rough-cut and lacked precision, but they were the features of Rachel Steed. The hair, down to the shoulder and soft with curls, was also clearly Rachel's.

"It's me, Mama. It's me."

"I know, Rachel." Jessica turned to Matthew. Her eyes were filled with surprise and wonder. "It really is marvelous, Matthew. I had no idea you could carve like this."

He shrugged, his cheeks coloring a little at the praise. "I always carve when I'm trying to get my thoughts away from other things."

She handed the doll back to Rachel. "When we get back home, perhaps we can make her a dress."

"Would you, Mama? Would you?"

"Yes. Did you thank your Uncle Matthew?"

Rachel nodded, but all the same, she whirled and in a moment had her arms around Matthew's neck, hugging him with all her strength. "Oh, thank you, Uncle Matthew. Thank you. I love her so much."

"You're welcome, Rachel. I'm glad you like her."

Jessica watched them for a moment, filled once more with gratitude that Matthew was with them. "Rachel," she called softly, "it's time to get ready for bed. Climb up in the wagon and get your nightgown on, then we'll read in the Book of Mormon for a few minutes before we say prayers."

Rachel immediately complied, setting the doll down carefully against the side of the wagon box where it could watch her as she climbed up the wheel and into the wagon. As she disappeared behind the canvas, Jessica moved over and sat down on the log beside Matthew. "That was very sweet of you, Matthew."

He was looking up at the wagon. "It was fun for me."

She gave him a sidelong glance. "Are you lonesome out here?"

That brought his head around quickly, but he only looked at her in surprise.

She reached down and picked up a branch that was half in and half out of the fire. For a moment she looked at the tiny flame consuming one end, then spoke again. "Do you wish you hadn't come?"

His eyes again registered his surprise. "To Missouri? Of course not. I have no regrets."

"None?"

"Well, I miss my family, of course. But no, I like it here. I get to farm my own land." He grinned. "I get to be the man of the house."

"I'm glad," Jessica replied, "because we're sure glad you're here."

Matthew reached out and touched her arm briefly. "Well, so am I. And if you'd like to know the truth, I—" He stopped as he caught sight of a figure out of the corner of his eye. He turned, then stood quickly. "Brother Knight. Hello."

Surprised, Jessica stood quickly, brushing at the back of her dress. Newel Knight was smiling nervously as he came over and joined them, shaking hands first with her, then with Matthew. At that moment, Rachel stuck her head around the corner of the wagon's canvas top. "I'm ready to read the Book of Mormon, Mama," she called.

"Just a moment, honey. We have company. You go ahead and play with your doll, and we'll be with you in a minute."

When Jessica turned back, Newel was watching her closely. He had swept off his hat and was twisting it round and round in his hands. "I'm sorry to intrude like this."

"No intrusion at all," Jessica smiled. "Matthew and I were just visiting. Won't you sit down? We have a little corn dodger and stew left."

He raised a hand quickly. "No, Sister Knight and I just had our supper. I'm fine. I . . ."

His discomfort was so obvious that Jessica felt embarrassed

for him. "Is there a problem, Brother Knight? May we help you in some way?"

He seemed relieved that she was that direct. "May I speak with you plainly, Sister Steed?"

"Of course." But his question surprised her. Brother Knight and Nathan Steed were such close friends, she had supposed he might have come to make sure Matthew was surviving all right without his family.

Matthew started away. "I'll see to Rachel, Jessie."

"No," Newel blurted. "Please stay, Matthew." He took a quick breath. "You're kind of the head of the house now. I think you need to hear this too."

Puzzled, Matthew nodded and stayed where he was. Jessica was perplexed too. She peered at Newel more closely, which did nothing to relax him.

"I come at the behest of another," he started. "I mean, I'm acting as his representative. He felt it improper to approach you directly."

One eyebrow came up and Jessica's perplexity deepened. "And who might that be?"

"Brother John Griffith. Do you know him?"

"Yes, we have met." John Griffith had come to Clay County a short time before the Saints had started to move north. Several weeks after Jessie had moved to Shoal Creek, he too came to Haun's Mill. He spent almost a month in the settlement with one of the families before coming over to Far West, where job opportunities were better. But that had been during her illness, and she had seen little of him or anyone else. He was a recent convert. She also remembered that he had lost his wife on the journey out from Indiana. He had two boys, both under five years of age.

"He's a good man," Newel continued. "An honest man and a hard worker."

"Yes, that is how I remember him."

"Good," Newel said with obvious relief. "He'll be pleased to hear that."

Jessica started. *Why would that please him?* But she had no chance to finish the thought.

"Brother Griffith knows this is a most unusual way to approach this. But he knew you were leaving first thing in the morning. He wanted you to have some time to consider it."

"Consider what?" she managed in a small voice.

Newel looked a little startled, as if he thought he had already made that clear. "He would like to propose marriage to you."

On January sixth, 1837, four days after the meeting in which the nature and the name of the Kirtland Safety Society were changed, the Kirtland Safety Society Anti-Banking Company began circulating its notes. Brother Jacob Bump, a former pugilist and recent convert, was the first person to receive the newly printed notes. Joseph came and declared to all present that if they would give heed to the Lord's commandments to be honest and faithful, all would be well. Others quickly followed in buying up the notes, and soon considerable amounts of the new currency were in circulation.

But almost immediately trouble began to rear its head. Other banks in the Western Reserve publicly announced that they would not accept the new notes as valid currency. Several newspapers, some vociferously anti-Mormon, called the new notes nothing more than "rags." When merchants in Kirtland refused to accept them in legal trade, the price of the notes began to fall. Rumors started to fly that Grandison Newell, one of Kirtland's wealthiest businessmen and a bitter opponent of the Prophet Joseph, was organizing the opposition. Non–Latter-day Saints began to buy up the notes at reduced prices, then brought them to the bank and demanded full payment in specie. Quickly a speculator's market in the notes began to form, and the bills were traded back and forth with no one knowing exactly what they were worth.

On the morning of January twenty-first, the *Painesville Telegraph*, one of the most virulent newspapers in its opposition to the Church, was distributed in Kirtland. The lead article announced that because the Church was violating the law and operating a bank without a charter, it was illegal to trade the notes of the Kirtland Safety Society. Anyone caught doing so would be heavily fined by the state. It wasn't true, but as is often the case, truth was the loser in the contest with emotion. The news raced through Kirtland like a mighty wind.

Nathan and Benjamin returned to the house just after noon of the twenty-third of January. Both looked exhausted. Lydia had come to wait with Mary Ann for the news. Rebecca sat with them, searching the men's faces anxiously. Young Joshua was playing a game with Emily on the table beside them. Little Nathan was asleep.

Lydia took one look at her father-in-law's face and turned to her son. "Joshua, will you take Emily out for a few minutes? You can play in the bedroom for a while, but not the one where Nathan is asleep."

Sensing something beyond his comprehension, without a word Joshua took Emily's hand and they left. Benjamin took off his coat and flung it in the direction of the coatrack. It missed, but he completely ignored it. "Two weeks!" he burst out. "Just barely over two weeks."

"What?" Mary Ann asked in alarm.

"They're in business two short weeks, and the system collapses."

Lydia turned to Nathan, her eyes wide and questioning.

He shucked off his coat wearily. "Sidney announced it just about an hour ago now. I tried to stop them. Get them to wait for Joseph. But they wouldn't."

"What?"

"They've suspended all payments in specie. The cash reserves have been seriously threatened."

———

On February tenth, another application for a bank charter for the Kirtland Safety Society was considered in the Ohio Senate. In this second application, the proposal for capital stock was reduced to three hundred thousand dollars. Along with six Church members (including Joseph Smith, Sidney Rigdon, and Oliver Cowdery), five influential non-Mormons attached their names to the application. In spite of that, the application was denied. Had the charter been granted, it would have accomplished two significant things. It would have done much to restore confidence in the bank and its legality. It also would have put Joseph and the other officers of the Society on firm legal ground and eliminated their vulnerability to lawsuits. But the charter wasn't granted, and that meant that in the eyes of the state of Ohio the Kirtland Safety Society Anti-Banking Company was not a legal banking institution.

———

In the early spring of 1837 the United States was fully caught up in an artificial boom economy, and Kirtland was right in the mainstream of it. In northern Ohio, land prices were rising at a dizzying rate. One piece of prime development land sold for ten thousand dollars. Four or five weeks later it sold again for twice that. Two days later the new owner was offered twenty-five thousand dollars and turned it down with a sniff of disdain.

In tandem with these dazzling opportunities for profit came the cheap money of the Kirtland Safety Society. Even the poorest were able to acquire some of the heavily devalued notes. One brother bought ten thousand dollars' worth of stock for $52.50. Suddenly people were "rich," and it was heady wine indeed. Borrowing heavily from the bank, many people bought more and more land in order to turn around and sell it for huge gains. With so little "real money" and so much paper available, inflation—already running wild—approached astronomical amounts. Prices on food and other commodities rose as much as a hundred percent in a few months. Unfortunately there was no corresponding rise in wages. Men who held thousands of dollars' worth of stock, land deeds, or bank notes couldn't purchase enough food to feed their families.

Instant "wealth" and crushing poverty. These were common neighbors in Kirtland by mid-March of 1837.

On May tenth, just sixty-seven days after the inauguration of Martin Van Buren as the nation's eighth president, the banks in New York City suspended payments to stop disastrous runs on their funds. Other northern city banks followed suit the next day. In what would later come to be known as the Panic of 1837, the conflagration spread like a prairie fire before a whistling wind. Eight hundred banks closed their doors and suspended payments before the end of the month. The U.S. government lost over nine million dollars in deposits held in some of its pet banks. Not all of these banks would fail, but during the panic money became extremely scarce. Creditors were no longer able to extend credit or postpone dates when loans were due. Prices—especially land prices—plummeted. What had been paper fortunes the day before were now worth less than the paper on which they were printed. Financial institutions found their bank notes worthless, irredeemable for even the most minimal purchases.

America was reeling. The infant nation, barely half a century old, was experiencing its first major financial crash and hurtling full tilt into its first full-scale economic depression.

Jessica Roundy Steed had only one Sunday dress, and it was showing signs of wear. Across the shoulder blades, where the dress pulled when she leaned over, the fabric was shiny and thin. The lace trim on the belt that tied at the back was starting to look frayed.

It didn't really surprise Matthew to see the dress in such a condition; he just hadn't paid attention to it before. He calculated quickly. Nathan had brought Jessica and Rachel back with him from Missouri when Zion's Camp had been disbanded in the summer of 1834. It had been only a few days later that Matthew's mother took Jessica and her daughter down to the Newel K. Whitney store and bought them both new dresses. That was the same dress that Jessica now wore, which meant that the dress was not quite three years old. But in a wagon, large wardrobes—even if Jessica had had one—were an unacceptable luxury. So for the last year it had been Jessica's only good dress.

But worn dress or no, Jessica looked as lovely as Matthew could ever remember seeing her. Her hair was a light brown, and she had always worn it straight and cut square at the neck. But a few months earlier Matthew and Rachel had teased her into letting it grow longer. Now it reached just slightly below her shoulders. She had brushed it until it gleamed, and it almost glowed in the subdued sunlight coming through the open cabin door.

Earlier that morning Matthew had gone walking along Shoal Creek until he found a patch of wild roses. He had cut several, carefully whittled the thorns off the branches, and brought them to her. It would be the only present he would be able to give her on this day. As she turned to face him, he was pleased to see that she had pinned one of the flowers in her hair. It was an appealing effect. It not only made her eyes seem a richer, deeper brown but also heightened the natural color of her cheeks.

Matthew looked at his sister-in-law more closely. There was so much color in her face that for a moment he wondered if she had somehow been hiding a supply of rouge from him all these months. But finally he saw that Jessica, who rarely showed any emotion, was nearly bursting with excitement.

Rachel was standing by Matthew's side. She too was in her only Sunday dress, a white and blue cotton gingham with little bows on the front. Her hair, half again as long as her mother's, was pulled back away from her face by a blue bow and hung down her back in long, dark brown ringlets. She looked up at her mother in wonder. "Oh, Mama, you look beautiful."

Pleased, Jessica did a small curtsy, then twirled around once, laughing softly in her self-consciousness. "Why, thank you, Rachel."

"You really do, Jessie," Matthew said. "You look lovely."

"Thank you for the flowers, Matthew. That was so sweet of you."

He nodded, then reached down and picked up the two bags she had packed the night before. As he did so, the smile on her face slowly faded and she looked around the cabin. It was plain, almost Spartan, in its furnishings, but it had been home to her and her daughter. Now she was leaving it.

She turned to Matthew. "Am I doing right, Matthew?" she half whispered.

"Of course."

She reached up and touched her face. "I'm too old to be a bride," she murmured.

He laughed right out loud. "You're only thirty-two, for heaven's sake. Now, if you were thirty-three, I'd have to agree with you."

It was the perfect response, this not taking her seriously, and she slapped him playfully. "But I *will* be thirty-three in just over a week." She laughed now too. "You're hopeless, you know that, don't you?" Then she sobered again. "I feel bad, leaving you here alone. You're still only sixteen."

"Seventeen in two more months," he corrected her. He lowered the bags to the floor again. "Look, Jessie," he said earnestly, "I'll be fine. I want to show Pa that I'm man enough to run my own farm."

"You are that, Matthew. You've been a marvelous help." She smiled warmly at him, thinking of what it had meant to her to have him with her and Rachel these past eight months. Then suddenly the reality of leaving hit her again—this time with even greater force. Her face fell as she looked around for one last time. "What am I doing, Matthew?" she whispered. "I barely know this man."

Matthew turned to his niece, who was looking up at her mother with sudden concern. "Rachel, you go make sure Old Red isn't pulling those reins loose from the hitching post, will you, hon? You can take the smaller bag out and put it in the wagon."

Pleased to be entrusted with such a task, Rachel picked up the carpetbag and lugged it out of the door. Matthew watched until she was out to the horse, then he swung back around. He gave Jessica a stern look. "He's a good man, Jessie."

"So you have no reservations?"

His mind started a little at that. It had been April sixth when Newel Knight had shocked them both with the news that John Griffith, a widower with two young boys, was proposing marriage to Jessica. Twice in the seven weeks since that time, Matthew had driven her to Far West. Once he had served as "chaperon" when Brother Griffith came to Haun's Mill and spent three days in the village. He had watched with mixed emotions as the gentle, quiet man courted his sister-in-law. At first, he had been filled with questions and concerns. Jessica had suffered so much, seen so much heartache. What if the marriage didn't work out? Was this just prelude to more sorrow? What if this man didn't treat her as she deserved? What if Rachel was given second place behind his own two natural children? What if? What if?

Then gradually his doubts had vanished. Part of that was due to his having come to know that John Griffith was a good man—quiet, but decent and filled with integrity. But more important, Matthew had seen Jessica change. She sang to herself, laughed right out at times, and sometimes her eyes were positively radiant. He would miss her and Rachel fiercely, but it was Jessica's time for happiness, and he wasn't about to stand in the way. "No, Jessie," he said firmly. "I have no reservations."

She shook her head ruefully. "I wish I could say that."

"Do you love him, Jessie?"

For a long time she looked up at him, her eyes wide and thoughtful. Then finally she shook her head. "I don't know."

One eyebrow came up, but Jessica was staring out of the door now and didn't see his reaction. Finally she spoke. Her voice was soft and far away. "Everyone talks of love these days, like it was the only thing that mattered in marriage." Pain darkened her eyes for a moment. "I loved Joshua, Matthew. I truly did. It didn't seem to make much difference."

Matthew nodded soberly at that.

"Is love such a great thing? It seems to me if a woman finds a man who is a good man, a man who is gentle with children, a

hard worker, a man who's honest, a man who believes in God
. . ." Her voice trailed off. Finally she looked up at Matthew.
"Maybe sometimes it's best to put love out of your head and
take what's there and be grateful."

Matthew watched her closely for a moment, then awkwardly he stepped to her. He put one arm around her and pulled
her up against his shoulder. Her eyes widened in surprise. This
was not Matthew. He was looking at her with a gravity far beyond his years. "You know this is right, Jessie," he said firmly. "I
can see it in your eyes."

That took her aback, but almost immediately she nodded.
"Yes," she admitted. "It does feel right. And I guess I'm ready for
a little happiness. It doesn't have to be a lot. Even a little will
do right now."

He smiled at her wisely. "You're overdue, Jessie. Way overdue." He stepped back and picked up the larger bag. "So let's get
you in that wagon and get on over to Far West and get you married."

"Oh, Lydia, look!"

Nathan and Lydia were returning from the Whitney store
and were just passing in front of Sidney Rigdon's home on their
way to see Nathan's parents. Across the street and slightly behind them was the temple. The front door had just opened, and
a small group of people were filing out. They were looking up at
the building, pointing and talking excitedly. It was this group of
people that had caught Nathan's eye. "It's Joseph Fielding!"
Nathan cried.

Lydia looked blank. The name didn't register.

"From Canada!" he blurted. "And those are his sisters, Mary
and Mercy. And look!" He took a step forward, the excitement
gripping him. "There, in the front. That's Brother John Taylor
and his wife." He grabbed her hand. "Parley said they were coming. Oh, Lydia, come on. I want you to meet them."

"That was a wonderful meal, Sister Steed," John Taylor said in that wonderfully rich and measured British voice that was so much his trademark. "You were most generous to have us for supper."

Mary Ann waved away the compliment. "After hearing so much about all of you, do you think we could pass up this chance to get to know you better?"

Only two of the families from Canada, the Taylors and the Fieldings, had accepted the invitation to supper at the Steeds. The others had other friends they wanted to see.

Mary Fielding, the older of the two Fielding sisters, looked at Mary Ann. "It is we who are pleased to meet you. We owe a great deal to Nathan and Brother Parley, and so it is a special pleasure to meet Nathan's family."

Six-year-old Joshua, Nathan and Lydia's oldest child, leaned forward over the table so he could see the two Fielding sisters. "Is it true you ran away from my pa the first time you saw him?"

Lydia's mouth dropped open at her son's boldness. "Joshua!"

But Joseph Fielding only laughed merrily. "Aye, lad, that's true. When my two sisters heard the Mormons were coming, they left the house and ran for the neighbor's. We had heard such terrible things about the Mormons, we didn't want to countenance any of it."

"And you, Brother Fielding," Brother Taylor laughed. "You said you didn't want to listen because the name 'Mormonism' had such a contemptible sound to it."

The Steed family chuckled at Brother Fielding's obvious discomfiture. Leonora Taylor looked at Joshua and smiled that quiet, gentle smile that Nathan had come to know well. "Brother Fielding said he wasn't about to listen to any new revelations, or about some religion that was contrary to the Bible." She turned now to Lydia and Nathan. "But Brother Pratt just took that as a challenge, of course. 'Now, Mr. Fielding,' he says, 'why don't you call your sisters home and we'll have supper to-gether. Then we'll all go to the meeting that has been called for this evening. And I promise you that I'll do nothing but preach the old Bible gospel, and I give you my word I won't say any-thing about any new revelations that are opposed to that old Bible gospel.' "

Mercy Fielding, much more the quiet one than her sister, spoke up. "We did come home. We fixed them some supper. We went to the meeting." Her eyes softened. "Not long after that, the three of us were baptized. That was just a year ago now."

Nineteen-year-old Rebecca Steed was sitting next to her mother, across from Mercy and Mary Fielding. "That's what makes this thing with Brother Pratt all the more troubling," she said sadly.

John Taylor's head came around sharply. "What thing is that?"

Rebecca was suddenly flustered. She thought they knew. Nathan jumped to her rescue. "You haven't heard?" he asked.

Brother Taylor shook his head. "Heard what? I was told that Brother Pratt has learned we are here in Kirtland and has asked to see me, but we stopped at his house this afternoon and he wasn't home. We plan to see him first thing in the morning."

Nathan sighed. He and Parley had been good friends before the mission to Canada, but the experience there had created an even stronger bond between them. Having to report this pained him greatly. "Well," he started slowly, "as you will learn soon enough, there are many problems right now in Kirtland." Nathan took a quick breath. "Ever since the bank started hav-ing difficulties and all the accompanying financial problems began to spring up, a spirit of contention and apostasy has swept through the Church here. There is hardly a quorum that is not affected by it to one degree or another."

John Taylor was nodding soberly. "I have heard that even some of the Quorum of the Twelve have become disaffected, that they are criticizing Joseph."

Lydia shook her head sadly. "They aren't just criticizing.

Some are saying he is a fallen prophet and want him to step down."

Leonora Taylor seemed shocked. Her husband was shaking his head.

Nathan's voice slowed, "Sadly, I must report that since his return from his latest trip to Canada, Parley has been caught up in that same spirit."

Joseph and Mary Fielding spoke almost as one. "No!" they exclaimed.

Mary Ann, always one to give people the benefit of the doubt, jumped in quickly. "I still think the death of Thankful has affected him deeply. And then, in his absence, there were some false accusations brought against him. Some of Joseph's enemies have said that these accusations came from Joseph himself. That really hurt Parley."

"But surely he didn't believe them!" Mary Fielding cried.

Nathan shook his head slowly. "I have tried to speak with Parley since his return, but he is filled with bitterness. He feels that Joseph has tried to profit, at Parley's expense, from some land sales they are working on. Also he claims that Joseph has turned some of the notes he holds on Parley's indebtedness over to the banks, which will put more pressure on Parley financially. He has even written a letter severely censuring Brother Joseph and Sidney Rigdon for their actions in relation to the financial affairs of the kingdom."

"I can't believe it," John Taylor breathed, the shock evident on his face. "Not Brother Parley. Not Brother Parley."

Rebecca looked at him. "That's what we said. But now a non-Mormon has taken that letter and is circulating it. The enemies of the Church are making much of the fact that Joseph is being condemned by one of his closest associates."

"Parley claims the letter has been tampered with," Mary Ann said, giving Benjamin a sharp look, disappointed that he had remained quiet through all of this. "He says it is a highly garbled version of what he actually wrote."

John Taylor stood abruptly. He looked down at his wife and

the Fieldings. "You stay here for a while." He turned to Nathan. "Nathan, would you accompany me?"

Nathan stood, the surprise evident on his face. "Of course. Where are we going?"

"We're going to go see Brother Parley."

Parley Pratt looked drawn, haggard, exhausted. He was also quite defensive. There had been a brief, warm reunion between him and John Taylor, but almost immediately Taylor had begun to question him, and Parley bristled like a cornered badger.

"Don't be too quick to judge, Brother John," he said curtly. "You have not been in Kirtland long enough. You do not know all that has gone on."

"Do you think I don't know what is right?"

Parley drew a hand across his eyes. "Who knows what is right anymore?" he whispered.

"You know that Joseph is a prophet," Nathan burst out.

"Is he?" Parley said, whirling on Nathan. "Is he? He prophesied that the Kirtland Safety Society would never fail. Now look at it." There was a derisive explosion of air. "Look at us who believed in that prophecy and invested in the Society."

"Did you ever hear Joseph make such a prophecy, Parley? Did you hear it from his own lips?"

"I . . . well, no, but others—"

Nathan cut him off, his voice tinged with a disgust of his own. "Those 'others' are men like Warren Parrish, Lyman Johnson, John Boynton. All of them filled with bitterness and hate toward Joseph. And no wonder. Joseph told me the other day he thinks that as much as twenty thousand dollars may have been embezzled from the bank." Nathan made no effort to hide his contempt. "Warren Parrish is one of the chief officers. Are you going to believe that kind of man? All Joseph has ever said was that if we followed correct principles, the venture would succeed. His enemies are saying this other thing about the prophecy to discredit him."

Parley opened his mouth to respond, then let it slowly close again. He turned to Brother Taylor. There was deep anguish in his eyes. "I deeply regret writing that letter. I do not know how it got into the hands of our enemies, but they have twisted it to their own purposes. I have never said that Joseph should be replaced or that God has rejected him. But he has made foolish mistakes. He has not acted in all ways in keeping with his high and holy calling. This disaster we are now facing, he should have foreseen it, warned us against it."

Nathan threw up his hands. "He did, Parley. Over and over. He told us that if we didn't put off this spirit of speculation and covetousness that has gripped us, we would see the results of our apostasy."

Parley stood, moving away from them. He started to pace the room. His shoulders sagged and his head dropped as he did so. "I do not know what to believe anymore," he said half to himself. "One part of me says that this situation must be corrected. Another part of me feels absolutely terrible about the feelings I'm harboring for Brother Joseph."

Standing now too, John Taylor stepped in front of Parley, blocking his path. He reached out and took his friend by both shoulders, peering steadily into his eyes. "Parley, listen to me. I cannot tell you how much your words surprise and sadden me. Remember that night at Mr. Patrick's house, the last one where you preached so powerfully? Mr. Patrick grew angry and said you could preach there no longer."

"Yes."

"You bore a strong testimony to the fact that Joseph Smith was a prophet of God. I heard you bear that testimony that night and many times afterwards, and was deeply touched by it. And that, more than anything else, convinced me the gospel was true."

Parley finally looked up to meet Taylor's gaze. "I know. Back then I *was* sure. I—"

John Taylor cut him off. "You also bore strong testimony to the truthfulness of the work Joseph Smith inaugurated. I heard you bear just such a testimony before you left Canada. You said you knew these things by revelation."

Brother Taylor shook him gently. "You said you knew these things by the gift of the Holy Ghost, Parley."

Parley's shoulders straightened a little. "I did."

"And you gave me a strict charge to the effect that though you or an angel from heaven was to declare anything else than that to me, I was not to believe it."

Parley's voice lifted a little with a touch of hope. "That's right. I did say that." Yet almost instantly his face fell again. "But that was then, Brother John. Things change. You don't know all that has happened. My brother Orson has told me things. . . ." He shook his head.

"Your brother is being fed a pack of lies," Nathan cut in sharply. "Warren Parrish is poisoning everyone's mind."

John Taylor still had one hand on Parley's shoulder. "Now, Brother Parley," he said with great solemnity, "it is not a man I am following, but the Lord Jesus Christ. The principles you taught me in Toronto led me to Him, and now I have the same powerful testimony that you then rejoiced in. If the work was true six months ago, it is true today. If Joseph Smith was then a prophet, he is now a prophet. You must not leave those feelings you once had, Parley. You must not!"

For a long moment Parley looked into the eyes of the man he had helped to convert. Then he looked away. "I don't know what I feel anymore," he said softly. "I just don't know."

———•———

Mary Fielding was what some people might have uncharitably called an "old maid." She and her sister Mercy were both in their thirties and, as some would say it, past the "marrying age." It had always been said of both sisters up till now, but Mercy was finally going to escape the dreaded title. Robert Thompson, who was another one of the converts resulting from Parley and Nathan's mission to Upper Canada the previous year, had come to Kirtland also. He and Mercy were to be married the following week by the Prophet Joseph.

As they walked along, Rebecca Steed wondered if the thoughts of her sister's marriage depressed Mary a little. There were no prospects of Mary's changing her own single status that Rebecca could see, and as old as she was, the future could not hold a lot of promise. But almost instantly Rebecca decided that Mercy's getting married would not likely make Mary unhappy. Mary seemed to accept what life had given her cheerfully and without regrets.

Rebecca had turned nineteen on the second of March, which meant that Mary was almost twice as old as she. But in spite of the age difference, the two of them had developed a closeness just since meeting each other the day before. Mary was more verbal than her sister Mercy, sometimes to the point of being quite forceful if she felt something strongly. Both sisters had a quick sense of humor; but Mary's was more subtle, and that made hers also the more delightful, because it had a way of sneaking around behind a person, then jumping out at them. Rebecca could tell right away that Mary was an intelligent and thoughtful woman and that she was filled with a deep commitment to the gospel. She and Rebecca became fast friends literally overnight.

About an hour before sundown on the twenty-sixth of May, 1837, Mary Fielding accompanied Rebecca Steed to the home of Joseph Smith, Sr., and Lucy Mack Smith, the Prophet's parents. As they came up the walk, Mary was quiet and quite reserved, something unusual for her. As Rebecca lifted her hand to knock on the door, Mary reached out and caught her hand.

"I don't have to do anything?" she asked.

Rebecca smiled. "Just bow your head and sit quietly while Father Smith gives you the blessing."

Mary bit her lip. Her hair was dark brown and straight. She wore it back, parted down the center, and pulled into a twist fastened with a silver clasp at the crown of her head. On someone else it might have looked severe, but on Mary it heightened the fineness of her features and the liveliness that played in her brown eyes. She was slight of figure and looked quite a bit younger than her nearly thirty-six years. "What if I'm not worthy?" she asked.

Rebecca looked grave. "Then the Lord will warn Father Smith. He'll stop right in the middle of the blessing and give you a listing of all your sins."

Mary's mouth dropped open. She looked horrified. "Really?" she breathed.

Rebecca couldn't hold it in. A giggle came bubbling up inside her. "Of course not, silly. I'm just teasing you."

Mary looked so relieved, Rebecca laughed all the more merrily. "You are worthy," she chided her new friend from Canada. "Besides, a patriarchal blessing is to help you. It will give you guidance for your life."

Rebecca knocked firmly on the door. "It's a wonderful thing when you think about it," she went on, as she stepped back to wait. "Imagine, our own personal counsel from the Lord. I can hardly wait to see what he has to say to each of us." In her mind she was remembering the thrilling experience she had had a little over a year ago, when she had attended a meeting and heard the patriarchal blessings that Father Smith gave Lydia and several others. Because she had not felt quite ready, Rebecca had not received hers on that occasion. But now she was sure the time had arrived to have the Patriarch to the Church lay his hands on her head.

There were footsteps and then the door opened. Lucy Mack Smith, Joseph's mother, was standing there in a dress and apron. She was barely four foot eleven, and had to squint up at them into the last rays of the setting sun.

"Hello, Mother Smith," Rebecca said. "We're here for the blessing meeting."

"Oh, come in. Father Smith is waiting in the next room."

"My dear sister, Rebecca Steed, in the name of Jesus Christ and by the power given to me as a patriarch in his church, I lay my hands on your head and give you this special blessing."

Rebecca felt a great calm begin to settle inside her. She loved Father Smith's voice. It was so deep and so resonant. And so dignified. He spoke very slowly so that the scribe could record the words with exactness. It was almost as if the Lord himself were speaking to her.

"You come through the lineage of Israel, even Jacob, the son of Isaac, who was the son of Abraham. You are of the tribe of Ephraim, which is of the house of Joseph. As a descendant of Abraham, you are entitled to all the privileges and blessings which were pronounced upon the heads of these great patriarchs of old. And just as Jacob gathered his sons and blessed them, so do I now bless you under the direction of the Lord.

"As a member of the house of Israel, you are privileged to come forth in the morning of the first resurrection. Be faithful and the time shall come that you shall be called up and crowned with glory and immortality and shall be privileged to live with your Savior and Master, Jesus Christ.

"You have been born of goodly parents, just as was Nephi of old. Stay close to them, follow their counsel, support them in their trials and they shall support you in yours."

A great sense of affection swept through Rebecca as she thought of her mother and father. On more than one occasion in her daily prayers she had thanked God for the privilege of being born into her family. She also prayed for her father daily. She knew he was struggling, and it frightened her. With an effort, she forced her mind away from that and concentrated on Father Smith's words.

"You have found the Church of Jesus Christ early in your life, and this is a blessing to you. Give of yourself to build up his kingdom on the earth and you shall lay up for yourself sheaves in heaven."

He paused, and she could feel his hands shift slightly on her head. When he continued, his voice seemed to deepen even further. "The Lord is mindful of the sacrifice you have made in order to prepare yourself for marriage."

Her eyes flew open in surprise. Many people knew that Arthur Wilkinson and she had broken off their relationship. But she had sworn her family to secrecy about her reasons for doing so. All she ever said was that it hadn't worked out.

"You have made the right choice. Be not discouraged with the results. Be patient. Be trusting. In his own due time, the Lord shall reward you for your goodness. You will find a good man, a righteous elder, who will make you the queen of his home. When that time comes, and you must be patient until it comes, you shall know of a surety that the Lord has heard and answered your prayers, for he has heard the cries of your heart."

Unbidden, tears had come to Rebecca's eyes and were trickling down her cheeks. Off to her left, she heard someone sniffing. *Mary Fielding*, she thought. And that made her cry all the more, for Mary Fielding had no husband, and Mary Fielding was almost thirty-six, not nineteen.

"You shall have children, both boys and girls, and they shall become the jewels in your crown. They shall be a joy to you. I give you this blessing in the name of Jesus Christ, amen."

Rebecca stood slowly, wiping at her cheeks with the back of her hand. She turned to the white-haired man who had just removed his hands from her head. "Thank you, Father Smith," she whispered.

He nodded, and took her hand in both of his. "That is a wonderful blessing, Sister Steed," he said. "You must live for it so that every one of those promises becomes yours."

"I will," vowed Rebecca Steed. "I will."

I don't like this, Father," Nathan said gloomily as they approached the temple. "We shouldn't be having a meeting without Joseph present."

Benjamin gave his son a quick look, then looked away again. "I think they are having this meeting because Joseph *is* away."

Nathan broke stride, looking at his father sharply. Benjamin saw the look of dismay but chose not to say anything.

"Is this another idea cooked up by Martin Harris and his little group?" Nathan did not try to disguise his contempt.

"Martin is not alone on this, Nathan, nor is he the leader."

"Oh, I know," Nathan shot back. "He's got the likes of Warren Parrish goading him on."

"*And* David Whitmer," Benjamin said quietly. "Not to mention at least three members of the Quorum of the Twelve. Five, if you count Parley and Orson."

"Parley is struggling right now," Nathan said flatly, "but he's not one of them."

"That's what you say. Others don't believe it. And there is some question as to where Oliver Cowdery stands."

Nathan started to retort, feeling his blood rising. But they were just coming up the walk to the great doors that were the east entrance to the temple. There were others there, some standing and talking, some just entering. Nathan took one last, whispered shot out of the corner of his mouth. "And where do you stand, Father?"

Benjamin didn't answer. They were almost to the nearest group of brethren. They stopped and shook hands. They greeted several others, then started for the door. As they stepped forward, for a moment they were alone again. Nathan looked across at his father. "You can't sit on the fence forever, Pa. Already there are people saying that your silence means that you are in agreement with them."

"Come on," Benjamin said, as though Nathan had not spoken. "Let's get upstairs or we're going to be late."

"Joseph is not a bad man," Warren Parrish said, his voice nearly oozing with charm. "No one is saying that. He has meant well, and he has tried hard." Suddenly his voice shot up in both volume and pitch. "But I say he has lost the prophetic gift." His fist crashed down on the pulpit, startling one of the older men near the back of the room who had started to doze. "He is a fallen prophet, and what has happened to the Kirtland Safety Society is proof of that."

"Hear, hear!" someone cried from the back.

Brigham Young was the senior Apostle present and felt compelled to speak. He swung around in his seat, his brows pulled down in a deep furrow, his eyes spitting fire. "We'll have order in this meeting, brethren, or we'll immediately dismiss and continue it at another time."

Parrish pounced on that. "Oh, no, Brigham. Now is the

time for action. We have already let this drag on, and look where it has gotten us. Only deeper and deeper into trouble."

John Taylor raised his hand, but Parrish shot him a withering look. "I have the floor at present, Mr. Taylor." Without waiting for a response, he swung back to the assembly of priesthood leaders. "We have several members of the Twelve present. We have both counselors in the First Presidency. We have leaders from the various priesthood quorums. I say we have sufficient leadership present here now to make a decision."

He stopped, his chest rising and falling. His eyes narrowed into two dark points of glittering triumph. "I hereby propose that this body act to solve the problem once and for all. I propose that Joseph Smith be removed from his office as prophet, seer, and revelator to the Church, and that our good brother David Whitmer be sustained to take his place."

The room broke out in instant pandemonium, but John Boynton, one of the Twelve, shot to his feet. "Second the motion!" he shouted into the noise.

"Strike the motion!" "Second the motion!" "Vote! Vote!" The cries rang out like shots from a volley of muskets.

Nathan looked around the room in horror. He had expected the opposition to bring forth their usual charges against Joseph—but remove him from office? He was stunned. He looked at his father. Benjamin returned the look, his face grim. He just shook his head.

Brigham Young was on his feet now too. He stepped to the podium, elbowing Parrish aside. He turned and faced the group, staring down at them with such fierceness that gradually the bedlam subsided a little. But there were still angry mutterings, and several individuals were in heated conversation.

"Brethren," he thundered, "we shall have order, or we shall clear this room."

As Brigham waited for silence, Nathan suddenly remembered something he had heard Joseph say some years before. There had been a meeting with some of the brethren. Brigham was asked to give the prayer, and when he did so he spoke in tongues. After the meeting, Joseph had said to some of those close by, "Someday, Brother Brigham will lead this church." It was clear now how that could be possible, for he stood like a lion, his eyes sweeping the room and daring anyone to resist further.

Finally, even the last undertones of whispering and muttering stopped. "Brethren." His voice had dropped again, and the contrast was such that several leaned forward to hear him more clearly. "I find it no accident that this meeting has been called while Brother Joseph is away. I wonder why it is that we do not have the courage to do this when Joseph is present."

Several heads ducked, or eyes turned away. "This is a crisis, brethren," Brigham went on. "This is a time when earth and hell are in league together to overthrow the Prophet and the Church of God."

Out of the corner of his eye, Nathan saw a man two rows behind him stir. He half turned. It was Jacob Bump, a small but wiry man who had been a boxer some years before. He was known for having a fiery temper and for being one of those most virulent in his attacks against Joseph.

Brigham ignored him. He had a fire of his own inside him at the moment, and he wasn't about to let someone make him hold it in. "It is obvious that the knees of many, even some of the strongest in the Church, have faltered."

His eyes raked those along the front two rows. There were nearly twenty of the opposition seated together. Among them were David Whitmer and Martin Harris. Next to these two sat the Pratt brothers, Orson and Parley (it had pained Nathan greatly to see the two brothers sitting with the dissidents). On the row behind them were Luke and Lyman Johnson, John Boynton, and William Smith. To the sorrow of the Smith family, Joseph's younger brother William, always headstrong and arrogant, had become sympathetic to the opposition, who, of course, milked that with great effect, for William was also a member of the Quorum of the Twelve. Between them, they represented a substantial portion of the leadership in Kirtland. But if Brigham was intimidated by either their numbers or their callings, it did not show.

There was a strong core of support for Joseph as well. Sidney Rigdon, First Counselor in the First Presidency, sat alongside Heber C. Kimball. And there were others who, though not in the Quorum of the Twelve, were part of the growing leadership in the Church. There was Wilford Woodruff, fearless and solid; Brigham's cousin Willard Richards; John Taylor and Joseph Fielding from Canada; Newel K. Whitney, the bishop of Kirtland; Lorenzo Snow, brother to Eliza Snow; John Smith, the Prophet's uncle; and others. While it was true that Brigham had formidable opposition to deal with, he also had a group of stalwarts behind him.

"Well, I tell you this," Brigham went on, the anger making his voice tremble slightly as he looked at the men who were trying to depose Joseph, "Joseph Smith is a prophet. He was called of God, and only God can release him. You may rail at him and slander him as much as you please, but you cannot destroy the appointment of a prophet of God."

Jacob Bump was up now, his mouth working in spasms. "This man is nothing but a lick skillet to Joseph Smith," he cried. "Who is he to speak like that to us?"

Brigham completely ignored him, still speaking to the group that composed the core of the opposition. "I'll tell you what you can do if you choose. You can't cut off Joseph's authority, for it comes from God, but you can cut off your own authority. You can cut the thread that binds you to the Prophet, and you can sink yourselves to hell, if you choose."

"Let me at him!" Bump yelled. He was dancing around, his fists up now. The men on both sides of Bump leaped to their feet and grabbed him by the shoulders. They were trying to restrain him, but he was writhing and squirming beneath their grasp. "How can I keep my hands off that man?" he kept saying over and over.

Brigham looked at him calmly. "Brother Bump, if you think

it will give you any relief, why don't you come forward and try and lay your hands upon me."

Jacob Bump continued to splutter and fume, but Nathan saw that the men restraining him were not having to struggle very hard to do it now. Nathan smiled a little. Brigham was not much taller than Bump. It would have been a good match. But suddenly the old pugilist didn't seem quite so enthusiastic about venting his frustrations.

Lorenzo Snow raised his hand, and Brigham immediately called on him. He was a younger man but held in great respect by many of the brethren. He stood slowly, then faced the group. "Brethren, I wish to speak in defense of Brother Joseph. I know that he has human frailties. Which of us does not? I am keenly aware of my own, but does that mean I cannot continue in service to God? Which of you are free of weaknesses and—"

Nathan was startled as his father suddenly stood. He looked up, for one instant panicked. He was afraid Benjamin was going to cut in, try to contradict what Lorenzo was saying. But Benjamin was not looking at Lorenzo. In fact, he was not looking at anyone. His head was down, and his eyes were fixed on the floor. "Excuse me," he mumbled to the man sitting next to him. And then he was out of the row and moving toward the door.

For a long moment Nathan stared after him, keenly aware of the other eyes that were doing the same. But then, almost without thinking, he was up and on his way out as well. Brigham gave Nathan a questioning look as he passed him. Nathan could only shrug and then move quickly after his father.

They walked up Chillicothe Road—or Smith Road—away from the temple, Benjamin taking long steps, Nathan hurrying to keep pace with him. Benjamin had not spoken a word since his abrupt exit. He had given Nathan a sharp look when his son had caught up with him on the stairway leading down to the front entrance, but he had said nothing.

Nathan couldn't bear it any longer. "Pa," he started tentatively.

His father swung his head around and glared at him. Nathan ducked his head a little but wasn't about to be deflected. "Pa, we have got to talk about this."

"I didn't leave that meeting because I wanted to talk," came the retort.

"I just want to—"

Benjamin made a sharp cut to the left, leaving Nathan on the pathway as he cut across the road. He looked over his shoulder. "Tell your mother I'll be home after a while. Tell her not to wait up for me."

Nathan came to a stop. He stared after the retreating back of his father. Benjamin did not turn around again, just strode off into the night.

The meeting in the temple took place on the twenty-seventh of May. Joseph returned to Kirtland in time for Sunday worship services the next day. During the services, Warren Parrish, supported by other dissidents, could not resist standing up once more and speaking out against the Prophet, even pronouncing a curse upon his head. Joseph—very much aware of the opposition movement that was afoot, but nevertheless exercising great patience in dealing with it—stood and spoke calmly but powerfully to the congregation of Saints, defending his position and simply stating that ultimately he would stand and his enemies fall. Several others expressed their support of Joseph as God's prophet. As one faithful Saint put it, "Joseph acted wisely, while all saw the spirit of his foe."

A group of well-meaning Church members sought to bring charges against some of the dissidents the following day, but procedural disputes frustrated those efforts, and no action was taken. And so for now the opposition appeared to have calmed somewhat, or at least it went underground again. The Saints seemed to breathe a collective sigh of relief, for the tension had reached a fever pitch in Joseph's absence.

On the first Sunday in June, the Saints gathered again for their Sabbath worship services in the temple. Nathan and Lydia sat on the third row back. Young Joshua—hair slicked back, and dressed in knickers, white shirt, and suspenders—sat next to his father. Little Emily, so much the image of her mother with her dark, long hair and wide, inquiring eyes—sat proudly next to him. Her mother had finished a new dress for her just the day before, and she was sure every eye in the room was taking note of it. Lydia held baby Nathan on her lap. He would be two in October, and looked with wide-eyed wonder on everything around him.

Nathan idly watched the people coming in. He and the family were seated near the west end, where the Melchizedek Priesthood pulpits rose in three grand tiers above the sacrament table. Already seated on the stand on one side of the pulpits were all the members of the Twelve who were presently in Kirtland. Joseph was moving among them, smiling and shaking hands. Nathan felt a flash of anger as he watched Luke and Lyman Johnson smile up at him as though there were not a thing wrong. And John Boynton and William Smith—it was as if there were not a problem in the world between them.

Brigham Young and Heber C. Kimball were seated side by side, being next to each other in seniority in the Quorum. There was a warm exchange between Joseph and Brigham, and Nathan guessed that Joseph had gotten a full report of Brigham's role in the meeting held while Joseph was away, and now Joseph was undoubtedly again expressing his gratitude to the faithful Apostle. Then Joseph turned to Heber. They too shook hands. Suddenly, Joseph leaned over and whispered something in Heber's ear. Heber's head jerked up so sharply, he nearly cracked Joseph's chin.

Nathan's eyes narrowed, intent on the interchange he was witnessing. It was obvious this was far more than a casual greeting. Heber's eyes were wide and filled with shock. He shook his head quickly. Joseph smiled and nodded firmly. Heber shook his head again, this time more slowly. Joseph said something else, smiling even more broadly, then reached down and patted him on the shoulder. Then he moved away.

A moment later Joseph went to his place in the pulpits, and the meeting began. But throughout the worship services Nathan's eyes kept stealing back to look at Heber C. Kimball. The Apostle did not seem to recover from his encounter with Joseph. He looked pale, dazed, as though he had been struck hard in the stomach and was having a difficult time breathing. Nathan wasn't sure what had happened, but he determined that immediately after the meeting he would find out what it was.

———•◆•———

Outside the temple there were still small groups of Saints here and there, but most of the eight hundred or so who had been in the meeting had left by now. Lydia had sent the children home with Benjamin and Mary Ann and then had joined in a conversation with Emma Smith, Elizabeth Ann Whitney, and Mary Ann Young.

Nathan stood by himself, watching the door to the temple. He had hoped to go right up and corner Brother Kimball after the meeting was over, but Heber had made an immediate bee-line for Joseph, and they fell into deep conversation. Now he had about decided Heber wasn't coming. But as he turned to call to Lydia that it was time to go, the door opened and Vilate Kimball stepped out. Her husband was right behind her.

Good, thought Nathan, they were alone. As he started toward them, the group of sisters called their greetings to Vilate. She smiled and moved over to join them. Heber stood for a moment, squinting in the bright sunshine. Nathan quickened his step and walked over to him.

"Ah, Brother Nathan," Heber said with a big smile. "And how are you on this fine day?"

"Fine, thank you." They shook hands, then Nathan gave his friend a sharp look. "Better than you, it seems." Nathan went on quickly. "I saw Brother Joseph lean over and whisper in your ear before the meeting. You haven't looked well since."

Heber managed a wan smile. "You're very observant, Brother Nathan. I have to admit, the rest of the meeting is a bit of a blur to me."

Nathan waited. He had been more bold than he should have been and felt that he could not pry further without exceeding the bounds of common courtesy.

Heber sighed. It was a sound of deep pain. "I am a man of such stammering tongue. I am altogether unfit for a work of such magnitude. How can I go preach in that land, which is so famed throughout Christendom for its learning, its knowledge, and its piety. It is the nursery of religion. The intelligence of its people is proverbial." He shook his head in despair. "How can one such as I expect to succeed in such a land?"

Nathan was staring at him. "What land?"

Heber looked surprised, then it hit him that Nathan couldn't have known what passed between him and Joseph. He put a hand on Nathan's arm. "You weren't present, Nathan, but the other day I heard Joseph make a most interesting statement. He said that something new must be done for the salvation of the Church."

"Yes, my father told me about that."

"Well . . ." Heber reached up and rubbed his temples with his fingertips. "Well, today he revealed what that new something is to be."

"What?"

The dazed looked came into his eyes again. "When Joseph leaned over, this is what he said to me. 'Brother Heber, the Spirit of the Lord has whispered: Let my servant Heber go to England and proclaim my gospel and open the door of salvation to that nation.' "

Nathan's jaw dropped. "England?" he echoed.

"Yes. England. Me! Heber C. Kimball. Son of a blacksmith. A man who makes clay pots with his hands. Heber C. Kimball, going to England, seat of an empire on which the sun never sets."

"That's wonderful, Heber! England! What a marvelous thing!"

"I felt intimations of this calling some months ago. In fact, I told Brother Willard Richards about it and promised that he would accompany me. But now that the call has come, I am overwhelmed."

Another thought hit Heber, and his eyes widened with wonder. "Nathan," he said with sudden eagerness, "do you remember the blessing you and I gave to Brother Parley more than a year ago now?"

"Of course. I'll never forget that." Nathan could not help but feel a twinge of sorrow at the mention of Parley's name, for there had been no sign that the Apostle had relented any in his disaffection.

"Do you remember what I said about yours and Parley's mission to Canada?"

Suddenly understanding dawned, and now Nathan's voice was tinged with awe. "You said our mission would lead us to a people who had been prepared by the Lord for our coming. And then you said . . ." He stopped, trying to recall the exact words.

"I said that out of your mission the fulness of the gospel would spread into England and cause a great work to be done in that land."

"Yes, but . . ." Nathan was confused now. "What has our mission got to do with your going to England?"

Heber gripped his arm more tightly. The full realization of all this was still hitting him. "After the meeting I asked Brother Joseph if Brigham could accompany me. I feel so inadequate for this task, and Brigham is so forceful. But Joseph said no. He has need of Brigham to stay here. But"—his voice rose in excitement—"guess who he *is* going to send with me!"

"Who?"

"Brother Joseph Fielding. Isaac Russell. John Goodson. John Snyder."

Nathan was staring at him. "The Canadians. The brethren we converted on that mission to Toronto."

"Yes, exactly right. Joseph Fielding has a brother living in a town called Preston, England. Near Liverpool. He's a minister.

Brother Fielding has written to him about the Church, and his brother has asked for more information." He stopped, suddenly a little overwhelmed. "I always wondered why it should have been me who was impressed to give Parley that blessing that night. Now I'm beginning to understand."

————◆————

Martin looked around furtively, then turned back to Benjamin. "I'd feel better if we were inside with the others, Ben. I don't like being out here in the night."

Benjamin's voice was flat and hard. "I'm not going in with that bunch, Martin."

John Boynton had come out with Martin to try and persuade Benjamin Steed to join the meeting going on inside Boynton's house. He looked offended. "No one is going to make you do something you don't want to do, Steed."

"I don't like Warren Parrish." He shot a look at Boynton. "I don't like it when members of the Twelve sit on the stand in the meetings with their pious faces, smiling and shaking hands with Joseph, then meet in secret to call him every name in the book."

Boynton reared back, his face contorting with anger. "Just who are you to be sitting in judgment?" he exploded.

But Martin cut in swiftly. "I don't like some things either, Benjamin. I know there are excesses in the group." He shook his head in bewildered weariness. "Some of them are even calling for a resolution that we reject the Book of Mormon." He too shot a fierce look at Boynton. "But I won't stand for that, Ben. You know that. I saw those plates. I saw the engravings. How could I ever deny that?"

Ben sighed. "But you do believe that Joseph is wrong?"

"Yes!" It was said fiercely. "Now especially. How dare he resign from the Kirtland Safety Society? He's the one who led us into it in the first place. He prophesied that if we invested our money, the bank would never fail. Now he resigns and transfers all his stock to others."

Benjamin turned away. "Nathan says Joseph never made that prophecy."

"I heard him," Boynton said flatly.

He swung around. "Did you? Did you actually hear it with your own ears?" This was an important point to Benjamin, and he had been trying to confirm it now for several weeks.

Boynton hesitated. "Well, I . . . Warren Parrish did. And Lyman Johnson."

"Two men of such high integrity," Benjamin said, with no attempt to hide his sarcasm.

Boynton bristled, but Benjamin turned away from him, deliberately ignoring him. "Did you hear Joseph say that, Martin?"

"No, but I believe Parrish." Martin decided to jump to the offensive. "What about what happened in those few weeks before the banks started suspending payments? You did hear some of those things for yourself. Right up to the last, Joseph continued to encourage people to invest in the bank. You heard him tell us to accept the bank's currency at face value so that it wouldn't add to the problems."

Benjamin's mouth opened and shut again. Martin knew full well this was the heart of what was eating at Benjamin. The Kirtland Safety Society had been caught in a situation that was causing banks to struggle all over the nation. That was understandable. But why hadn't Joseph foreseen what was coming? Why hadn't he warned them? Fortunes had been lost. Benjamin's investment of several thousand dollars—over three hundred in cash and two of his farms as collateral—was now worth less than a hundred, and even that was falling fast. If Joseph really was a prophet, why hadn't he told them to get out before the roof fell in?

"And what about Salem, Benjamin?" Martin pressed in hard, sensing his friend's uncertainty. "I was there in that meeting. You told Joseph it was pure foolishness to go off treasure hunting. Yet he still did it."

"Yeah," Boynton sneered. "How great was his prophetic gift then?"

"I . . ." Benjamin blew out his breath, not sure of anything anymore.

"I'm telling you," Martin said with great fervency, "Joseph has lost his authority. He's a fallen prophet, Benjamin. Even a blind man can see that."

Benjamin was suddenly tired. He had gone over it so many times. Back and forth. This side and that. Charges and denials. Fervent testimonials from both sides. Whispered innuendos and heated rebuttals. "I've got to go, Martin. Nathan and I are going in the morning to see Heber C. Kimball off on his mission. We'll go with him as far as Fairport Harbor."

Brother Boynton hooted in derision. "That fool. He asked if I might help him out financially, since he has so little money. I told him that if he's fool enough to answer the call of a fallen prophet, I won't give him a dime of help. And if he gets stranded over there, he'd better not look to me for help."

Benjamin looked at the younger man in disgust. "Well, he asked me too, and I gave him five dollars. I would give him more if I could spare it."

"Then you're a fool too."

"I can see, Brother Boynton," Benjamin said dryly, "that you are filled with the spirit of love for Heber, one of your fellow Apostles." Boynton's eyes instantly narrowed with anger, but Benjamin went on smoothly. "Brother Lyman Johnson doesn't think Heber should go either, but when Heber said he was determined to do so, at least Lyman gave him a cloak."

"Lyman is a fool too."

Benjamin had had enough. "Everyone's a fool but you, right, Boynton?"

"Look, Steed," Boynton said, stepping forward menacingly, "I don't have to—"

Martin stepped between the two men quickly, his back to Boynton. He grabbed Benjamin's arm. "You've heard that Joseph is deathly ill?"

Benjamin turned back slowly. "No, I hadn't heard that."

"Came on him just this morning. He can't even lift his head off the pillow. Some say he won't live through the night. It's that bad."

That was really a surprise to Benjamin. "I'd better go see him."

Martin was shocked. "Don't you understand?"

"What? What should I understand?"

Boynton's face was lit with triumph. "Joseph is being punished for his transgressions."

Benjamin snorted in open derision. "Come on!"

"Do you think this is all coincidence?" Boynton cried. "Joseph resigns his position in the bank and within a week he's on his deathbed? Warren Parrish pronounced a curse on his head for his wickedness. Now the curse is being fulfilled. You think about that," he added archly. "God is trying to tell us something."

Benjamin just shook his head and started to move off. As he moved across the front yard, his old friend and neighbor called after him. "Ben?"

He stopped but didn't turn around.

"The day's coming when every Saint in Kirtland is going to have to make up his mind which side he's on."

Benjamin smiled sadly to himself. His son had said the very same thing just a few days ago. "I know, Martin. I know."

Heber C. Kimball left on his mission to England on June thirteenth, 1837. He was accompanied by Orson Hyde of the Quorum of the Twelve, Willard Richards, the recently converted cousin of Brigham Young, and Joseph Fielding, a priest in the Aaronic Priesthood and a recent convert from Canada. The three other Canadian brethren who were to accompany them had returned to Toronto with the promise that they would meet the Kirtland party in Buffalo, New York.

At a little before nine on that morning, Nathan and Benjamin Steed arrived on Heber's doorstep. A small party of friends and family were going to escort the missionaries as far as Fairport Harbor (a twelve-mile journey), where the missionaries —in company with Robert B. Thompson and his new bride, Mercy Fielding Thompson, who were bound for Canada— would then catch a steamer to Buffalo. Heber lived east and north of town, so Nathan and Benjamin had agreed to pick him up at his home, then they would meet the others at the cross-roads next to the Whitney store.

As they came up the walk, the sun was already getting hot, and the front door of the Kimball home had been left open halfway. Benjamin stepped up to the door and raised his hand to knock, but the sound of a man's voice coming from inside stopped him. He listened for a moment, then quickly put a finger to his lips.

Nathan moved slightly to the left to get a clearer view inside. Through the partly opened door he could see the Kimball family. They were in a circle in the middle of the room, all on their knees, all with bowed heads. Heber was praying with his family. Embarrassed to have intruded, father and son stepped back a little, but Heber's voice still came to them clearly.

"O beloved father, thou who carest even for the sparrow's fall, and who feedeth the young ravens when they cry, I beseech thee now to provide for this good wife and for our little ones as I depart across the mighty ocean to the shores of a far distant land."

There was the sound of a stifled sob. Nathan thought it came from Vilate. Then as he listened more closely, he could tell that Vilate was not the only one crying. Benjamin swept off his hat and placed it against his chest. Nathan followed suit quickly. It was as though they had entered a cathedral. Suddenly it was too intensely personal and sacred for them to stand by as observers. They moved back away from the house. Heber's voice was still evident, but they could no longer hear the words.

After a few moments the voice stopped. Nathan saw the family stand. Heber looked out of the door and waved briefly, but he did not come out. A chair was secured and placed in the center of the room. In a moment Nathan understood why. Like the great patriarchs of old, Heber was taking his children one by one and giving each a father's blessing. That touched Nathan deeply. The memory of such farewells with Lydia and his own children was all too real. And the most he had ever been away was around six months. Heber would be gone perhaps as much as a year, maybe more.

Finally, there was a sound at the door, and Nathan turned. Vilate had come out now and was brushing at her eyes. Heber was right behind her, surrounded now by his three children. Eight-year-old Helen suddenly broke free from her older brother. "No, Papa, no!" she wailed, clinging to his legs. "Don't go. Don't go."

The brother gently pulled her free. She buried her face against his shoulder. Then, sobbing, Heber gathered each child into his arms one last time. He hugged them fiercely, smothering their hair and faces with kisses. Finally, he turned away blindly, waving through his tears. "Good-bye, dearest children."

The tears and sobbing became even more intense. "Good-bye, Papa." "Write to us, Papa. Please write to us." "Hurry home, Papa."

Heber groped for Vilate's hand, and they hurried over to where Nathan and Benjamin stood waiting. Vilate would be going with him as far as Fairport. "Come," Heber whispered, "I cannot bear another moment."

They went out of the gate and halfway down the block. Seeming to know exactly where he would get his last glimpse of his children, Heber stopped and turned. They were gathered in a little cluster, still at the front door. He waved once, then turned away, his head down, his lips trembling.

They walked on for several steps in silence. Finally, Heber looked up, turning to Benjamin and Nathan. "There is nothing—" His voice caught and he had to turn away again. When he finally got control he started again. Now he was filled with fierce intensity. "There is nothing, *nothing* that could ever induce me to tear myself from such a loving and affectionate family group except it be a great sense of duty and love for God."

His eyes filled with tears again, and he put his arm around his wife. "Nothing."

———•———

Caroline Mendenhall Steed watched her husband with a sense of wonder and amazement. Joshua had taken the baby from her as soon as she had finished nursing her. Now he sat in the rocking chair across the room. The baby was propped up in the crook of his left arm, so she was nearly sitting up, and with his free hand Joshua was gently pulling on the tuft of bright red hair, wrapping it between his two fingers and shaping it into a curl.

Caroline smiled, her eyes glistening. Donovan Mendenhall had never reacted to one of the children like this. "Joshua," she chided gently, "she's got to burp."

He looked up. "She's sitting up. This'll work just fine."

"On the shoulder is better."

He shook his head, then dropped his hand to rub gently up and down the center of Savannah's back. "I used to watch my mother do this with Matthew."

She looked up in surprise, then looked down again quickly before he saw her reaction. She waited for a moment, then casually she asked, "Matthew? Was he the youngest?"

Joshua nodded. "Yes." His head raised for a moment as he calculated. "Let's see, he'd be . . ." He gave it up. "I don't know, fifteen or sixteen now."

"Oh." She felt her heart race a little. This was the first time he had volunteered any kind of detail about his brothers and sisters. About five and a half months before this, when he had finally opened up and told her of his past, he had said little about the specifics of his family. Once or twice since, when she had tried to talk about it with him she had seen the walls go up again and so had not pushed him. "Did it work?" she asked after a moment, keeping her voice half-disinterested.

His thoughts had gone elsewhere. "What?"

"Rubbing the back like that."

At that instant Savannah exploded with a huge burp.

Joshua looked at her in surprise, then up at Caroline, an immense grin splitting his face. "Yeah," he said. "It worked."

Caroline laughed merrily, thrilled at the love and pleasure she saw in his eyes. She laid her head back against the chair's cushion, watching her daughter and husband. Savannah's eyes were wide open, and in the sunlight coming through the window they were already looking like they were going to go blue for sure.

Again Caroline held her breath for a moment. "Who was next?"

He shot her a quick look, and for a moment she thought he was going to shut her out again; but finally he looked back down at his baby daughter and began stroking her hair again. "Rebecca." His hand slowed its movement. "We all called her Becca. She had long brown hair and eyes that could just make you melt. She was probably most like my mother."

Caroline reached down and picked up the piece of sewing she had been working on before Savannah had awakened. She didn't want Joshua to see the excitement in her eyes.

"Then there was Melissa," he went on. "She was just four years younger than me." His eyes softened as he stared out of the window. "I heard she got married. Probably has three or four children now."

Still not looking up, pretending to concentrate on her sewing, Caroline waited for several moments; then, again as if she were half musing, asked, "So you had only the one brother?"

Joshua jerked around, his eyes suddenly hard. She felt her heart drop, but did not look up, just kept sewing as if she had already forgotten the question. She could sense him gradually relax again. But she knew somehow she had touched a nerve. There would be no more questions.

"I'll bet if you walked her, she'd go right to sleep again."

He nodded and stood up. He shifted Savannah so that she was now cradled in his one arm, then began walking slowly back and forth. For almost two full minutes the room was silent.

Then finally he spoke again, startling her with the answer to her previous question. "I have one other brother."

She glanced up, then back down quickly. "Oh."

"His name is Nathan. He's two years younger than me."

She could feel the tension in him, even across the room. She nodded nonchalantly. "Hmm," she murmured, going right on with her sewing.

"You're right," he said again after a few moments. "She's asleep."

"Do you want me to put her down?"

"No, I will."

He walked up the broad staircase that led to the upper floor of their new home. He was up there for nearly five minutes, and Caroline had to smile. She knew what he was doing. Supposedly he lingered to make sure she was asleep, but in reality he just loved to stand and watch her.

When he finally came down he walked to the coatrack and got his hat. "Well, I'd better put some time in at the freight office. Cornwell is beginning to think I don't remember we've got a business to run anymore."

He came over and leaned down to kiss her on the cheek. She looked up, her eyes filled with warmth. "That makes me very happy, Joshua."

He looked suddenly wary. "What?"

She had thought about saying something about his opening up about his family. She immediately thought better of it. "Your loving our daughter so much."

He laughed, the relief evident in his eyes. He reached down again, and this time he kissed her firmly on the lips. "It makes me very happy, Mrs. Steed, that you have given me such a beautiful little girl."

It was nearly eleven o'clock at night when Benjamin turned in at his gate and came up the path to his door. He was exhausted. They had walked all the way to Fairport, then stood around for nearly two hours waiting for the steamer to depart. Then they had walked the twelve miles back again. His feet ached, his eyes burned, and his back hurt abominably.

He opened the door quietly, then slipped inside. As he started down the hallway, he stopped. In the sitting room, outlined against the lighter square of the window through which the moon shone, he saw his wife's silhouette.

"Hello, Ben." He could hear the smile in her voice.

He moved into the room. "I told you not to wait up. I knew we would be late."

"I wanted to." She stood and came to him, putting her head against his chest. She was in her night robe and dress, and her hair was let down for sleeping. "How is Vilate?"

"Being brave."

"But having a difficult time?"

"Yes. But she's a good woman. She'll be fine."

"I know." She stepped back. "Do you want something to eat before you go to bed? Some bread and milk maybe?"

He shook his head. "I'd fall asleep over the table."

She took his hand. "Come on, then. Let's get you in bed."

They went upstairs. She slipped into bed, sitting up against the pillow, and watched him remove his boots in the darkness. As he stood and went to the basin of water to wash his face, she spoke. "Ben?"

He half turned.

"Joseph is worse."

He straightened slowly. "Worse than this morning? The missionaries wanted to bid him farewell, so we saw him for a minute. He wasn't good."

"Did you talk to him at all?"

"Not really. He wasn't even able to raise his head off the pillow to say good-bye to Heber and the brethren."

"Emma says he's been in excruciating pain all afternoon."

"Still no idea what it is?"

"No, not yet."

"That's too bad."

There was silence again for several moments. Then, "Ben?"

"What?"

"You need to go see him, Ben."

There was no answer.

"Whatever else your feelings are, Ben, you need to go see him. You owe him that much."

He reached for a towel and dried his face. Finally he sighed. "I know," he said. "I'll go see him tomorrow."

———◆———

Just before Benjamin turned in at Joseph's gate, the door to the house opened. Doctor Levi Richards, older brother to Willard Richards, stepped out onto the porch. His back was still to Benjamin as he spoke to someone in the house. Benjamin slowed his step. Finally, Richards turned and the door shut behind him. Benjamin met him just as he reached the front gate.

"Good afternoon, Brother Steed."

"Good afternoon, Brother Richards. How is Joseph doing?"

He blew out his breath and shook his head. "Not good."

"Any idea what's ailing him?"

The doctor shook his head. "It came on as sudden as a thunderclap."

Benjamin looked away, remembering John Boynton's gleeful response to that news and his diagnosis of the reason for Joseph's sickness. A curse from Warren Parrish, they were claiming.

"But Joseph has asked me to come both as doctor and priesthood holder," Richards continued. "I've laid my hands on him and blessed him. And, at his request, I have nursed him with some herbs and mild food. Don't know what more I can do for him now."

"Is he—" He stopped. "Someone said he was near death."

"Good heavens, no. At least I don't think so. He's a very sick man, but he's got a strong constitution."

"Thank you." Benjamin shook hands with him, then walked on past the gate and down the street, not looking back.

———•———

Benjamin walked the streets of Kirtland for nearly an hour, arguing with himself. If Joseph was that sick, he would not be up to visitors. He certainly hadn't been yesterday. Perhaps tomorrow he'd be better. And yet Mary Ann's words kept echoing in his mind. *"You owe him that much."*

He knew she was right. He just wasn't ready to face Joseph yet. He wanted to silence the questions first—the questions that had been haunting him now for months. The questions that Martin Harris and his friends were so sure they had already answered.

He swatted at nothing in the air in front of him, disgusted at himself for even listening to them. That's what irritated him so greatly about those who had turned against Joseph. They were so certain they had all the answers. They weren't questioning anything anymore, except how to get Joseph out. And yet he couldn't totally dismiss them either. Some of their reasoning was persuasive. Too persuasive!

As he always did when he reached this point in the dizzying spiral of his thoughts, Benjamin backed away. This part always shook him. For if Martin Harris and the others were right, then a whole new set of questions loomed before Benjamin Steed. And those questions were truly frightening. They not only struck at the very core of his own testimony but also threatened the entire fabric of his family life. And that left him feeling very cold and very alone.

He looked up. He was approaching the temple again. That meant that a block beyond that he would be to Joseph's home again. He stopped and started to turn, then stopped again. *"Whatever else your feelings are, Ben, you owe him that much."*

Suddenly he made up his mind. There would be no more vacillating. No more wandering the streets like a lost mongrel dog. *"You owe him that much."* "Yes, I do," he said aloud. He started walking swiftly northward, past the temple. He crossed the street, and this time when he reached Joseph's gate he turned in. Not allowing even so much as a moment's hesitation, he strode up to the door and knocked firmly.

There were footsteps inside, and then the door opened. It was Emma.

For a moment she blinked into the sun, which was behind Benjamin, then she smiled. "Why, Father Steed, how good to see you. Come in."

"I've come to inquire about Joseph. Perhaps see him, if he's up to receiving visitors. If not—"

Smiling even more broadly, she took his elbow. "Please do come in. If you had come two hours ago, I would have turned you away, but now . . ." She shut the door behind him.

Benjamin's eyes widened slightly. "He's better?"

"Come and see."

Joseph was propped up in his bed, a copy of the Doctrine and Covenants open on his lap. When the door to the bedroom opened and Benjamin stepped in, his face was instantly wreathed in smiles. "Why, Brother Benjamin, what a pleasant surprise." He started to get up.

Benjamin hurried quickly across the room. "No, don't get up, Joseph." He stopped as Joseph reached out and took his hand. He couldn't help staring. Joseph's color was good, his eyes had life in them, his grip was strong and firm. He couldn't believe it was the same man he had seen the day before.

Joseph saw the look and laughed heartily. "A little different than yesterday, eh?"

Benjamin nodded.

"Truly said. I am a new man. Doctor Richards was in this afternoon and attended to me with all tenderness and good will, and almost immediately the disease turned." He slapped his stomach. "Now look at me. I am still weak, but I can't believe the change in me."

Benjamin reached out for the wooden chair beside the bed. He pulled it to him and sat down slowly. So much for the idea that Joseph was cursed for his "transgressions."

Joseph seemed to discern his thoughts. "This should put down some of the rumors that are going about town, I'd say. Wouldn't you?"

Benjamin nodded in wonder. "I certainly would say."

Joseph's blue eyes twinkled merrily. "Some of the brethren are going to have to put their black suits away. There's not going to be any funeral tomorrow that I know of."

Benjamin gave a short laugh, thinking about John Boynton. Then the more he thought about Joseph's remarks, the more amused he became. "And who's going to pay the undertaker?" he chortled. "Warren Parrish?"

Joseph roared at that. That was about the only thing they hadn't done—built the coffin and hired the undertaker.

They chatted for nearly an hour. Twice Benjamin made as though he were going to leave, but Joseph insisted that he stay. He fired questions at him concerning the group's trip to Fairport. Who had gone? Did they get on the steamer all right? How was Vilate holding up? Wasn't that Mary Fielding a wonderful woman? Too bad she wasn't married. The Fieldings were good blood. Through it all, Benjamin marveled. This was the old Joseph. Though still showing some signs of having been seriously ill, he had his old vitality, seeming as though he would bounce right off the bed at times. Twice he laughed so loudly at something Benjamin said that Emma stuck her head in and gave them both stern looks—which only caused Joseph to beam all the more broadly.

Finally, Benjamin stood. "I really have to be going, Joseph. And you need to rest. Even if you are doing better, you shouldn't overdo."

"I know, I know," Joseph boomed cheerfully. The smile faded, and he grew suddenly earnest. "It was so good of you to stop by, Benjamin. I mean that. It's been wonderful to talk with you."

"It has been for me too."

Joseph gave him a sharp look. "I was beginning to fear that my old friend Benjamin Steed was starting to have doubts about Joseph too."

Benjamin couldn't keep a startled look from crossing his face. Then instantly he looked away, not able to meet those piercing, searching eyes. Joseph reached out and patted the chair seat. "Come on, Benjamin. Sit down. Now let's really talk."

———•———

"That really doesn't help much, does it, Ben?"

Benjamin let out his breath slowly, then finally looked Joseph right in the eye. "If you tell me you never prophesied that the Kirtland Safety Society would not fail, I believe you."

"Well, I didn't. I did say that if we would live by the principles God had established, the bank and our other financial efforts would prosper. And I still believe that to be the case. Had we only . . ." He raised his shoulders in a sign of resignation. "But we didn't, did we? Even now in the midst of disaster there are some who cannot see the connection between their actions and what is happening." He sighed. "That's why I resigned. I cannot countenance their actions any longer. I don't want them using my name to make people think that I do."

Benjamin shook his head in frustration. "But your leaving takes away the last confidence anyone has in the bank. There is no hope for it now."

Joseph looked at him sadly. "You really think I can save it now, Benjamin?"

For a moment he considered that, then finally shook his head. "No."

"What I feel most terrible about is that people—good people like you and Mary Ann—are going to lose a lot of money."

Benjamin looked away. "We already have."

Joseph nodded slowly. "I know. Would it help if I tell you that I have lost heavily too?"

With a start, Benjamin remembered a conversation he and

Joseph and Hyrum had had some months previous to this. "The funds you borrowed?"

Joseph's head bobbed once. "Gone."

Now Benjamin was understanding something else. "That's why you've been trying to sell off your land, isn't it?"

"Yes. The loans are overdue."

"Will you get enough to pay them off?"

"Not completely." It was said without rancor or bitterness.

Benjamin leaned back. Some of the brethren were saying that Joseph was selling off his land because he was trying to capitalize on other's misfortunes. But wasn't that how it always was? Twist the truth, shave off the corners here and there, then sell it as though it were clear and unvarnished reality.

Joseph cleared his throat. "I want to say something, Ben, but before I do I want you to know that you haven't been a murmurer. You haven't gone around whispering behind my back, making false accusations to everyone about me. The fact that you're here, asking me these questions straight to my face . . ." He nodded, the appreciation clearly written in his eyes.

"That isn't my way," Benjamin mumbled.

"I know. And I thank you for that. More than you know." He adjusted the covers across his legs for a moment. "But I want to teach you a principle, Benjamin. It is one of the keys to the mysteries of the kingdom. It is an eternal principle that has existed with God from all eternity."

"What is it?"

Now Joseph looked at him fully, the wide blue eyes filled with solemnity. "That man who rises up to condemn others, finding fault with the Church, saying that the leaders are out of the way while he himself is righteous, then know most assuredly that that man is on the high road to apostasy. And if he does not repent, he will apostatize, as surely as God lives."

Benjamin felt a chill run across his back. He had never seen Joseph so grave.

"And it matters not if that man has seen angels, or if he sits in the highest councils of the Church. The principle is still true."

Benjamin nodded slowly. Martin Harris and the others thought they were being so secretive, meeting at night behind closed doors, swearing others to silence. But Joseph knew. Benjamin felt a stab of shame. If Joseph knew that, he probably also knew that while Benjamin maybe hadn't joined them, neither had he rejected them.

Joseph was watching him closely. "Now, the Lord doesn't say that because his servants are so tender they can't handle a few lumps. You've known me for a long time, Ben. You're one of the few from the old Palmyra days. Criticism, ridicule, mockery— they've been my lot since that day I came out of the woods in the spring of 1820. A man can't be much of a prophet unless he's got a pretty thick skin."

"I can see that."

"It's not his servants God is trying to protect with this principle. There is something about murmuring that kills the Spirit of God. It was true of the Israelites. It was true of Laman and Lemuel in the Book of Mormon. You cannot turn against God's anointed without it grieving the Spirit."

Joseph was musing now. "It's not so much that God cuts off the murmurer; it's that the murmurer cuts himself off from God." For several moments the room was quiet, both men lost in their thoughts. Then Joseph finally turned back to face Benjamin. "There's something else I want to say to you, Ben."

"I'm listening, Joseph." And with a start, Benjamin realized he really meant it. He was listening now. Finally.

"Do you remember that meeting we held just prior to the departure of Zion's Camp, in which Brigham and his brother Joseph Young were concerned about whether or not Joseph should accompany us?"

"Yes. I remember it well. You promised them that if they would go, and follow your counsel, not a hair of their heads would be harmed."

"Yes, and what else, Benjamin?"

The memories of that meeting were still vivid in his mind. He and Nathan had been sitting side by side and had stared at each other in amazement at what followed. He looked into Joseph's face. "Then you startled every one of us by talking about the Church going to the Rocky Mountains."

A tiny smile played around the corners of Joseph's mouth. "Actually I startled myself a little when I said that. But the statement about the Rocky Mountains was only part of what I said that night. I said something about the destiny of the Church."

"You said that we knew no more about its destiny than a baby in its mother's lap." The memories were coming back sharply now. "You said that although we were only a little handful of priesthood brethren gathered there that night, the time was coming when the Church would fill North and South America and the whole world. You said there would be tens of thousands of Saints in the Rocky Mountains and that that would open up the way for the gospel to go to the Lamanites."

"That's exactly right, Benjamin." Joseph sighed. "It is hard to imagine now, isn't it? But that is our destiny."

Suddenly he pulled himself up into a full sitting position, leaning forward to peer at Benjamin intently. "Satan understands that destiny as clearly as I. And that causes him to rage, for when the kingdom fills the earth it will signal his final defeat." Now his voice took on a strange and powerful tone. "But let him rage. Let him bellow and roar and gnash his teeth. Let him stir up the hearts of wicked men against us. Even let him turn the hearts of those who have been faithful, those who sit in some of the highest quorums in the Church. It will not deter us from our destiny, Benjamin." He paused, his chest rising and falling now with the intensity of his words. "It will not. Indeed, *it cannot!* The Lord has his work, and no unhallowed hand can stay the hand of the Lord."

He leaned back against the pillow, as if the effort of sitting up had suddenly drained him. "You know Brother Ebenezer Robinson, don't you?"

Benjamin nodded.

"He visited me a while back and made a most interesting comment. We were speaking of these gloomy days. He said he knew that the gospel was true and that truth and righteousness will ultimately prevail."

Benjamin nodded again. "Yes, ultimately it will."

"That's right," Joseph burst out fiercely. "The gospel will prevail, Benjamin! I'm not just talking about gospel principles. They will always remain true and endure. I'm talking about the Church, Ben. God's kingdom on the earth. He didn't restore it to the earth to have it undone by men like Warren Parrish. This church will not fall! As surely as God exists, God's work—his church, his priesthood, his gospel—*will triumph!*"

Slowly the fire in him died, and he looked at Benjamin with some sadness in his eyes. "But all of this doesn't help you much, does it, Ben? It doesn't really get at what's eating away down inside you."

Once again Benjamin was a little taken aback by this man's perceptiveness. "It helps," he said lamely.

Joseph chuckled. "Bless you, Brother Benjamin. You make a terrible hypocrite."

Benjamin wasn't sure how to respond to that, so he looked away. Joseph reached down to the foot of the bed and retrieved the copy of the Doctrine and Covenants from where he had tossed it when Benjamin had first come in to see him. He opened it up to a place about midway through the book, turned a page or two, then finally looked up. "I'd like to read you something." He let his finger run quickly across the page, then began. " 'Although a man may have many revelations, and have power to do many mighty works, yet, if he boasts in his own strength, and sets at nought the counsels of God, and follows after the dictates of his own will, and carnal desires, he must fall and incur the vengeance of a just God upon him.' "

Joseph's eyes raised, and a sad and wistful smile pulled around the corners of his mouth. "Do you know who the Lord was speaking to there?"

Benjamin remembered that revelation well. "To you," he answered softly.

"Yes. It came not long after I gave the one hundred and

sixteen pages of manuscript from the Book of Mormon translation to Martin Harris and he lost them."

He looked down and picked up where he had left off. " 'Behold, you have been intrusted with these things, but how strict were your commandments.' " His eyes skipped further down the page. " 'Behold thou art Joseph, and thou wast chosen to do the work of the Lord, but because of transgression, if thou art not aware thou wilt fall.' "

He closed the book and lay back against his pillow. "There is hardly a day that goes by that I don't remember that warning, Benjamin. It is a heavy burden to act as God's servant. I do not take it lightly."

"I have never thought that of you, Joseph," Benjamin said firmly. He meant it. His questions were of a different nature.

"I know, Benjamin. Don't you think I know what's bothering you? Is Brother Joseph still a prophet of God or is he not? Isn't that it?"

Benjamin's head came up slowly. Count on Joseph to hit something head on and not try to dodge.

"Has God rejected Joseph? Oh, he's a fine fellow and all that, but has he lost it? The power? The calling? Isn't this at the nub of your problem, Ben?"

Benjamin swallowed quickly, trying to collect his thoughts, to come up with an appropriate response. "Joseph, I—"

"No, I don't want you to try and answer that. I just want to say this to you, Ben. I've sensed your doubts. I know the whole Salem experience raised many questions in your mind." He laughed briefly. "And you've always thought I was such a wonderful businessman."

Benjamin laughed in spite of himself. "Especially when it comes to being a storekeeper."

Joseph smiled in agreement, then slowly sobered. He lifted the book he still held in his hand and turned it over slowly. "When I gave Martin that manuscript back in the summer of '28, the Lord had told me two different times not to do it, but I did not listen. I would not follow his will. That's why I lost the power to translate."

Now he turned his full gaze on Benjamin, and his eyes seemed to pierce right through to the very soul. "I have never claimed to be anything but a man, Benjamin. I am more keenly aware of my weaknesses than any five of my bitterest enemies. But I tell you with all the candor of my soul that this time it is different than it was back in '28. I have been"—he smiled that sad smile again—"human. But this is the Church of Jesus Christ. He is my Master. It is him I have to please. Not Warren Parrish. Not the clamoring voices of men blinded by their own greed and wickedness. I tell you, I have not been unfaithful to my Savior. So I care not what others may say. *I have not been unfaithful!*"

Benjamin was deeply moved. He had never seen Joseph speak so frankly of himself and of his calling. "I . . ." He shook his head. "Look, Joseph, I don't know what I feel anymore. I'm not trying to be difficult. I just—"

Joseph reached out and laid a hand on Benjamin's knee, stopping him. After a moment he spoke very slowly. "Benjamin Steed, I want you to listen to this carefully. Some who have stood by my side in the most holy and sacred of experiences are now turning their faces away. Even some of the Twelve and the Presidency are wavering. But all that matters not one whit to you. There is only one thing you must deal with. There is only one issue for Benjamin Steed. Is Joseph still God's chosen?"

He pulled his hand away, but his eyes never left Benjamin's. "And no one can answer that for you. Martin Harris can't tell you if God is pleased with Joseph. Oliver? Frederick Williams? David Whitmer? Brigham Young?" He shook his head. "None of them can. Not even *Joseph* can tell you if God is pleased with Joseph."

For a long moment the room was silent as the two men looked at each other. Then Joseph, suddenly weary, lay back on his pillow. "Only God can tell you that, Benjamin. Only God."

Nathan looked up in surprise. He and Lydia were sitting on the grass in front of the house of the Lord. They had
gotten Emily and little Nathan to sleep, then gone out for a
walk, leaving young Joshua to watch them. It was an evening in
early July and nearly full dark now. The air was pleasant, still
carrying some of the heat of the day but cooling off quickly. So
they had stopped to talk, neither one anxious to return to the
stuffiness of their little house. Now across the street from them
Nathan saw a man walking along slowly. His head was down,
and his hands were behind his back.

"Is that Brother Parley?" Lydia asked, noting that Nathan's
attention had been diverted.

"Yes, I think so."

As they watched, the man stopped. He had just passed the
Sidney Rigdon home. The next home on that side of the street,
another few rods further north, was that of the Prophet Joseph.
The man seemed to be staring in that direction. He took an-

other step or two, moving even more slowly now. Again he seemed to be peering at the spot some yards ahead where the lights of Joseph's house were burning.

"What's he doing?" Lydia asked softly.

The man had stopped again, turned, and started back the way he had come. Then he stopped again, obviously agitated.

"I don't know," Nathan said, standing to get a better look. "It is Parley. There's no mistaking that walk of his. Maybe we should go over and speak with him."

Lydia stood now too. "He seems exercised about something."

"Let's go across and see if everything is all right."

Lydia nodded, and slipped an arm into her husband's, but after a few steps she pulled him to a stop. "On second thought, you'd better just go."

Nathan was surprised for a moment, but then quickly he saw the wisdom of it. Since Parley's disaffection with Joseph, Parley's relationship with Nathan had been strained. "Are you sure you don't mind?"

"No, I'll just go on home. You take what time you need."

He gave her a quick kiss on the cheek, grateful for her sensitivity. "Thank you." With a quick wave, he bid her farewell and cut across the street. Parley had moved forward again, still slowly, but was now some yards ahead of where Nathan and Lydia had been sitting.

Nathan strode out quickly, and as he approached, the sound of his footsteps on the path brought Parley around with a start.

"Parley, it's me. Nathan."

There was a quick look of surprise, followed by one of relief. "Oh. Good evening, Brother Nathan."

"I'm sorry to intrude, but I was across the street. I saw you pacing. Is everything all right?"

The heavy brows that covered those normally piercing eyes lowered quickly. "No. I don't think that is how I would choose to describe my current situation."

"What is it, Parley? Can I help in any way?"

There was a short exclamation of disgust, aimed at himself—a characteristic that, Nathan had learned while they were together in Canada, was typical of Parley's personality. "You tried once and it didn't seem to take," he muttered.

"I beg your pardon?"

"You and Brother John Taylor. Surely you have not forgotten that night the two of you came to my door and tried to help me."

Nathan understood now. "No, I haven't forgotten."

"Nor have I," Parley said in a low voice, his eyes on the ground. "Do you remember what Brother John said to me that night?" He didn't wait for an answer. "'Parley Pratt, when you were in Canada you bore a strong testimony to the fact that Joseph Smith was a prophet of God. I was deeply touched by your testimony. That, more than anything else, convinced me the gospel was true. And you gave me a strict charge to the effect that though you or an angel from heaven was to declare anything else than that to me, I was not to believe it.'"

He finally looked up and peered into Nathan's face. "Thomas B. Marsh has been laboring with me and Orson." There was a short, mirthless laugh. "I guess as senior Apostle he thought the Pratt brothers might need a call to repentance."

"Maybe he thought the Pratt brothers were not as far gone as they thought they were," Nathan corrected him softly.

"How could I have been such a fool, Nathan?" It came out in a burst.

Nathan felt a peculiar thrill as he saw the look in his friend's eyes. It was a glimmer of the old Parley—the Parley who stood undaunted and unflinching in the face of a large crowd hurling insults and epithets, the Parley who could open the Bible and preach a two-hour sermon on the prophecies of the Restoration. And then, to his surprise, Nathan thought of that night—so long ago now, it seemed—in a room above a saloon in Independence, Missouri, when he had flung angry words at his brother, trying to goad him into repentance. "Most of us are fools about one thing or another at some point in our lives, Parley," he said, smiling sadly.

"But to turn against Joseph . . ." Parley's voice was heavy with anguish. "I am one of the Twelve. How could I have been caught up in the lyings and railings so easily?"

Nathan reached out and grasped his hand. "Does that mean you are convinced of your folly?"

"Aye," Parley murmured, "and tormented by it."

"Then go to Brother Joseph. Tell him."

Parley's head snapped up and he stared at his friend. Then he turned and looked to where the windows in Joseph's house were alight. "That was the very thing on my mind," he said. "But I am so ashamed. How can I face him after what I have done?"

Nathan gripped his hand tighter. "But you must, Parley. You must!"

For a long moment, Parley stared into the eyes of the man who had gone with him to Toronto and with whom he had shared so many incredible experiences. Then a great shudder shook his body. He fell on Nathan's shoulders. "You're right, of course," he cried in relief. "Of course you're right. Will you come with me, Nathan?"

Nathan held his friend in a crushing grip. "Of course, Parley."

It was Joseph who came to the door. He was barefoot, and his shirt was pulled out of his trousers. It was past nine-thirty, and he had obviously begun his preparations for bed. When he saw who was at the door, his eyes widened, then immediately a smile crossed his face. "Brethren, come in, come in."

He invited them into the sitting room, and for several minutes Joseph chatted warmly about nothing of consequence, mostly talking to Nathan. Through it all, Parley remained subdued, saying little except when asked.

Finally, Joseph turned to Nathan, then to Parley. "I sense this is not simply a social call," he said with an encouraging smile.

Nathan shook his head. "No, Joseph, it is not. Parley wanted to come to you. He has some things to say. He asked if I would accompany him."

Joseph turned to Parley, his clear blue eyes curious but also open and supportive. "Yes, Parley?"

Parley's hands were twisting around and around. His head was down, his eyes on the floor. Finally he looked up. A great sob welled up inside him, then burst out in one anguished cry. "Oh, Brother Joseph, can you ever forgive me for what I have done?"

The two of them stood outside the front gate to Parley's house. To the east of them the dark shape of the temple loomed against a moonlit sky. Each seemed lost in his thoughts, but then at last Parley spoke.

"He easily could have removed me from the Quorum."

Nathan gave a quick shake of his head. "That is not Brother Joseph's way."

Parley's voice was tinged with wonder. "Instead he frankly forgave me. No bitterness. No recriminations. Just that wonderful, sincere 'I forgive you, Brother Parley. Thank you for coming back with a sincere heart and a contrite spirit.'"

"You did that, Parley," Nathan said, his heart filled with gratitude. This night had relieved a terrible burden from his shoulders. His friend's near defection had troubled him deeply. "You *have* shown a broken heart and a contrite spirit."

Parley nodded, looking at Nathan. "My dear friend," he began, but his voice caught and he had to stop. Finally, swallowing hard, he went on. "How can I ever thank you for caring enough to come with me? The feelings of darkness and oppression are gone. I am filled with light and joy. I see now so clearly the contrast between the spirit that has been over me these past weeks and the spirit I now feel. I shall ever more be able to discern more clearly between those two spirits." He sighed, and it was a sound of happiness, relief, and regret all at once. "I think now, because I myself have been tempted in all points in this matter, I shall be better able to bear with, excuse, and succor those who are tempted in a like manner."

Nathan looked at his friend sharply, but Parley did not see his reaction. They shook hands and said good night. Then Nathan started towards his home. He walked slowly, troubled by his thoughts. There was one in his own family who was "tempted in a like manner," as Parley had put it. That was Nathan's own father. Martin Harris, Parrish, Boynton, and the Johnson brothers were all wooing Benjamin Steed incessantly. It would be a great coup if they could persuade him to throw in with them. And the fact that his father had thus far refused to totally repudiate them infuriated Nathan. It was a source of considerable tension between father and son.

Could he, as Benjamin's son, say as Parley had just said, that he was able to bear with and succor those who were tempted as Parley Parker Pratt had been? It was a question Nathan could not immediately and honestly answer, and that troubled him deeply.

———————————•◆•———————————

There is an old but hallowed saying in England. "The king is dead. Long live the king."

On the twentieth day of June in the year of our Lord, one thousand eight hundred and thirty-seven, William IV—king of the United Kingdom of Great Britain and Ireland and king of Hanover—closed his eyes in death. He was in the seventh year of his reign and the seventy-second of his life. In this case, the saying had to be slightly modified. "The king is dead. Long live the queen."

Next in the line of succession was an eighteen-year-old girl. She was the only child of Edward, duke of Kent, and Princess Victoria, daughter of Francis, duke of Saxe-Coburg.

At the time she came to the throne, the monarchy was neither liked nor respected. The royal family had spawned a succession of weak and selfish leaders, and most Britishers held the crown in low esteem. But this young woman would go on to rule England for sixty-three and a half years, the longest reign in the history of the British monarchy. She would usher in an age so shaped by her influence that it would be named after her. She would preside over Great Britain when it was at the apex of its power. She would hold herself so much above reproach and prove to be such a wise and capable monarch that the throne would once again be raised to a position of veneration and respect. Few queens in England's history would die more beloved than Queen Victoria.

On the twentieth of June, 1837, England lost a king and gained a queen. Exactly one month later, on July twentieth, after eighteen days and eighteen hours on the Atlantic, the British packet ship *Garrick* anchored in the Mersey River, opposite the city of Liverpool. On board were seven elders of the Church of the Latter-day Saints. Soon they would be standing on the pier at Prince's Dock.

———◆———

It was two days before Election Day in Preston, England. The new queen had ordered a general election for members of Parliament, which would be held on Monday. By midafternoon on Saturday, the 22nd of July, the streets of Preston were thronged with thousands of people. It was overcast, but the temperature was in the low seventies, and the day was quite pleasant—more pleasant than staying in the sweatboxes that passed for houses. The factories had declared a half-day holiday—something almost unheard of—and the population had turned out to celebrate. Candidates from the two parties were noisily vying to call attention to themselves. There were flags flying everywhere. Ribbons and posters were in abundance. Here and there, hastily erected booths offered the populace a chance to talk face-to-face with the hopefuls.

But the pubs outdrew the booths ten to one. They were islands of pandemonium in a sea of chaos, and it was obvious that, for the most part, the people had turned out because of the holiday and not because of a great interest in the elections. For those not in the pubs, vendors worked their way through the crowds, adding their shouts to the bedlam. They offered candy, nuts, apples, dried plums, or, most commonly, fish and chips wrapped in newspaper—the fish cooked whole with the heads and scales and fins still on, the potatoes cut in thick wedges and deep-fried in boiling oil.

As Derek and Peter Ingalls pushed their way through the sea of humanity, Peter's eyes were wide and shining with excitement. Derek smiled, but not without a touch of sadness. He hadn't seen Peter this excited since he had been a little boy waiting for a spoonful or two of Christmas trifle, too little to understand how desperately poor they were and how long it would be before there would be another. Derek, who would be twenty in October, had long ago lost his capacity for getting excited over things like today's festivities.

"Oh, look, Derek," Peter breathed, pointing eagerly. Derek turned. A group of nearly a hundred children were marching toward them down the middle of the street. Some of them clutched upside-down pots and pans against their stomachs and banged away on them with spoons. They had been told that they were to get the attention of the crowd, and they had set themselves to the task with great enthusiasm. They were making a most wonderful racket, and most of the crowd stopped what they were doing to watch them pass. Behind the percussion section some older children held up hand-lettered placards, all of which read: "Mr. James Cogglesworth, Tory, House of Commons."

"What do the Tories believe again, Derek?"

"The Tories—or, as they now prefer to be called, the Conservatives—want to keep the power with the Church of England and with the crown. The Whigs want to give more power to the common people."

Derek tried not to look smug. Three months ago he knew little more than Peter about English politics, but then Derek had noticed that at the end of each week Mr. Morris, the factory owner, took all the newspapers he had accumulated out to the trash. It took several days, but Derek finally worked up his nerve and asked if he might have them. Morris seemed pleased and gave him his blessing. Derek now spent a good part of each Sabbath day voraciously reading them while Peter played with his friends. It had been a wonderful boon, not only because it helped satisfy his natural hunger for knowledge but also because it was polishing his reading skills at a rapid rate.

Peter looked up at his brother. "So we'll vote for the Whigs, then?"

Derek gave a short, bitter laugh. "Poor folk like us aren't allowed to vote, Peter. We're too ignorant to know anything, don't you know? Only the gentry and the lords and the ladies have enough savvy to do that."

"Oh." In a moment any thoughts of politics were gone from Peter's mind. The children were passing them now, and the racket was actually painful to the ears. But Peter didn't care. He wiggled his way in so that he was right up next to the passing parade. Derek moved up behind him, amused and pleased. It was little enough pleasure a thirteen-year-old factory worker got out of life. Let him enjoy the moment, no matter how brief.

Peter's eyes were dancing with excitement as the rows of children trooped past. These were obviously the children of Preston's upper and middle classes. They were all in school uniforms. There was not a dirty shirt or dress or a bare foot among them. A handsome lad of about Peter's age was looking at the faces of the people. His eyes came to rest on Peter for a moment. Peter's nature was to be cheerful and friendly. He smiled broadly at the boy and sang out, "Afternoon, mate."

A look of distaste instantly darkened the boy's face. He turned his head, studiously avoiding looking further in Peter's direction, and banged all the harder on his steel kettle.

Derek saw the crestfallen look on his brother's face as he stared at the boy's retreating back. He reached over the shoulder of one of the boys and touched Peter's shoulder. "Come on, Peter. I have tuppence in my pocket. Shall we have a go at a candy stick?"

They crossed the street and plunged into the throngs on the

far sidewalk. Derek caught the eye of one of the candy vendors. In a moment they both were sucking on sticks of peppermint candy.

The two brothers fell in with the crowds, letting themselves be carried along for a minute or two. As they turned and moved down another street, a clatter behind them drew their heads around. "Make way! Make way! Stage is coming! Clear the way!"

A black carriage, drawn by four horses whose necks and flanks were flecked with sweat, was making its way slowly toward them. The people in the street were giving way but not fast enough, and the driver had his team reined in tightly. The press of people was making the animals nervous. Their eyes were wide behind the blinders, and their hooves struck an occasional spark off the cobblestones as they danced their way slowly forward.

"It's the stage, Derek."

"Yes." He glanced up at the sky. Through the overcast he could see that the sun was down about halfway toward the sea. That meant it was about four o'clock in the afternoon.

"From Liverpool, I'd say," Peter said knowingly.

Continuing another half block down the street, the carriage approached the front of the building where it made its usual stop. The driver pulled the horses over to the curb and reined them to a halt. "Preston!" He leaned down to call into the coach. "This is it, gentlemen!"

Peter and Derek continued up the street until they reached a spot near where the carriage driver had stopped. There had been seven men inside the coach. Now they had gotten out and were standing around and stretching, waiting for the driver and his assistant to get the luggage down from the carriage. Half-curious, Derek stopped to watch. The men were different, a little peculiar in a subtle way, but he couldn't decide why.

One of them, a balding man built somewhat along the lines of a large barrel of rum, turned to the driver. "We seem to have come on a holiday, sir," he said. "What's the occasion?"

Derek leaned forward. The man spoke strangely, his voice flat and nasal sounding. It was not a Lancashire accent, that was for sure.

"Election Day is coming up, day after tomorrow," the driver said. "The new queen has called for general elections for members of Parliament."

"Oh."

Another man, slightly younger than the first, shook his head. "And I thought elections in America were a wild affair."

Peter clutched at Derek's arm. "Did you hear that, Derek? They're from America."

That was it, Derek realized. Their dress was different, their boots, the way they brushed their hair, their bearing—nothing dramatic, but definitely not British. He had seen an American or two before, but he had never been this close to one before. He and Peter edged a little closer.

Return passengers had come out from the coach station now, and the driver and his companion were loading their luggage on the top of the coach. Finally they were loaded and the carriage moved off. For a moment the seven men stood around, looking a little confused. Then the barrel-chested man looked up. As the coach had pulled up, two men on ladders had been unfurling a large banner and hanging it over the entrance to the building. Preston was the hub of a significant temperance movement that fought the excessive drinking problems so common to Britain's working classes. They were taking advantage of the holiday crowds to put up a temperance banner. It was that banner that caught the American's eye now. The others, seeing him, tipped their heads back as well.

Derek looked up too. The banner was made of canvas, and on it, in large gilt letters, three words had been painted: "Truth Will Prevail." The Americans seemed transfixed by it.

The large man read it aloud. "'Truth Will Prevail.'" He turned and looked at his companions, his eyes filled with amazement. "Do you see that, brethren? Truth will prevail!" He turned to the younger man standing next to him. "Brother Hyde, can you think of anything more seasonable? Could there be any sentiment more appropriate to our arrival here than this?"

"No, Brother Kimball, I cannot think of anything more fitting."

The first man, the one they called Brother Kimball, looked up again, his face infused with joy. "Amen!" he cried aloud. "Thanks be to God! *Truth will prevail!*"

Derek was sitting on the front step of the two-story red brick house, the cellar of which he and Peter shared with two other men. In foul weather he would have been forced to stay in the cellar, squinting to read in the dim light that came through the two narrow and filthy windows. But on this Sabbath day the morning overcast had burned off by ten, and now it was a bright, clear, wonderful day in Preston. Derek was methodically working his way through the newspapers he had brought home from Mr. Morris's office the day before, enjoying the warmth of the sun on his arms and head.

"Derek! Derek!"

He lowered the newspaper and looked around. Peter was coming down the street at a dead run, eleven-year-old Jenny Pottsworth in tow behind him. They slid to a stop at the bottom of the step. Peter's chest was rising and falling in great gasps. Jenny was panting like a winded puppy.

"What is it, Peter?"

"The Americans!" He gulped in a quick breath. "At Vauxhall Chapel."

"What?"

"Those men we saw yesterday."

"Yes, what about them?"

"The Rev'rend Fielding . . ." Jenny pitched in, but then she too had to catch her breath.

Derek nodded, trying not to smile at their excitement. The Reverend James Fielding was the pastor of a congregation that met in the Vauxhall Chapel. Mrs. Pottsworth, Jenny's mother, had recently started to attend the reverend's church. "Yes, I'm familiar with Mr. Fielding. What about him?"

Peter was starting to get his breath. "Those men are preachers," he blurted. "Mission'ries."

Derek's eyebrows lifted. "You mean the Americans?"

"Yes. Except they ain't all from the United States. Some are from Canada." He had to stop for breath before plunging on. "One of them is the Rev'rend Fielding's brother."

"Hmm," Derek said, still not seeing what had got the two children so worked up.

"Me mum and me went to church this morning," Jenny said, obviously proud to be the source of their information. "Those men were all there. Mr. Fielding had invited them. At the end of the services, he stood up and—"

"Who stood up? The rev'rend or one of the strangers?"

She realized Derek was teasing her a little. She put her hands on her hips, jutting out her lower lip. "The Rev'rend Mr. Fielding," she said, shocked that he could jest about something this important, "stood up at the end of the services, and he said there was gonna be a meetin' this afternoon at three o'clock. And one of them elders from America would be doin' the preachin'."

Derek feigned surprise. "They didn't look that old to me."

Both children looked blank. He fought to hide a smile. "You said he was an elder. They looked pretty young to me."

Peter looked offended. "Derek! It ain't funny."

"Sorry." He was fast losing interest. He lifted the paper again.

Peter came up the steps and grabbed his arm. "Can we go, Derek? Can we, huh?"

That brought Derek's head up. "What for?" he asked bluntly.

"I want to hear them," Peter said in exasperation.

Derek shook his head firmly. "I've told you before, Peter. Church ain't for no poor people like us."

"Yes, 'tis," Jenny burst out. "Me family and me go all the time now."

Mrs. Pottsworth had always been inclined to run after this church or that, but Derek didn't say anything, just shook his head again.

"Tell him about the dreams, Peter," Jenny urged.

"Oh, yeah," Peter said, relieved that there was something more to revive Derek's interest. "Mrs. Fielding told Mrs. Pottsworth that her husband's brother—the one from Canada, Joseph Fielding is his name—and others have written letters to them from Canada during the past year. In the letters they claim they've found a new church that's just like Christ's church in the Bible. It has prophets and Apostles and everything."

Jenny darted up the steps and slugged Peter on the arm. *"Tell him about the dreams!"*

"I am, Jenny, I am." He took a deep breath. "When Rev'rend Fielding got the letters, he read them to his congregation. They decided they would pray for these men to come and bring them the gospel."

The newspaper lowered again.

"Since they started praying, some of the people have had dreams. In the dreams they saw men coming from across the sea to give them the gospel."

Derek was impressed in spite of himself. "And?"

Peter's eyes grew wide and filled with awe. "Well, the people are saying these men are the same men they saw in their dreams. Especially the big man who's the leader. The one we saw yesterday."

"The one they called Kimball?"

"Yes, that one. A lot of people say they recognized him the moment they saw him."

Derek leaned back, the doubt heavy on his face.

Jenny's right hand jerked up to the square. "Swear it!" she said solemnly. "Me mum heard the people say that with her own ears."

"It's true, Derek." Peter was pleading now. "That's why I

want to go hear them preach. Can we go, Derek? Oh, please."

For a long moment Derek looked at the two innocent, ex-cited faces. Finally, he shrugged. "I suppose it can't do any harm."

By quarter of three the chapel was packed, and Derek and Peter had to wiggle their way forward through the crowd—win-ning themselves several nasty looks—before they found seats on the edge of one of the side pews where they could slip out easily if this proved to be what Derek expected. Twice in the next fif-teen minutes Derek nearly changed his mind and got up and left. He felt completely out of place. While many in the assem-bly were obviously factory workers—more than one from his own shop—there was also a generous sprinkling of the middle classes. Neither Derek nor Peter had any kind of Sunday best. They had been hard-pressed to put a little polish on their shoes, wash their faces, and run a comb through their thick hair. Derek had even gotten a sliver from a stick and tried to clean out the dirt from beneath his fingernails. But now when he looked around at some of the others in their Sunday finery, he felt as conspicuous as a beetle on a tablecloth.

Peter spotted Jenny and Mrs. Pottsworth near the back and gave a little wave. Derek wished they hadn't seen them. Mrs. Pottsworth could talk the tail off a monkey, and he was sure she would be over to discuss their mutual experience when the meeting was over.

Finally, the meeting began. The Reverend James Fielding led them in a hymn and offered a brief prayer of invocation; then, thankfully, he went right to the task at hand. "We have come to hear the mission'ries from North America. They claim to have the gospel restored to the earth. We shall now turn the time over to Elder Heber C. Kimball, from the land of Ohio."

A man stood up and walked to the pulpit. It was the same man who had been so impressed with the banner yesterday at the coach stop. "*'Truth Will Prevail.'*" Derek could still hear the joy in his voice as he read the motto.

Derek watched Kimball closely. He had a deep mistrust of those who claimed to be pious. Too often he found it only ran Sabbath-deep. During the rest of the week some of God's most vocal "friends" were small and petty at best, mean and vicious at worst. But he was pleased to note that Kimball carried no air of haughtiness or arrogance. He was a plain man with an open face and wide, pleasant eyes that seemed to hold no guile in them.

"My dear brothers and sisters," he began. His voice was deep and rich, and foreign-sounding to Derek's ears. Kimball turned briefly and nodded to the pastor. "We—my companion missionaries and I—are most grateful to the Reverend Mr. Fielding for this opportunity to preach to you. Mr. Fielding, I can't thank you enough. We hope to make this a most profitable hour and a half for all in attendance."

As the pastor acknowledged the thanks, Derek was fascinated by the distinctness of the American's voice. The short vowel sounds Kimball pronounced were flat and nasal. He said "can't," not "cahn't," and it was "Deehr brothers and sisters" instead of the softer "deahr." And the way some of the words came out with more syllables was strange: it was "mish-u-nair-ies" rather than simply "mish-un-ries." But what sounded the strangest of all, he breathed sound into his *h*'s, so that it came out "have" rather than "ahve," and "half" rather than "ahf."

But then as the American preacher continued to speak, Derek stopped listening to the sounds and began to listen to the words.

"We have come from across the sea to share with you a most important message. Mr. Fielding tells us that you have prayed with much faith that you might find the truth. Well, we have come to share the truth with you. In the Old and New Testaments we often read of angels ministering unto men. We are here to tell you that angels have again come down from heaven to restore truth and bring back the authority of the priesthood. The Church of Jesus Christ has been restored to the earth again. It is patterned after the church that Jesus founded while he was here on earth."

There were one or two murmurs as people leaned over and whispered to each other. They seemed impressed.

Kimball reached inside his ample coat and withdrew a small brown book and held it up high. "We have come to tell you about a sacred book of scripture that has been translated by the gift and power of God. This book comes from ancient records, hidden up in the earth under the direction of God. They were brought forth by an angel, an angel come from the presence of God, and translated by a man named Joseph Smith."

"Glory to God," a woman behind Derek breathed. "Amen," said the man sitting beside her.

Derek was mesmerized. He had heard probably only one or two sermons preached in all his life. The memories were dim and clouded now, but he could remember that he was frightened. He couldn't recall now whether the fear came from what was said or from how it was said; he just remembered the feelings of being afraid. There was none of that now. Kimball did not pound on the pulpit or speak with great dramatics. He spoke simply. He spoke plainly.

He gave a brief history of the man he kept referring to as Brother Joseph. Derek had not read the Bible. He knew virtually nothing about it except what he had heard others say in idle conversation. But he was deeply interested as Heber Kimball called their attention to what he termed the "first principles of the gospel," and told of the restoration of the priesthood, which was the power to act in God's name. He was intrigued as Kimball walked them through various New Testament passages which described what the Church of Jesus Christ was like in ancient times. Then he testified that this new church was organized following that same pattern. And when Kimball said that he and one of the other missionaries were two of the Twelve Apostles in the new church, Derek was very impressed.

When Kimball finished, Elder Hyde, the other Apostle, arose. Like Kimball, he was a young man, just in his early thirties. He didn't add much new but spent his time bearing witness to the truthfulness of what Kimball had taught. The crowd was hushed and attentive, and Derek was amazed when he glanced at the windows to see that the sun had lowered noticeably. He had sat in church, had listened to two sermons for more than an hour, and had been scarcely aware of the passage of time.

Hyde stepped to "Brother Kimball," as he kept referring to him, and took the book from him. "This book," he said, holding it up high, "is called the Book of Mormon. It gets its name from the prophet Mormon, who wrote most of what we find in the pages of this book." Still holding it high, he opened it with one finger so they could see the pages. "It contains the fulness of the gospel of Jesus Christ. It contains many things which have been lost or taken out of the Bible over the centuries since it was written." He grew very sober. "Most important, it testifies of Jesus Christ. It contains a most glorious account of his visit to the people who lived in America, after his resurrection in Palestine."

That created a small stir among the people.

"That's right," Hyde said, lifting his voice higher. "There was a people who lived in Palestine many years ago. They were led to the promised land by God. The promised land is in America. And after he was resurrected and showed himself to Peter and Thomas and Mary and all the others there in Jerusalem, Jesus came to the people in America. He came down from heaven. He walked among them. They saw and felt the prints of the nails in his hands and feet. They were allowed to thrust their hands into his side where the spear had pierced him through."

His voice grew thick for a moment, and Derek was amazed to see that the man was deeply touched. "It is a wonderful account, my brothers and sisters," he said huskily. "It is my favorite part of the Book of Mormon."

Finally he lowered the book. "But that is not the part I want you to read first." He opened it to what looked like the last few pages. "Here," he held it up again, "this is what I want you to read. It is a promise given by the last prophet to write on the plates. Let me read it to you. It is on page 586."

Derek glanced at Peter. He was transfixed and didn't even see that Derek was looking at him.

"Here is the promise. 'And when ye shall receive these things, I would exhort you that ye would ask God, the Eternal Father, in the name of Christ, if these things are not true; and if ye shall ask with a sincere heart, with real intent, having faith in Christ, he will manifest the truth of it unto you, by the power of the Holy Ghost.' "

As Derek had expected, Jenny's mother had come right outside and located him and Peter. What Derek had not expected, though, was that he didn't mind at all. They talked eagerly of the afternoon's experience and of what they had heard. Like him, Mrs. Pottsworth had been very impressed with the message of the Americans. Finally they prepared to leave, but Derek wasn't ready, and he asked Mrs. Pottsworth if she would see Peter home. He promised he would follow shortly.

At last the missionaries came out of the Church. In the lead was Joseph Fielding, the reverend's brother. He was talking with the reverend's wife. Then, a moment later, the others came out. Heber C. Kimball was deep in conversation with the minister and another couple, but to Derek's relief, Orson Hyde was at the rear, pretty much alone. Derek also saw that he still held the book in one hand. He sidled up to him carefully. "Mr. Hyde?"

Hyde turned and sized Derek up quickly. What he saw was a broad-shouldered, strapping fellow with the features of a twenty-year-old and the eyes of a much older man. "Yes, lad."

"I . . ." He shoved his hands into his pockets, suddenly embarrassed by his boldness. "I was wonderin'. That book . . ."

"Yes?"

"Where might I get a copy that I might read it?"

Hyde nodded thoughtfully, looking him up and down with new interest. "Can you read, lad?"

"Aye." Derek thought of the leather bag of coins carefully hidden away in the coal pile in the cellar where they lived. It was still pitifully light. If the book was too much, he'd have to pretend that he wasn't that interested after all.

Hyde held out the book to him. Derek stared at it. "Go on, take it, young man. We've got only a limited number of them, so I can't let you have it permanently. But as you heard, we'll be preaching here again tonight and then on Wednesday night. Do you think you could have some of it read by Wednesday?"

Derek took the book, holding it carefully so as not to drop it. He looked up into Hyde's face. "Yes, sir! I could have it nearly all read by Wednesday, sir."

"Then it's yours. Take it, Master . . . ?" He let the sentence hang.

"Ingalls. Derek Ingalls."

"Take it, then, Master Ingalls, and return it read to me by Wednesday evening."

Derek whirled around and ran down the church steps. As he got to the bottom, he suddenly remembered his manners. He stopped and turned. "Thank you, sir. Thank you very much."

"You're welcome," Hyde laughed. And then as Derek raced away, he called after him. "Don't forget the promise at the end of the book. Page 586."

"I won't," Derek called over his shoulder. "I won't."

The little stub of the candle had finally melted down into a puddle of wax in the bottle lid. The flame began to sputter and crackle softly.

Derek looked at his younger brother, whose eyes were closed. "Peter?" he whispered. The two men who shared the cellar with them were long since asleep, and waking them up would only bring a stream of curses and maybe a hurled boot or something.

Peter's eyes opened immediately. He hadn't been asleep.

"The candle is nearly burned out."

"I know."

Derek frowned, looking at the flickering remains of the only light source for their side of the cellar apartment. "The meeting t'morrow night starts right after supper. There's no way we can finish the book by then."

Peter's shoulders rose and fell. "Maybe they'll let us keep it longer."

"Maybe." Derek didn't have much hope for that. Brother Hyde had said they had only a few books with them, and with the large crowds they had drawn to both Sunday services, they would almost certainly have many requests for books.

He closed the Book of Mormon and set it down on the small crate that served as their only table. The scrap of paper he was using for a bookmark was stuck in the book not quite two-thirds of the way through. They had read steadily all of Sunday afternoon and evening, and then had done the same last night and tonight as soon as they got home from work. But it was difficult reading for two who were still mastering the art of reading. There were many strange words. And they often stopped to talk about what they had just read. Derek's greatest disappointment was that they had not yet come to the story of Jesus appearing to the people in the Americas that Brother Hyde had talked about.

The sputtering and crackling had ceased now. The melted wax was nearly consumed, and the flame had shrunk to half its normal size. Peter turned over on his side so that he could look at his older brother. His eyes were large and dark in the flickering light. "Derek?" he said softly.

"What?"

"Would you pray with me?"

Derek straightened, fighting a sudden sense of panic. "What?"

"The mission'ries said we should pray about whether the book is true."

"I know. I . . . well, I've been kinda doing that inside."

Peter looked pleased. "Me too," he confided. He hesitated. "Is that good enough?"

Derek looked away. "I don't know."

Peter looked up at him until Derek finally turned and met his gaze. Peter's eyes were filled with longing. He didn't have to put words to it; Derek read him perfectly.

"I ain't never prayed before, Peter," Derek whispered.

The disappointment filled Peter's eyes. "I know," he said.

After a moment, he turned over and snuggled down against the mattress. "It's all right."

Derek sighed in exasperation. Peter knew full well how to get his brother to do his will. But then, Derek realized, he was glad in a way, for he was filled with a longing of his own. "All right, Peter, I'll try it."

Awkwardly he climbed off the bed and knelt down. Grinning with pleasure, Peter scrambled off to join him. He knelt beside Derek, his shoulder pushing up against that of his brother.

For several moments, Derek knelt there, feeling beneath his arms the roughness of the straw under the mattress ticking and with his knees the hardness of the brick flooring. His tongue felt like a piece of stone inside his mouth. He took a quick breath, then another. Then he plunged in.

"God . . ." He stopped. That didn't sound right, but for the life of him he couldn't remember how the pastor had started his prayers at the meeting. Perplexed to be stopped at his first word, he rushed on. "Peter and me, we ain't been much for church." He swallowed quickly. "We hope you'll forgive us for that. It's not that we don't believe in you, it's just that . . ."

It occurred to him that if God really existed, he didn't need Derek to be giving him any excuses. He decided to get on with what they wanted to say. "God, Peter and me, we been reading this book. We like it. There are some things we don't understand, but we feel good when we read it."

He felt beads of perspiration starting to form on his forehead. This was sheer agony. "We was wond'rin' if you would tell us if the book is true. The missionaries—" He stopped as he realized that he had pronounced the word in the American fashion. "The mission'ries told us that if we asked you, you'd tell us. So we're askin'. We really want to know, God. We—"

His voice strengthened as he realized that he really meant what he had started to say. "We want to do what you want us to do. 'Cause we don't want to go to hell, God. So tell us, please. Then we'll know what to do." He stopped again, his mind racing with a thousand thoughts. But he could put none of them into the form of a prayer, so he simply finished. "Amen."

"Amen," Peter whispered.

Derek opened his eyes to darkness. During the prayer the candle had gone out. He stood slowly and felt Peter stand beside him. He put his arm across his younger brother's shoulder.

"Thank you, Derek."

"Thank *you*, Peter. I wanted to, I just didn't know how."

"It was a real good prayer, Derek."

"You think so?"

"Yes."

"I hope so."

"Do you know how I know it was a good prayer?"

Derek looked down in surprise at the small figure in the darkness. "No, how do you know that?"

Peter slipped his arm around Derek's waist. " 'Cause I feel so happy, Derek. I feel happier than I can ever remember."

Derek squeezed his shoulder. "Me too, Peter."

On Wednesday evening, the twenty-sixth of July, the elders from America held their third meeting in the Vauxhall Chapel in Preston. For the third time they preached to a capacity crowd. Word spread quickly after the Sunday afternoon meeting. Sunday evening's session was bigger than the afternoon's had been, and now Wednesday's was the largest of all. As usual, the missionaries preached stirring sermons, and afterwards several of those who attended requested baptism. A date was set for the following Sunday.

To the elders' surprise and dismay, that set the Reverend James Fielding into a spin. Even though he had written to his brother in Canada and begged him to bring someone from the new church, even though he had been the one to invite the missionaries to speak in his chapel, now everything changed. It was members of *his* congregation that were abuzz with the new doctrine. It was *his* people requesting baptism. Claiming that the missionaries had violated their trust by preaching baptism contrary to their arrangement with him, the pastor said he could no longer tolerate their preaching in his church. Heber C. Kimball vehemently denied that there had ever been such an arrangement, pointing out that he would never consent to remain silent about the one ordinance by which membership in the kingdom was obtained. But Fielding was adamant, and practically overnight their ardent supporter became their violent opponent.

Fortunately, the "damage" had already been done. Many of the congregation followed the Reverend Mr. Fielding's lead, of course, but many others did not. He had spoken too glowingly of what his brother and others had written about a restored Church of Jesus Christ. Many had prayed fervently that the Lord would send someone to them, and Fielding himself had said they had come as an answer to those prayers. And then there were the dreams. Word of the remarkable fulfillment of the dreams went through Fielding's group like news of a raise in salary at the factory. Many were as dismayed and frustrated at the reverend's change of heart as were the elders from North America. They opened their houses to the missionaries now, and the meetings simply shifted to new locations.

But the powers of darkness had determined that the gospel would not take root in the Old World. In America, Satan raged in the Church, making significant inroads even into the highest quorums. The infant Church, barely seven years old, was being shaken to its very roots. In those dark and terrible days, the Lord told Joseph, "Something new must be done for the salvation of my church." A few days later Heber C. Kimball was called to take the gospel to England. Within days of his and his companions' arrival, a beachhead had been successfully established, and the work was rolling forth with remarkable success. When the reversal and opposition of James Fielding failed to halt the progress, the adversary decided on more drastic measures.

The time for the first baptisms in England was set for the

morning of July thirtieth at the River Ribble, which ran along the southern edge of town. Heber C. Kimball would later relate what happened in the early morning hours of that Sabbath day.

"By this time the adversary of souls began to rage, and he felt determined to destroy us before we had fully established the kingdom of God in that land. I witnessed a scene of satanic power and influence which I shall never forget.

"Sunday, July 30th (1837), about daybreak, Elder Isaac Russell, who slept in the same room with Elder Richards in Wilfred Street, came up to the third story, where Elder Hyde and myself were sleeping. He called out, 'Brother Kimball, I want you should get up and pray for me that I may be delivered from the evil spirits that are tormenting me to such a degree that I feel I cannot live long, unless I obtain relief.'

"I had been sleeping on the back of the bed. I immediately arose, slipped off at the foot of the bed, and passed around to where he was. Elder Hyde threw his feet out, and sat up in the bed, and we laid hands on him, I being mouth, and prayed that the Lord would have mercy on him. And we rebuked the devil.

"While thus engaged, I was struck with great force by some invisible power, and fell senseless on the floor. The first thing I recollected was being supported by Elders Hyde and Richards, who were praying for me, Elder Richards having followed Russell up to my room. Elders Hyde and Richards then assisted me to get on the bed, but my agony was so great I could not endure it, and I arose, bowed my knees, and prayed. I then arose and sat up on the bed, when a vision was opened to our minds, and we could distinctly see the evil spirits, who foamed and gnashed their teeth at us. We gazed upon them about an hour and a half (by Willard's watch). We were not looking towards the window, but towards the wall. Space appeared before us, and we saw the devils coming in legions, with their leaders, who came within a few feet of us. They came towards us like armies rushing to battle. They appeared to be men of full stature, possessing every form and feature of men in the flesh, who were angry and desperate; and I shall never forget the vindictive malignity depicted on their countenances as they looked me in the eye. Any attempt to paint the scene which then presented itself, or to portray their malice and enmity, would be vain.

"I perspired exceedingly, my clothes becoming as wet as if I had been taken out of the river. I felt excessive pain, and was in the greatest distress for some time. I cannot even look back on the scene without feelings of horror. Yet by it I learned the power of the adversary, his enmity against the servants of God, and got some understanding of the invisible world. We distinctly heard those spirits talk and express their wrath and hellish designs against us. However, the Lord delivered us from them, and blessed us exceedingly that day."

Elder Hyde described it thus: "After Elder Kimball was overcome by these evil spirits and had fallen, their awful rush upon me with threats, imprecations, and hellish grins amply convinced me that they were no friends of mine. After we laid Elder Kimball on the bed, I stood between him and the devils and fought them and contended with them face-to-face, until they began to diminish in number and to retreat from the room. The last imp that left turned round to me as he was going out and said, as if to apologize and appease my determined opposition to them, 'I never said anything against you!' I replied to him thus: 'It matters not to me whether you have or have not; you are a liar from the beginning! In the name of Jesus Christ, depart!' He immediately left, and the room was clear. That closed the scene for that time."

By the time the horrifying experience had been withdrawn, the sun was just rising in the east. With its coming came also the Spirit of the Lord to comfort and strengthen the elders after their ordeal. They had tasted of the bitter; now they partook of the sweet. They had been encompassed about by the powers of darkness; now they were enveloped in the peace and joy "that passeth understanding." Still shaken and exhausted but rejoicing greatly, the elders dressed, and prepared to take the first converts outside the North American continent into the waters of baptism.

"I'm telling you, Mr. Kimball, I forbid it. I absolutely forbid you to baptize these people."

The Reverend Mr. Fielding was livid—in a "fine frenzy," as Willard Richards whispered to Elder Hyde. They were outside the residence of the missionaries. A few people had already gathered there, even though for a Sabbath day it was still early, not yet quite nine a.m. The Anglican church believed in infant baptism by sprinkling. The Baptists baptized by total immersion, but they had baptismal fonts in their chapels and kept their services private. So the news that the Americans would be baptizing out in the open—in the river, no less—had caught the fancy of many in Preston, and there was already a crowd of seven or eight thousand lining the riverbanks around the designated site. That was, in large part, a good deal responsible for the Reverend James Fielding's apoplexy.

The nine candidates for baptism were already outside and waiting for the short trip to the river. Derek and Peter had come with Jenny and Mrs. Pottsworth. Mrs. Pottsworth somehow knew the place where the elders had rented their rooms, and so they had come to Saint Wilfred Street in order to accompany them from the first. And thus they had come upon the confrontation between Kimball and Fielding as the elders came down to the street.

"Do you hear me?" Fielding shrilled. "You cannot baptize these poor souls."

Mr. Kimball looked drawn and weary, and yet there was a quiet majesty about him. He looked at Mr. Fielding, then with quiet patience he simply said, "They are of age, Mr. Fielding, and they can act for themselves. I shall baptize all who come unto me, asking no favors of any man."

He pushed past the angry minister, and the other missionaries followed. The candidates for baptism fell into step behind them. The Ingalls brothers, the Pottsworths, and the others did the same, leaving the pastor trembling and spluttering as though he had a terrible chill.

A stir swept through the assembled crowds as the party came out of the narrow side street and into Avenham Park, which ran along the riverbank. The River Ribble was a broad but quiet stream, lined with trees and greenery. In the bright sunlight of this next to last day in July, the waters shimmered and sparkled. It was a glorious day indeed.

"You may prepare yourselves here," Elder Kimball said to the candidates. Then, without waiting, he quickly stripped off his coat. He sat down and removed his boots and stockings. He unhooked his suspenders, then fished in his pockets, removing a few small items he carried there. He handed them to Willard Richards, then strode over to where there was a small path down to the water. A ripple of sound swept through the crowd as he hesitated not at all but waded out until he was waist deep. There were one or two catcalls, but also a light smattering of applause. The crowd was certainly not going to be hostile.

"Come on, Peter," Derek said. "I want to see better. Let's go over by the riverbank."

As they moved down to the grassy slope that dropped off into the river, they came near to two men who were still in the process of readying themselves for baptism. The taller one worked in Derek's factory in the carding sheds. Derek did not know his name. He was speaking to another man whom Derek had met a couple of times. He lived several houses up the street from where Derek and Peter did. His name was George Watt.

The taller man turned and gazed across the short distance to where Heber C. Kimball stood waiting in the river. "I shall go down first," he said to Watt. "I shall consider it a privilege to be the first soul baptized into the restored Church in the British Isles."

Watt was just finishing shucking off his outer shirt. He looked up in surprise, then grinned. "Sorry, mate," he said, "but I have chosen that honor for myself."

The other man whirled. "I say not, sir."

Watt's grin only broadened the more. "Shall we say that the better man wins? Eh, what?"

It took only a second for the other to grasp the import of what Watt was suggesting. "Indeed, sir!" he cried.

In an instant they were at a dead run, dashing across the cobblestones and then the grassy riverbank. It was several rods from the starting place to the path that led down to the water. The man who worked in the mills had the longer legs, but Watt was the younger and the swifter. Watt was at the path, and then into the river, sending forth a great spray as he hit the water at breakneck speed. The loser pulled up, the disappointment evident on his face. A cheer went up from the crowd.

As Watt waded out to join the American elder, the watching throngs quickly quieted again. Heber Kimball pulled Watt around so that they half faced each other. There was a quick whispered interchange, then Kimball raised his right arm to the square.

"Brother George Watt," Elder Kimball said loudly, "having been commissioned of Jesus Christ, I baptize you in the name of the Father, and of the Son, and of the Holy Ghost. Amen."

He took him by the hands and leaned him back. Down under the water he went. Elder Kimball held him there for a moment, looking quickly to make sure he was totally immersed, then brought him up. Watt came up beaming like a schoolboy, the water streaming down his face. He looked at Elder Kimball, and then they embraced.

The man who had lost the race was waiting to shake Watt's hand as he came out of the river, and the crowd greeted that with enthusiasm. They loved a good loser.

"Derek?"

Derek turned and looked down at his brother.

"I . . ." Peter looked away.

Derek smiled at him. He was closer to this boy-turned-man than anyone else in the world. "You want to be baptized too, don't you, Peter?"

Peter looked up. He had been afraid that Derek would laugh. "Yes."

"Oh, Mama," Jenny Pottsworth said, "I do too."

Mrs. Pottsworth was weeping quietly. "We shall, Jenny girl, we shall."

Derek looked grave, and he saw Peter's face fall. Slowly a smile stole over his face. "I have only one regret."

"What?" Peter said, the hope rising in his eyes.

"I wish we had decided to do it t'day. I think I could have beat Mr. Watt to the river."

It was a hot August afternoon in Independence, Missouri, and though Caroline Steed had the windows open, there was not even a stirring of the curtains. She felt the dampness around her forehead and the stickiness of her dress. "Come on, little one," she said. She quickly finished doing up Savannah's diaper. "Let's go back downstairs where it's a little cooler."

Downstairs there was the sound of the front door crashing open, followed immediately by a shrill voice crying, "Mama! Mama!" Caroline's face registered surprise. She hadn't expected them back this early. "I'm up here, Olivia."

She lifted the baby to her shoulder, then turned just as Olivia came bursting through the door. She slid to a stop, gasping for breath.

"My goodness, Olivia," Caroline said with a smile. "Did you run all the way home from Westport?"

She shook her head, panting hard. Below, Caroline heard

heavier footsteps and the front door closing. Joshua and Will had arrived home too.

"Mama, Joshua let me drive the team." Her eyes were wide, and the green in them was alive with excitement. "All by myself!"

"No," Caroline said, feigning complete shock.

"Yes, Mama. I got to drive all four horses." She cocked her head, causing the auburn hair to bounce lightly on her shoulders. At nearly ten, she was already starting to show the beauty that would be hers as a woman. "Will said I couldn't do it, but I showed him. I took them right down Main Street."

"Well, good for you."

Olivia instantly changed focus, looking up at her baby sister. "Hello, Savannah," she cooed. "Hello, baby."

The baby, now five months old, stared at Olivia wide-eyed, then finally smiled. Olivia opened her arms, and Caroline handed the baby to her. She turned at the sound of footsteps. Will came through the door first. "Hello."

Caroline stepped across to him and opened her arms for a quick hug. As she held him close she could smell the dust on him and a trace of the horses. She touched his hair. He had turned thirteen in March, and the top of his head was nearly up to her nose now. Another year and he would be well past her in height. "Hello, son," she whispered.

Joshua came in now too. She smiled at him across the top of her son's head but still spoke to Will. "Olivia tells me you were a doubting Thomas."

Will looked up, his face puzzled.

"You said I couldn't drive the team by myself," Olivia said.

Will looked up at his mother and winked. "I didn't think she could," he said soberly, "but she did, Mama. And she did real good too."

"Yes, she did," Joshua said with equal solemnity.

Olivia beamed.

"I'm real proud of you, Olivia." Caroline let go of Will and stepped to Joshua. She went up on tiptoes and kissed him. "You made good time."

He nodded. "The riverboat arrived almost an hour ahead of schedule. They had the freight already on the dock when we drove up."

"I'm glad."

"Let me hold Savannah," Will said, stepping to Olivia.

"No," Olivia wailed, "I just got her."

"I want to see her too." He held out his arms. "Come on, Savannah. Come see Will." Savannah eyed her brother without blinking.

"No," Olivia said, jerking away. "It's my turn."

"Hey," Joshua said easily, "I know how to solve this." He walked to Olivia and took the baby. "We'll let Papa take her." He held her out at arm's length, then lifted her up high above him. "Hello, little carrot head." He looked to Caroline. "I swear her hair gets redder with every passing day."

"I think so too." She reached up and touched the baby's cheek. "And she's getting to be so much fun now." Finally, she turned back to her other children. "You hungry?"

"I am!" Will cried.

"Me too," echoed Olivia.

"I didn't expect you for another hour or more, but it shouldn't take too long. Olivia, you come help me. Will, you go out in the smokehouse and fetch that side of pork and slice me off some thin strips." As they started toward the door, she looked over at Joshua. "The mail's down on the table in the hall. The newspaper from Richmond also came this afternoon. It's there too."

He nodded absently, then looked at the baby as he lowered her down again. "Is it time for her to sleep?"

"No, she just woke up."

"Good." He tucked her in the crook of his arm. "Then what say, young lady? Shall you and me go for a walk while your mama gets some supper on?"

Joshua swore and slammed the newspaper down on the table. Will and Olivia looked up in surprise from where they were playing a game of tic-tac-toe with a slate board and a piece of soapstone. Caroline was in the adjoining room folding the clothes that Will had gathered in from the clothesline after supper.

Joshua leaned over the paper, read some more. His heavy brows came almost together as the anger swept across his face. He swore again, this time bitterly and in a stream of curses.

"Joshua!" Caroline said sharply.

His head came up. "What?"

"You have children present."

There was a quick glance to where the two were sitting. The game had stopped now and they were watching him with dismay. But it was as if their presence wasn't registering with him. He shook the paper at Caroline. "I knew we should have finished it! I told them that we had to finish it!"

She set down the trousers she was folding, stood, and came into the room. "Should have finished what?" There was an edge of warning in her voice.

He missed it totally. He turned the paper around, thrust it out toward her, and jabbed his finger at a spot on the lower part of the page. She came closer, peering at the place where he was pointing. After a moment, she straightened, her mouth tightening into a hard line. "So?" she said.

"So!" he exploded. "So the Mormons are taking over again. Look at that!" He slapped the paper with the back of his fingers. "They say there's over four thousand of them now and more coming all the time. They've completely taken over Caldwell and Daviess counties." He snatched up the paper and began to read furiously. "'With their growing numbers, the Mormons now control most political offices in both counties. It is estimated that there are now fifteen Mormon constables and six or seven county judges who are Mormon. Reports received in

Richmond indicate they have even started to form their own militia.'" He slammed the paper down. "And you say, 'So?'"

Caroline moved so that she stood between Joshua and the children. "Yes," she said quietly. "So? You said that's why they went north. So they could be alone and not bother anyone. What do you care what they're doing up there? That's two days' ride from here."

He looked at her incredulously. "They're forming their own militia, Caroline. Do you know what that means?"

Her head came up slightly. "Maybe after what happened to them in Jackson County, it means they want to protect themselves."

He slapped the table hard, making the lamp on it jump. "It means they're gonna be comin' back here to claim their precious land of Zion again. Is that what you want?"

At that point Caroline made a mistake. She laughed, openly scoffing at the idea. "You surely don't believe that."

Joshua shot to his feet, nearly knocking over the chair in which he had been sitting. His eyes were blazing. "You don't know them, Caroline," he shouted. "Mormons are like a swarm of lice. If you don't squash 'em one by one, before you know it there's gonna be ten thousand more."

"*Joshua!*" She snapped it out hard and angrily. "You are speaking in front of your children. I won't have you talking like that."

Joshua looked beyond her at Will and Olivia. They were staring at their parents, their mouths half-open in shock. Olivia shrank back against her brother, her eyes large and wide and frightened. Joshua turned back to Caroline. "Then I suggest they find somewhere else to be while we talk."

Her shoulders came back. "Or maybe you'd better find somewhere else to be until you can calm down enough to stop talking like a wild man."

His mouth opened, then clamped shut again. The muscles along his jaw stood out like cords of rope. For a long moment he stood there, chest rising and falling. Then without another word, he spun on his heel, and without bothering to get his hat, he stalked out of the door, slamming it behind him.

———————

Joshua was playing a desultory game of small-stakes poker in the far corner of Clinton Roundy's saloon on Main Street. When Joshua had come storming into the bar like a Missouri twister, Roundy knew instantly that his former son-in-law was in a black mood; but he had long ago learned that with Joshua you didn't ask questions until he let it be known it was all right. Roundy just drew large mugs of beer for Joshua and himself, then gathered up three or four other regulars and started a game. Now, two hours later, he could tell that Joshua's mood had flattened out considerably.

It was a warm evening outside, and Roundy had propped the two front doors open. A movement there caught his eye. He had been about to call for more cards, but he stopped short. Caroline Steed was standing just outside, looking in. Lowering his cards, he shot Joshua a warning look. For a moment Joshua was too busy concentrating on his own hand and missed it, but finally his head came up. Roundy motioned slightly with his head toward the door. Everyone at the table turned to look. Slowly Joshua put his cards down too.

For a long moment their eyes locked. The sound in the barroom dropped to an instant hush. Finally, Joshua shoved his chair back. "Give me a minute," he grunted. As he stood, Caroline backed away and disappeared again.

When Joshua stepped outside, Caroline was a few feet down the board sidewalk, her back to him, hugging herself as though it were cold. He moved quietly up behind her and stood without speaking.

After a moment she stirred slightly. "Is that what it's come to?"

"What?"

"Whiskey and poker again?"

He stiffened. "I've won a whoppin' seventy-five cents in the last two hours," he said sarcastically. "And I've drowned my sorrows in about three-quarters of a glass of warm beer. If that qualifies as 'whiskey and poker,' then I guess I'm guilty as charged."

Slowly she turned around. In the half-light from the windows behind them, he couldn't tell if she had been crying or not, but now she definitely was not. Her eyes were luminous but unreadable. Finally, she dropped her chin a little. "All right, that was uncalled for. I'm sorry."

He nodded slightly but didn't say anything.

"And shall I take the children and move into the hotel for the night?"

One eyebrow went up. "Why would you do that?"

"So you won't have to wait around here all night to be sure I'm asleep before you feel like it's safe to come home."

Again he bit his tongue and waited for a moment until he could speak calmly. "You're the one who told me to go find someplace to be until I could stop talking like a wild man." A tiny hint of a smile toyed at the corners of his mouth. "How am I doin'?"

A little of the tightness in her face softened. "Much better."

"I was going to come home in a little while."

"After I was asleep?"

He started to protest, then finally shrugged. "Probably."

"So?" she said, her eyes challenging him.

He grinned more openly now. "As I recollect, that was the word that got us into trouble in the first place."

This time she didn't smile. "So? Do I go to the hotel or not?"

He peered at her more closely. "You're serious, aren't you?"

"Joshua, when Donovan Mendenhall found me working in my mother's dress shop and took me away, everything was wonderful between us. He was handsome, he was rich. I never challenged him on anything." She shook her head, looking away, the pain evident on her face. "Then the troubles with Boswell and Berrett began. When I found out what was happening, for the first time there were sharp words between us. I wanted to know what was going on between him and his two—partners." She spat out the last word with utter contempt. "I was worried sick. Donovan would get angry and tell me the business was his business. He'd stomp out of the house, and I'd lay there in bed for hours on end, brooding and practicing my lines over and over for when he returned. But he never would, not before he was sure I was asleep. Then the next morning, we'd kind of tiptoe around each other, talking nice and trying to smile. It was too painful to go through it all again, so we'd just pretend everything was all right."

She stopped for breath, a little surprised at her own intensity. "Well," she finally said, more slowly now and with soft bitterness, "it doesn't work, Joshua. Donovan ended up dead, and I ended up trying hard not to hate him for leaving me—a widow with two children—totally dependent upon the tender mercies of Mr. Theodore Berrett and Mr. Jeremiah Boswell."

She tipped her head back, the challenge evident in her eyes. "So, I'm not going to sleep alone tonight, Joshua. If you're not coming home, then I'll get a room and sleep with my children."

He looked away, not wanting her to see his face. Two conflicting emotions were struggling in him. Part of him wanted to strike back at her. She was the one who'd started it all. All he'd done was make a couple of innocent comments about those wretched Mormons, and she'd come at him like a mother badger protecting her young. But another part of him was watching her with wonder. She rarely spoke of her marriage to Donovan Mendenhall or of her life back in Savannah, and he knew she avoided talking about those things out of respect for his feelings. So this was like a revelation to him.

Once again he felt a familiar sense of awe at the thought that he—Joshua Steed, mule skinner and Missouri wildcat—had been bold enough and lucky enough to convince this woman to marry him.

"Well?" she said.

He pulled a face. "I'm not sure it was a good idea that I

stepped in between you and Boswell and Berrett. At the time I thought I was helping you. Now I'm beginning to think I was saving their hides."

For a moment she looked startled, then instantly her lips compressed into a thin, hard line. She whirled around and started away, her shoulders squared, her back stiff. Joshua swore under his breath and went after her. He reached out and grabbed her arm. "Caroline!"

She jerked away. He grabbed her again, this time turning her around to face him. "Caroline," he said more gently.

Finally her head came up. "I guess I'm not in much of a mood for jokes right now, Joshua."

He shook his head in frustration. "Listen—," he started. But again she pulled free and started away from him, her shoes making sharp staccato sounds on the boards.

"So that's how it is," he snapped. "You can tear into me, and I have to stand here and take it, but the moment I try to talk to you . . . How about *you* listening for a minute?"

She stopped. She didn't turn around, but finally she nodded. "All right, I'm listening."

He took a breath, feeling like he was fighting a losing battle. "I ain't very—" He caught himself and started again. "I'm not very good with words, Caroline. I always feel like I've got a mouthful of prairie sod when I try to talk with you." He shrugged helplessly. "All I was tryin' to say was, you are some kind of woman, Caroline Mendenhall Steed. And you're right. I shouldn't have stomped out, and I shouldn't have stayed away."

He paused, then spoke more softly. "It was my way of tryin' to say, don't go to the hotel, Caroline. I don't want you sleepin' alone either."

He dropped his hands to his sides. "That's what I was hopin' to say. I'm sorry if it sounded like I was making a joke."

Slowly she turned around. Her eyes were shining in the faint light. "No, Joshua," she murmured. "I'm the one who's sorry. I . . . I'm just wound up so tight right now." She came back to him. After a moment, she reached out and touched his hand. He opened his arms and she came against him, laying her head against his chest.

"I'm sorry, Caroline."

"So am I, Joshua. I *wasn't* listening, and I'm sorry." She looked up at him and smiled faintly. "But promise me one thing."

"What?"

"Don't ever say you're bad with words, Joshua. Sometimes you are absolutely wonderful in what you say."

———————•———————

"I think I understand at least some of your feelings about the Mormons, Joshua."

He swatted impatiently at a mosquito that was humming around his ear. "No," he said wearily, "I don't think you do, Caroline, or you wouldn't ask me to change how I feel."

She was sitting on their front step. He was leaning against the hitching rail that ran about half the length of their porch. When they had arrived home, she had stepped inside only long enough to make sure the children were still asleep, then suggested they stay outside in the pleasantness of the summer's night.

She watched him for a moment, then leaned forward, looking down at her feet. "Have you never wondered how I feel about religion, Joshua?"

The question caught him by surprise. "I . . . no, I guess I haven't. You never talk about it."

"I know." She folded her hands in her lap, still looking down. Her voice took on a faraway sound. "My mother was a devout Methodist. My papa too before he died. So when Donovan and I were married in the home of a justice of the peace in Baltimore, I thought I had risked my eternal salvation." She gave a quick, soft laugh. "It was probably the most 'terrible' thing I had ever done in my life."

She finally looked up at him. "I guess what I'm trying to tell you is that during all the time I was growing up, religion was very important to me. I went to church services every Sabbath day. I said my prayers night and morning. I read from the Bible usually at least once a day, often more."

He was really surprised, almost shocked. They had been married for well over a year now, and she had never—not once—made even the slightest reference to her feelings about church or religion or God. "What happened?" he asked.

She looked away again. "Donovan was much more liberal about religion than I was. To him, church was more of a social thing than a religious one, so he didn't mind if I continued in my beliefs. When Will was born he said I could teach him whatever I chose. Then we moved to Savannah. It seemed like all the people who were important to us were members of—" She shook her head quickly. "Well, it doesn't matter. But it wasn't the Methodists. Suddenly, Donovan got 'religious.' We became very involved in the congregation there. I still gave money to the Wesleyan Methodist church. Donovan didn't mind as long as I didn't make too much fuss about it. After a while I decided it really didn't matter so much which church you belonged to, as long as you believed in God."

She shook her head, her eyes half closing. "Jeremiah Boswell and Theodore Berrett were pillars in that same congregation. In fact, they were the ones who got Donovan and me involved there."

"Oh," he said slowly.

She didn't seem to hear him. "It couldn't have been more than a month after Donovan's death. The minister got up that Sunday. He was so excited, he could barely contain himself. The church was adding a new wing. It seems that Mr. Berrett and Mr. Boswell had just given a very substantial contribution to the church. *Very* substantial." There was a short, bitter laugh of derision. "Why not? They had plenty to spare with what they had taken from Donovan and me."

Now her voice dropped to a low, mocking whisper. "The minister preached a whole sermon that Sunday on what God-fearing men these two fine gentlemen were. He said the Spirit testified clearly that mansions on high awaited them. Whatever minor sins they might have committed would surely be swallowed up by this one grand act of generosity."

She looked up at Joshua. "I never went back. I quit praying that very day. I took the Bible and locked it in a chest."

He was nodding slowly. "I understand."

She whirled now, her voice filled with sudden passion. "No, Joshua, you don't understand. That's what I'm trying to tell you. I was so filled with hate, so torn with bitterness. It wasn't aimed at just those two. I hated the minister. I hated the congregation for how they gushed all over them after the services." She took a quick breath. "I hated God for doing this to me. He'd already taken my husband. Now it was like he had to drag it beneath my nose. Well, I thought, I'd show him. I'd withhold my devotion. I'd turn my back on him."

He was beginning to see now where she was going. He didn't like it and started to speak, but she went on quickly. "I don't know much about the Mormons, Joshua. I don't know much about what they did to you, except for the little you told me. I don't know what they believe. It doesn't matter. What matters is what my hatred did to me and what your hatred for them is doing to you."

"There's a difference between the hypocrisy of those two fancy-dressed blowhards and downright evil, Caroline. The Mormons are not just another religion that doesn't practice what they preach, they're—"

"It doesn't matter, Joshua!" she burst out. "That's what I'm trying to tell you. What matters is what's happening to you."

His eyes hardened. "There are some things you can't change, Caroline," he said stubbornly.

She gave an incredulous laugh. "Did I hear you right?"

His jaw tightened. "Yeah, you heard me right. I haven't begun to tell you all that has happened to me because of Joseph Smith and those who follow him. You don't know—"

She cut him off. "You're telling me that the man who came out to Missouri with nothing but a few dollars and naked willpower and built one of the largest freight businesses in the western United States can't do anything about how he feels?" She stood now, her eyes softening. "You're telling me that the man who came to Savannah and convinced an independent-minded, bitter-hearted widow to marry him and run off with him to Missouri is helpless in the face of what's inside him?" She smiled, her lips barely touching. "Sorry, Mr. Steed, but I find that hard to accept."

He shook his head. He couldn't debate her. She had a way of turning him inside out with her logic and her quickness. He turned away now too, leaning on the hitching rail as he stared out into the night. Behind him, Caroline spoke again. Now her voice had taken on a pleading note. "Joshua, I want you to close your eyes and picture something for me."

He shook his head. He wasn't in a mood for any of her games.

"Remember Olivia's eyes this afternoon?" she asked softly. "After you let her drive the team? Do you remember what they looked like?"

He turned slowly.

"They were so full of love and adoration." A tear welled up in the corner of one of her eyes and started slowly down her cheek. "She loves you, Joshua."

She brushed at the tear with the back of her hand. "Last night, while you were working late, Will and Olivia and I talked about having their names changed."

He blinked in surprise. "You did?"

"Yes," she whispered. "They want your name, Joshua." She had to stop, and she looked away quickly. "They want you to be their father."

"Why didn't you tell me?" he said huskily.

"I was going to tonight."

He felt as if he had been punched in the stomach. Again she shook her head quickly. "That's not the point I'm trying to make. I want you to think about Olivia's eyes today. Do you remember?"

"Yes," he said softly. "I remember."

She nodded. She took a deep breath. "Now I want you to picture those same eyes tonight, when you were talking about the Mormons being like lice. Did you see them, Joshua? Did you? Did you see Olivia's eyes?"

He looked down, unable to meet the piercing power of her gaze.

"They were terrified, Joshua. She saw the ugliness that's eating away at you down inside, and it frightened her. It even frightened Will." She sat back down on the step, heavily. "It frightened me, Joshua."

He didn't know what to say. There was nothing to say.

After the silence had stretched on for several minutes, Caroline looked up at him. "I got my Bible out of that chest a few weeks ago."

His head came up sharply.

She watched him steadily. "The day after Savannah was born, I prayed again for the first time in nearly two and a half years. I thanked God for our beautiful, healthy little girl. I thanked him that you loved her so much." She smiled sadly. "I'm glad to report that while I turned my back on God, he didn't respond in like manner. I felt like he'd been waiting—just waiting for me to heal enough to see what a fool I've been."

She stood and moved over to Joshua's side. "I'd like to start taking the children to church." There was a pause. "Would you mind terribly if I did that?"

He hesitated only a moment. "No, I suppose not."

She slipped her arm through his. "Thank you." She laid her head against his shoulder. Finally, he slipped his arm around her and just held her.

Again, after several minutes had passed in silence, Caroline spoke. "My papa died when I was seven. I can barely remember him. But Mother told me once something Papa taught her."

"What?"

"He said that if you're bitten by a rattlesnake, you can do one of two things. You can grab an ax and try and chase that rattlesnake down and kill him. But all the time you're chasing him, the venom keeps pumping deeper and deeper into your system. Or . . ." She took his hand and pulled it more tightly around her. "Or you can forget about the snake and sit down and try and get the venom out of your system quick as you can before it kills you."

"Caroline, I—"

She put a finger up to his lips. "I'll not be saying anything more to you, Joshua. You've got to work this out yourself. But I am telling you, what you're harboring down deep inside you is poison. I know, because I've been doing the same thing." Her voice caught. "I never thought I could change either, Joshua, but I have. In these past few months I've felt what it's like to put the hate away. I'm hoping for your sake that someday you'll be able to do the same. That's all."

Isaw Martin Harris at the saddle shop. He said he wants to see you before the meeting tomorrow morning."

Benjamin looked up, then away again. There was no mistaking the disapproval in Mary Ann's eyes. "Did he say what for?" he asked.

She watched him steadily, knowing exactly why he wouldn't meet her gaze. "You know very well what for. Joseph's gone to Canada. Most of the Twelve are on missions. It's the perfect time for them to move."

He had an ax handle he was smoothing down with a wood rasp. He held it up and eyed it carefully, then lifted the ax head and tried the fit. It was close but not close enough. He picked up the rasp again and began to stroke it across the wood methodically.

"Nathan was talking to Lyman Johnson this morning. They've been having secret meetings. They're still trying to make David Whitmer president."

He didn't look up. "They've been talking about doing that for a long time now. They don't have the stomach for it. Besides, now that David has gone back to Missouri, it will die out."

"That's essentially what Nathan said too, but Brother Johnson swears things are different now. They've found a girl who has some kind of black stone that supposedly has magical powers. Using that, she's prophesied that Joseph has fallen because of transgression and that the leadership will now fall on David Whitmer or Martin Harris. They say David can preside from Missouri. Or Martin's name has been mentioned too. Martin likes that idea, of course. This girl has told them that the time for action has come. They have to get rid of Joseph."

Benjamin set the rasp down and finally looked up at his wife. "What they do is their affair. Let them wallow in their own stupidity. They can try and call up the dead, for all I care. I'm not part of it."

"But they think you are!" she burst out.

"Well, they're wrong," he shot back. "My feelings about Joseph are my affair, and I've never given that bunch one minute's encouragement."

She sat down on the bench to face him. She took a deep breath, knowing she could well be pushing him too far, but there was too much at stake now to let it go without saying something. "Ben," she started tentatively.

He had picked up the rasp again and was studying it carefully. He did not look up.

"You know they're just using Martin to get at you," she went on. "They think they can still convince you they're right, that Joseph has to be replaced. They want your support."

"Well, they don't have it."

"But they don't have your opposition either. You can bet they're not still trying to get Brigham Young to listen to them. Why? Because he has come out foursquare against them. There's no doubt about what his position is."

"I'm not Brigham Young," he muttered.

"Ben, you know that's not what I'm saying. But we're coming to a crisis. These men are becoming bolder. I understand that, before he left, David Whitmer was bragging that he has been given the power to either raise Joseph to the highest heaven or thrust him straight down to hell."

"David Whitmer doesn't have the power to raise a handkerchief off the table. They're blowhards, every one of them. They bow and scrape and smile when Joseph's around, then the minute he's gone they start talking real big."

"Then say that, Ben. There are so many people who respect you and look up to you. And right now they're taking your silence to mean that you agree with the opposition."

He picked up the handle again and began working it, pushing the rasp across the oak in hard, vicious strokes. She had to move back a little, away from his flying elbows.

Mary Ann shook her head slowly, sensing that once again she had lost. "At least tell Martin you won't see him as long as he continues to associate with them," she finished quietly.

There was a momentary pause in his strokes. "Martin's my friend, Mary Ann. Whether or not I agree with him, he's still my friend."

"Not if he's doing things that can harm you."

His head came up sharply, and for a long moment he met her gaze steadily, his face a mask. Mary Ann felt a chill run through her. Once before she and this man she loved so fiercely had stood on opposite ground about Joseph Smith. It had not been a happy time for either of them. These past few years since Benjamin had joined the Church had been the best of their marriage. But now the spectre of apostasy hung heavy over Kirtland. Evil men were poisoning the minds of many of the Saints toward the Prophet. Even former stalwarts were wavering. Ben hadn't gone over. Not yet. But he was teetering perilously close to the edge, and it frightened her more deeply than anything she could ever remember.

Finally he looked away, staring out of the small window of

the toolshed into the August sunshine. "That's not what's really bothering you, is it?"

"What do you mean by that?"

"What's really worrying you is that you're not sure where *I* stand yet."

Her chin came up. "Are *you*, Ben?" she asked softly. "Are you sure?"

For several moments there was no sound in the toolshed. He continued to stare out of the window, not turning to meet her probing gaze.

She stood quickly, turning away from him, afraid he would see the bitterness of her disappointment. She hugged herself, feeling the chill deepen somewhere down inside her. Finally she turned back around. "Ben, do you remember how Carl said the Mormon church breaks up families? It was while you were gone to Missouri. I told you about it."

"Yes, I remember."

"Do you remember what I said to him?"

"You told him he and Melissa ought to make it a matter of prayer, ask God which church they should join so they could be united in their family."

"Yes," she murmured. "And isn't that what Joseph told you to do? You have to find out for yourself, Ben. No one else can give you the answers you're looking for."

For a moment a flash of anger darkened his face, then almost instantly it turned to melancholy. "Not everyone gets their prayers answered as easily as you do, Mary Ann."

"If you ask, the Lord will answer."

His breath exploded softly in an expression of frustration, then he shook his head. "I have asked, Mary Ann. Over and over. Nothing has come."

She leaned forward, not trying to hide her surprise. She knew of the challenge Joseph had given him to pray about whether Joseph was still God's prophet, but he had never said anything more about it, and she had assumed he had decided against taking that challenge. She took a quick breath. "Benjamin, back in Palmyra, when you were still bitter about Joseph, and everybody was preparing to move to Ohio . . ."

He looked up.

"It was prayer *and fasting* that finally brought me my answer."

Again he totally dumbfounded her. "I know. That hasn't helped either."

"You have been fasting?" she blurted.

As he nodded, her mind was suddenly remembering. Three different times in the past two weeks Benjamin had been gone when she came down to fix his breakfast. She had thought it odd, for he never missed breakfast, but she had finally attributed it to their current financial pressures. Ben had lost as heavily in the bank failure as most any two other men, and she just assumed . . . She felt a stab of shame. She had been so sure she knew the heart of this man. "Why didn't you tell me? I would have fasted with you."

He shook his head quickly. "This isn't your problem. It's not your fault your husband is too hard-headed—or maybe too hard-hearted—to get an answer from the Lord."

"That's not true," she cried. "You are as close to the Lord as any man I know."

He stood up with one swift movement, knocking the ax handle to the floor with a sharp clatter. "Right!" he exclaimed. "That's why it's been two months and I'm still no closer to knowing than I was before."

She moved up to him, putting her arms around his waist and laying her head against his chest. Suddenly, along with the shame inside her, there was a feeling of pride and caring and love so intense that she could barely speak. "Don't give up, Ben," she finally managed. "Some things just take more time."

He sighed. It was a sound of great weariness and discouragement. "There is no more time, Mary Ann. I need to know now, because this thing is tearing me apart."

The next morning Benjamin decided he did not want to see Martin. Not before the worship services. His wife was right. Martin was simply mouth for Warren Parrish and John Boynton and the others. They were desperately trying to win allies to their cause. But while inside himself he was a turmoil of questions, there was one thing about which Benjamin Steed was very sure. Even if he decided Joseph had lost his calling from God, even if he determined Joseph had been a fool and was no longer fit to govern, he would not join the men who were howling for Joseph's head. He wasn't sure what he would do yet. Maybe move. Find another wilderness to tame. Get a fresh start. He didn't know what he would do. But he was very sure about what he would not do. He would not join them. And he also knew it was time to tell Martin that much, at least. And that would not be easy. It could wait until after the meeting. Martin would seek him out soon enough.

He walked to the small table by his favorite chair. On it were three books—the Book of Mormon, the Doctrine and Covenants, and the Bible. He picked up the thinnest of the three. Since it had been published in the fall of 1835 the Doctrine and Covenants had become Benjamin's favorite work of scripture. He enjoyed the Book of Mormon and the Bible—especially the New Testament—but there was something about the compilation of revelations given to Joseph over the years that particularly resonated with his practical nature.

He stood there for a moment, holding the book in his hand, but then he set it back down again and picked up the Bible. The questions in his mind revolved around Joseph. In this case perhaps there was some wisdom in staying with something totally independent of Joseph. Feeling a little foolish, and not without a twinge of shame for being disloyal to Joseph, he tucked the Bible under his arm and walked to the bottom of the stairs. "Mary Ann," he called up.

He heard her moving in their bedroom, then down the hall. She stopped at the upper landing. "Yes?"

"I don't want to see Martin before the meeting. It will only depress me. I'll see him after. I think I'll walk a while before the services."

One eyebrow came up, then he saw her eyes drop to the book he was carrying. She immediately nodded, understanding. "All right, Ben. Rebecca and I will just meet you at the temple."

———•———

Most of the town of Kirtland was built on high bluffs that overlooked the meandering path of the Chagrin River valley. Not far south of where the Steeds lived, a thick woodlot of natural forest still lined the edge of the bluff. Benjamin had found the spot over a year ago and sometimes went there to be alone or to think things through. He loved the deep shade and freshness of the air. There was also one spot, under a huge oak tree, where he could look out across the valley and the patchwork of farmland and forest to the east. So it was to this spot Benjamin came with his Bible on this Sabbath morning in August of 1837.

For several minutes he picked his way idly through the four Gospels, stopping here and there to read a parable or a brief sermon. He didn't know what he was looking for, wasn't sure where to begin. For almost half an hour he got swept up in the final chapters of the book of Luke. For a time the stirring account of the Savior's arrest, trial, and crucifixion and the marvelous events of the Resurrection held his attention, and any thoughts of Joseph Smith and Martin Harris and the troubles in Kirtland were pushed aside.

When he finished, he leaned back against the tree and closed his eyes. There had been no answers there, but it felt good to focus on the Savior. It was as though he had come back to something fundamental, something that in the past few weeks he had neglected. But the feeling lasted only a few moments, then the other questions came pressing back. There was an immediacy to his current situation that could not be ignored. Once again he opened his Bible.

This time he turned to the beginning pages of the Gospel of St. Matthew. Across the top of each page there were running heads, a line or two of text that summarized the content of the chapters below. As he turned the pages, he saw that the first chapters covered the birth and genealogy of the Savior, the coming of the Wise Men to Herod, and then the baptism and the temptation of Jesus. He didn't pause to read any of those things.

He turned the page. He was now to chapter five. The running head said, "The Sermon on the Mount; gospel laws replace Mosaic codes." He glanced briefly at the text below, then went on. The next heading read, "Sermon continues; Lord's Prayer given; treasures in earth and heaven." For a moment he paused, half closing his eyes as he recited the Lord's Prayer softly to himself. His mother had made him memorize that prayer before he had reached the age of five. It was probably the only scripture he had ever memorized. He smiled to himself, strangely pleased he could still remember.

But it was a momentary pleasure, and he turned the next page. Suddenly he was peering at the top of the page. Something in the running head had leaped out at him. "On judging; the strait and narrow way; *false and true prophets.*" He looked more closely at the final words: *false and true prophets.* He could hardly believe what he was seeing. Eagerly he dropped his gaze and started skimming through the chapter, looking for the relevant text. He found what he was looking for beginning in verse fifteen of chapter seven:

> Beware of false prophets, which come to you in sheep's clothing, but inwardly they are ravening wolves.
>
> Ye shall know them by their fruits. Do men gather grapes of thorns, or figs of thistles?
>
> Even so every good tree bringeth forth good fruit; but a corrupt tree bringeth forth evil fruit.

A good tree cannot bring forth evil fruit, neither can a corrupt tree bring forth good fruit.

Every tree that bringeth not forth good fruit is hewn down, and cast into the fire.

Wherefore by their fruits ye shall know them.

"By their fruits ye shall know them." He lowered the book to his lap, gazing out across the valley below him. He had heard that phrase many times before, but he had had no idea it was given in the context of a discussion on true and false prophets. He picked up the Bible again. Carefully, more slowly now, he read through the whole passage again.

———————

Benjamin's mind was still racing as he walked swiftly up the street toward the Kirtland Temple. There were still many things to sort out, some questions he had to think through, but he knew he was on the verge of getting his answer, and his spirits were soaring.

He took out his pocket watch and glanced at it. It was two minutes before the hour of nine. He frowned in disappointment. That meant there would be no time to talk with Mary Ann. And he was anxious to do that. He needed her gentle wisdom and her practical good sense. She would listen to his questions, point out any flaws in his reasoning. And, being completely honest with himself, he knew he was also eager to see the look in her eyes when he told her that her granite-headed husband had finally broken his impasse with the Lord.

Suddenly he remembered Martin Harris. His mouth pulled down into a heavy frown. He didn't want to face Martin yet. Not until he had come to a clear resolution. In that sense, the lateness of his arrival might be to his advantage. He could already see that there were very few Saints still on their way to the temple. Most were already inside and seated.

But to Benjamin's surprise it was not Martin Harris who waited for him on the temple steps, but his own son. The moment Nathan spotted him coming up the walk, he came in a half walk, half run to meet him. "Pa," he said, even before he reached him. "There's going to be trouble."

Benjamin was surprised at the grimness on Nathan's face. "What kind of trouble?"

"Parrish and his followers are armed."

"*What?* Are you sure?" Benjamin had long ago learned that wild rumors had a way of multiplying like rabbits in a meadow of clover.

"I saw them, Pa." Nathan shook his head, and the depths of his alarm now touched off Benjamin's anxiety. "They've got pistols and bowie knives."

"In the temple? Why didn't someone stop them?" But even as he said it he realized it was a foolish question. He took Nathan's elbow. "Let's get inside."

"Yes. Mother and Lydia and Rebecca are saving us a place." He looked at his father. "I was afraid you weren't going to make it in time."

———— • ————

The tension inside the great assembly hall on the main floor of the Kirtland Temple was thicker than smoke inside an Indian wickiup. The congregation had started the opening hymn as Benjamin and Nathan stood at the back of the hall for a moment before moving to their seats. But this was not the usual opening hymn. Benjamin always thrilled with the power of eight hundred Saints lifting their voices in songs of praise to the Lord. But now the singing was half-hearted, tentative, almost frightened. He saw that many people kept turning away from their hymnbooks to look nervously over their shoulders. The congregation was facing west, toward the Melchizedek Priesthood pulpits. But the attention of the audience was being drawn to the Aaronic Priesthood pulpits that occupied the east end of the hall, just to the left of where Nathan and Benjamin were standing.

As Benjamin turned to see what they were looking at, it

became instantly obvious what was causing the stir. Warren Parrish and his followers had taken over the eastern pulpits. There
were fifteen or sixteen of them, all leaning forward on their elbows, glaring menacingly at the faces below them. Benjamin felt
his heart drop. The man closest to him had a long bowie knife
stuck in his boot. Beyond him, Benjamin could see the handle of
a pistol jutting out from Lyman Johnson's belt. John Boynton,
who sat in the second row but in the seat closest to Benjamin,
had a cane across his lap and a pistol in his hand. Benjamin felt
suddenly sick. He was familiar with that cane. In reality it was
hollow. It was nothing more than the scabbard for a long, razor-
sharp steel blade. The end of the cane served as the handle for
the sword. Nathan was right. This was a dangerous situation.

Warren Parrish suddenly turned and looked at Benjamin.
For a long moment their eyes locked. Then Boynton turned as
well. He sneered at Benjamin, motioning with his head for him
to come and sit with them. Benjamin pretended he had not
seen it. "Come on," he whispered to Nathan. "Let's sit down."

The relief on Mary Ann's face as Benjamin sat down beside
her was so obvious that he would have smiled if the situation
weren't so serious. "Ben," she started to whisper, "did you see
those—"

He took her hand and squeezed it quickly. "I saw," he murmured. "It's going to be all right."

The congregation finished singing the hymn, and a brother
on the front row rose to give the invocation. All heads bowed,
and for a few moments the assembly was united in prayer. When
the man finished and was seated again, Joseph Smith, Sr., rose
from his place in the western pulpits. He was evidently in charge
of the meeting and conducting it in Joseph's absence. Benjamin
nodded. He didn't know who had made that choice, but it was a
good one. Joseph's father, now in his sixty-seventh year, was a
venerated figure in Kirtland. His bearing was always one of dignity and wisdom. As Patriarch to the Church and father to the
Prophet, he was almost universally beloved and respected.

"Brothers and sisters," he began in a voice that was surprisingly strong for his years, "we shall begin our meeting today by calling on Brother Zebedee Coltrin to address us."

He sat down, and Brother Coltrin immediately stood. Again Benjamin nodded. This too was a wise choice. Zebedee Coltrin had been one of the seven presidents of the First Quorum of the Seventy for a time. Earlier in the year he and four others had been released from their positions in the presidency so that they could join with the high priests quorum. Zebedee was a faithful follower of Joseph and a man of unflinching courage.

For a moment he looked out across the congregation, then finally let his eyes come to rest on the brethren on the opposite end of the hall. "My dear brothers and sisters, fellow citizens with the Saints, it is with a grave heart that I rise to speak to you this Sabbath morning. These are sobering times in the Church. These are times of great sorrow."

Behind him Benjamin heard an angry mutter. He half turned and could see Boynton and Parrish whispering urgently to each other.

"Apostasy has reared its ugly head among us," Coltrin was continuing, "and it is eating at the very foundations of the Church."

Parrish shot to his feet. "Objection!"

Every head in the congregation turned. Eyes were wide with shock at the blatancy of the interruption. Parrish was leaning forward, breathing hard. "We bitterly resent the insinuations being made by Brother Coltrin. He speaks of apostasy and looks directly at us."

"Rightly so," someone in the congregation called out.

Now Boynton leaped up. "I heard that," he shouted. "Who said it? Who dares to accuse us of apostasy?"

Zebedee Coltrin's mouth was a tight line. "Brother Parrish, may I remind you that I have the floor. I referred to no one by name. I wish only—"

"You didn't have to," Parrish yelled. "We know who you are referring to with your subtle accusations and condescending innuendos."

Father Smith rose, his eyes blazing. "Brother Parrish," he called out across the congregation. "I have turned the time over to Brother Coltrin. If you wish to speak, I will call on you as soon as Brother Coltrin is finished."

Instantly all the men surrounding Parrish were up. Some were waving pistols in the air, others were pounding on the tables. "Let him be heard!" "We won't be silenced!" "Unfair! Unfair!"

The congregation sat in stunned silence, their heads jerking back and forth between the two groups. Benjamin and his family were seated just two or three rows back from the pulpits where Father Smith and Zebedee Coltrin were standing. Benjamin saw Father Smith turn to a brother near him. He leaned forward, trying to catch what was said.

"Go fetch the police," Father Smith called to the man. "We shall not tolerate this outrage one moment longer."

The man nodded and hurried out. Benjamin looked to Mary Ann, whose face had gone white. Lydia and Rebecca were staring at the Parrish group in shock and horror. Benjamin grabbed Nathan's shoulder and pulled him close. "Be ready to get the women out of here," he said. "Things are getting out of control."

"Silence!" Father Smith suddenly roared. It was like dumping a bucket of water on a burning stick. The shouting on the far east end sputtered out to angry mutterings and then to quiet.

Father Smith turned and motioned for Brother Coltrin to sit down, which he did. At that, Parrish and his party also sank back into their seats. Their faces were angry, but for the moment they were silenced.

"I cannot believe what is happening," Father Smith said, his voice trembling. "This is the house of the Lord. This is a place of reverence and worship. Have we lost all respect for God? Have we no shame?"

Benjamin saw Parrish stir, but Father Smith overrode him, his voice like the thunders of heaven, his eyes raking the group in the eastern pulpits. "You make this house a den of robbers and thieves and armed thugs! You are all rabble-rousers. And you, Warren Parrish—you are a known adulterer. How dare you come into the Lord's house and demand to be heard!"

Parrish screamed out one foul obscenity and was out of the pulpits, running up the aisle toward Father Smith, his hands outstretched, his fingers formed into claws. Boynton leaped to his feet, brandishing his pistol. "I'll blow the brains out of any man that moves!" he shouted. The other men around him were up now too, pistols out, knives drawn.

The effect was just the opposite of what Boynton demanded. Women and children screamed. A man on the far aisle leaped up and dove out of the nearest open window. People were ducking down between the pews, husbands were grabbing for their wives and children, people were stampeding for the doors.

Benjamin turned to Nathan. "Let's get them out of here! You take Lydia." He grabbed Mary Ann, then leaned forward to see beyond her to Rebecca. "Take your mother's hand," he cried. "Come on!"

As they pushed out into the masses of people frantically fighting their way up the aisle, Benjamin glanced up. On the first level of the Melchizedek Priesthood pulpits, Warren Parrish had reached Father Smith. He had him by the lapels of his coat and was screaming into his face. Father Smith had his head turned and was shouting over his shoulder. "Oliver, Oliver! Help me!"

Benjamin raised his eyes a little higher. Oliver Cowdery was in the row of seats just behind Father Smith. For a moment Oliver stared at the old patriarch, then dropped his eyes and looked at the floor. Benjamin felt a great surge of anger. Oliver Cowdery was a justice of the peace. Oliver Cowdery had been appointed to act in just such cases of lawlessness. But Oliver Cowdery was among the number who had become disaffected, and now he did nothing.

"Nathan!" Benjamin yelled.

His son turned around. He had his arms around Lydia, shielding her against the press of the people. Benjamin elbowed a man aside roughly and pulled Mary Ann and Rebecca forward next to Lydia. Rebecca was sobbing openly now. Mary Ann was pale, her lips pressed into a tight line. "Take your mother and your sister," Benjamin shouted. "I'm going to help Father Smith."

He turned. It was a scene from a nightmare. Screams rent the air. People crushed forward. For a moment, just in front of the pulpits, the crowd parted and Benjamin saw the face of Mother Smith. She was reaching out for her husband, crying piteously for help. Then the crowd pushed in again.

Roaring for people to make way for him, Benjamin thrust his way forward. In a moment he was to her. He threw up his arms to shield her, blocking off the pushing mob. "Father Smith! Father Smith!" she cried over and over.

Benjamin leaned down. "To the pulpits, Mother Smith. We've got to get out of the way."

She looked up. There was a flash of recognition and then a quick nod. Again using his body as a shield, he moved forward, shoving people out of his way. Finally they reached the western pulpits, which had largely emptied now. With a surge of relief, he helped Mother Smith up on the risers. Almost instantly she turned and began searching the crowd for her husband. Benjamin did the same.

Joseph's father was about ten feet away, still in the grip of Warren Parrish. But at that moment a great cry rent the air. Down the aisle, bumping people out of the way like a horse shouldering his way through tall weeds, came William Smith, one of the Prophet's younger brothers. William was a large young man, nearly as big as Joseph, and he had a fiery temper. Parrish was so intent on his task of dragging Father Smith back to his group that he did not see or hear William coming. William was like a man possessed. He lunged forward, throwing his arms over Warren Parrish, breaking his grip on Father Smith and grasping him in a huge bear hug. Stunned, Parrish tried to see who his attacker was. But William lifted him clear off the ground. Parrish's feet and hands flailed wildly but harmlessly in the air. Walking backward with heavy steps, William moved down the aisle, intent on getting Parrish out of the building altogether.

Gasping frantically for breath, Father Smith turned and stumbled back to where Benjamin and Mother Smith stood waiting. Mother Smith threw her arms around him and buried her face against him.

The aisle between the pulpits had cleared almost magically when William started carrying Parrish toward the doors. While there were some people still trying to get out of the doors or crawl through the windows, those inside the hall saw what was happening and a sudden hush fell over them. Then at the far end of the aisle, near where the doors to the entry hall were opened to the outside, a group of men moved forward to block the aisle again. In the forefront was John Boynton, flanked by Lyman Johnson and another man.

"William, watch out!" Benjamin yelled.

Boynton had drawn his sword out of its cane holder, and it gleamed in the light from the windows. William dropped Parrish and whirled to face the new danger. In one swift movement, the tip of the sword was touching William's chest. "One step further," Boynton screamed hysterically, "and I'll run you through." Instantly the other men had William surrounded, yelling and shouting at him, warning him that if he lifted so much as a finger to harm Parrish further it would go most severely with him.

Then from the other side of the hall there was a shout. "The police! The police are here!" Benjamin turned around in time to see several men pouring through the entryway. A cry went up from Parrish's group as some panicked and fled for the door. The Saints still in the hall tried to seize them, while others shouted, pointing out the offenders to the incoming officers. As one officer made a dive for a running figure, he slammed into the potbelly stove that sat in one corner. The stovepipe jarred loose and came crashing down, sending clouds of black soot billowing up.

Feeling a great sorrow and a great rage, Benjamin turned back to the couple next to him. "Father Smith, Mother Smith, I think it might be wise if we got you out of here."

———•———

For a long moment, Benjamin Steed stood at the front gate to the Warren Parrish home, located two doors north of the Newel Whitney store. It was past nine o'clock at night. How like them to hold their meetings so late, after most decent men had gone to bed. Benjamin's heart was pounding and his mouth was dry. Twice he nearly changed his mind and went back to accept Nathan's offer to accompany him. But then, as he had when Nathan made the offer earlier that afternoon, he shook his head. This wasn't Nathan's problem. And it wasn't Nathan who needed to clear things up once and for all.

Suddenly the door opened. Benjamin straightened and stepped forward. "Martin?"

"Benjamin, is that you?"

"Yes."

"Good. I expected you before this. Come in. Everyone is waiting for you."

Benjamin walked forward to the edge of the step, then stopped. "Martin?"

"What?"

"You know why I'm here, don't you?"

Martin's face twisted with concern. "Now, Ben, don't be hasty. What happened today got out of hand. Just come in and listen to what they have to say."

"I heard what they had to say today," he said bitterly.

"I don't cotton to that either," Martin said, suddenly morose. "I told Parrish to get a grip on his temper, but . . ." He shrugged, as if there were nothing more that could be said.

"A sixty-six-year-old man!" Benjamin exploded. "He attacked a sixty-six-year-old man. How can you excuse that?"

"I'm not excusing it, Ben," Martin snapped, irritated that Benjamin was being difficult. Instantly his voice softened.

"Look, Ben, I don't like everything that is going on. Some of the people inside there are even suggesting that we throw out the Book of Mormon. I won't stand for that."

"But as long as they're willing to throw out Joseph, you're willing to crawl in bed with them."

"Joseph is the real issue here," Martin said angrily. "Don't forget that. Joseph has fallen, and we have to do something about it. You even said that yourself, Ben."

Benjamin's head shot up. "No, I didn't, Martin. I never said that. I said I had questions, that I wasn't sure. But I never said Joseph is fallen." He looked away. "And I don't appreciate you twisting my words."

That seemed to hit the older man hard. His eyes narrowed. "We've been friends a long time, Ben. Are you going to turn your back on me now?"

Benjamin gave him an incredulous look, then saw that his task was hopeless. He took a deep breath. "Martin, I've been struggling with this a long time. But this morning things started to fall into place. I found a scripture. I thought it might possibly be the answer I've been looking for, but I wasn't sure. Then I went to the meeting." He shook his head, still shocked by the events of the morning. "Now I'm sure."

"No, Ben," Martin said, grabbing his arm. "Come inside. Just listen to what they have to say."

"I don't care what they say," Benjamin said wearily. "All that matters is what they do. All I'm looking for anymore is fruit."

Martin stared at him blankly. "Fruit?"

Benjamin gave a short, mirthless laugh. "Yes. Remember the promise? 'By their fruits ye shall know them.'"

"What's that supposed to mean?"

"I wasn't sure at first. I mean, Joseph has produced some remarkable fruit, wouldn't you say? The Book of Mormon. The restoration of the priesthood. A church that is like the one Christ organized on the earth. A temple. The Doctrine and Covenants." He shrugged. "How much time do you have? I could keep going."

"That's beside the—"

"No, let me finish," Benjamin rushed on. "And what fruit does this group have to show me? Threatening a sixty-six-year-old patriarch? Pistols in the house of God? Foul language? Rejection of the Book of Mormon?" He snorted in disgust. "Girls with black rocks giving you your revelation?" He passed a hand before his eyes. "I can't believe I've been so blind. It is so simple, and I couldn't see it."

"Benjamin, you're oversimplifying things. You have to—"

"Martin!" The voice from inside the house was sharp and angry. It was Warren Parrish's voice. "Are you bringing him in here or not?"

Martin turned around, his face flashing momentary anger. "We're comin', we're comin'. Just hold your horses."

Benjamin moved right up to the step. "There's nothing more to say, Martin, except to them. I need to let them know it's over for me. No more questions about where I stand."

A look of genuine panic flitted across Martin's face. "Ben, you can't go in and tell them that. They're expecting you to throw in with us. They're mad, Ben. Real mad."

Benjamin just nodded and started for the door.

Martin grabbed at his arm. "I'm warning you, Ben. As your friend. It's not wise to go in there like this."

For several moments Benjamin searched his friend's face. "It's got to be done, Martin." He pulled free and stepped to the door. He hesitated for only a brief second or two, then squared his shoulders and walked inside.

———◆———

Ben had finished his task at Parrish's house and was on his way home. It was as though a great burden had been lifted from him, and he walked slowly, savoring the feeling. He had been under the cloud for so long, it was as if he had been given new life. Now he had only two desires, both of them so keen that they burned inside him. The first was to get back to Mary Ann. He had told her of his decision this afternoon, and she had wept with joy. Now he wanted to lie beside her and talk it all through. His second wish was nearly as strong. He wished that Joseph were in Kirtland. If he were, he would go to him this very moment, late as it was, and beg for his forgiveness.

Benjamin stopped. He was passing a vacant lot filled with high weeds, now dry and brown in the late summer. There was a rustling sound a few yards off, as though something large were passing through the undergrowth. He peered more closely, but almost immediately the sound stopped.

After a moment, when it wasn't repeated, he moved on. Almost immediately he heard it again. Again he stopped. "Hello," he called. "Is someone there?"

But once more there was no other sound but the chirping of crickets and the soft rustling of the breeze. Feeling a sudden uneasiness, Benjamin started again, no longer dawdling. He passed one house that was darkened, then approached another large open field. Even though this was the side of the street his house was on, he considered crossing the street where there were other houses.

Smiling at his own childishness, he pushed the thought aside. Suddenly his heart jumped. A dark figure had stepped out from behind the hedge that separated the yard from the open field. It was a large man, but he had a hat on, pulled down low so his face was in blackness. Benjamin slowed his step. His heart was suddenly pounding in his chest like a bass drum. "Good evening," he said, peering at the man.

"Good evening." It was a deep voice, soft but menacing. There was a noise behind him. Benjamin whirled. Two figures had stepped out. They could have come only from the vacant lot. They were still ten yards away, but were walking swiftly now toward him.

"What do you want?" he demanded, his voice harsh with the fear that had swept over him.

"We want you," the voice behind him said. Benjamin started to spin around, but before he could turn, a crushing blow sent him staggering to his knees.

"We want the man who doesn't know what's good for him," the same voice said again. There was a fiendish laugh from someone else, and then something slammed into the side of his head.

Benjamin threw his hands up across his face as he went down hard. *Protect your head,* his mind shouted at him. He felt the toe of a boot catch him hard under his right arm. It sent incredible jolts of pain shooting through his body. *Protect your head,* his mind cried again, *protect your head.*

And then mercifully, as the blows and the kicks began to come like pelting rain in a thunderstorm, the blackness took him, and he no longer knew what was happening to him.

Peter took the stairs that led down into the cellar three at a time, his feet barely touching the cement. "Derek! Derek! Derek!" Derek was nearly asleep on the bed, the weekly newspapers from Mr. Morris draped across his chest. He sat up. "I'm right here, Peter."

Across the room, one of the men who shared the cellar with them came up with a jerk. He had been stretched out on the small bed, snoring heavily. Now he looked wild for a moment, trying to get his bearings. His chin was covered with black stubble, his eyes watery and red.

"Elder Kimball's back!" Peter screeched as he darted into their half of the room. "Elder Kimball's back."

"Hey, you," the man cried angrily, "shut yer bloomin' trap. How's a man supposed to sleep with you makin' on like a banshee or somethin'?"

Peter ignored him. "Come on, Derek. There's gonna be a meeting at Mrs. Dawson's house in ten minutes."

The man swore heavily. "Knock it off, kid, or it'll be the toe of me boot connecting with yer backside."

Derek stood up. "Let's go outside, Peter. Wouldn't want to wake ol' Charlie here until he's had a chance to sleep off a hard day at the pub."

———— ◆ ————

The missionary work in Preston had gone so well in the little over two weeks since the arrival of the brethren from North America that on August sixth Heber organized a branch of the Church in Preston—the first branch to be organized outside the North American continent. The "dippers," as all the townsfolk were calling them by then, had baptized twenty-eight souls in Preston. And many more were flocking to the meetings and listening to their preaching.

With that kind of success taking place, four of the missionaries were sent on August first to nearby communities—Willard Richards and John Goodson to Bedford, and Isaac Russell and John Snyder to Alston, in Cumberland. Then an unusual set of circumstances took Elder Kimball to Walkerfold, a small village about fifteen miles from Preston. A young woman by the name of Jennetta Richards had come to Preston to visit the Thomas Walmsley family. She soon met Elder Kimball and had a lengthy discussion with him about the gospel. At his invitation, she went to an evening meeting and listened to him preach. Much impressed, she came a second night and then, the next morning, requested baptism. She was baptized that morning, along with Peter and Derek Ingalls and Mrs. Pottsworth and her daughter, Jenny. That night, Heber C. Kimball penned a letter to Willard Richards in Bedford. "Willard," he wrote, "it may interest you to know that I baptized your wife today."

The day following her baptism, as Jennetta prepared to return home, she burst into tears. Surprised, Heber inquired as to what was wrong. She was the daughter of Walkerfold's most prominent minister. She was fearful at what her father would say when he learned she had joined another church without consulting him. Elder Kimball took Jennetta by the hand and said firmly, "Sister, be of good cheer, for the Lord will soften the heart of thy father, and I will yet have the privilege of preaching in his chapel, and it shall result in a great opening to preach the gospel in that region."

That prediction had created a small stir among the members. Word of the success of the Mormon missionaries was spreading among the English clergy, and opposition was mounting. But a few days later a letter came from Jennetta. With it was a letter from her father inviting Heber C. Kimball to come to Walkerfold and preach to his church. That had been over two weeks ago, and the Preston branch had been anxiously awaiting word ever since.

Now more than fifty people were packed into Mrs. Dawson's sitting room, listening eagerly as Elder Kimball reported on his labors. He had started by giving them the details of his trip there on foot and of how the Richardses had received him warmly and given him supper. He even began to tell them what the Richardses had served at the meal.

Mrs. Dawson was the landlady of the small boardinghouse in which the missionaries were staying, and was therefore close enough to them to be quite open with them. She wagged her finger at Heber. "Brother Kimball, all of these details are most interesting, but what we're all waiting to hear is, did you or did you not get to preach in the reverend's church as you promised his daughter?"

Heber just gave her an impish smile; then, imitating their own west Lancashire accent, he said, "I cahn't believe you bloomin' Englishmen. Ya got no patience at all. Won't even let a gentleman tell a proper story, ya won't."

Good-natured laughter rippled through the group as Mrs. Dawson blushed. Heber was well liked, and his teasing with them endeared him to them all the more. He waited for things to quiet again, then went on. "The next morning, being the Sabbath, I accompanied the reverend and his family to his church at the hour appointed. It was a goodly congregation.

Fine people." He smiled as Mrs. Dawson stirred again, then hurried on. "When the meeting started, the reverend gave out the hymns and prayed, and then he called on me to preach to those present."

There were numerous exclamations of satisfaction.

"I preached to an overflowing congregation on the principles of salvation. I likewise preached in the afternoon and the evening. By the time we finished, nearly the whole congregation was in tears. I preached again on the following Monday and Wednesday." His voice softened. "And on Thursday six individuals came forward for baptism. That seemed to alarm Mr. Richards. I think he was beginning to see all of this as a threat to his livelihood. But fortunately, unlike the Reverend James Fielding here in Preston, I'm pleased to say that Mr. Richards did not turn bitter—at least, not for now. He continued to manifest a kindly spirit and warm hospitality toward me. The following Sunday he once again gave out an appointment for me to preach. I baptized two the following day, and more are awaiting my return and will enter the kingdom soon."

A murmur of excitement and gladness swept through the group. Heber turned to Elder Orson Hyde, his fellow Apostle. "Brother Hyde informs me that he has received a letter from our companions in Cumberland, and as you can see"—he motioned to where John Goodson sat—"Brother Goodson has come down from Bedford and brought us a letter from Brother Richards there. I am happy to report that the work progresses well in both places. They have already baptized nineteen in Bedford and formed a branch there. And in Alston, the brethren there have baptized about the same number. Not to mention the success that Brother Hyde and Brother Fielding have continued to have in this area."

Now the group buzzed with excitement. Derek felt it too. The work was growing. Already nearly a hundred baptisms and that many more coming to meetings. That thrilled him. He was so on fire with the joy of the gospel, he wanted to shout it to the world. He had already started to quietly share the message with some of his fellow workers at the factory. Two of them, both women, were here tonight. One had her husband and two sons with her.

His thoughts were pulled back as he realized Heber was talking again, but now his face had grown very sober and his voice was subdued. "My brothers and sisters, the news is gratifying in many respects. The work rolls forward like the stone Daniel saw which was cut out of the mountain without hands. But it does not go unopposed. We know that the adversary is violently opposed to what is happening. He is starting to rage in the hearts of men. In Walkerfold, for example, some of our people are being ill treated by their neighbors because they have joined those 'Mormons from America.' In Cumberland, some of the younger brothers and sisters who have requested baptism are being thrust from their homes by their parents unless they renounce the faith."

As cries of shock and disappointment erupted, Derek felt a tug on his sleeve. He turned. To his surprise, Peter was smiling at him. "What?" he mouthed.

"At least we don't have that problem in our family," Peter whispered.

Derek smiled back. "No, Peter. That's one problem we don't have."

When Joseph returned from Canada in the closing days of August 1837, he was greeted with the grim news of what had been happening in his absence. The report of the near riot in the temple grieved Joseph deeply. Such actions could not be ignored. He called for a conference of the Church to be held on the following Sabbath, September third. One of the primary items on the agenda was the sustaining of the Church leaders and dealing with those who had violated the sanctity of the house of the Lord.

Brigham Young—who had been away on a business mission and had returned to Kirtland on August nineteenth—knew that the opposition was determined and organized. He feared they would try to get enough support so that Joseph would not be sustained. So early that Sunday morning Brigham rose and dressed, and then went quietly from house to house, visiting every brother whose vote could be relied on. He asked that they be to the temple early and occupy the pulpit seats and the most prominent benches.

When Sidney Rigdon, First Counselor in the First Presidency, stood and called for a vote by the priesthood quorums, Joseph Smith was unanimously sustained as the President of the Church. The vote for Sidney as First Counselor also carried unanimously. But the Saints refused to sustain Frederick G. Williams as Second Counselor. For months he had openly, and sometimes bitterly, criticized the Prophet. The Saints had had enough and found him unworthy of such a high office. Joseph then proposed that four assistant counselors be chosen. Joseph Smith, Sr.; John Smith, an uncle to the Prophet; and Joseph's brother Hyrum were accepted without hesitation. But the fourth name, that of Oliver Cowdery, was not. Oliver had not completely broken with Joseph, but the congregation had serious reservations about him too. Joseph asked the priesthood brethren to pray for him so that he might yet "humble himself and magnify his calling," and finally he was sustained.

John Boynton and Luke and Lyman Johnson, of the Quorum of the Twelve, were rejected and disfellowshipped for their general apostasy and also for their part in the attempt to take over the temple. Several other troublemakers, including Warren Parrish, the man who had once served as scribe to Joseph, were also disfellowshipped.

Another conference was called for later in the month, and the meeting was adjourned. To the vast relief of most present, things had gone with comparative smoothness, and relative calm seemed to settle over Kirtland again.

Dinner later on that same Sunday afternoon was not much like the usual Sabbath gatherings that had become traditional at the Steed house. The lighthearted bantering, the lazy conversation, the happy melee of the children racing around the house and yard—all of those were missing. Benjamin Steed had sent word to both of the married couples that they should make arrangements for someone to take the children immediately after dinner. There was to be a council of the Steed family, and it would be best if their attention wasn't diverted by the activities of the children. Sensing that something significant was happening, both couples—Lydia and Nathan, and Melissa and Carl—independently decided not to bring the children at all.

The mood through dinner was quiet and subdued. Rebecca barely said a word. Carl Rogers, Melissa's husband, was particularly restrained. Melissa looked as if she had been crying before she arrived. Nathan seemed preoccupied with his own thoughts and only responded with a murmur or grunt when directly spoken to. Benjamin and Mary Ann kept looking at each other, but neither chose to give any hints about what was coming, and both kept what conversation there was directed toward general topics.

Lydia kept finding herself stealing glances to where Benjamin sat at the end of the table. And each time she did, she winced inwardly. It had been exactly three weeks since that night he had gone to the Parrish house. Most of the swelling around his eyes and mouth had disappeared. But the bruises, once a shocking black or deep purple, were now a sickly yellow or dull brown. He still moved slowly, especially when he sat down or stood up. Occasionally, if he forgot himself and moved too quickly, the pain would slash across his face. The doctor said his three broken ribs and a punctured lung were healing well, but it would be another month before he was back to normal.

Finally dinner was done, to everyone's vast relief. Mary Ann stood and reached over for Benjamin's plate. Immediately, Rebecca, Melissa, and Lydia started to rise. Benjamin raised his hand, looking up at his wife. "The dishes can wait. Let's move into the sitting room."

Mary Ann gave him a quick look. "Do you want pie?"

He shook his head and pushed his chair back. "Let's talk first." For the first time, a tiny smile played around the corners of his mouth. "If we stay around this table much longer, someone's going to have to start singing a funeral dirge."

Mary Ann smiled, then nodded in agreement. She turned to her children and in-laws. "Let's go in where we can be more comfortable."

Benjamin stood by his favorite chair until they were all settled, then he moved around and sat down. He reached across to the small table where he kept his scriptures and picked up the copy of the Doctrine and Covenants. For a long moment he held it, his eyes looking down, his finger stroking the spine of the book slowly. Finally he looked up. He seemed surprised to find everyone watching him intently.

"I've been doing quite a bit of reading in the last couple of weeks," he began. He turned to Nathan. "Should have been out with you helping with the harvest, but . . ." He shrugged.

"We're makin' on fine, Pa. You're in no shape to be doing hard work."

Benjamin acknowledged that, then looked to his wife. "We used to spend a lot of time worrying about our properties here in town, but we've lost all those too now, so I seem to have a lot of time on my hands of late."

"You need to take it easy," Melissa said. "You've been through a lot."

Again he absently acknowledged the comment with a nod, then he opened the book and began thumbing through it. He found what he was looking for almost immediately. He read silently for a moment, then looked up. "I love the Doctrine and Covenants," he said. "It's really our book. Even the Book of

Mormon was given to an ancient people." He held up the book. "This book was given directly to us."

Carl Rogers stirred slightly, and Melissa reached out quickly and laid a hand on his knee. If Benjamin saw the little interchange, he gave no sign. He lowered the book again and found the place he wanted. "I'd like to read you something the Lord said around seven months after Joseph came to Kirtland." His finger went down to the page, moved quickly for a moment, then stopped. His voice softened as he began to read. "'I willeth not that my servant Frederick G. Williams should sell his farm, for I the Lord willeth to retain a strong hold in the land of Kirtland. . . .'" He paused, then more slowly, and with greater emphasis, continued. "'I the Lord willeth to retain a strong hold in the land of Kirtland, *for the space of five years.*'"

Now there was not a sound in the room. Every head was turned toward him, every eye watching the tiniest movement of his face for clues as to where this was going. Every eye, that is, except for Mary Ann's. She sat beside him, her hands folded calmly in her lap, her head turned so she could watch him, but without anxiety, or without questions.

Again there was a tiny flicker of a smile on Benjamin's face. "That was given in September 1831. Now it is September 1837. We're a year overdue."

Nathan leaned forward. "Overdue for what?"

Benjamin looked at Mary Ann, then reached across the table and took her hand with his free hand. He still held his copy of the Doctrine and Covenants in his other hand, one finger marking his place. "We've been thinking a lot about Missouri lately, your mother and me."

"Missouri?" Rebecca blurted.

"Yes. We're pleased that things are going so well for Jessica since her marriage, but your mother has been much concerned about Matthew. He's still quite young to be all by himself, running a farm, with no family close by."

Lydia sat back in wonder. "You're not thinking of . . ." Then she laughed softly. That was exactly what they were thinking of.

Benjamin smiled at this daughter-in-law who had become as close to him as either of his natural daughters. "It's been six years since the Lord said we could expect five years in Kirtland. With what's happening now, I think we all see the handwriting on the wall. Kirtland's heyday has passed."

Carl Rogers looked angry. "Kirtland is doing just fine."

"Oh, Carl," Benjamin said, with just a touch of impatience, "I'm not talking about Kirtland as a town, but Kirtland as a place for the Latter-day Saints." He turned and looked at Nathan and Lydia. "Now let me read you what the Lord says in this same revelation." He opened the book again and read quickly. "'And after that day'—after those five years are up—'I the Lord will not hold any guilty, that shall go, with an open heart, up to the land of Zion.'"

Melissa shot forward. "You and Mama are thinking of going to Missouri?"

"You can't!" Nathan cried, not waiting for the answer that was now quite obvious.

"Why not?" Mary Ann said calmly. "What is there left for us here? The farms are gone. The crops you are harvesting now will only go to the new mortgage holder. Our property in town has gone into foreclosure. All we have left now is this house."

"And your family!" Melissa cried.

Mary Ann looked away, her lip suddenly trembling. "Yes. And our family. But we have family in Missouri too."

Rebecca was shaking her head, half-incredulous and yet instantly accepting. Kirtland held no special attraction for her, not since Arthur Wilkinson had started spreading his stories about her. "Joseph is talking about *all* of the Saints gathering there," she said to Melissa. "They've called a conference for later in the month to talk about that very subject." Suddenly a thought hit her. "Maybe if we go, we could even find Joshua."

Benjamin's head jerked around sharply, and his eyes were suddenly cold.

Mary Ann jumped in quickly. "I don't think so. First of all, it's not safe to go to Jackson County. But if you remember, in one of Jessica's letters almost a year ago she said that Joshua has gone, moved to Georgia or somewhere."

Rebecca's face fell. "Oh, that's right."

Out of the corner of her eye, Mary Ann saw Nathan look away, though whether in gratitude or disappointment she could not tell.

Benjamin cut in brusquely. "Your brother has nothing to do with this. He's never answered our letters. He's not been a part of our family for years. That's not going to change." Then, before Mary Ann could contradict him, he changed the subject. "After the meeting this morning, Joseph told me that he and Brother Rigdon are planning to go to Missouri after the next conference. Your mother and I are seriously thinking of going with them."

"In less than a month?" Lydia said softly, her eyes suddenly tearing. "So soon? So terribly soon?"

Mary Ann swung around to Nathan and Lydia. "Come with us. There's nothing to hold you here either, now that we've lost the farms. You don't want to farm them for someone else."

Lydia was shaking her head slowly. "I . . ." She reached for Nathan's hand. "Actually, we've been talking about going to Zion too. But . . ." She turned to her husband.

Nathan gave her a questioning look, and she nodded. He looked at his parents. "Lydia is with child."

All three of the other women burst out together. "You are?"

Lydia nodded happily. "Yes. The baby's due in late April or early May."

"That's wonderful, Lydia," Benjamin said.

Instantly, Rebecca was to Lydia and kneeling in front of her, clasping her hands. "It *is* wonderful, Lydia. I'm so happy for you."

Nathan touched his younger sister's shoulder. "We're very happy too, but we've already traveled once when Lydia was carrying a child. From Palmyra to here. It wasn't much fun for her. We'd have to wait until spring."

Benjamin leaned forward, obviously pleased. "By spring we could have a place ready for you."

Mary Ann had turned to watch her oldest daughter. Melissa was staring at Lydia, forcing a smile, but her eyes were bleak. Mary Ann spoke very softly. "Melissa?"

She turned.

"We know what this means. But we also know that things are different for you. Carl has the livery stable here, and—" She stopped. And what? What else could she say? Carl despises the Mormons. Carl rejects everything that would draw us to Zion. Carl would laugh in our faces if we asked you to come with us.

Melissa closed her eyes. "I know, Mama, I know."

Carl startled everyone by standing abruptly. His mouth was set in a tight line, and his eyes were grim. "I'm sorry, Benjamin, but there's something we have to say."

Benjamin looked up at his son-in-law calmly. "Say on, Carl."

He blew out his breath, looking quickly at his wife, then away. "Melissa and I have been talking a lot about things lately too. We were glad when you said the family was going to meet to talk tonight."

And then in the face of Benjamin's steady gaze, he lost his nerve. He reached down and pulled at Melissa's arm. "Tell them, Melissa."

"Not now, Carl. Not with all this."

"Tell them!"

Mary Ann stood and went to her daughter. She took her by the hands and pulled her up. For a long moment she looked into her eyes, holding her hands tightly. "I think your father and I already know, Melissa," she said, fighting to keep her voice steady. "You can tell us."

There was a stifled sob, a looking away, then slowly Melissa's head came back to face her mother. "I can't go on any longer, Mama. It's tearing me apart."

Mary Ann bit her lower lip. "I know."

Melissa swung around, suddenly angry, turning on her father. "After what they did to you, Papa, how can you still be one of them?"

His head came up slowly. "I'm not one of them who did this to me."

"How can you still stay a Mormon?" she burst out. "The Church is falling apart. You're fighting amongst yourselves. Even three of the Quorum of the Twelve have turned against you."

"You claim to be the only true Church," Carl snorted in derision. "But look at what's happening. Bickering, infighting, one group turning against another." His eyes were hard and challenging. "Beating up one another."

Benjamin watched his son-in-law steadily for a moment, and then spoke slowly, choosing his words very carefully. "That's true, Carl. And I can see why that would upset you and Melissa. But I assume, then, that you'll want to give up on Christianity altogether."

Carl's eyebrows lifted sharply. "Why would you say that?"

Reaching over to the table, Benjamin set down the copy of the Doctrine and Covenants and picked up the Bible. "I told you I've been doing a lot of reading lately. I've always mostly read in the Gospels when I've read the New Testament. But these past two weeks I've been reading a lot in the book of Acts, and in the writings of the Apostle Paul. It's been most interesting."

Carl was wary now.

Benjamin pressed on. "After the Resurrection, the church Jesus organized saw fantastic growth both in numbers and in the areas where the Church went. But all was not wonderful. Over and over there were challenges. Some were challenges from the enemies outside the Church." He gave Carl a sharp look. "But some were challenges *within* the Church. For example, Paul warned Church leaders from Ephesus to watch out for 'grievous wolves' who would enter in among the flock, leading away many. He even predicted that some among the leadership would arise and lead away disciples after themselves."

Carl said nothing. Melissa was looking at the floor. Benjamin sighed, not liking what he was doing, but knowing it had to be done. "Again and again Paul talked about false teachers in the Church who went around trying to deceive people. Almost every one of his letters was sent to correct problems among the Saints."

Subconsciously he let one hand steal up to rub at the spot where his ribs had been broken. "Paul was beaten and stoned and scourged. And sometimes that was done by members of the Church."

Now he looked directly at Carl, challenging him openly. "So with all that, Carl, I just hoped you'd be fair. If you're going to reject the Mormon church because it has these kinds of problems in it, then I assume you'll reject Christianity altogether, for the early Church had exactly the same kind of problems."

Carl was breathing heavily. His face had turned sullen, but he had no answer. Melissa watched him and her father for a minute, then stepped forward. "Papa, I don't know what is right and wrong anymore. I don't like what I see happening in the Church. But I don't know who or what is to blame. All I know is that Carl and I can't go on like this, fighting among ourselves, jerking the children back and forth."

Benjamin turned to his daughter, his eyes dark and filled with an immense sadness. "I understand, Melissa." He turned to Carl. "Did you ever pray about finding a church that you both could be united in?"

"You mean did I pray about whether the Mormon church is true or not?" Carl said, almost sneering.

"That's not what Mary Ann suggested you do. What she said was—"

"You don't pray about something you already know the answer to," Carl cut in bluntly. "No, I didn't pray about it."

"I see." There was a great weariness in him.

Melissa stepped between these two men whom she loved. Now her cheeks were wet, and she was fighting hard to keep her voice under control. "Papa, I've started going to Carl's church. It's . . ." A slight shudder shook her body as she fought back her emotions. "It's just easier." She tensed, waiting for his reaction.

But to her surprise, he did not get angry. Instead, he opened his arms and took her into them. He pressed her head down against his shoulder, wincing for a moment, with the movement. Then he began to pat her shoulder softly. "I understand, Melissa," he whispered. "I understand."

"Don't go, Papa. Please don't go."

He pulled back, reached out and lifted her chin, looking deep into her eyes. "We have to, Melissa." He stopped. His Adam's apple bobbed twice, and then to everyone's shocked surprise, there were tears in his eyes. Benjamin Steed was crying! "We have to. We just have to."

Melissa began to sob openly now. Benjamin shook his head, trying to shake away his own emotions. Failing in that, he pulled her to him again and held her tightly to him. He buried his face in her hair. "But I want you to know that the thoughts of leaving you and your family behind—" His voice broke, and he had to stop for a moment. Finally, he took a deep breath, and in a strained whisper finished his sentence. "That will be the hardest thing your mother and I have ever done."

———————

Jessica Roundy Steed Griffith was softly humming one of the hymns to herself as she moved about the small, one-room cabin picking up after Rachel and the boys' hasty departure to go out with their father for a load of firewood. The early September sunshine came through the south window, filling the room with brightness. This was her favorite time of the year. Indian summer was in its full strength on the Great Plains, and she loved its warmth and golden brightness.

Suddenly she stopped and dropped a hand to her stomach. She probed carefully. Had she felt something there? But instantly she shook her head. At most she could be only three months along. It was too early to feel life. Much too early. And yet she thought about it every day. Ever since she had realized she was with child again, she had anxiously awaited the time when she would feel life. She was growing, swelling slowly but steadily now, and that encouraged her. But she had grown in those first times too, back with Joshua in Independence. But there had never been any stirrings of life, and eventually she had miscarried.

But while she lived daily with the worry, somehow it was not the same as back in those times with Joshua. There was a feeling of peace, of steadiness. It was as though the Lord were comforting her, telling her that the days of lost babies were past.

And there was something more. The losses back in those days when she had been married to Joshua not only had been bitter personal tragedies but also had brought a great strain into the marriage. If she did lose this baby—heaven forbid!—she knew it would be different with her and John. They were still developing their relationship. The awkwardness had not yet fully disappeared between them—they had been married for only four months—but to her constant surprise and wonder the marriage had brought her a joy that she had never known to this point. John Griffith was a gentle and kindly man. He treated her with respect, and she could sense that something was developing between them. It would take time, but when it fully bloomed it was going to be a source of great joy to them both.

A sharp knock sounded at the door. A little surprised to have company this early in the day, she walked over to it. She opened it, then stepped back in pleased surprise. "Matthew?"

"Hello, Jessica."

———————

"No," Matthew said firmly, looking John Griffith straight in the eye, "I've thought this over very carefully. My mind is made up."

Jessica's husband shook his head. "It's not a fair trade. You get a cabin no bigger than what you already have, smaller maybe. And I get a cabin and five acres of land."

"So, I'll sell the land to you. Two hundred dollars. You pay it off whenever you can. No interest on the mortgage."

Griffith was a small man, not more than an inch or two taller than Jessica, but he was strong and wiry. And while he was a quiet man, he was not of a weak mind by any means. "You would make a terrible businessman, Matthew. You are far too generous."

"You are a farmer, John, not a day laborer. You also have three children to care for, with another one on the way. I'm single. I can do what you're doing here and earn more than sufficient for my needs. But I can't do that in Haun's Mill. The work is here in Far West."

"I know all that—"

Matthew held up his hand. "Now, listen to me. I don't want to be that tied down. I want to do missionary work. This will give me that freedom."

"I can't do it. Your father got the land for you."

"No, my father got that land for Jessica and Rachel. I just came along to help Jessica." He turned to Jessica. "Tell him, Jessie. What will Pa say when he finds out what I've done?"

Jessie smiled, her eyes shining. "He's right, John. You didn't get to meet Benjamin Steed. He's one of the most generous men you'll ever meet. He'll put an arm around Matthew's shoulder and tell him he did right in this."

John Griffith sat back, obviously still very uncomfortable. Matthew grinned at him. "Then it's settled. I brought my stuff with me in the wagon. I'll help you pack tomorrow." He turned to Rachel and the two Griffith boys, who had been watching the proceedings with wide, curious eyes. "Get your stuff together, kids. You're going to Haun's Mill."

"Mr. Morris wants to see you in his office."

Maggie Stumps dropped her eyes as Derek looked up in surprise from the ledger book. "He does?"

"Yes, immediately."

Surprised and a little flustered, Derek stood, putting the quill pen back in the inkwell. He brushed off his shirt and trousers and checked himself quickly. Mr. Morris almost always came out into the clerk's area when he had something on his mind. Derek had been in the back office only two or three times.

As he came out from behind his table, Maggie cleared her throat quickly. She was just two years older than Derek but already a mother of two. She worked at the table beside him, and they had become good friends. She was one of the people he had talked to about the gospel. "Derek?"

He slowed his step. She glanced nervously in the direction of Mr. Morris's office, then concentrated her gaze on her ledger book. "I won't be comin' to the meetings anymore."

He stopped, peering at her. "Why?"

Again her eyes darted toward the back office. "I just won't."

Derek was stunned. She would not look up again, and finally he made his way slowly toward the back office.

Alexander Morris was looking at some papers on his desk when Derek stepped inside his office. He did not lift his eyes, though Derek knew he was aware of his presence. For almost a full minute he kept reading, leaving Derek standing there awkwardly. He kept frowning as he clamped his teeth on his unlit cigar.

Finally, he pushed the papers aside and leaned back. His eyes were cold and his jaw set. "Ah, Mr. Ingalls." It came out oozing, but beneath the veneer his voice was hard and challenging.

"Yes, sir?" Derek tried to force himself to breathe normally.

"How old are you now, Ingalls?"

"I'll be twenty next month, sir."

"You're a strapping lad for twenty. How long did you work shoveling coal in the boiler rooms?"

"Four years, sir."

"Did you enjoy that?"

He smiled faintly. "Not especially, sir." *Where is this leading?*

"You prefer working here in the office?"

"Yes, sir. I really enjoy what I'm doing."

"Good. You wouldn't want to leave, then."

Derek felt his heart plummet. "No, sir. Of course not, sir."

Morris took the cigar from his mouth and laid it in the ashtray. "Then you'll not be doing anything more with those Mormons, will you?" he asked softly.

Derek rocked back, too flabbergasted to comprehend what he had just heard.

"The stories are true? You have been listening to the Mormons?"

"Uh . . . yes, sir, but—"

"No buts, Ingalls," Morris snapped. "Either you have or you haven't. Which is it?"

"I have, sir, but I don't see what that has to do with my work. I—"

Morris leaned forward, cutting him off. "I'm a deacon in my church, Ingalls. Our minister called us together yesterday. He told us what has been happening. We've already lost four of our congregation." He shook his head in disbelief. "When he told me some of my own factory workers—"

"Sir, it's not what you think. I can tell you sure, sir, Mormonism—"

"Silence!" the man roared, slamming his fist down against the desk hard enough to make the inkwell jump. "Do you think I brought you in here to preach to me?"

"No, sir," Derek stammered. His mouth had gone dry, and he felt his knees trembling.

Morris leaned back, his tiny eyes glittering and narrow, his mouth pulled back into a grimace of a smile. "Tell you what, Ingalls. You've been a good worker. I understand how easy it is to be misled. Don't let me hear any more about this, and I'll forget the whole thing."

Derek's jaw dropped. He didn't know what to do except stand there and stare at the man.

After a moment, the veneer smile faded away. "Do you understand what I'm saying to you, lad?"

Derek felt dizzy, as if he might faint. He shook his head slowly.

Morris leaned forward, his hands spread-eagled out on the desk top. "I'm saying you've got until lunchtime to tell me you're going to stop this ridiculous flirtation with these Mormons. And by the way, there'll be no more preaching to Mrs. Stumps or any of the other workers either. If that's not to yer liking, then you're out of a job. Now, is *that* clear enough?"

"But I've already been baptized," he blurted.

"Then renounce it!" he thundered. "You've got until lunch. I'll want your answer by then."

Something snapped in Derek. He straightened slowly, squaring his shoulders. "I don't need until lunch to make that decision, Mr. Morris."

Morris was starting to rise, to dismiss him. He froze in position. His face went almost instantly livid. "Then get your things and get out!"

Derek didn't answer, just spun on his heel and started for the door.

"Ingalls!"

He stopped but didn't turn around. "On your way out, stop at the cutting shed and pick up your little brother. He's fired too."

The September mist was heavy in the air as dawn began to break over Preston. Peter came creeping up the cellar stairwell, looking cold and tired and frightened. Relief instantly crossed his face when he saw Derek sitting on the upper stairs.

Derek slid over without a word and then put his arm around his brother's shoulders and held him tight up against him.

"Have you been up all night?" Peter asked.

There was a quick nod.

Peter's lower lip started to tremble, and he bit down on it hard.

"It's going to be all right, Peter."

"What will we do? Mrs. Pottsworth says other factory owners are saying they won't hire any Mormons."

"I've thought about it all night, Peter."

"And what have you decided?"

Derek reached down and picked up a small leather bag. It was black with coal dust, and Peter knew it was the bag his brother had kept so carefully hidden in the coal bin below them. Derek bounced it up and down, and there was the soft jingle of coins.

"How much do we have?" Peter asked.

"Not quite ten quid."

Peter's eyes went wide and round. "Really? I didn't know we had anywhere near that much. We can live for quite a while on ten quid."

Derek immediately shook his head.

"We can't? Why not?"

Derek raised his head, let his eyes run down the dingy row of workers' housing that stretched on down the street for as far as the eye could follow it. "Do you remember when we were reading from the Book of Mormon, Peter? About how Lehi and his family left Jerusalem?"

"Yes."

"Where did they go?"

"To the promised land."

"Yes."

Peter's eyes widened. "But the promised land was in America."

"Yes, Peter, it was." He tossed the bag up in the air and caught it neatly with a sweep of his hand. "It not only *was* in America, Peter. It still *is* in America."

How much money do you have, lad?"

Derek's mind raced quickly. The captain of the American clipper ship seemed kindly enough. But after a week in the harsh environment of the Liverpool waterfront, Derek had learned that caution was required at all times. He also knew that human nature sought to make the best deal possible.

"Not nearly enough, sir," he finally said carefully.

The captain eyed him for a moment, then chuckled. "Normal steerage-class passage is eighteen American dollars. That would be . . ." His head bobbed back and forth for a moment. "About six pounds each."

That didn't surprise Derek. He had been asking around now for the past week about passage fare. Five to six pounds was about average. He had just slightly more than that. When the missionaries had announced Derek and Peter's determination to go to America, Heber C. Kimball had asked for a collection from the branch. Even from their poverty the Saints had collected more than three pounds. That gave them a total of about thirteen quid. But since their arrival they had spent almost a pound for a place to stay and eat—a shocking price for the filthy room and awful gruel they were receiving—and Derek knew that every day they stayed in Liverpool took money from the purse. And besides that, if they spent it all on passage, there would be nothing on which to live when they arrived in New York. And there was still the problem of getting from there to Ohio.

The captain was watching him closely. "Your family can't help you?"

"Both of our parents died of cholera."

The captain nodded, already expecting some such answer. His mouth softened. "My parents indentured me when I was eleven," he said. There was a quick shrug. "They had eight mouths to feed. Boston was not a good place to do it. By the time I was thirteen I had crossed the Atlantic six times." He eyed Derek up and down. "You a good worker?"

"I shoveled coal twelve hours a day for four years."

There was a quick nod. "All right, tell you what. I'll give you twenty-five cents a day as a deckhand. Figure eighteen days passage, two days unloading the cargo. That's five dollars. I'll lower passage for the two of you to thirty dollars. Make it an even ten pounds."

Derek's face was impassive. He didn't want to seem ungrateful, but he sensed they were still in the bargaining phase. "My brother, he's thirteen. He's been working in the mills since he was seven. He's very quick."

The American shook his head. Then when Derek didn't flinch, he finally laughed. "Can he cook?"

"He's been cooking for us since he was ten."

"All right, all right. Ten cents a day for him being a cabin boy. That's"—he calculated quickly—"about two dollars more. Eight pounds for the two of you. But if you're seasick and can't work, you owe me that many more days on arrival. Fair enough?"

Derek felt an immense rush of relief. "More than fair, sir."

———•———

"Do you think she'll ever learn to crawl like a normal baby?" It was said not as a criticism but with evident pride. Joshua was watching Savannah scoot across the woolen carpet that covered all but the outer edges of the parlor. He had rolled a ball across her line of vision, and she had immediately changed directions and gone after it, pulling herself forward rapidly by her elbows, but not pushing with her legs at all.

Caroline laughed. "For a child who is barely six months old, this one has a mind of her own. I think she will do what she darn well pleases, whether it's the traditional way or not."

As though she had understood exactly what her mother said, Savannah stopped and turned her head to gravely survey her parents. Her eyes were a deep blue, like the surface of a lake in the afternoon sunshine. Her cheeks were losing their baby chubbiness, and she was becoming quite a beautiful little girl. She had never lost her baby hair, and new hair was coming in thick and fast. And it was as red-orange as the leaves on the maple trees behind their home.

Joshua stood. "Thanks for dinner. I'd better be getting back. We've still got that load of fabric from St. Louis to unload. I'll be—"

A knock on the door cut him off. "I'll get it," he said. As he moved to the entryway, Caroline stood and retrieved Savannah from the floor.

"Hello, Joshua."

Joshua blinked in mild surprise. "Well, hello, Clint."

Clinton Roundy had his hat in his hand and was fidgeting nervously. He looked past Joshua. "Good afternoon, Mrs. Steed."

"Good afternoon, Clinton." She was obviously surprised too. Feelings were still quite awkward between her and the father of Joshua's former wife, and so Clinton Roundy had come to their home only once before.

Joshua stepped back. "Come in, come in. Would you like some johnnycake?"

Clinton shook his head quickly. "No, thank you anyway. I've only a minute." He reached inside his jacket and withdrew an envelope. Again he shot a nervous glance in Caroline's direction before turning to Joshua. "I got a letter from Jessica this morning."

"Oh?" Joshua watched him closely, also wanting to see Caroline's face but not daring to turn around and look. Jessica still occasionally wrote to her father, and from time to time Clinton would get someone to help him write her back. Sometimes when Joshua was at the saloon, Clinton would tell him what was going on with her. But Joshua had strictly forbidden Clint from saying anything to Jessica about him. Somehow Jessica had heard about his trip to Georgia and thought it was permanent. That suited his purposes fine, and he hadn't let Clint correct her thinking.

One time Clint had tried to suggest that Joshua come north with him to see Rachel. They could even look up Joshua's younger brother Matthew. Joshua had cut him off bluntly before the suggestion was half finished. He often thought of Rachel— she would be six in January—and there was something deep down inside him that ached to see her, but seeing Rachel meant seeing Jessica, and that was not appealing at all. There was too much pain. He was glad that Jessica had married again. Glad for her. Glad that it put a bad chapter in his life to rest. And the idea of seeing Matthew was equally unappealing. Sometimes when he thought of his little brother—still six and towheaded in his mind—he physically hurt inside. But seeing Matthew or Rebecca or any other family member meant all kinds of other complications as well, complications he was not willing to face.

Clinton had started to open the envelope and take out the letter. When he saw Joshua's face, he thought better of it and pushed it back inside the envelope. He knew perfectly well what it said anyway. He cleared his throat, looked down at the address for a moment, then slowly raised his eyes. "Jessie got a letter from your family, Joshua."

Joshua's eyes narrowed slightly. "My family?"

"Yes, your mother." He took a quick breath. "They're moving out here, Joshua. They're coming to Missouri."

Behind him, Joshua heard a quick intake of breath from his wife. But he was barely conscious of it. "When?" he asked slowly.

"The letter was written the first part of September. They said they were leaving with some others the last part of the month."

Caroline came forward and stood by Joshua. She looked up at him. "That's wonderful, Joshua."

He didn't turn his head. "What about Nathan?" he said, his voice almost a whisper. "Did they say whether my brother would be coming?"

Clinton nodded. "His wife is with child, but Jessica said they would come in the spring. Your sister that's married, she won't be coming, but everyone else will."

Joshua suddenly felt more bleak than a prairie sleet storm. "Thank you, Clint," he finally managed. "Thanks for coming to tell us."

———————

It was a biting-cold day in mid-October. The sky was a deep gray and was threatening snow. As Emma Smith hurried up the walk to the door of Nathan and Lydia Steed's home, her breath puffed out in little explosions of mist. She knocked sharply, then knocked again almost immediately.

There were the sounds of footsteps, then the door opened. It was Lydia. Instantly a look of concern crossed her face. "Hello, Emma. Is it Jerusha?"

"Yes." Hyrum Smith's wife was very ill. With Hyrum gone to Missouri, the sisters in Kirtland had rallied around to help her.

"Even worse than yesterday?" Lydia asked in alarm.

Emma looked away. "Yes."

That was not good. "We'll get our coats and meet you there."

Jerusha Smith had always been a favorite of Lydia's. She had the same gentle and gracious disposition as Hyrum. She was cheerful and positive in her outlook. She never spoke meanly of others. And when Hyrum was gone—as he often was with Joseph, conducting Church business—she never complained. Like now. Joseph had requested that Hyrum accompany him and Sidney Rigdon to Missouri to strengthen the Church there. Hyrum had gone straight to Missouri while Joseph and Sidney stopped off to visit some of the branches of the Church along the way. That left Jerusha to care for five children by herself in a time of increasing tensions and grim economic conditions in Kirtland. Yet not once had Lydia heard her murmur about her lot. And then the week following Hyrum's departure, Jerusha's health failed.

Rebecca hurried alongside Lydia as they turned into Hyrum's yard and walked up to the door. "I hope she's going to be all right."

Lydia was tight-lipped with worry. "She was terrible yesterday. Totally listless. She could barely lift her head off the pillow. The fever was raging inside her. If she's gone downhill from there . . ." She didn't finish, just raised the door knocker and rapped it sharply.

After a moment the door opened. Mother Smith was standing there, a towel in one hand. She looked very tired and very small, as though life had finally beaten her down. "Hello, Sister Lydia. Thank you for coming." She turned, looking a little surprised. "Rebecca. I thought you were going to Missouri with your parents."

"No. I was going to, but then we decided I should stay with Nathan and Lydia until spring so I can help her with the baby." She stepped forward. "I thought maybe I could take Jerusha's children for a time, Mother Smith."

The wrinkled but kindly face fell. "That's very kind of you,

Rebecca, but . . ." Her shoulders lifted and fell. "Jerusha has called for the children to come to her bedside. They've just gone in to see her."

That sent a jolt of alarm through Lydia. Was it that bad?

Mother Smith ushered them in and started immediately down the hallway. As they came into the bedroom, they both stopped, struck by the scene before them. The five children, three girls and two boys, were gathered around the foot of the bed. Jerusha's face looked as gray as stone against the whiteness of the pillow. The children ranged in age from ten down to a small baby which Lovina, the oldest daughter, held in her arms. Emma was standing by the head of Jerusha's bed, her eyes red and swollen. She looked at Lydia, then away, shaking her head. All hope had gone from her face.

Jerusha looked up as they entered. Her eyes smiled for a moment at Lydia, and there was gratitude there, but then three-year-old Hyrum—his father's namesake and already destined to look like him—came forward. His lower lip was quivering, but he was trying fiercely not to cry. Behind him, little Jerusha, nearly two years old, started to whimper softly. That was too much for Hyrum, and he dove forward, burying his head against his mother's arm.

Instantly Lydia's eyes were burning, and a great clutching sensation gripped her chest. Behind her, Rebecca stifled a sob. Emma was weeping silently, one hand touching her sister-in-law's shoulder. Mother Smith stared at the floor, her body trembling slightly.

For a long time, Jerusha just held her son, letting her hand caress his hair gently. Then she pulled him close and whispered for several moments into his ear. Finally he straightened, nodding. He squared his shoulders and stepped back, tears squeezing out of the corners of his eyes. But his jaw was set, and he fought to look brave.

"All right, children," Mother Smith said softly, "I think we'd better let your mother rest."

Rebecca came forward. "Come children, come with me."

Jerusha pulled up slightly, straining desperately to make herself heard. "I'd like Lovina to stay for a moment."

"Here," Rebecca said, "let me take the baby."

Lovina handed the baby over to Rebecca, who then gently shooed the children forward and out of the room. As the door closed, Lovina came forward to her mother's side. Jerusha reached out and grasped her hand, holding it tightly. "Dear Lovina," she whispered.

"Yes, Mama," she answered in a quavering voice.

"Tell your father when he comes home that the Lord has taken your mother home and left you and the others for him to care for."

Lovina started to cry uncontrollably. "I will, Mama. I will."

Satisfied, Jerusha fell back, letting go of her daughter's hand. "Come, Lovina," Lydia said, putting her arm around the shuddering young body. "Let's go out with the others."

Even as Lydia left the room, Jerusha Barden Smith closed her eyes and fell into a deep sleep. Within the hour her breathing became shallow and labored. Finally, there was a great sigh, and then her body was still.

———————————

"Listen to this, Peter."

Peter rolled over on his side in the narrow bunk above Derek's.

Derek sat up a little straighter, adjusting his shoulder so that it did not block the light coming from the one lamp above their heads. "This is the one I was telling you about. The one I was looking for. It's the book of Ether."

He opened the Book of Mormon wider and let his eyes run down the page, automatically letting them adjust themselves to the gentle rolling motion of the ship. "It's speaking about the Jaredites." He looked down and began to read. "'And the Lord would not suffer that they should stop beyond the sea in the wilderness, but he would that they should come forth even unto the land of promise, which was choice above all other lands, which the Lord God had preserved for a righteous people.'"

He leaned out of his bunk, looking up. "Did you catch that, Peter? It's a land choice above all others."

"Yes," Peter said dreamily.

"Here's one more part. I like this the best. 'Behold, this is a choice land, and whatsoever nation shall possess it, shall be free from bondage, and from cap—'" He peered more closely, struggling for a moment with the word. "'From cap-tiv-i-ty, and from all other nations under Heaven, if they will but serve the God of the land, which is Jesus Christ.'"

"What does that mean, Derek? What is bondage?"

Derek sat back, closing the book. How grateful he was to Elder Orson Hyde! When Elder Kimball had taken up the collection to help the Ingalls brothers make the journey across the sea, Derek had determined to use part of the money to buy his own copy of the Book of Mormon, even though they did not have the money to do so. But before he could even ask, Elder Hyde had stepped forward and given him a copy. Inside the front cover it was signed by each of the missionaries. It was the first time Derek could remember wanting to cry.

He lay back, putting his hands up beneath his head. "Bondage is when . . . well, it's like being a slave to someone. They're your master."

"Like Mr. Morris?"

Derek started to laugh, then caught himself. "Well," he said, suddenly sobered by the idea. "I'd not thought about it that way, but yes, I guess in a way we were in bondage."

"And we won't be in America?"

Derek let out his breath slowly. That was a constant worry, now that they were only one more day out of New York City. Had they left an intolerable situation merely to fall into something equally desperate?

"That's what it says," Peter said, troubled by Derek's lack of response. "It says if we serve Jesus Christ, we'll be free from bondage."

Derek smiled. Everyone kept telling him what a good brother he was to Peter, what a blessing it was for the younger boy to have a brother to care for him. Few realized how often it was just the other way around. This boy with a heart as pure and unsullied as mountain air was constantly proving to be a great blessing to his older brother. "Yep," Derek said finally, forcing a cheerful note into his voice. "That's what it says." He felt the slip of paper sewn inside the lining of his jacket. "We have the names Elder Kimball gave us of people in Ohio. I don't think they'll put us in bondage."

"It worked on our seasickness."

Derek reared up in surprise. "What?"

Peter turned over on his stomach and leaned his head over the edge. "When the captain said we'd lose a day of work for every day of seasickness, I prayed that Jesus would bless us not to get seasick."

"You did?"

"Yes," Peter said matter-of-factly. "I prayed for both of us. It worked."

Shaking his head, Derek stared at his brother in wonder. For the first six days out of Liverpool, Derek had fought a constant queasiness, but fortunately the weather had been almost perfect and the seas calm, and the nausea had not been sufficient to take him from his work with the crew. By the time the weather changed and they went through two days of stiff winds and rain squalls, he had developed enough of his sea legs that he saw it through with no more than an hour or two with his head between his legs. But from the beginning, Peter took to the rolling deck as if he had been born to it, and he never had a moment's trouble. It had irritated Derek a little, but now he was strangely humbled. "I'm glad you prayed, Peter. It did work."

"Then all we have to do is make sure we serve Jesus Christ as long as we're in America and we'll be all right."

Derek went to speak, then suddenly couldn't. He took a breath, then another, swallowing hard. Finally, he looked up at those large blue eyes so filled with innocence and excitement. "I think you're right, Peter. I think you're absolutely right."

———•———

Rachel Steed turned to the older of her two stepbrothers. "All right, Luke. Don't start until I'm on top."

Luke Griffith screwed his five-year-old face into a look of pure disgust. "I know that," he said.

There were eight or ten children gathered around the wooden stile, or steps, that allowed human passage over the sturdy rail fence but kept animals from passing. This was the pasture where the Griffith cow and horse were kept. The children were seated in the dust, oblivious to the dirt that was clinging to their clothing. It was the last day of October, and the late autumn sunshine was bright and warm.

Rachel took a cloth from her dress pocket and carefully pulled her long dark hair back, tying it with the cloth so that the cloth became a headband. She reached for a second prop, one she had gathered from the small chicken coop behind the cabin. With great care she stuck the point of the feather into the headband, just behind her left ear.

"You're an Indian," one of the girls cried.

"Pocahontas," an older boy said, blurting it out even as he raised his hand eagerly.

Rachel was most put out. "Just wait!" she commanded. "We haven't even started yet." Then, very solemnly, she climbed up the three wooden steps of the stile. Once on top, she turned around. "All right, Luke." He stepped forward and instantly began making motions as if he were shooting a bow and arrow. Rachel ducked or flinched or twisted away as the unseen arrows flew past her. All the time she was moving her lips, raising her arms, or shaking her finger at her audience below.

The children seemed baffled. They watched. The same boy tried again with Pocahontas. Rachel was thoroughly disgusted.

"I'm not Pocahontas. Watch what Luke's doing." Again the two of them acted out the charade carefully.

Suddenly from behind them a deep voice boomed out. "Samuel the Lamanite, preaching to the Nephites from the top of the wall."

The children swung around in surprise. A tall man with broad shoulders was standing near the edge of the toolshed. He wore a large hat and was smiling broadly. Rachel was startled by the new player but was nevertheless ecstatic. "Yes," she cried, turning the heads of the children back around in her direction. "The Nephites are angry with me 'cause I'm telling them they're bad. They're trying to kill me."

The other children now started to nod, one or two looking sheepish. The stranger stepped forward, smiling broadly. "That's one of my favorite stories from the Book of Mormon."

Rachel suddenly leaned forward, staring. This was a face she had not seen for more than a year, but it was a face with which she was very familiar. Her eyes flew wide open. "It's Brother Joseph!" she cried.

"Indeed, it is," the man replied. "And could this lovely, grown-up young lady really be Rachel Steed?"

"It's Joseph Smith," Rachel shouted joyously. "Joseph Smith's here."

As the children all scrambled to their feet, two other figures—a man and a woman—stepped out from behind the shed. The man swept off his hat and dropped to one knee. "He's not the only one who's here, Rachel."

For a moment Rachel was stunned, then she gave a piercing squeal of joy. In one bound she was off the stile and running hard toward the kneeling figure. "Grandpa! Grandpa!" she shouted. With one flying leap she hurled herself into his arms.

Benjamin buried his face against her lean little body, hugging her tightly to him. Then he stood and held her at arm's length. "Say hello to your grandmother, Rachel. Then let's go find your mother."

Matthew was around the back of the small cabin in Far West, chinking mud in the cracks between the logs. John Griffith had not fully finished the cabin when Matthew had made the trade with him for the farm in Haun's Mill. In the intervening seven weeks since then, Matthew had finished the last few major items and had started an addition of two small rooms off the back of the house, but the jobs had often been pushed aside as he took whatever jobs he could find in order to get enough food or goods to see him through the coming winter. But today was the first day of November. He knew that the pleasant weather would shortly turn, and he could not keep putting off completing what he had begun.

He had a flat board on which was a pile of thick mud mixed with dried chopped prairie grass. He was trowelling the makeshift mortar into the gaps between the logs, some of which were as much as three or four inches wide. A soft noise behind him brought his head around. He nearly dropped the trowel when he saw Rachel standing there alone. "Rachel?"

"Hello, Uncle Matthew."

He straightened, looking around. "Rachel, what are you doing here? Is your mother with you?"

Gravely she shook her head, her blue eyes dark and concerned.

He felt a lurch of fear. "Brother John?" Maybe her stepfather had brought her to Far West. It was twelve miles, not a journey a five-year-old made by herself.

But again there was the solemn shake of her head.

He set the mortar board and trowel down quickly. "What's happened, Rachel? What's wrong?"

Then she couldn't hold it any longer. An impish smile stole across her face, and the blue eyes were suddenly dancing. "I came with somebody else."

Matthew had started toward her. Now he stopped dead as Mary Ann stepped around the corner of the house. His jaw dropped and his eyes widened. Then, in two great strides, he was to his mother, sweeping her up in his arms. "Hello, son," she said huskily.

"You made it," he said, as his father and Joseph Smith and Sidney Rigdon stepped out now too. "You made it."

------◆------

The arrival of Joseph Smith in northern Missouri was a great cause of rejoicing to the Saints in Missouri. It had been almost two years since they had last seen him, and with hundreds of new converts pouring into Missouri from the various branches established by missionaries throughout the East and the South, there were many who had never met the Prophet. Oliver Cowdery and David Whitmer had both arrived in Far West earlier (David, sometime in July; Oliver, sometime in October), and their arrival too had been greeted with rejoicing. That meant that two of the three special witnesses who had seen Moroni and the gold plates of the Book of Mormon were now in Missouri.

A meeting of some of the Church was held on the sixth of November in Far West. Joseph had been shown around the countryside by then, and it was determined that there was sufficient room in Daviess and Caldwell counties for additional stakes and that Missouri should be the place of gathering for the Saints. Joseph determined that the building of a temple in Far West should wait further instructions from the Lord.

At a general assembly of the Church held on November seventh in Far West, the leadership of the Church was to be sustained as directed by the Lord in the earliest beginnings of the Church. All the business of the Church was to be done by the principle of "common consent." Common consent meant that the leadership of the Church proposed which officers were to serve in various callings, then the general membership—both men and women—voted as to whether they would sustain those proposals. They could choose not to sustain them if there was good reason not to. Joseph was unanimously accepted as the

President of the Church. Sidney Rigdon was again sustained as First Counselor. But as had happened at Kirtland, the Saints rejected Frederick G. Williams as Second Counselor in the First Presidency, even though Bishop Edward Partridge and other leaders spoke warmly in his defense. Hyrum Smith was sustained in his stead. David Whitmer was nominated to be president of the Church in Missouri. There were immediate objections by some, but David had confessed the error of his ways in the events in Kirtland, and several spoke on his behalf. He was finally sustained. Sustained as assistant presidents for the Church in Missouri were John Whitmer, David's brother, and W. W. Phelps. Other Church officers were sustained and other Church business conducted, and the conference adjourned.

On the tenth of November, another meeting was held. It was unanimously voted to enlarge the town plat of Far West from one square mile to two. A short time later, Joseph and Hyrum bid the Missouri Saints farewell and started back to Kirtland to return to their families.

Rebecca threw open the door, a wide smile splitting her face. "Hello," she started, "come . . ." The smile froze on her lips. "In," she finished lamely. Mary Fielding had promised she would come over in the afternoon to help Rebecca and Lydia make a quilt. But it was not Mary Fielding who stood on Nathan and Lydia's porch. It was two men—or rather a young man and a boy.

At the sound of the knock, Lydia's children had come running. Joshua slid to a stop at the sight of the strangers. Emily collided with him, intent on the men at the door. Little Nathan, just two now, came toddling up behind them, not sure what all the excitement was about but not wanting to miss out.

"Yes?" Rebecca asked, trying to cover herself. She noted quickly that the two were poorly dressed. The weather had finally turned, and there had been snow the previous day. It was late in the day, and the sky was leaden and lowering for another storm. Yet both had on only light jackets, and those were tattered at best. She glanced down. They did not wear boots but only thin leather shoes. The younger one had a scarf around his neck but nothing on his head. The older one wore a small woolen cap that perched on his head but did not cover his ears, which now were tipped with bright red that matched the redness of his nose.

He swept off his hat, a little startled by the warmth of the greeting. "Excuse me, ma'am, but would you be Sister Steed?"

Rebecca was struck with three things all at once. His features were congenial—open and pleasant with a hint of a smile around his mouth. The second thing was his eyes. They were a striking blue—like Brother Joseph's. And they had that same clearness, the same gentle intensity. And most noticeable, he spoke with a strange accent. Suddenly she remembered he had asked her a question. "Yes," she said quickly, "I'm Sister Steed."

There was a momentary look of surprise, as if he had expected her to say no, but then he quickly nodded. "And is your husband at home?"

That really startled Rebecca. Emily, who had pressed up against Rebecca's leg and was peering up at the strangers, erupted into giggles and answered for her. "Rebecca's not married, silly."

"Hush, Emily," Joshua commanded, embarrassed by his sister's boldness.

"Oh." Flustered now, the young man blushed deeply. "I wondered. You look too young to be married and have children."

For some reason that stung Rebecca. "I'm probably as old as you," she retorted.

"I didn't mean it that way," he apologized hastily. His cap was going around and around as he twisted it in his hands. "It's just that . . ." He could see that that was not going to do anything but get him in deeper, so he thrust his hand in the pocket of his jacket and drew out a slip of paper and looked at it quickly. "We were looking for Brother and Sister Nathan Steed."

"He talks funny, Joshua," Emily said, trying to whisper but still speaking loud enough that everyone heard it.

The young man smiled at that. He bent down slightly, looking into Emily's dark brown eyes. "Where we come from, everyone would say that it is *you* who talks funny."

Being inhibited had never been a problem for Emily. At five, she felt completely comfortable conversing with adults. She screwed up her face into a puzzled expression. "We don't talk funny. You talk funny."

He laughed pleasantly and turned back to Rebecca, who was embarrassed by her previous curtness. "I'm Rebecca Steed," she said. "I'm Nathan's sister." Then she looked at the two of them more closely, realization dawning. "You're from England."

"Yes, from Preston. My name is Derek Ingalls, and this is my brother, Peter. Elder Heber C. Kimball gave us some names of people to see when we got here. He said to be sure and find Nathan Steed."

Joshua was staring up at Derek in open awe. "From England?" he said. "Did you come on a ship?"

Derek laughed. "Only across the ocean. We walked most of the way from New York City."

"Why didn't you take a stagecoach?" Emily asked bluntly.

"Emily!" Rebecca said sharply. Then she gave Derek an apologetic look.

He just laughed and looked down at her. "Because stagecoaches cost a lot of money."

Rebecca took Emily by the shoulders and turned her around. "Go find your mother, Emily. Tell her we have visitors." As Emily started off, Rebecca picked up little Nathan and then opened the door more widely. "Nathan is not here right now. He's down at the livery stable helping my brother-in-law with some repairs."

"I'll go get him," Joshua volunteered eagerly.

"Yes," Rebecca said. "Tell him we have visitors from England." Joshua grabbed his coat from the rack and shot out of the door. Rebecca stepped back. "Come in. You must be very cold."

Derek smiled gratefully. "Only from the toes up and the head down."

Rebecca laughed. "Then come in and sit down. My brother will be very pleased to meet you."

———————

Nathan rolled over onto his side. He peered carefully at his wife in the darkness, but the bedroom was almost totally black and he could not see if her eyes were open. He rolled back.

"I'm awake," she said.

"Good." He turned again and took her hand. "I've been thinking."

"About what?"

"About Derek and Peter."

"Aren't they wonderful boys? The children adore them."

"They're both fine young men. I can't believe they've come all this way completely on their own."

Lydia smiled sadly in the darkness. "They've been on their own a good deal of their lives."

"I know." He fell silent, thinking through again the whole situation. In the two days since their visitors had arrived, the Steeds had grown surprisingly fond of Derek and Peter. He took a quick breath, fearing how his idea was going to be received. "I think they need to go to Missouri."

There was a quick intake of breath, and Lydia turned her head to him. "No, Nathan. They just got here."

"I know, I know. And it's not that I wouldn't love to have them stay with us all winter, but you've seen Derek's reaction to that. He's not about to take any charity. He wants to make it on his own."

"And that's bad?"

"No, of course not. It shows what kind of young man he is. But you know what the situation is in Kirtland now. There's no work. Prices are impossible. Far West isn't a paradise, but from all reports, at least there's work. And . . ." He sighed. "And the problems in the Church here." He shook his head. "Over a hundred people have been excommunicated or disfellowshipped now. There's so much bitterness. It's not a healthy environment for two young men so new in the Church."

"I don't think you need to worry there. When I listen to their testimonies—so simple and yet so strong—I think they'll be all right."

Nathan had not come to this conclusion lightly. "Joseph has said that Missouri is the place of gathering for the Saints now. If they don't go now, they'll want to go with us in the spring. Now will be a better time for them."

"They don't have enough money for steamboat fares," Lydia said. "They'll have to walk." She hesitated. "That's eight hundred more miles."

Nathan lay there for a moment, then squeezed his wife's hand. "Not if we gave them enough from our savings."

He felt her body stiffen. "We've got almost fifty dollars now," he went on in a rush. "I think half of that would get them there. And with Carl's giving me employment . . ." He smiled ruefully. "I think Carl's feeling guilty about taking Melissa away from us. He's got enough work to keep me going most of the winter."

"I hate for you to be dependent on him," Lydia said softly. "It's like it proves his point that we can't take care of ourselves."

He moved over closer and took her in his arms. "I know, but he's being good about it. And all I care about is getting enough money so that we don't have to have you and the children walk next spring. I know that twenty-five dollars is a lot of money, but I can—"

She put one hand up to his lips. "I don't care about the money," she said. "I think it's wonderful that you are willing to share with the boys."

Nathan chuckled. "I'm not sure that Derek qualifies as a boy anymore. He's a man. Been acting like one since he was twelve, it sounds like."

For several moments Lydia was quiet. Then softly she came to the heart of her objection. "Rebecca will be very disappointed."

Nathan turned his head, puzzled. "About what?"

She laughed, poking at him. "Are you so blind?"

"What?"

She shook her head.

He came up on one elbow. "You mean her and Derek?"

"Yes," she said in mock exasperation, "I mean her and Derek. I know my instincts for matchmaking are maybe acting up, but I think there are some definite possibilities there." She shrugged. "But if Derek and his brother go now, it's not like it would cut things off completely for Rebecca and Derek. Just delay them a little."

He lay back, smiling in spite of himself. "That would be nice. For Rebecca *and* Derek."

"Have you forgotten so soon?"

"Forgotten what?"

"The night you and Heber went and blessed Parley."

He was startled. "No, of course not. Why?"

"Don't you remember what Heber said to you afterwards?"

Suddenly realization dawned. His eyes opened wide, and he turned to stare at his wife. "He said that not only would our mission to Canada open the way for the work to go to England, but out of that mission things would come that would . . ." His voice trailed off in wonder.

"That would be a great blessing to our family as well," she finished for him. "And if you remember, he said that you would live to see the fulfillment of his promise."

Nathan laughed softly, the amazement filling him with joy. "Well, I'll be," he exclaimed. "Rebecca and Derek. Wouldn't that be something?"

She snuggled up against him. "We can't say a word to her yet. Maybe we are wrong in this." Then she had a thought. "But maybe it would be good to wait a little before they leave. Derek is so anxious to meet Brother Joseph. They should be back in a few weeks."

Nathan shook his head. "By then the rivers could be frozen and the steamboats no longer running. No, if they're going to go, it's got to be now, or else they're going to have to walk all the way. And in the winter . . . no, that's not good."

Lydia sighed. "I guess you're right, but Rebecca is going to be very disappointed."

Rachel Greets Her Grandfather

January 20th, 1838, Kirtland, Ohio

Dear Father and Mother Steed,

I have much news, some of an urgent nature, so I hope this letter makes its way swiftly to you. We received your letter saying that our two wonderful boys from England arrived safely there early in December. That was a great relief to us. They found their way into our hearts so quickly, and we trust they will have done the same in yours. We prayed for their safe journey and were much comforted to learn the Lord watched over them. By the way, Rebecca said to be sure and send her greetings to Derek and Peter along with ours.

We are all in good health. Little Nathan still asks where "Gamah and Gampah" are. Emily and Joshua miss you fiercely and are counting the days when we can go west, but Nathan is too small to understand and just knows that you're no longer around to play with him (and spoil him!).

Nathan thinks he has sold the house. We will get about ten cents on the dollar, but we shall do it anyway. Such things are of passing value anyway. If successful, this will give us some cash money to help with our removal to Far West. I have more to say about that, but first the news from here.

Not all is bad, so I will share some of the better things first. I wrote you in my last letter about Jerusha Smith. Her death was a shock to all of us, as I'm sure it was to you, Mother Steed. You can imagine Hyrum's grief when he returned from Missouri. But a most interesting thing happened. A few days after their return, Joseph and Hyrum were together and happened to see Sister Mary Fielding passing by. Joseph turned to Hyrum and nearly bowled him over with his next words. "Brother Hyrum," he said, "it is the will of the Lord that you marry this English girl without delay so that you may have a mother for your offspring."

Well, you can imagine Mary's surprise when she learned that. She was somewhat deterred by the thoughts of becoming the stepmother of five children, but she is of great faith and said that if it was the Lord's will, she would accept it. Joseph married them on Christmas Eve, and so now it is no longer Mary Fielding, but Mary Fielding Smith. So far, she seems very happy.

Be sure and share the following with Peter and Derek. Just last week, Sister Vilate Kimball received a letter from her beloved Heber. The work continues with great success in England. They have baptized upwards of seven or eight hundred people since arriving in July. He said that there are nearly three hundred members now in Preston alone, and branches have been organized in several of the surrounding villages.

On Christmas Day they held a conference in the "Cock Pit," a large hall in Preston once used for cock fighting (can you imagine anything so horrid?). They preached the Word of Wisdom publicly for the first time there, which was well received. The temperance movement that has swept across England and the United States is strong in Preston, according to Heber. He believes it is an important factor that has helped prepare the people for the coming of the gospel. In fact, I found this interesting. Heber says it was a man in Preston who first coined the word "teetotaller." Many in the temperance movement called on the people to reduce their drinking, but this man said that they should "totally" abstain from liquor. He wanted them to be tee (for "total") totallers in swearing off spirits of any kind. It was already well known by then that the Mormons did not use tobacco, liquor of any kind, or tea and coffee. So when the missionaries read the Word of Wisdom to the people, it was really very well received.

In fact, Heber said they are having such great success, the English clergy keep complaining that the missionaries are taking the very best of their flocks. You know Brother Heber. He just smiles and tells them that all we want is the wheat, they can keep the chaff.

Now for news of a blacker sort. With every passing day it becomes more evident that Satan's opposition is without mercy. The Lord's Spirit more and more whispers, "Get ye out of this place." Kirtland has become a madhouse. The dissenters become more and more brazen. Parrish and company have now openly and publicly renounced the Church of the Latter-day Saints. They claim to be the "Old Standard," and call themselves the Church of Christ, excluding the word "Saints" from their title. Joseph points out that they seem to have forgotten Daniel's prophecy that in the last days it would be the Saints who possessed the kingdom. They publicly attack Joseph and anyone who remains true to him and the Church. They say we are heretics. Heresy seems a particularly ironic charge since it was reported that in a recent meeting, one of their number even went so far as to say that Moses was a rascal, all the prophets tyrants, Jesus a despot, the Apostle Paul a liar, and all religion fudge.

Such blasphemy would be bad enough, but they have become increasingly violent as well. They have now seized control of the temple, threatening to kill those who had the keys to the building if they did not give them up. And what happened to you, Father Steed, is now almost a daily occurrence. Men are beaten, women terrorized, even children threatened. The streets are no longer safe at night for any sympathetic to our cause.

A recent development has become particularly alarming to us. In just the past few days, several fires have been started in the cellars or basements of various houses—always of the faithful. Nathan believes it is nothing more than a shameless attempt to drive us from our property so the greedy and covetous can get it for little or no cost. So arson has been added to all the other terrors. Four nights ago, we were all awakened from our sleep when we realized it was as light as day outside. We ran to the window and to our horror we saw that someone had set fire to the printing office behind the temple. By then the building was almost totally consumed. Sparks and burning cinders were flying everywhere, and for a moment we thought it would catch the roof of the temple. But fortunately (or was it Providence!) the wind was blowing the flames away from the house of the Lord and it was spared.

Conditions are so terrible that even the leaders are leaving in order to save their lives. Just before Christmas, Brother Brigham stood in a meeting and fearlessly confronted Joseph's enemies. He bore testimony that he knew by the power of the Holy Ghost that Joseph was God's prophet. That so infuriated Warren Parrish and his group that Brigham had to flee for his life late that same night. He is now in Indiana. Sidney Rigdon has also been driven out. The powers of darkness truly reign in much of Kirtland now.

Brother Joseph had an especially close brush with death. There was a plot laid to assassinate him and Sidney. A member of the group, one of Joseph's former friends (probably Luke Johnson) and thankfully someone whose rebellion stopped short of murder, ran to warn Joseph. Before Joseph could escape, however, a mob surrounded the house where he was. Luckily, there was a coffin in the cellar of the house. Those present nailed Joseph inside it and carried him out, saying that someone had died. Because the coffin was sealed, they were able to pass through the mob without Joseph's being detected. We just received word this morning that he and Sidney are both safe. Emma and the children, along with Sidney's family, have left to join them. They will spend some time with Brother Brigham, then plan to remove permanently to Far West. I'm sure you, and the rest of the Saints, will greatly rejoice at that news.

Mother Steed, I cannot help but say something of Emma here. Remember when Joseph and Emma came to Kirtland? It was early February. It was the dead of winter. Emma was carrying the twins and was only about three months from delivery. You'll remember that, I'm sure, Father Steed. You were very critical of Joseph for taking Emma so far in winter weather when she was in that kind of condition. Well, as you know, Emma is with child again. She is now about four or five months along. And once again she is on her way to a new home in the dead of winter. So as she came to Kirtland, now does she leave. Only this time it is not in answer to God's call, but in response to the howling cries of murderous men who would take the life of her husband. How much shall that marvelous woman be called upon to endure?

Which brings me at last to my real purpose in writing. Nathan and I sorely debated whether to write you in advance or whether to just show up on your doorstep and save you having to worry about us while on our journey. Yes, Mother and Father Steed, we are coming to Missouri. The situation has deteriorated so badly that we feel waiting until the baby comes and I am fit to travel is no longer acceptable.

Though our home is not one of those which the arsonists have struck, last week Nathan was awakened in the middle of the night by some noise. He discovered two men outside the back of our home and drove them off with a rifle. We know not their purpose, but we are certain it was not to our good. Rebecca, myself, and the children have moved in with Carl and Melissa. Nathan still sleeps at the house with two or three other brethren to stand guard, but each night is a terrifying experience, and I barely sleep until I see him safely again each morning. I simply cannot bear the strain of it for another two or three months. I would rather face the arduous journey even with the weather than live with this awful dread that hovers over us.

(By the way, I'm happy to report that while Carl is still very critical of the Church, he has been wonderful in this crisis. He has taken us in—all six of us—cheerfully and without a murmur. Melissa still stands firm on her decision to keep the Church at arm's length. We shall miss them terribly.)

I can just hear what you are saying by now about the dangers of traveling when I am this far progressed in carrying another child. But if you remember, I too traveled to Kirtland when I was heavy with child, so I think I have an understanding of what this choice means. It will not be easy. But the thought of being with you in a place where there is safety and peace makes it worth whatever price is required to get there. Rebecca concurs fully in this decision. She will be a great blessing to us as we travel.

Our plan is to leave in a day or two. Every day's postponement now will only add to our challenges, both here and on the journey. Nathan is out today trying to complete the sale of the house. But if we cannot sell it, we shall turn the key in the door and simply walk away. He is also trying to secure some form of transportation for us. We know not how long it may take us, so please be patient and remember us in your daily prayers. We mention you in ours both night and morning.

We long to see you and to stand together in the family circle again. Oh, how excited we are to see Matthew again!

> With tenderest affections,
> Lydia

St. Joseph, Missouri, lay about fifty-five miles north of, or upstream from, Independence. Founded in 1826 by a French fur trapper named Joseph Robidoux, it was situated on the east bank of the Missouri River and was the first major settlement one encountered on coming down the river from the rich vastness of the Rocky Mountains. Though John Jacob Astor had established his headquarters for the fur trade in St. Louis, that was another three hundred miles downriver, and many of the mountain men preferred to do their trading in "St. Joe."

A trapper's prime time in the high country was in the dead of winter when the snows were deep. This forced the beaver, muskrat, fox, marten, mink, and other furbearing animals to stick to easily discernible trails and runs. Each spring along with the mountain runoff came the fur trappers. The waters flooded the Missouri River plain, and the mountain men flooded St. Joe.

Joshua Steed finished cinching up the girth of his saddle

and fished a cigar out of his pocket. He turned to watch a group of three trappers go by as he lighted it. One had a jug of whiskey, the other two an Indian squaw on each arm. Their buckskin shirts and breeches were filthy, their hair greasy and matted from months without a bath. Joshua shook his head, fighting back the temptation to grimace. When he had first come to Independence he had seriously flirted with the idea of becoming a mountain man. He had decided against it finally and turned to hauling freight instead. So now he came to St. Joseph every spring to buy the mountain men's furs and wrinkle his nose at the smell of them.

Garrick Harris, Joshua's wagon master, came striding up to him, tapping the big bullwhip against his leg as he walked. "All set, Mr. Steed. We're ready to roll."

Turning, Joshua surveyed the line of eight wagons. He squinted a little, feeling a great sense of satisfaction. It was still early April, and the Missouri River was at near-flood stage. But once the waters subsided a little, the steamboats would be coming upriver and taking the furs at a cheaper rate than he could haul them. But until then, he would roll them all the way into St. Louis and get a premium price for the first furs of the season. He had learned that trick almost seven years before, and it had been a profitable venture for him every year since.

He puffed on the cigar once, then grabbed the reins of the sorrel stallion that he was riding and swung up. "All right. Get 'em movin'."

"Yes, sir."

Joshua reined the horse around, holding him in. He was dancing beneath him, eager to be started. "When you get to Independence, send someone round to my wife and tell her I'll be no more than a day or two behind you."

"Yes, sir." Harris was a man as hard as the rutted roads that stretched out across the prairie before them. He squinted up at his boss with a look of disgust. "You really ridin' through Mormon country?"

Joshua laughed. "Worried that I won't be safe?"

The teamster spat out a stream of tobacco juice. "No, that you'll be converted." He hooted raucously at his own joke.

"Think they could keep my cigar dry while they baptized me?" Joshua asked straight-faced.

Harris roared, slapping his knee and causing a tiny puff of dust to spurt out from his trouser leg. "Now, there'd be a sight to see. You underwater with just your nose and a cigar sticking up." He guffawed again, pleased with the image. Then after a moment he sobered a little. "What do you want me to tell your wife if she asks where you are?"

The smile instantly disappeared from Joshua's face. He considered the question for a moment. He had almost said something to Caroline before he left, but then decided against it. First of all, he hasn't been sure if circumstances would be such that he would have to accompany the wagons back. Second, he hadn't been sure exactly what he was going to do, or if he was going to do anything. Even now he wasn't sure of that. And yet it would please her to know.

He looked down at his wagon master. "Just tell her I'm comin' home by way of Far West. She'll understand."

"And how's Lydia doing?"

Nathan smiled in satisfaction. "Fine. She swears she's big enough to deliver two full-size colts, but all in all, she came through the journey very well. We were really blessed to get steamboat passage most of the way."

Oliver Cowdery nodded. "That's good. Give her my regards and Elizabeth's as well."

"I will, thank you."

"By the way, who was that stranger who was looking for your family?"

Nathan had leaned down to pull at a blade of prairie grass. He straightened and stuck it in the corner of his mouth. "What stranger is that?"

Oliver shrugged. "I never saw him. David just said there was a man in town this morning asking questions about several things, but particularly about your family."

"Your brother-in-law David, or David Patten?" Nathan asked. Oliver had married Elizabeth Ann Whitmer, youngest sister of David Whitmer. David Patten was one of the Twelve Apostles and was in the presidency of the Far West Stake.

Oliver frowned. "Not David Patten," he said shortly.

Nathan winced a little at his error. David Patten was a very sensitive issue with Oliver right now. In February, just before Nathan and Lydia had arrived in Far West, the high council of the Far West Stake had charged two members of the stake presidency, John Whitmer and W. W. Phelps, with misusing Church funds. According to the charges, they were once again trying to sell Church lands and pocket the profit. David Whitmer was accused of willfully violating the Word of Wisdom. Oliver and others were also cited as being in contempt of Church principles and in opposition to the Prophet Joseph. John Whitmer and W. W. Phelps had been excommunicated and David Patten and Thomas B. Marsh put in as acting presidents until Joseph could arrive from Kirtland. It was also decided to wait until Joseph came to press the charges against Oliver Cowdery and David Whitmer. The Church court date for Oliver had been set for the twelfth of April, which was tomorrow morning; David Whitmer's case would be considered on the thirteenth. David Patten, a man whom Nathan found to be of the highest integrity, would be pivotal in the proceedings, and Oliver and the Whitmers held intensely bitter feelings against him.

Nathan decided to move on quickly. "What did David say about this man?"

Oliver's mind had gone elsewhere, probably to David Patten, for his face had now darkened. "What man?"

"The stranger."

"Oh. Not much. He said he didn't think he was a Mormon. He was tall, well dressed, wore a full beard. Rode a fine piece of horseflesh. David told him where both you and your father are living. I thought he would have sought you out."

"No. At least I didn't see him, and Pa didn't say anything."

Oliver nodded absently. After a moment he looked more closely at Nathan. "Are you going to vote against me, old friend?"

Nathan was startled, and yet he knew instantly what he had reference to. He took out the blade of grass and flipped it away. "I'm not on the high council, Oliver. You know that."

Oliver Cowdery gave him a long and searching look. "I know. But are you going to vote against me?"

For a moment Nathan was puzzled, then he understood. From the first day he and Oliver had met in Harmony, Pennsylvania, back in the late spring of 1829, almost instantly there had developed a strong bond between them. From that time to this, their friendship had never waned. But in the past year it had been strained considerably as he and Oliver drew farther apart on the issues that were tearing Kirtland asunder. It had sickened Nathan to watch Oliver become more and more disillusioned with the Church and more and more bitter against Joseph Smith. And it had angered Oliver that Nathan would give no serious consideration to the evidence—"as obvious as the whiskers on a raccoon"—that Joseph had lost the prophetic gift and fallen out of favor with God. More than once they had talked late into the night, neither making a dent in the other's position, but still grateful they could speak honestly.

Now Oliver was asking where Nathan's vote was—not in priesthood council, but in his heart. Nathan wanted to look away. Oliver's eyes were like a hot wind across his face. They were challenging, probing, demanding. Nathan decided to probe back a little. "Did you try and sell your land in Jackson County?" he finally asked softly.

"Jackson County is a dead issue anymore. We're never going to redeem Zion. Not in our lifetime. Maybe never."

"But in the revelations, God specifically said it was his will that we should hold claim on our properties and not sell them off to our enemies. People are saying that you and Frederick G. Williams and members of the stake presidency here in Far West tried to sell your land. Did you?"

Again Oliver ducked the question. "That's only one of many charges against me," he said wearily.

Nathan nodded. He had heard about the charges from Joseph—who was as sick at heart about the whole thing as Nathan was. The Church court was going to investigate Oliver Cowdery on the following accusations: bringing vexatious lawsuits against the brethren, trying to destroy the character of Joseph Smith, not attending his meetings in the Church, refusing to be governed by the revelations, selling his land in Jackson County, sending an insulting letter to the high council, leaving his holy calling to work for filthy lucre, and participating in business ventures of an unsavory nature.

There was little doubt in Nathan's mind that some of the charges were unsubstantiated and probably the result of the heated emotions over Oliver's defection. There was also little question but what there was sufficient truth to several of the accusations. By tomorrow at this time, Oliver Cowdery would very likely be excommunicated from the Church.

Nathan reached out and laid a hand on his friend's shoulder. "No matter what happens, Oliver," he said softly, "I want you to know that your friendship is still important to me. Even if you leave the Church, I want it to continue."

Touched, Oliver reached up and gripped Nathan's arm. "Thank you, Nathan. That means a great deal to me as well."

Nathan straightened. There was not much more to say after that. "Well, I'd better be getting on."

"Thank you for stopping." Oliver smiled warmly but ruefully. "Not many people stop by to say hello anymore."

"Well, I will." Nathan clapped him on the shoulder, then lifted a hand in farewell. "Good luck tomorrow."

Oliver's eyes were hooded, but he nodded, and Nathan turned and walked to the gate. "Nathan?"

He turned back around. "Yes?"

"The truth of modern revelation is not the issue here, Nathan. I want you to know that."

"What do you mean?"

"I'm challenging what Joseph is now, what he has become of late. But I have never questioned the reality of what he did in restoring the Church. I stood on the banks of the Susquehanna River and saw John the Baptist in broad daylight. I know that Peter, James, and John restored the priesthood of Melchizedek to Joseph. I saw the angel Moroni and heard the voice of God declare that the Book of Mormon was translated by the gift and power of God. Some people are saying I'm denying my testimony of those things. I want you to know that it absolutely is not true."

Nathan started to speak, but Oliver's mouth softened and his eyes got a faraway look in them. "I stood on the pulpits there in the Kirtland Temple and saw the Lord and Savior, Jesus Christ." He held out one hand. "He was no further than this from me. It was an experience which words cannot describe." He took a deep breath, then looked directly at Nathan. "I cannot now, nor will I ever, deny those experiences, Nathan."

Nathan couldn't help what he blurted out next. This was at the very core of his frustration with his friend. "Then how can you now turn against Joseph?" he cried.

Instantly Oliver's face hardened and the light went out of his eyes. "Because Joseph Smith is a fallen prophet," Oliver said. "I have no choice."

Matthew Steed heaved the last gunnysack of wheat seed up into the wagon with a grunt. He pushed it into position, then stepped back, taking off the straw hat he wore. He dragged a piece of muslin from his pocket and mopped his brow. "Well, that's it."

Derek Ingalls eyed the wagonload of sacks dubiously. He was sweating as heavily as Matthew. "Is that really enough to plant five acres?"

"It is," Matthew replied. "Probably with some to spare." He walked around to the front of the wagon and climbed up onto the seat. Derek followed and climbed up beside him. As

Matthew took the reins, he stopped and looked at Derek. "I was thinkin'."

"What?"

"I'll bet young Joshua would love to go to Haun's Mill with us. He and Rachel are very close."

"Rachel is your sister-in-law's daughter?"

Matthew nodded. "Yes. Joshua also gets along very well with his two little stepcousins, Brother Griffith's two boys."

"Fine," Derek said. "Let's go see if Lydia will let him go with us." He turned and looked around. Peter Ingalls was just inside the barn, still talking animatedly with the man who had sold them the wheat seed. "Peter," Derek called. "Let's go."

As Peter came trotting out, Matthew grinned mischievously at Derek. "I'll bet if we asked Lydia real nice she'd let Rebecca come with us too."

Derek blushed instantly and furiously. There was only about three years' difference between him and Matthew in age. Derek would be twenty-one in October; Matthew would turn eighteen in July. Physically they were in no way alike. Matthew was now an inch or two over six feet and lean as a weathered fence post. Derek was three or four inches shorter and heavier through the shoulders and body—the legacy of four years as a shoveler in the boiler rooms. Matthew was fair of skin, his hair was a lighter brown, and his eyes were blue and clear. Derek was darker in complexion, with almost black hair, and though his eyes were also blue, they were darker than Matthew's, deeper and harder to fathom. They were just as different in their temperament and personality. Matthew had a natural cheerfulness and optimism that lifted all around him. He loved people and was open and friendly with everyone. Children adored him. Derek was of a more sober and reserved nature. In groups he usually sat back, speaking only when called upon or on those rare occasions when he felt that he had something to say.

But the differences between them made no difference. From the day Derek and Peter had arrived in Far West—cold, hungry, tattered, and with a letter from Nathan and Lydia—Derek and

Matthew had become fast friends. The two brothers from England were staying with Benjamin and Mary Ann, and Derek and Matthew shared a bedroom. Rebecca had opted to stay with Nathan and Lydia to help with the children and the housework until the baby was born. By then, Nathan would have his new cabin nearly completed. With it would be a smaller cabin out back where the two English boys would stay.

Matthew laughed and slugged Derek on the shoulder. "Is that all right with you, mate?"

Peter had climbed into the back of the wagon and was following the conversation now. "I'll bet it's all right with Rebecca," he exclaimed.

Derek grinned, feeling foolish. "Yes," he said, "I think that's all right with me too."

"Look, Matthew," Rebecca said in a low voice. "It's that man who passed us a while back."

Matthew had already seen the man and the horse in the road about a hundred yards or so in front of them. The man had dismounted and was looking in their direction. He seemed to be waiting for them.

"Yep, it sure is," Matthew said. He flipped the reins gently, keeping the team moving steadily toward the man. Peter and Joshua got up from their makeshift bed on the wheat sacks and stood behind the seat where Matthew, Derek, and Rebecca rode, peering over their shoulders at the stranger. Since they had left Far West they had not passed another person on the wide expanse of rolling grasslands, and so this provided a break in the monotony.

As they drew a little closer, Rebecca looked more closely at the man. "That's the man who was in town yesterday. I saw him at the dry goods store trying to buy some tobacco."

Young Joshua hooted. "I'll bet he was surprised."

"Shh," Matthew said. They were nearly to the man now, and he was watching their approach with a steady gaze. He was dressed warmly for the weather, with a full coat on and a long-sleeved white shirt with a fancy collar. His beard was thick and black. His eyes were shaded by the brim of his hat, but Matthew guessed they were dark also.

Matthew reined in the horses as they came up to him. "Good mornin'," he said cheerfully.

"Mornin'," came the reply. His eyes moved from Matthew to Derek and the two boys, then lingered longer on Rebecca. There was a flash of recognition, then a quick look of surprise. "Good mornin'," he said to her. "You were in the store yesterday."

"Yes."

He shook his head, almost as though in disbelief. Then he quickly turned back to Matthew. "You know your way around here? I seem to be lost."

"What are you lookin' for?"

"I'm headed back down to—" There was a quick hesitation, then he went on smoothly. "Down Richmond and Liberty way. They said in town I'd find a road that turned south about five or six miles out. Have I come far enough?"

"No. It's another mile or so further on from here."

He nodded. "Well, that's probably why I haven't found it yet." He put one finger to his hat. "Much obliged." As he swung up on his horse, his eyes still kept coming back to stare, first at Rebecca, then at Matthew.

"We're going right past there," Matthew volunteered. "It's not much of a road. It's easy to miss. We'll be happy to show you where it is."

Again there was the briefest moment of hesitation, then he made up his mind. "All right. If you don't mind, I'll ride along behind you."

"This is it," Matthew said, pointing to the faint wagon track that went off at a right angle. He swung around to the east. "This goes on to Haun's Mill, but if you follow that one it will take you right into Liberty. Ain't much between here and there, either."

The man on the horse turned his head and looked south. "I can find it. Again, much obliged for the help." He reined his horse around but did not move it forward. He seemed reluctant to leave them.

Matthew had a sudden idea. "We've got some dinner. Ain't much. Cold chicken and some hard rolls and a block of cheese. But we've got plenty."

For the first time, the man seemed caught off guard. "I . . ." He shook his head quickly. "That's very nice of you, but no, thank you."

Rebecca felt a quick sense of relief. Matthew's invitation had caught her by surprise as well. There was something about this man that left her feeling strangely uncomfortable. His eyes kept coming back to her, searching her face. It was not a flirtatious thing, like the looks she got from some men—she sensed that somehow—but there was something in his eyes that still left her vaguely disturbed. She was glad they had reached the crossroads.

But Matthew was Matthew. He jumped down from the wagon seat, as if the issue were already decided. "It's a long ride to Liberty. Won't hurt you none to start it with a full belly."

For a long moment the man looked down at Matthew, who grinned up at him with open invitation. Then he seemed to make up his mind. "Well, maybe just for a few minutes, then I really have to be on my way."

"Good," Matthew said. "Rebecca, you get the blanket. We can eat right over there." He looked up at the boys in the wagon. "Peter, you fetch the jug of water. Derek, pull the wagon over so the horses can graze while we eat. Joshua, get that basket your mother packed for us."

The man had started to swing down off his horse. He froze, one foot still in the stirrup. He was staring at the two boys. Matthew looked up in surprise. Rebecca was also caught by the expression on the man's face. It was as though he had been struck from behind by an unseen hand. He saw their faces and recovered quickly, stepping down. Ignoring their questioning looks, he turned to his saddlebag, quickly took out a set of hobbles, and fastened the devices to his horse's two front legs. Then he gave the animal a soft whack on the rump and sent it into the tall grass. Without another word he stepped back, watching quietly as the lunch preparations were completed.

When all was ready, Matthew suggested that Derek offer grace, which he did. The stranger seemed uncomfortable for a moment, but immediately as Derek finished he asked if Derek was from England. They laughed. Almost everyone teased the two boys about their accent. That led to a brisk conversation between the man and Derek. He was particularly interested in the English textile mills and questioned Derek at length about the industry there.

As they finished the last piece of chicken and washed it down with mugs of tepid water, the man looked at young Joshua, then turned to Matthew. "This your brother?"

Matthew shook his head. "No. Becca and I are brother and sister, but this is our nephew. He'll be seven in just over a month from now."

The man nodded thoughtfully. "Yes." He turned. "And did they say your name was Joshua?"

"Yes. Joshua Benjamin Steed."

Again Rebecca was surprised at the look that crossed the man's face. He seemed taken aback, puzzled, and, in a way, filled with a quiet sadness, and she couldn't fathom why. Her sense of disquiet, that all was not quite right with this mysterious stranger, went up another notch. "We're mostly Steeds," she said, wanting to know whom they were talking to. "My name is Rebecca. This is Matthew. And Joshua, of course. Our friends are Derek and Peter Ingalls."

He nodded at each in turn. It was a perfect opening for him to introduce himself, but instead he looked to Matthew. "And do you have family in Haun's Mill?"

"Kind of. We have a sister-in-law. Or she used to be our

sister-in-law. She was divorced from her husband and has re-married."

The man looked down at his plate, then with studied casu-alness he said, "Oh, and does she have any children?"

Joshua spoke up. "There's my cousin Rachel. She's six. And two boys, Luke and Mark Griffith. They're five and three. They're my stepcousins."

"Our sister-in-law, her name is Jessica," Matthew said, "she just had a baby about a month ago. A little boy."

"Really?" The man nodded, seeming pleased. "And is every-thing well with her and the baby?" he asked, still as though he were only making light conversation.

"Well, he was a whopper—weighed nearly ten pounds. But both are fine."

"That's good." He seemed to really mean it. Then before anyone could say anything more, he abruptly stood. "Well, I'd better be going. Thank you again. You've been very kind."

They all stood and followed him as he went to his horse and unhobbled it. As he gathered up the reins, he turned to Re-becca. He stuck out his hand. "It's been very much a pleasure to meet you, Miss Rebecca." She took it and was surprised at the softness of his touch and the pain she saw in his eyes. He turned quickly to Matthew. "And you as well, Matthew Steed. You are a fine young man now."

Before either could answer, he nodded briskly to Derek and Peter. "A pleasure to meet you as well." He put a foot in the stirrup and swung up into the saddle. Now he was looking in-tently at the youngest Steed. "Good-bye, young Joshua," he said softly.

"Good-bye, sir."

He lifted the reins, then let them drop again. There was in-decision in his eyes for a moment. Then, still looking at the boy, he asked, "Were you named for your father?"

Joshua shook his head. "My father's name is Nathan."

Matthew looked up. "He was partly named for his grandfa-ther Benjamin Steed."

"Ah," the stranger said, as if it didn't really matter. Then as an afterthought, "And Joshua, where did you get that name?"

For a moment Rebecca was inclined not to answer, then she decided she wanted him to know. "You're not a Mormon, are you?" she asked.

There was a momentary flash of anger, instantly followed by a small smile. "No, hardly."

"Well," she went on, "in the Mormon church we give names to our babies in a special blessing ceremony. Our brother Nathan had planned to give their first boy his own name, but when he stood up to bless him, suddenly the Spirit whispered that he should change that and name the boy Joshua." Her voice went suddenly quiet. "It's the name of our oldest brother."

She stopped for a moment, surprised at how intensely the man was listening to her story now. "It was a shock to all of us. Our brother Joshua ran away from home almost eleven years ago now."

The man stared at her for what seemed like the longest time. "And what ever happened to him?" he finally asked in a voice so low it was barely discernible.

Rebecca looked away. "We don't know. He came to Missouri for a while. Then he went to Georgia, we heard. He never answered our letters."

Again the silence stretched out for a long moment, then the man nodded, his eyes hooded and unreadable. "That must have been hard for your parents," he finally said slowly.

Rebecca's eyes were suddenly filled with tears. "Mama still prays for him every night and every morning." Her voice caught. "So do I."

The man stiffened, then quickly reached up and pulled the hat down lower over his eyes. "Well," he said brusquely, "I've got to go. Thanks again for the food." Without waiting for a reply, he reined the horse around sharply, put the spurs to it, and loped off, cutting across a corner of the prairie, then turning south on the road that led to Liberty and on across the river to Jackson County.

———•——

Olivia Mendenhall Steed was the envy of every girl in the small two-room schoolhouse in Independence. She was beautiful; she was poised and confident; she was the smartest in the class; her father was one of the richest men, if not *the* richest man, in Jackson County; and she had the most stunning hair of anyone in the school.

For a ten-year-old, it was pretty difficult not to have one's head turned by such things, but fortunately Olivia's mother and her brother, Will, constantly worked with her to convince her that while she might be more blessed than others, she was no better than they were. For the most part it was working, and unlike some favored children, Olivia had not triggered the jealousy of her classmates.

When Joshua road into the school yard, it was recess time. Some of the boys were off against the wall of the school building playing "huzzlecap," a game in which pennies were pitched at a mark and the one coming closest won points. But most of the children, including almost all of the girls, were involved in a game of "blindman's buff." Olivia had been chosen as first one "it," and was moving about slowly, arms outstretched, a cloth tied around her eyes, trying to catch someone. The children were darting in and out, coming within inches of her grasp, shrieking in alarm as they barely eluded her clutches.

Joshua swung down and tied his horse, then put a finger to his lips as the children turned and recognized him. Now they squealed all the more, thrilled to be in on this new conspiracy.

In blindman's buff, one of the players, while blindfolded, tried to catch another person and then identify that person without removing the blindfold. Joshua moved directly in the line of Olivia's path and stood stock-still. She sensed that there was a change in the nature of her playmates' cries, and stopped for a moment.

"Go on! Go on!" they shouted. One placed a hand on her back and gave her a gentle shove. She moved forward, cautious now. Then her outstretched hand touched Joshua's arm. "Got you!" she yelled. She threw her arms around him to make the identification and instantly realized she had gotten something very different from what she expected. One hand went up to the blindfold to take it off, but the children shrieked all the louder. "No! No! You have to guess. You have to guess who it is."

She began to reach out, tentatively feeling. She patted his chest, then his shoulders. When her hand touched his beard, she started jumping up and down. "It's Papa! It's Papa!"

Thrilled to hear her use that title, Joshua reached out and swept her into his arms. He dropped his head and put his mouth next to her ear. "Hello, Olivia. I'm back."

Now she whipped off the blindfold and hugged him happily as the children applauded. The schoolteacher, hearing the commotion, came to the door. "Hello, Mr. Steed," she said. "Welcome home."

He looked up and smiled. "Would it put my daughter's grades in jeopardy if she were to miss a half day of school?"

She smiled. "With Olivia, I think we'll be just fine."

He took the blindfold from her and tossed it to the nearest child. "Then let's go home and find your mother," he said.

———◆———

"And you didn't tell them who you were?" Caroline said in total disbelief. "You were right there with them, and you didn't say anything?"

Joshua blew out his breath, realizing how foolish it now sounded. "I couldn't."

"Your own brother and sister and you didn't say a word?" She shook her head. "I'm surprised they didn't recognize you."

"I would have been surprised if they did," he answered. "It's been about eleven years. Matthew and Rebecca were just kids when I left." He reached up and rubbed one hand across his beard. "And I don't think they ever saw me with a beard before I left Palmyra. Even if they did, it wouldn't really help them recognize me now. I didn't have much of a beard back then; I kept it short and trimmed."

Caroline was still shocked at his news. When the wagon master had come and told that her Joshua was going to Far West, she had been thrilled. Now her hopes had been dashed. "And you didn't see any of the rest of your family?"

His head went back and forth slowly. "You've got to remember that I was very conspicuous there. There are about five thousand people in Far West now, and only about a hundred of them are not Mormons. I felt like a gopher stuck on a rock." There was a brief smile. "I made the mistake of trying to get some cigars. You wouldn't believe that place. A man really has to work to find any liquor or tobacco there."

"That's one point in favor of the Mormons." Caroline did not like his cigars and would not let him smoke them in the house. She sighed. "I can't believe you were right there and didn't see your parents."

"I can't," he said softly.

"But why? It's been over ten years. Surely they've forgiven you by now."

He shook his head slowly, not meeting her eyes.

"Joshua," she pleaded, "they can't be that unreasonable. They keep writing to you. I know you and your father came to blows, but it's done. It's over. It's been nearly eleven years!"

He was staring at his hands. "It's more than that." The fingers clenched into fists. "That night when I told you about my past . . ." He opened his hands and spread them out, palms down. "I didn't tell you everything."

The hurt in her eyes was like a spear thrust in his side.

"It is something I can barely bring myself to think about," he added, knowing how totally weak it sounded.

Now it was she who looked away from him. "Then maybe it's time you did, Joshua."

It took him almost ten minutes. It came out in halting, stammering, pain-filled phrases. About how his brother Nathan had come to Jackson County looking for him in the summer of

1834. About his shock and yet his elation at seeing a family member again. Then had come the bitter words, the terrible recriminations, the blind fury. And Joshua had walked out, turning his own flesh and blood over to the men with the bullwhips.

For a long time after he finished, the house was completely quiet. Finally, Caroline stood and walked to the window. She pulled the curtain back and stared out. After several moments, he spoke. "I'm sorry I didn't tell you before. It's not that I was trying to hide it. It's just . . ." He took a breath. "Even after four years it makes me ill to think about what I did."

She didn't answer, nor did she turn around.

"Now," he said, his voice bleak, "now do you see why I can't face them?"

At last she turned. She shook her head. "No, Joshua. Now I feel all the more strongly about it. You have to face them. You have to face Nathan. Tell him what you're feeling. Tell him you're sorry."

"Sorry!" he exploded. "I am responsible for having my own brother—the brother I was closest to all the time I was growing up—I am responsible for having him beaten senseless, whipped until his back was a bloody pulp, and I'm supposed to go and say I'm sorry! Doesn't that seem just a little inadequate to you?"

"You have to," Caroline said, her voice trembling in response to his own anguish. "You have to, Joshua."

He dropped his head into his hands. "I can't, Caroline. I'm sorry, but I can't."

On April twelfth, 1838, the high council court in Far West, Missouri, found Oliver Cowdery guilty of six of the nine charges brought against him. Two were not proven and one was withdrawn. He was excommunicated from the Church. When his brother-in-law, David Whitmer, learned that charges were being drawn up against him, he withdrew his name from the records of the Church rather than face the high council court.

In Kirtland, the faithful Saints were abandoning the city in droves now, leaving or preparing to leave for Missouri. Martin Harris, completely disaffected and disheartened by what had happened during the past several months, had been excommunicated the previous December. He decided that Missouri held nothing for him and stayed behind to salvage what he could in Ohio.

And thus within a period of a few short months, all Three Witnesses to the Book of Mormon were excommunicated from the Church of Christ, or the Church of the Latter-day Saints, as it was variously called.

On the twenty-six of that same month, April 1838, Joseph Smith received a revelation from the Lord calling on the members of the Church to gather to northern Missouri and build the kingdom there. Among other things the Lord also declared that his Church should officially be called The Church of Jesus Christ of Latter-day Saints.

Ⅰt was Sunday, the third day of June, 1838, and with the final worship service of the day finished, the Steeds had gathered to the home of Benjamin and Mary Ann. Even on normal occasions the Sunday gatherings taxed the home's capability. Benjamin had lost almost everything in the financial difficulties in Ohio, and so far they had been able to secure nothing more than a few acres west of town and the cabin Matthew had received from John Griffith in trade for the farm at Haun's Mill. Matthew had started to add two small rooms at the back by the time Benjamin and Mary Ann had arrived the first part of November. Over the winter Benjamin and Matthew had finished those rooms, but the cabin was still small and only modestly furnished. And today there were more Steeds than normal.

The previous day Jessica and John Griffith had driven over with their children from Haun's Mill to spend the weekend, which meant there were eighteen people in all at the Steed home—counting the two new babies. And that really tested the limits of the small three-room house. But fortunately the weather had stayed pleasant, and they had eaten outside. Now things had settled a little. Both babies were asleep, and the children were out back playing a spirited game of "statue tag," with Peter serving as referee. The adults had gathered on the front porch or around the steps to visit. They chatted lazily, not wanting to rush the time when John and Jessica would have to start for home.

As Mary Ann looked around, she reflected on what an odd collection the family circle was turning out to be—two grandparents, three natural children, two daughters-in-law (she still thought of Jessica that way, though she had not been married to their son now for several years), a step-son-in-law, six natural grandchildren, and two stepgrandchildren. That made sixteen Steeds in all. Their two "adopted" sons from England, Derek and Peter, made up the total of eighteen.

The men, including Matthew and Derek, were talking about the weather and the need for rain now that they had the wheat and corn crops in. The women were talking about Emma Smith's new baby boy born the day before, and that naturally led the conversation to Jessica's and Lydia's newborns. As they went on, a great contentment settled over Mary Ann. She noted that John reached out and took Jessica's hand while she was speaking. She did not stop, but turned and smiled warmly at him. Nathan and Lydia were already touching, her hand resting lightly on his arm.

Mary Ann had worried herself nearly into exhaustion over these two women of hers. When Jessica announced she was with child, the nagging fears started immediately. In several pregnancies, only once had she been able to carry a child full term. Mary Ann went to the settlement on Shoal Creek and spent the last three weeks of Jessica's time with her. On March fifteenth, when the baby came out as healthy as a lumberjack and weighing almost as much, Mary Ann had dropped to her knees and wept out her thanks to the Lord. They named him John after his father and Benjamin after his grandfather.

And Lydia had been no less an emotional drain on Mary Ann. When the letter came in late January announcing that she and Nathan were leaving Kirtland to come to Missouri as soon as possible, Mary Ann had a whole new source of concern. Here Lydia was, less than three months from delivery and traveling eight hundred miles with three young children in the worst of the winter season. But in late February they had finally arrived, and there had been no ill effects. Elizabeth Mary Steed came out pink as a Vermont sunrise and with a pair of lusty lungs that could be heard three houses away in any direction.

There was still the empty ache inside whenever she thought of Melissa and Carl and the three grandchildren in Kirtland. But while she had lost a daughter, she had also regained a son. Her eyes moved to her youngest, and something deep inside her smiled. It was so good to have Matthew back with them. His natural cheerfulness and perpetual love for people always cheered her. And he was always sneaking up behind her and surprising her with a hug or a quick peck on the cheek. And to see him working the land side by side with Benjamin gave her great satisfaction.

She turned slightly. Derek was standing at ground level, looking down at Rebecca, who sat on the step. He was talking animatedly about his recent trip with Brother Joseph and some of the brethren to the northern part of Caldwell County and into Daviess County to scout out new locations for settlements. As she watched her daughter, Mary Ann's thoughts turned to Arthur Wilkinson, the young man who had proposed marriage to Rebecca about two years before. How grateful she was that Rebecca had had the foresight—and courage—to tell him no. It had cost her. Mary Ann had wept over that pain too, a pain that didn't end like the pain of delivering a baby, because Arthur Wilkinson turned viciously bitter. Mary Ann had prayed much over this sweet and gentle daughter of hers. She wanted her to be happy. So it was wonderful to see what was starting to happen between her and Derek.

Rebecca's face was a study in concentration. She would watch

Derek intently, nodding or murmuring at the right places, then suddenly she would smile softly to herself as he dropped his *h*'s or used some other peculiarly English expression. It was too early to make solid predictions, of course, but both Mary Ann and Benjamin were cheering Derek on. He was so painfully shy around Rebecca, and strangely, she was much more reticent around him than she was with anyone else. And so the relationship was developing very slowly. But Derek was a fine young man. The world would probably call him simple and unlearned, but his spiritual depth was remarkable, and his openness to life in America and as a Latter-day Saint was constantly refreshing to all of them.

With a sudden start Mary Ann remembered the patriarchal blessing Rebecca had received from Joseph Smith, Sr. After her experience with Arthur the words had been particularly comforting both to Rebecca and her mother. "You will find a righteous man," the Lord had promised through Father Smith, "a worthy priesthood holder who will make you the queen of his home." Sudden tears sprang to Mary Ann's eyes. She had not thought of it before, but here, not two feet away from Rebecca, stood Derek Ingalls from Preston, England. In the blessing the Lord had told Rebecca to be patient, but promised her if she was, the blessing would be forthcoming. And now Derek was here, had come within the very circle of the family so that he could not possibly miss her. Mary Ann shook her head, marveling. How great was the goodness of God!

Derek was making some comment to Rebecca about "Adam-ondi-Ahman," which brought Jessica's head around. "What was that you called it?" she asked.

"Adam-ondi-Ahman."

Jessica looked puzzled. "What is that? I know there's a hymn about it, but I've never really understood what it's all about."

"That's right," Nathan said, "you and John haven't heard Derek's report. Derek went north with Joseph and some others to check out the lay of the land. Tell them what happened, Derek."

Derek was a little flustered to be the center of attention, but he was also pleased. "Well, we went up into Daviess County, up where Lyman Wight has a settlement and a ferry service across the Grand River."

"Yes," Jessica said, "I know Colonel Wight."

Derek glanced quickly at Rebecca, then back to Jessica. "It's beautiful country. So green." His voice turned wistful. "It reminds me in some ways of England. Peter would love it."

"So," Nathan broke in, "tell Jessica about Di-Ahman."

"Di-Aham?" she said, looking confused.

"That's short for Adam-ondi-Ahman," Derek explained. "Anyway, the morning after we arrived, Joseph took us about a half mile upriver, near Wight's Ferry, to a place the brethren there call Spring Hill."

"Spring Hill," Rebecca corrected him, her eyes teasing him. Derek had dropped the H as he often did, pronouncing it 'Ill. "This is one time your Lancashire pronunciation loses something of the meaning."

Derek pulled a face at himself. "Spring Hill," he said, forcing out the H with exaggerated breathiness. "Anyway, that's where Brother Joseph wants to start a settlement. But then he surprised us all. 'You may call this Spring Hill,' he said, 'but the Lord has named it something else.'"

"Adam-ondi-Ahman?" Jessica guessed.

"Yes."

"But what does it mean?" her husband asked.

"Ah, that's what was so exciting," Derek went on eagerly. "Brother Joseph said the Lord revealed to him that Adam-ondi-Ahman is the place where Adam, or the Ancient of Days, shall come just prior to Christ's second coming, as was seen in vision by the prophet Daniel."

John Griffith shook his head. "I guess I'm not familiar with that."

"It's in the seventh chapter of the book of Daniel," Lydia said. When Derek had returned to report what had happened, the family had gathered together and found the account in Daniel and read it together. It had thrilled them all deeply. "It will be a wonderful thing," she went on. "Christ will come and receive the kingdom the Saints have been preparing for him. Then he will assume his rightful power and dominion over all the earth in preparation for the millennial reign. Daniel says there will be ten thousand times ten thousand of the Saints there."

Jessica was suitably impressed, as was her husband. He looked at her. "When we get home tonight, I would like to read that. It sounds wonderful."

Derek again looked at Rebecca, then away quickly. "Now that Sister Emma has had the baby, Brother Joseph is going back up north again to lay out the city plat. They're going to call the new settlement Adam-ondi-Ahman."

"Hmm," Benjamin said. "I didn't know he was leaving again that soon. But it's a good thing they're establishing another place. With Kirtland emptying out and new members coming in from all over, Far West just can't handle everybody anymore."

"I'm going with him," Derek said quietly.

Rebecca looked up quickly. "Again?" she asked.

He looked away. "I'm going to ask for an inheritance up there."

"What?" Matthew blurted.

"You're what?" Lydia exclaimed.

Mary Ann's head had come up sharply, and she was staring at him in dismay. But no one was as shocked as Rebecca. She looked stunned. And betrayed.

Derek rushed on. "I've thought a lot about it. It's good farmland up there. And there are just too many families here in Far West who need land. It's easier for us to go, Peter and me." He finally looked at Rebecca. "Up there I can get a start." He laughed, but it came out hollow and forced. "There ain't— isn't—much call for coal shovelers out here. I know I'm not much of a farmer yet, but Nathan and Matthew and Father Steed have taught me a lot."

He stopped. Rebecca had turned her head away from him, as if she were no longer listening. His face colored slightly. "I need to make my own way if I'm ever going to have my own family." She didn't turn.

Benjamin came to his rescue. "Nathan and Matthew and me just planned to have you work our land with us, Derek."

"I know, and I thank you for that. But . . ." He shrugged.

Benjamin nodded slowly. "I understand." He looked at the faces around him, studiously avoiding looking at Rebecca. "Well, it's only about thirty miles from here. It's not like we'll never see him and Peter." But everyone knew that thirty miles was a full day's travel one way. It would happen, but not frequently.

Rebecca got up quickly. "I'd better go see what the children are doing," she said. "I haven't heard them for the last few minutes."

John Griffith stood, pulling Jessica up too. Though he was the newest addition to the Steed family, he sensed immediately what was happening. "We'll come too," he said to Rebecca. "It's time to round up our kids and start for home. We've got a three-hour ride ahead of us."

Rebecca nodded, and as the three of them walked away, going toward the back of the house, Derek stared after them, his face drawn and his eyes desolate.

———— ✦ ————

Nathan and Lydia lived three blocks away from Nathan's parents in a small cabin on the north edge of the town. With Derek and Peter staying at her parents' house, Rebecca still lived with Nathan and Lydia as she had since they had arrived in Far West. Originally the plan had been to build a small cabin behind Nathan and Lydia's so that the two Britons would have a place to live; but limited funds had not made that possible, and Rebecca had stayed with Nathan and Lydia so that Derek and Peter could stay at her parents' home. All that would change now, she thought, as she walked steadily toward her parents' house. Derek and Peter were leaving, and she would be able to return home again. It did not cheer her.

Suddenly she pulled up. A familiar figure was coming down

the street toward her. The sun had gone down now, and the final minutes of twilight were fading, but there was no mistaking the broad shoulders, the strong, sure gait, or the thick-cut hair on which a small woolen cap was precariously perched.

Derek's head was down, and he seemed to be deep in thought as he strode along. She waited, smiling to herself. As he nearly reached her, she spoke sharply. "I beg your pardon."

It was as though he had walked into the side of a barn. He fell back a step, eyes wide and startled.

"Do you always go around running people off the sidewalk?" she said gravely.

"Rebecca. I didn't even see you. I—"

"Good evening, Mr. Ingalls." Her voice was as sweet as maple sugar. "And where might you be going in such a hurry?"

"I . . ." He swept off the cap. "I was comin' to see you, actually." He jammed his hat into his pocket. He always felt like such a dolt around her. "I . . . I wanted to speak with you."

That pleased her greatly, and the desire to tease him quickly died away. "That's interesting," she murmured. "Actually, I was coming to see you."

"You were?"

"Yes." She turned and started walking slowly again. "Yes, I was."

He fell into step beside her. They walked along for a time, neither one speaking, but he kept giving her quick, sidelong glances. Finally, he cleared his throat. Instantly she stopped, holding up one hand. "No, Derek," she said. "I would like to speak first."

"All right," he said tentatively.

"I wanted to say . . ." She took a quick breath. She had rehearsed this over and over in her mind, but now it wouldn't come out quite as easily as it had then. He was leaning forward slightly, watching her intently. "I wanted to apologize for the way I acted this afternoon," she said. "It was childish of me. I think it's wonderful that you're going north with Joseph."

He blinked. "You do?"

A tiny smile played around the corners of her mouth. "Well . . . I kind of do. It just took me by surprise when you announced it like that."

"That's what I wanted to come say to you," he said eagerly. "I'm sorry. I wanted to tell you first today, but there was never a chance."

She looked up. "You had no obligation to tell me first."

He looked a little hurt by that. "I know, but I wanted to."

She nodded, pleased. "I understand why you want your own land."

He shuffled his feet, looking at the ground. "Your family has been very good to me, Rebecca." His eyes raised quickly, then dropped again. "Nathan lent me that money to get me and Peter out here. Your father and mother have been giving us board and room free of charge. I've got to make my own way."

"There's nothing wrong with letting people help you. And neither Nathan nor my parents expect you to pay them back."

"Well, I do. Peter and me didn't come to America to live off'n others."

She watched the stubborn set of his lips and the squareness of his jaw. "Are all Englishmen this proud?" she asked lightly.

His head came up sharply. "In England, at least where Peter and me come from, only the ladies and gentlemen could afford such a thing as pride."

She was taken aback by the fierceness of his reaction. "You're a gentleman, Derek."

He hooted in disbelief. "I'm an unlearned and unschooled working-class donkey. Good for shoveling coal or writin' notes in a ledger book. There aint' nothin' to be proud about there."

"Unlearned and unschooled are not the same thing, Derek Ingalls, and you know it."

He was angry now, and it surprised her. "Look at your family. You've all been to school. You talk nice and act nice. You know how to do so many things."

She started to object, but he overrode her. "Take Matthew, for example. Not yet eighteen, and yet he can do almost anything—drive a team of horses, plow a straight furrow, shoot a rifle, build furniture, shoe a horse. He can read and write. He knows arithmetic."

"You can read and write," Rebecca exclaimed, "and you taught yourself to do it. You and Peter have made it completely on your own all this time. We all admire you tremendously for that. Stop berating yourself."

He pounced on that. "Berating? You see, that's a word I don't even know. Your family uses words all the time that I don't know. I watch them at supper. They set the table and say grace and pass the food one to another all polite like. Me and Peter, all we ever did was set out bread and cheese on a piece of metal plate and eat it with our hands."

"Stop it, Derek!" Her eyes were blazing. "My family has not tried to make you feel inferior. Not ever."

He was staring at her in disbelief. "Do you think that's what I'm saying? Your family are the most wonderful people me and Peter have ever known. That's what makes me feel so awful. I want to be like you. I want to know where to put the knife and where to put the fork. I want to be able to do what Nathan and your father and Matthew and John and everyone else in America seem to be able to do." He looked at her, pain pulling little lines around the corners of his eyes. "Then maybe I can come down and be among you and not feel like a donkey in a horse race." His gaze held hers for a moment. "Then maybe I can come down and see you and not be . . ." He shook his head and turned away.

Rebecca was staring at his back, shocked by his outburst. Finally, her head lifted. "You are a fool, Derek Ingalls."

There was a short, humorless laugh. "That's what I've been trying to tell you, Rebecca Steed."

"A stubborn, bullheaded English fool." Her mouth opened and shut. There was nothing more to say. She turned and walked away, not looking back.

———•———

Obadiah Cornwell had been hired to drive wagons for Joshua Steed when Joshua had first come to Independence. As the freight business expanded, Joshua made Cornwell his yard foreman, giving him responsibility for the stables, the storage sheds, and all of the live and the rolling stock. Then, as Joshua branched out into other ventures—the textile mills in St. Louis, the purchase of cotton from the South, investments in the fur trade—he had brought Cornwell into full partnership in the freight business. Though a rough man outwardly, Cornwell was a family man, full of integrity, totally dependable. And completely loyal to Joshua Steed. So now he looked at Joshua's wife with just a touch of panic. "Mrs. Steed, you know I can't do that."

Caroline had expected no less of him. "I'm not asking for anything more than a wagon with a team. Put some beds in the back and a few supplies. That's all I need." She laid a hand on her son's shoulder. "Will is fourteen now. He is a capable driver."

Cornwell looked at Will and smiled. If Joshua Steed had not legally adopted Will Mendenhall and given him his name, Obadiah Cornwell would have gladly done so. "Will's as fine a driver as I have. That's not the point."

"The point is, Obadiah," Caroline cut in swiftly, "I need a wagon. My husband is gone to St. Louis and can't give the yard foreman permission, so I'm asking you, as his partner, to authorize it."

He blew out his breath in exasperation. "Why didn't you talk to Joshua before he left?" He brightened. "Or why not wait until he gets back? He should return before the first of July. That's less than two weeks now. Why don't you wait?"

Caroline liked and respected Joshua's partner as much as Joshua did. She couldn't lie to him. Besides, he knew her well enough to know it instantly if she tried. She smiled briefly at him. "Because he will say no."

Cornwell threw up his hands. "Exactly! Do you know what he'll do to me when he finds out I've helped you in this?"

Her smile broadened. "He'll rant and rave and cuss a little. But I'm the one he'll be most angry with, and I'm ready to deal with that."

"I can't, Mrs. Steed. I just can't. He'll kill me."

Will stepped forward. "Mr. Cornwell, I know how you feel. But Mama's right. We need to do this."

Caroline tipped her head back, brushing a strand of hair away from her eyes. Her mouth turned down, and her voice lowered. "You know why I want to go up there, don't you, Obadiah?"

He looked all the more glum. "Yes."

"It's his *family*, Obadiah. And he's not going to do anything. He's afraid to. Someone has got to make the first move."

Cornwell's chest rose and fell. He was torn. He had tremendous respect for Caroline Steed and for what she had done for Joshua. There was very little resemblance between the man Cornwell had first started working for and the man he worked with now. But he also knew that Joshua was not going to like this. Not one bit. And he had seen Joshua Steed when he was angry.

Caroline's green eyes flashed with determination. "If you won't help me, I'll find someone who will. There are others with wagons here."

"And Pa wouldn't like that either," Will threw in.

Cornwell stared at her for several moments, then finally he passed one hand before his eyes. "All right," he said wearily. "All right."

Caroline was elated. "Thank you."

"I'd better send a man with you. You're going right into the heart of Mormon country."

There was a quick frown of irritation. "I wasn't here when the Mormons were in Jackson County, Obadiah. But if the reports are correct, it wasn't *them* who took up arms against you; it was the other way around. I'm not worried about going amongst them." She laid an arm across Will's shoulders. "Besides, I already have a man to go with me."

———•———

Nathan was at the small table reading. There was a knock, but to his surprise it was at the back door of the cabin, which was in the far corner of their one large open room.

Joshua jumped up from where he was working on a writing assignment. "I'll get it."

Lydia was on the wooden bench that served as their sofa now, teaching Emily how to sew a simple design on a pillowcase. She gave Nathan a questioning look. He shrugged, and they both turned to watch Joshua. He opened the door. There was no one there. He stuck his head out; then, to their surprise, stepped clear outside. In a moment he was back, looking suddenly spooked.

"Papa." His blue eyes were wide and frightened. "There's a man out back. He says he's got to see you right now."

Nathan shut the book and stood up. Lydia's curiosity had turned to anxiety. "Be careful, Nathan."

He smiled. "This isn't Kirtland, Lydia."

"There are many people from Kirtland here," she retorted, "and not all good ones. Be careful!"

He nodded, and walked swiftly to the door. Joshua followed behind him. Nathan opened it. There was no one there. Puzzled, he stepped outside, stopping for a moment on the landing. There was no moon and the night was dark. He peered into the blackness, feeling a sudden eeriness. Then a figure stepped out from behind the darker shape of the outhouse. "Nathan. It's me, Oliver. Can you come out?"

Nathan waved an arm, feeling a rush of relief. He turned to Joshua. "Tell your mother it's just Oliver Cowdery." As the door shut, Oliver came forward, looking around furtively. He had something white in his hand.

Nathan felt a quick jolt as he saw the fear on Oliver's face. "Oliver, what's the matter?"

Oliver thrust his arm out. It was a piece of paper he held. "Have you seen this?"

Nathan took it, turning so that he caught a ray of lamplight from the window. He recognized it immediately without reading it. "Yes," he said, handing it back.

"Yes," Oliver burst out. "That's all you've got to say, is yes?"

Nathan took his friend by the arm. "Come inside. Let's talk."

Oliver jerked away. "No. I don't want to be seen." He looked around quickly. "We're leaving. Tonight."

"What?" Nathan was stunned. "This paper is hogwash, Oliver. Something meant to scare you. Surely you don't believe anyone—"

"Well, it worked," he exclaimed. He thrust the paper right in front of Nathan's nose and shook it. "If this had your name on it, wouldn't you take it seriously?"

Nathan started to say something, but Oliver's question had brought him up short. Two days before, Sidney Rigdon had delivered a sermon that had left all of Far West buzzing. It had quickly been dubbed the "Salt Sermon," because Sidney had used for his text a verse from the Sermon on the Mount. "Ye are the salt of the earth," Jesus said, "but if the salt have lost his savour, . . . it is thenceforth good for nothing, but to be cast out, and to be trodden under foot of men." Sidney then compared the apostates who had left the Church and the dissidents still in it to the salt that had lost its savor.

The message struck a strong, responsive chord in some of the Saints. Many of the dissenters had come from Kirtland and were trying to stir up trouble in Missouri. But the situation in Missouri was much more precarious than it had been in Kirtland. The old settlers were becoming increasingly alarmed by the swelling population of Mormons. Anti-Mormon sentiment was strong, and there was considerable fear among the Church members that those who were disaffected from the Church might go into league with the Missourians. There was already talk in some of the communities to the south about the need for another "Mormon solution." The horror of Jackson County was still vividly fresh in the minds of many, and such rumors brought near hysteria.

Nathan was not sure Sidney had intended to suggest that those who opposed the Church should be trodden under foot, but that was how many had interpreted it. A short time later, a printed notice started to circulate—the one Oliver now held in his hand. It was addressed to five of the apostates—Oliver Cowdery, David and John Whitmer, W. W. Phelps, and Lyman Johnson. It was signed by more than eighty Latter-day Saints, including several of prominence. The message of the circular was blunt and plainly stated. The apostates would be wise to flee the state immediately or face the threat of bodily harm.

Nathan took the paper from his friend's hand and smoothed it out against his leg. "You don't see Joseph's signature on this, do you? He had no part in this. He has already condemned it, said it was not authorized." He jabbed a finger at the top name on the signers list. "Sampson Avard, a hothead if ever there was one, he's behind this."

From out in front of the house there was a laugh. Someone was passing by out in the street. Oliver shrank back into the shadows of the house, his face suddenly pale. Nathan was shocked to see the naked fear that twisted his face. When the sounds died again, Oliver spoke from the darkness. "I ask you again, if your name was on this paper would you take it seriously?"

Nathan finally sighed wearily. "Probably."

Oliver stepped out of the shadows and snatched the paper out of Nathan's hand. "Well, so are we. We're riding out tonight."

"All of you?" Nathan was reeling a little.

"Yes." His eyes half closed for a moment. "We dare not even wait to get our families out. You're the only one I can trust, Nathan. Will you see to Elizabeth and the two girls?"

"Of course. I—"

There was another noise from out in the street. Oliver's hand shot out and gripped Nathan's arm. "Thank you. I'll send word where we are." And then before Nathan could say another thing, he was gone.

———•———

Lydia looked up as a knock sounded at the front door. Joshua started to get up again, but Lydia raised her hand quickly. "No, Joshua, I'll get it."

Her son looked disappointed, but then shrugged.

"Just wait a moment, Emily, and we'll go on," Lydia said. She stood and walked quickly to the door and opened it.

"Good evening."

Lydia's eyes took several things in at once. The woman was well dressed and very attractive. She had a little girl in her arms, a girl with the reddest hair Lydia had ever seen on a child that young. On one side of her stood a handsome young man, almost as tall as the woman. On the other side was a girl, about ten, Lydia guessed, and obviously the woman's daughter, for she had the same wide green eyes and long auburn hair. "Good evening," Lydia said, recovering from her surprise quickly.

"Are you Mrs. Steed?" the woman asked.

"Yes," Lydia said, noting that it was *Mrs.* Steed and not *Sister* Steed.

"Is your husband Nathan Steed?"

"Yes."

"Is he here?"

Though the woman spoke calmly, Lydia sensed an underlying tension in her that was puzzling. "Yes, he's out back for a moment. Let me get him." She stepped back, opening the door more widely. "Won't you come in?"

"Thank you." She gave her daughter a gentle push, and they all came into the room. Since the cabin had only one main room, the family was now in clear view of Joshua and Emily, who were eyeing them with unabashed curiosity. Lydia motioned toward the bench. "Won't you sit down while I get my husband?"

The woman smiled briefly but shook her head. "We'll wait here."

When Lydia opened the back door, she was surprised to see

Nathan just standing there all by himself. As she opened the door, he turned. "It was Oliver," he said. "He's gone. He's leaving. I can't—"

She stepped out and half closed the door. "There's a woman here."

He stopped, surprised. "Who?"

Her shoulders lifted and fell. "I've never seen her before."

Nathan looked perplexed. This was certainly not a typical night at home. Still troubled by his encounter with Oliver, he followed Lydia back inside. He slowed for a moment as he saw the visitors, then walked across the room quickly. "Hello," he said.

Lydia immediately started for her own children. "Come, Emily and Joshua. We'll go upstairs."

The woman turned quickly. "No." She was embarrassed by her abruptness and smiled to soften it. "Please stay. I'd like you to hear this too."

Lydia nodded.

The woman turned back to Nathan and took a quick breath. "You are Nathan Steed?"

"Yes."

"I'm sorry to come this late. We've had a long journey today." She shifted the child to her other arm and held out her hand. "My name is Caroline Steed."

Nathan took her hand slowly, peering at her. "Steed?" he echoed. Lydia also was staring.

"Yes. My husband is Joshua Steed. I believe you and he are brothers."

Chapter Thirty-One

Obadiah Cornwell was waiting for Joshua when he came down the gangplank of the riverboat that had just tied up at the wharf at Westport, Missouri. Joshua slowed his step at the sight of him, then pushed his way through the disembarking crowd. "Didn't expect to see you here," he said abruptly.

From the lines in Joshua's face and the weariness in his eyes, Cornwell could tell it had been a wearing trip. And from the clipped tone of his voice, he knew his partner was in a foul mood.

"Did you bring the wagons?" Joshua asked.

"Yes. Six of them."

"That should be fine." He turned and started moving toward the nearest warehouse office. "Let's get the stevedores and get those bales of cloth goods transferred."

"I also brought your horse," Cornwell said.

Joshua stopped and turned around slowly.

"I think you'd better get on to Independence. I'll see to the shipment."

There was a quick flash of concern. "Is there something wrong with my family?"

Cornwell took him by the elbow and pulled him to a spot where they had some privacy. And then he told him. He told him about Caroline's demands for a wagon and her refusal to take no for an answer. He told him where she went and why. He rushed on quickly as he watched the disbelief in Joshua's eyes slowly turn to fury. "I tried to tell her you wouldn't like it, Joshua. But you know how she can be sometimes. There was no talking her out of it."

"Where's my horse?"

Cornwell pointed. "Tied there, second building down."

Joshua spun on his heel and stalked away. Cornwell watched him go, shaking his head. The one thing he hadn't told his partner was that it was Caroline who had sent him to Westport and told him exactly what to say.

"Caroline!" He stepped inside the door and shut it hard behind him. "*Caroline!*" His voice reverberated through the house. It was past seven o'clock now, and the last rays of the afternoon sunshine were coming through the west windows, leaving the hallway filled with softly muted light.

He flung his hat at the table and went in quick, stiff steps to the stairs. "Will! Olivia!" He thundered it up toward the second floor.

"They're not home, Joshua. Mrs. Payton has them."

He whirled. Caroline was standing another five feet down the hallway in the doorway that led to their sitting parlor. She had not been there moments before. "It's just as well," he muttered, moving toward her. "Obadiah met me at the dock. He told me you went to Far West."

"I know," she said calmly. "I told him to."

That took him aback some. "You what?"

But she had stepped back inside the room, out of his sight.

"*Caroline!*" In three strides he was at the door. He swung his head. She was standing near the window, her hands at her sides, her face composed. "Caroline, what have you done? What in the name of—"

"I know you're angry," she said quickly, "and I understand that. But swearing isn't going to change anything, Joshua. Neither will yelling at me."

His mouth opened and closed again. He stepped inside the room and shut the door with a bang, as if there were someone in the house whom he wanted to prevent from overhearing what was about to happen. He planted his feet, fighting to keep his voice under control. "All right," he demanded, "just what in the world possessed you to go to Far West?"

"I wanted to see your family."

He whirled. "She wanted to see my family," he mimicked, speaking to the wall.

"I went because you won't."

He spun back around. "You had no right! Do you hear me, Caroline? No right at all. I can't believe you've betrayed me like this."

"Joshua, I know what—"

He was still raging, not even looking at her now. "And you went deliberately while I was gone because you knew—" His breath exploded in disgust. "You *knew* I would say no."

"Yes, I did, Joshua, and I know that it was wrong now."

"Oh," he mocked, now addressing the nearest chair, "she thinks she did wrong. Ain't *that* wonderful?"

"Joshua, if you'll let me explain, I'll—"

"And did you and my family all get to sit down together?" he hissed. "Did you have a nice warm chat about good old Joshua and what you might do to smooth over all the wicked things he's done? I'll bet my father just hooted at that!"

She didn't even try to answer him, but moved slowly over to the rocking chair and sat down. He started striding around the room, speaking to himself, throwing out his arms as he talked.

"And you and Jessica? Did you two get to let your hair down and share horror stories about me? Or maybe you got to bring Lydia in on it too! I'll bet there were some good laughs out of that, comparing notes about the courting habits of Joshua Steed from the time he was just a boy."

"Are you through?" she asked quietly.

"Through!" he roared. "I'm just barely beginning."

"Joshua, I did not see your father."

"You get something in your mind and think that you can . . ." He stopped as he realized what she had said.

"I did not see your mother. I did not see Jessica or your daughter."

His eyes narrowed suspiciously.

"I didn't. I had planned on it, but then I realized that I had no right to do this without you."

"So you just drove by and waved?" he asked sarcastically.

"No. We only went to Nathan's house. I didn't—"

"*Only* Nathan?" he asked, feeling suddenly sick. "You *only* went to Nathan's house?"

"Yes. We stayed overnight. We were going to go to your parents' the next morning, but I didn't sleep all night. I knew I was wrong to do it this way, forcing your hand." She looked down. "So we left first thing in the morning without seeing anyone else."

His mouth was a tightly compressed line now, and his eyes had gone cold. "And did you ask Nathan if he would show you his scars?" he sneered.

"No, I did not," she snapped right back at him. "I didn't have to. I've already seen them."

He was already forming another withering comment, but that stopped him as sharply as if she had shoved a gag down his throat with a ramrod. "You have?" he said.

"Yes." Her eyes conveyed the sickness she was feeling inside. "I've seen them a thousand times in my mind since you told me. I don't need to see them again to know what you did to your brother."

"And you're going to fix all that too, right?" He shook his head in disbelief. "Well, who asked you?"

"No one," she answered, her chin lifting. "No more than anyone asked you to interfere in my affairs with Berrett and Boswell back in Savannah. But you did anyway because you said you cared for me."

"Well, I . . ." He stumbled over that one.

She pressed in. "And while we're at it," she continued, a touch of asperity hardening her own voice, "who are you to tell me my daughter has no right to meet her own grandparents? You know, Joshua, they aren't just your family anymore. They're Savannah's now too. She has grandparents. She has aunts and uncles and cousins. She has every right to know them."

Her chest was starting to rise and fall now as the anger began to build inside her. "You're furious because I tried to interfere in your relationship with your family. Well, what about you? What gives you the right to interfere with Savannah's relationship to *her* family just because you're living in your own private little hell?"

His jaw tightened, then jutted out. "Don't try and twist things, Caroline. I can't debate you, you know that. But what you did was down-deep wrong. You knew I would be furious, and you still went ahead and did it."

Suddenly her voice was pleading. "I told you, I know that now. I'm sorry I was so headstrong. But I'm not sorry I got to meet Nathan and Lydia." She looked up at him, her eyes filled with wonder. "Did you know they named their oldest son Joshua?"

"Yes," he snapped. "I met him that day on the road, remember?"

"They don't hate you, Joshua. Do you think they'd call their own son by your name if they still felt bitter towards you?"

"He was born before most of the things happened."

"He has your father's name too," she said, fighting down her impatience. "They could call him Ben if they detested you so much."

He shook his head stubbornly. "That's got nothing to do with the issue at hand."

Caroline looked up at him, her eyes suddenly hopeful, her mouth soft. "They're having a Fourth of July celebration in Far West on Wednesday. Jessica and her husband will be coming over. Everyone except your sister in Ohio will be there. Nathan suggested that maybe we could come up and meet—"

She stopped at the look of utter disbelief on his face.

"We could meet them all, Joshua," she rushed on. "I know it won't be comfortable. Not at first. But then . . ." She let her voice peter out into silence. His eyes were as hard and implacable as steel plates.

"You haven't heard a word I've said, have you?"

"I have, Joshua. I—"

He spun on his heel and stalked to the door. He yanked it open. "I've got six wagonloads of freight coming in. Don't wait up for me." He stepped out and slammed the door hard behind him.

Caroline stared at the door for a long moment, then slumped back in her chair, her face lined with weariness and filled with bitter disappointment.

———————◆◆———————

It was way past eleven o'clock when Joshua returned from the freight yard. He was exhausted and still seething inside. He felt as if he had been horsewhipped, then run over six or seven times by a Conestoga wagon. He stopped on the porch and removed his boots so that he wouldn't wake anyone. He was in no mood for additional battle. Not tonight. Morning would be soon enough.

As he moved slowly up the staircase, he winced as the third stair creaked loudly, as it always did. But he needn't have worried. When he entered the bedroom he saw in the faint light that the bed had not been slept in. He swore, and moved quickly to the table. Fumbling, he got a match, struck it, and lit the lamp. The room was empty.

He went out and down the hall swiftly, still carrying his boots. Olivia was gone. Will was gone. Savannah was gone. As he walked back to his bedroom he hurled his boots against the wardrobe. "You want to play the hotel game, do you? Well, fine." He started unbuttoning his shirt with vicious jerks. "You go ahead and sleep there. Then maybe I can get some sleep around here."

———◆———

"Gone? What do you mean she's gone?"

The desk clerk of the Independence Hotel was stammering like a kid getting ready for a "lickin'" from his teacher. "I'm sorry, Mr. Steed. She and the children were up early and checked out."

He felt a lurch of concern and a flash of anger at the same moment. "What time was that?"

"About six, sir."

Six! He couldn't believe it. Caroline hated early mornings. It took her almost an hour every day, sliding back and forth between sleep and wakefulness, before she finally came to life again. And Joshua, who was an early-morning person, had been so mentally and physically exhausted that he had slept straight through until nine-thirty that morning. He cursed himself for not waking up earlier, then looked at the clerk. "Did she say where she was going?"

"No, sir. Not to me, Mr. Steed. But you may want to ask Mr. Cornwell. I saw her with him a little over an hour later."

"*What?*"

The man's hands began to flutter. "I thought you knew that, Mr. Steed. Mr. Cornwell was helping her with the wagon and the horses."

Joshua slapped the counter so hard that it made the clerk jump, nearly dislodging the glasses perched on his nose. Joshua swore under his breath, then without another word he spun around and left the hotel. On the street he did not hesitate. He turned right, and ignoring the glances his angry muttering was garnering, he strode down Main Street toward the freight yard.

—◆—

"Will you shut up and listen for a minute?"

The sharpness in Obadiah Cornwell's voice shocked Joshua into silence.

"I didn't give her one of our wagons. I think she knew I wouldn't do that again."

"You mean she bought her own wagon and horses?" Joshua looked dubious.

"That's right. She's got her own money. And she used it. Paid out more than three hundred dollars."

"Why didn't you stop her?"

"Why didn't *you* stop her?" Cornwell shot right back at him.

Joshua glared at his partner. "Because I didn't know she was going!"

"Did you know she was gone last night?" Cornwell asked quietly.

"I . . ." Now he was suddenly defensive. "When I came home last night, I figured she had gone to a hotel. She threatened that once before."

"And you didn't go looking for her?"

Joshua bristled. "It was late. You know that. We were here until past eleven." He realized how lame he was sounding. "Then this morning I slept later than I planned," he finished sheepishly. "When I found where she'd stayed, she was already gone."

"Yeah, I know. She roused me out about quarter past seven. By that time she'd already been to the livery stable and picked out a wagon and team. She came to me and asked me to help outfit the rig."

"Why in the world didn't you come and get me?" Joshua asked, thoroughly disgusted.

Cornwell stood up slowly and leaned over the desk. "Look, Joshua," he said in a tight voice. "I'm not your mother and I'm not your employee anymore. Caroline is my friend as much as you are." He straightened, his face reproving. "She said to tell you that if you had come for her she might have changed her mind. But you didn't."

Joshua sat down heavily in the wooden chair across from the desk. "And she's going to Far West." It wasn't a question.

Cornwell nodded. "Ain't no secret about that. She wanted you to know so that if you change your mind you'll know where to find her."

"Well, it'll be a cold day in hell when I change my mind."

Cornwell gave him a long, appraising look, then shook his head at his old friend and partner. "It's a good thing I'm *not* your mother."

Joshua looked up, his thoughts only half on Cornwell.

"If I were I'd take you out in the woodshed and bust a stout piece of oak across your backside. Or maybe on your head."

Joshua shot to his feet. "Well, you're not my mother," he said hotly. "And judging from this morning, you're not much of a friend either." He kicked the chair back, almost knocking it over. He glared one last time at Cornwell, then left, slamming the door behind him.

On a gentle knoll that poked its nose into the valley of Adam-ondi-Ahman sat the beginnings of the new Mormon settlement which the Saints had affectionately named Di-Ahman. It was a striking setting. The valley—no more than a mile wide—followed the meanderings of the Grand River, whose course was marked by thick stands of willow, cottonwood, river birch, and heavy undergrowth. The valley floor was flat and rich and fertile, the results of the numberless times over the centuries that the river had flooded its banks. Once only grassland and low brush, now some of the valley's expanse was marked off in patches and squares stitched together by knee-high strips of prairie grass left to mark property lines. Some of the fields, plowed too recently to be planted this year, showed almost jet black. They would lie fallow over the winter to let the thick sod start to decay and break down. But elsewhere, where the earlier settlers had been given land, various crops were responding to the richness of the deep and fertile topsoil. Here there was waist-high corn, there the deeper green of a potato patch. Two or three fields showed a lighter yellow-green, the winter wheat just starting to turn toward the golden brown that would mark its harvest time.

On the bluffs north of the river, at a point not too far from the road that led south to Gallatin and Far West, signs of a vigorous human presence were everywhere apparent. Simple sod huts were the most frequent form of buildings; but there were also several log cabins, and there was one frame building that housed the store. The wagon tracks were quickly becoming roads, and the narrow pathways broadening to become hardened dirt sidewalks. About half a mile from the main center of Di-Ahman, on a small lot marked off not too far from the top of the bluff, a shell of a sod hut was nearly completed.

"All right. One. Two. Three. Heave!"

The two Ingalls brothers swung their arms in unison, and the chunk of sod—nearly a foot wide, and two feet long, and six inches thick, and weighing close to fifty pounds—went up and onto the top of the back wall of the hut. The wall was well over five feet high now, and Peter couldn't quite reach it. His end of the sod draped over the side and started to pull the rest of it over and down into his face. But Derek stepped to the side quickly, caught it, and pushed it back up into place. He lined it up carefully with the other sod bricks, then tamped it down into place.

Finally, he stepped back, wiping at his forehead with the sleeve of his shirt. "Done," he said with great satisfaction.

"Done?" Peter cried. "We've still got to do the whole roof."

"I know that," Derek replied, a touch impatiently, "but the walls are done. When we get back from Far West, Lyman Wight and the other brethren will help us put the roof on."

"And what if it rains while we're gone?"

"Then the inside will get wet. It's not like we've got a lot in there that will be hurt."

Peter had a petulant look on his face. "The Independence Day celebration isn't until Wednesday afternoon. That's five more days, countin' today. Why can't we finish the roof first and just go down on Tuesday?"

Derek sighed wearily. "The first reason is that it's not really five days. Today's already half over. Tomorrow is the Sabbath, and we can't work then. The second reason is that some of the brethren are leaving early too and won't be here to help us if we do stay. And you know we can't do the roof by ourselves. We don't know how to do it."

"And the third reason," Peter said, "is that yesterday my brother heard that there's a young man from Tennessee who's recently moved to Far West and is takin' a great interest in Miss Rebecca Steed."

Derek's eyebrows lowered and the irritation flashed across his face. "That's got nothin' to do with it. What Miss Rebecca Steed does is her business."

"Yeah, sure," Peter said soberly, mocking his brother's seriousness.

Derek bent over and wiped the Missouri dirt from his hands on the prairie grass. "What's got into you, anyway? I thought you wanted to go to Far West for the celebration."

"I do. But if we wait we can get a ride with one of the families. If we go today, we have to walk."

Derek suddenly laughed. "Is that all that's botherin' you? Didn't I tell you? Brother Wight is going down this afternoon. He says we're welcome to ride with him."

"Really?"

"Yes, really."

"Well, all right," Peter said happily. "Then let's go today."

Derek boxed at his ears playfully. "Since you've come to America you've gotten to be kind of a lazy bloke, you know that?"

Peter cocked his head. "Eh? What's that, mate?" Then he jumped quickly as Derek swung at him.

"Come on," Derek said. "Let's get down to the river and

wash up. Brother Wight said he'd be passing by here about two o'clock."

"We'd better," Peter said. "If we don't get some of that dirt and sweat off you, Rebecca isn't even goin' to let you into the same house with her."

He gave a yelp and darted away as Derek picked up a clod of dirt and sidearmed it at him, smacking him on the back. Derek stepped inside the sod hut and grabbed the one towel they owned between them, then with a shout started after his brother, who was hightailing it down the hillside and across the fields toward the trees that lined the riverbank.

It was Saturday night in Independence, and Jackson County's saloons were jumping with activity. The laughter and raucous merriment spilled out of the open doors and into the streets, beckoning any passersby to enter in and partake. But Joshua Steed passed them by. He didn't even raise his head. He was in no mood for merriment, and he was bone-tired from throwing himself into the work at the freight yard with an intensity that had shocked the boys and men who worked for him. Now all he wanted was to take off his boots and lie out on the bed. So he walked on swiftly, trying not to think about having to face an empty house for the second night in a row.

The spacious two-story house looked like a barn in the darkness. It looked particularly foreboding with all its windows dark. Caroline always left at least one lamp on for him so that there would be light in the house no matter what time he arrived home.

He pushed the thoughts of her aside angrily as he climbed the steps to the porch and opened the front door. He had vowed he was not going to mope. When she came home—and he knew she would eventually—there would be much to straighten out. His only fear was that somehow this time the rift would not completely heal. He wasn't sure it would for him. The duplicity she had shown in going to Far West was too deep, the perfidy too damaging. Once inside, he turned, and twisted the lock on the door with a hard snap.

For a moment he stood there, debating whether to go into the kitchen and find something to curb the hunger that was gnawing at his stomach. But then he shook his head. He could wait until breakfast. Tonight what he needed was bed. Without bothering to light a lamp, he climbed the stairs and went into his bedroom.

He walked to a basin and pitcher of water that stood on the night table and poured some water into the bowl. For a moment he stared balefully at himself in the small mirror hung on the wall, then he leaned over and scooped up handsful of water and started washing his face. Suddenly he straightened with a jerk. He cocked his head to one side, listening intently. There was nothing. He grabbed the towel in disgust. Was his imagination betraying him now too?

But then it came again. Someone was rapping sharply on the front door downstairs. With a surge of hope, he swung around, toweling his face rapidly. He had locked the door. If she had returned, Caroline could not get in. He threw the towel in the direction of the bed and walked swiftly out, taking the stairs two at a time. But as he reached the entry hall, his pace slowed. Through the glass he could make out a dark shape against the moonlit background. It was too big to be Caroline. He stopped, the disappointment in him sharp and hard.

He almost turned away. He couldn't imagine who might be calling—it was already past ten—and he had no desire to see anyone. But the shape through the glass moved and the knocking began again, this time even more sharply and insistent. Joshua realized that his nighttime caller had heard him come down and now was surprised that he had not yet opened the door. With an angry shake of his head, he stepped forward, turned the lock, and opened the door.

With no lamp on in the house, the man at the door was backlit by the moonlight, and his face was in deep shadow. "Yes?" Joshua growled.

"Hello, Joshua."

It was like that split second in time when the trigger pin is kicked out of a trap and you know with terrible clarity, even before the steel jaws slam shut, what you have done. The knowledge is almost more horrible than the actual physical pain that comes an instant afterwards. Joshua fell back, his jaw slack, his eyes gaping wide. He felt as if he were strangulating. "Nathan?" he cried in a hoarse whisper.

"Yes, Joshua. It's me. May I come in?"

———————

As the lamplight filled the room with a soft glow, Joshua blew out the match. He saw that his fingers were trembling slightly, and he dropped the match quickly, as though it had burned him. He stood there, looking down. He didn't want to turn. He didn't want to see that face in the light. It had haunted him, dogged his worst nightmares for four years. Now it was as though the reality would be even more terrifying than the chimera of his dreams. He laid his hands on the table and leaned forward, staring down at them, willing them to be steady. "Why did you come here?"

Joshua had not invited Nathan to sit down, and so he still stood in the center of the room. Nathan lifted his hands and stared at them, as though he might find the answer written on them. "That's what Lydia asked me, too. And Pa. They both think I'm insane."

Joshua whirled on him. "You *are* insane!" he exploded. "Do you think they won't remember who you are? This time they'll dump you in the cemetery instead of on a doorstep."

Nathan smiled wanly for a moment. "I don't exactly plan to parade myself through downtown Independence."

"I don't want you here. Please go."

It was as though he hadn't spoken. In fact, Nathan didn't react at all, just simply continued to watch his brother with a steady gaze. And then suddenly Joshua understood. His eyes narrowed and filled with fire. "This was Caroline's idea, wasn't it?"

That broke through. "What?" Nathan exclaimed.

"She put you up to this, didn't she?" His breath exploded in a burst of disgust. "What'd you do, agree to meet in Liberty?" The pieces were dropping into place like stones in a rock wall. "That's why she went to the hotel last night. She needed to get an early start to meet you."

Nathan just stared at him. When Joshua finally stopped for breath, Nathan shook his head. "I haven't seen Caroline since she came to our house last week."

Joshua's lips pulled back in a snarl. "Liar!" he shouted. "If you came down from the north, you would have passed her, seen her along the way."

"As you may remember," Nathan said evenly, "I wasn't received too warmly the last time I came to Independence. So this time I stayed off the main roads. I avoided everyone I saw coming." He let his breath out wearily. "I did not see Caroline. I have not seen Caroline. I assumed she would be here too."

The rage went into an icy calm. "I don't believe you."

Nathan shook his head, a sadness pulling at his mouth. "I know. Because that's easier than believing she left because of you." His eyes raised a fraction. "Just as it was with Jessica."

"You son-of—" Joshua leaped forward, one arm cocking back, his fist doubled.

Nathan didn't flinch, did not so much as even blink. He just stood his ground, awaiting the blow. Joshua started the swing, but at the sight of those eyes, watching him without fear or anger, he pulled up. His chest was heaving, his whole body trembling. For several moments—moments that seemed like full minutes—they stood there, eye to eye, rage and calm locked together in a contest of wills. And then Joshua spun away. His hands dropped to his sides, the fists came unclenched. "Get out of my house," he said. He walked across the room to the window. "Just get out of my house."

Joshua felt sick inside. Empty. As hollow as a cooper's new barrel. Without thinking, he raised his hands and began to massage his temples with his fingertips. He realized there had been no sound behind him. No footsteps across the floor, no opening of the door. He lowered his hands again. "Please go, Nathan," he said quietly. "I know what you're trying to do, but it's no good. Tell the family to forget it. There's too much trail behind the wagon now."

"Yes, there is. I should have come years ago. Before it went this far. But now it's time to settle it."

Joshua swung around. "Why won't you go?" he cried. "Don't you see, it's no . . ." His words died in his throat. Nathan was unbuttoning his shirt in slow, deliberate motions. Joshua's eyes locked on Nathan's fingers, appalled at the sight of what they were doing. "No, Nathan," he exclaimed, falling back a step. "Please!" He wanted to hurl something at Nathan, stop that dreaded, inexorable movement. Something shouted at Joshua from the dark recesses of his mind to throw his hands in front of his eyes, to turn and bolt out of the room. But instead he stood transfixed. Nathan's fingers moved in slow motion, like in a dream. And then, eyes wide with horror, Joshua watched as Nathan shucked the shirt from off his shoulders and pulled it down around his belt, baring himself to the waist.

Nathan stood for a moment, watching Joshua steadily, then turned so that his back was to him. In the soft glow of the lamplight the marks of the bullwhip were soft tracings against the smooth flesh, as if a child had tamped down a patch of dirt with his foot and then scratched out a random pattern of lines back and forth across it. It made Joshua gasp inwardly. Now the nightmare had become reality. He looked away quickly as Nathan turned back, pulled up his shirt, and started to button it again. "Nathan," Joshua whispered, "I—"

Nathan cut in quickly, "They're healed now."

"I didn't mean to—"

"Joshua," Nathan said more sharply. "Did you hear me? I said the scars are healed. They're getting less noticeable every year. That's why I came. I wanted you to see that they're healed." He took a deep breath, his eyes suddenly filling with sorrow. "But there are stripes inside you and inside me that are as raw and bloody as the night this happened. It's time to heal those too."

Joshua turned and sat down heavily in a chair. He dropped his head in his hands. "Some things are done. You can't change the past—not what's been said, not what's been done."

Nathan finished the buttons and tucked his shirt back into his belt. He walked to the corner of the room and picked up a spindle chair that sat in front of Joshua's desk. He brought it over in front of Joshua and set it down. He stood for a moment, looking down at the top of his brother's head, then he sat down facing him. "I want you to listen to me, Joshua. Just listen till I'm done. Then I'll go."

Joshua didn't look up, but neither did he protest. Nathan nodded slowly, then took a breath. He held it for a long moment, then it came out in a soft laugh filled with self-mockery. "Want to know the irony of this whole thing? I've been beating myself with the memory of that night for the last four years, just like you have."

Joshua lowered his hands and lifted his head, his eyes questioning.

"That's right, Joshua. All this time I've been kicking myself for being such a fool. I don't blame you. I blame myself."

"But it was—"

"No," Nathan went on swiftly, "let me finish. I came to Jackson County that night because I wanted to make peace with you. I was so filled with determination. We were going to bury this ugly thing that lay between us once and for all. Be brothers again. But what did I do instead? I lost my temper. I lashed out at you, goaded you into a fury. Your friends weren't the only ones with a whip that night, Joshua. I laid my words across your back as surely as they took the whip to mine." A weariness filled his voice now. "I wrote you twice. Tried to tell you that I was going through hell. Tried to beg your forgiveness."

"I tore them up," Joshua murmured.

"I figured as much. Then we were told you had moved to

Georgia. I thought I had lost the chance forever, that I'd never get a chance to tell you how terribly, terribly sorry I was." He sat back, his eyes looking at the wall behind and above Joshua's head. "And then Caroline came that night. We couldn't believe it. It was like an answer to prayers." He shook his head quickly. "It *was* an answer to prayers. I have begged God to let me find you again so we could make this right."

Joshua's eyes were wide with wonder and disbelief.

"I was so excited to tell Mother and Father. I wanted to tell Matthew it was you he saw on the road that day. I wanted the whole family to meet Caroline and the children. I wanted Pa to listen to her talk about you, to listen to her tell how you've changed." His eyes bored into Joshua's. "I wanted them to see the love this woman carries in her eyes for their son."

There was a long pause, and only the quiet chirping of crickets outside the window broke the silence. Then finally Nathan continued. "But Caroline left first thing the next morning. She wouldn't go see them. Said it wasn't right to do it this way, without you. That was a bitter disappointment, but I knew she was right." He stopped again, his eyes getting a faraway look in them. "For over a week now I've had nothing else but you on my mind. I knew this was the chance I had been pleading for. If I let it go, perhaps . . ." He couldn't finish. Finally, he swallowed quickly. "So I came. Risk or no risk."

"Pa didn't want you to, did he?" Joshua asked in a half whisper.

"No," Nathan said simply. He couldn't lie about that, not even soften it for him. "But Mother did. She wanted to come with me. So did Rebecca and Matthew and Lydia."

"But not Pa."

"No. The hurt runs pretty deep, and he's still as stubborn as a wet piece of oak. He's mellowed a lot. But some things . . ." He let it go unfinished.

"Deep feelings. That's something I can understand." Joshua glanced quickly at Nathan. "But I'm glad you didn't bring the others."

Nathan nodded. Then his eyes searched Joshua's face. "What I said earlier, about you driving Caroline out?"

Joshua looked away. "It's true."

"I didn't mean it as a gibe, Joshua. Lydia and I, we were only with your wife for a few hours, but it's like we've known her for years. That's a fine woman you've found for yourself, Joshua Steed. Don't let her get away from you."

"I'm afraid she already has."

Nathan shook his head. "She's hurting too. There's a cure for that." He sighed, then stood slowly. "I've got a long ride back. And it's best I go at night."

Joshua looked up at him, but before he could respond, Nathan went on. As he spoke, his fingers absently rubbed at the flesh beneath his shirt. "Whenever I remember that night, you know what makes me the sickest, Joshua?" Suddenly his voice caught and his eyes were glistening. "It's not the pain, not the horror of the whipping." He blinked quickly, angry that his emotions were betraying him. When he spoke, his voice was low and deep. "It's wondering how these four years might have been different if only I had held my tongue."

With that, he turned and walked swiftly to the door. "Good night, Joshua. I'll watch for Caroline. I'll tell her to come back. It's going to be all right." He reached out and took the door handle.

"Nathan?"

He stopped and turned, his eyes questioning.

"Why did you call your son Joshua?"

For a moment, Nathan hesitated. But there was only one answer. "I'm afraid it was the Lord's idea."

Joshua shook his head impatiently. "That's not good enough. Why did *you* call him Joshua?"

For a long moment Nathan just stood there, then his eyes softened. "Because it is a good name. And because—" Again his voice wouldn't hold for him. He looked down for a moment, fighting for control. Then his head came up again and his voice steadied. "Because it is the name carried by the man I have loved and admired since I was big enough to toddle around after him."

Joshua considered that, his face impassive. After a moment, when he didn't speak, Nathan opened the door. Joshua seemed a little surprised. "How long since you ate last?" he asked.

Nathan thought for a moment. "I had some hard biscuits and goat's cheese right after sunup."

"I worked right through dinner and supper," Joshua said evenly. "When I came in, I was thinking about warming up a pot of stew Caroline left in the icehouse. That interest you?"

Nathan smiled and shut the door again. "Yeah, I think it does."

The morning worship services had finished some fifteen minutes earlier, but the great open field that lay right in the heart of Far West was still jammed with people. Weather permitting, all public and religious meetings were held at the site designated for the new temple, since there was no building in the city large enough to hold even a fifth of the normal number of attenders—and today was certainly not a normal Sabbath. There had been nearly double the numbers at the services on this day.

Part of that was due to its being the first day of July. On Wednesday the town would turn out to celebrate Independence Day with a parade, picnics, speeches, games, and a few fireworks. For those that lived away from the main center of the Latter-day Saint community, the opportunity to mingle and worship with the main body of the Saints was strongly appealing, and they had come into town a few days early so as to be there for Sunday. But more important, they had come for the temple cornerstone laying.

Two months before, on April twenty-sixth, in a revelation given to Joseph Smith, the Lord had said: "Let the city, Far West, be a holy and consecrated land unto me. . . . Therefore, I command you to build a house unto me, for the gathering together of my saints, that they may worship me. And let there be a beginning of this work, and a foundation, and a preparatory work, this following summer." In obedience to that counsel, Joseph had announced throughout the scattered settlements that on July fourth, in addition to the other doings, the priesthood would lay the cornerstones for the new temple.

That announcement had been received with great rejoicing. The house of the Lord in Kirtland had been lost to the enemy, but now there would be one in Far West. And so the Saints had come, in their wagons and carriages, on mule- and horseback; and in many cases, whole families walking barefoot in the soft dust of the roadsides, Sunday shoes tied together and hung around their necks. They had come to worship together and would stay to see the start of a second temple.

Derek Ingalls stood a short distance away from Benjamin and Mary Ann Steed, who—along with Jessica and John Griffith and Lydia—were talking with Parley P. Pratt and Reynolds Cahoon. Lydia and Jessica both had their babies in their arms. But Derek was not watching the Steeds, at least not the ones who stood together nearby. His eyes were fixed on a spot about three or four rods away where Rebecca Steed and two other girls stood with their backs to him. All three of the young women were looking up at Isaiah Jensen, a twenty-three-year-old recent arrival from one of the branches in the South. Though he was speaking to all of them, Derek could see clearly that it was Rebecca who was drawing most of his attention. As he watched, Isaiah smiled down at her and Rebecca's head tipped back as she laughed back at him.

Derek looked quickly away, shoving his hands deep into his pockets, one finger absently poking itself through the hole in the bottom of one of them. The reports about the Jensen family and the eldest of their children had not been exaggerated. Derek's head came up and he stole another look, noting glumly the differences between him and the young man from Tennessee. Isaiah was tall and slender, with long, graceful hands. Derek was barely five feet nine, with a body built more like that of a Shetland pony. Isaiah's hair had been recently cut and had a natural wave to it. Derek's was thick and shaggy, whacked off with a sharpened knife by Peter in preparation for their trip here. Jensen's clothes, though not expensive, were obviously Sunday only. Derek had washed his best pair of trousers and shirt the night before they left, pounding out the prairie soil and grass stains as best he could against the scrubbing board.

"Grandma?"

Derek's attention was pulled back to closer at hand. Seven-year-old Joshua, Lydia and Nathan's oldest, was at the head of a troop of grandchildren. Rachel—Jessica's daughter—and her two stepbrothers, Luke and Mark Griffith, were right behind him. Emily, Joshua's sister, had little Nathan, now nearly three years old, by the hand just behind them. Derek's brother, Peter, seven years senior and a good foot taller than any of them, brought up the rear.

Mary Ann turned. "Yes, Joshua?"

"Can we go to our house and change our clothes?"

Lydia turned now too. "We'll be coming in just a moment, Joshua."

Joshua wasn't about to be deflected. "It's hot, Mama. Peter says he'll go with us."

Lydia looked at Mary Ann, who smiled and nodded. Lydia finally nodded too. "All right. But I want you to play quietly in the house. Remember, this is the Sabbath."

"Yes, Mama." He turned to his siblings and his cousins, who were grinning happily. "Let's go."

"Emily," Lydia called after them, "you watch Nathan close, now."

"Yes, Mama."

Derek watched them for a moment, then turned back in the direction of Rebecca. The girlfriends had moved off now to join another group of young ladies. Rebecca and Isaiah were standing together, just the two of them. Rebecca had changed position enough that Derek could see her face in profile. She was listening earnestly to whatever it was he was saying to her. Derek swung back around to Lydia and Mary Ann. "I'll go with them," he said.

"Oh, you don't have to do that," Lydia said. "They'll be all right."

"No, I don't mind," he said, trying not to sound too morose. "I'll help Peter keep them out of trouble."

"There you are," Matthew said as he rounded the cabin and saw Derek sitting on the back step.

"Hello, mate."

Matthew gave him a sharp look, then moved over and sat down next to him. "I've been looking for you. Brother Joseph came over to speak with us. He was particularly looking for you and Peter. He got a letter from Heber C. Kimball."

Derek looked up in surprise. "He did?"

"Yes. It just came yesterday. Brother Heber's back in Kirtland."

"Really?" Derek cried. "In Kirtland? They've come back from England?"

"Yes, he and Orson Hyde came home together. They're coming here."

He shot to his feet. "To Far West?"

Matthew nodded. "Yes, he said they and some others will be leaving Kirtland on the first of this month."

"But that's today!"

"Yes," Matthew agreed. "If all went well, they left this morning."

"That's wonderful news. Peter will be thrilled. How long will it take them to get here?"

"About a month, he thought." Matthew's face darkened slightly. "Brother Kimball says things in Kirtland are terrible. It's like a ghost town. He says most of the rest of the faithful are preparing to leave. They've formed what they're calling the Kirtland Camp. About five hundred Saints in a wagon train. They'll be leaving shortly after him. He said the wagon train stretches almost a mile and a half."

Derek considered that somberly. "That will pretty well empty the city of Latter-day Saints, then."

Matthew looked down at the ground. "Except for my sister Melissa."

Mentally, Derek kicked himself. He knew that. He knew that leaving Melissa and her family behind had been one of the hardest things the Steeds had ever done. They tried not to dwell on it too much. "Well," he said, trying to bring Matthew's mind to other things, "I'm so excited to think we'll be seeing Brother Kimball and Brother Hyde again. That's wonderful. I can hardly wait to hear how things have gone in England."

"They've gone wonderfully," Matthew said. "Brother Joseph said that Heber himself baptized nearly a thousand people in eight months. Add to that what the others have baptized and that means there are over fifteen hundred Latter-day Saints in England now."

"So did some of the other missionaries stay?"

"Yes. Brother Fielding and Brother Richards were left to preside over the Church there, along with a British convert named William Clayton. By the way, that reminds me of something Brother Heber wrote. Do you remember a young woman by the name of Jennetta Richards?"

"Aye. A fine young woman. Daughter of a minister in Walkerfold. In fact, after he baptized her, Brother Kimball wrote to Brother Richards and told him that he had baptized Brother Richards's wife that day."

"Yes, that's what Joseph said too. And though they have the same last name, Jennetta and Willard are not related, right?"

"No, there was no relation."

Matthew had a tiny smile around the corners of his mouth, savoring what he was about to report. "That's what made this so funny. Listen to this. Just this past spring Willard was visiting the branches of the Church in the various towns and met Jennetta. He offered to walk to a meeting with Jennetta and a friend. While they were walking along, Willard looked up and said, 'Jennetta, I have always liked the name of Richards. I never want to change it. How about you?' I guess that startled Jennetta a little, and she replied, 'No, I do not want to change it.' Then she smiled at Brother Richards and said, 'And I think I never will.'"

Derek laughed aloud, picturing both the lovely Jennetta and the mild-mannered Willard Richards. "How delightful. I'm glad for them both."

"It's a different way to propose marriage, I'd say." Matthew gave Derek a shrewd look. "Too bad my family's last name is Steed and not Ingalls."

Derek went instantly red. "What makes you say that?" he stammered.

"Then you could use that same line on Rebecca."

Derek felt his face burning, and he looked away quickly.

"She came looking for you, you know."

"She did?"

Matthew's nature was always to be scrupulously honest with himself and with others, so he pulled back a little. "Well, actually she came back to join the family, but she asked where you had gone."

"I'm surprised she even noticed," Derek muttered.

Matthew's eyes narrowed, then he laughed. "You mean Isaiah Jensen?"

Derek didn't answer, just pushed at the dirt with the toe of his shoe.

"He's a fine young man," Matthew said, a mischievous look in his eye.

But Derek wouldn't rise to the bait. "I know," he agreed dejectedly.

A look of mild disgust pulled down Matthew's lip. "Derek, I don't know how it is in England, but in America there's an old saying: 'If you don't put your sign on the gate, how are people supposed to know whose property is behind it?'"

Derek turned to his younger friend. "What's that supposed to mean?"

There was an answering look of total disbelief. "Let me ask you this—just what are your intentions with my sister?"

Derek stamped on the pile of dirt he had made with his shoe, sending a little puff of dust shooting out. "Until I get me some land and a way to make a living, I can't have any intentions. And by that time, Rebecca will probably have chosen another."

"Are all you bloomin' Englishmen this daft?" Matthew asked.

In spite of himself, Derek laughed that Matthew was picking up some of his and Peter's expressions. He sobered quickly again. "No, not all Englishmen. Just the ones in the Ingalls line."

"I didn't ask you what your assets are," Matthew retorted. "I asked you what your intentions are. Do you want to marry my sister?"

Derek was dumfounded by his directness. "I . . ."

"Well, do you?"

Derek looked away, his eyes suddenly filled with longing. "I don't know if she'll have me."

Matthew leaped up, throwing up his hands in frustration. "Will you just answer the question, mate? Do you or do you not want to marry my sister?"

There was only a moment's hesitation. "Yes."

"Then tell her."

The look of horror on Derek's face brought an explosion of laughter from Matthew. He reached over and slapped his British companion on the arm. "I'm not talking about saying it straight out like that, but you tell her. You let her know what your intentions are. You owe her that. If you don't, then you can't be moping around here like a kicked dog when she has the likes of Isaiah Jensen trying to find out if there's somebody's name hanging on the gate."

The thoughts of trying to express what was in his heart to Rebecca like that made Derek look positively sick. "I . . . how could I ever do that? We've barely talked at all."

Matthew straightened to his full height. "Tell you what," he said matter-of-factly. "I'll give you until Wednesday night. That's three more days. If you haven't told her by the time the Fourth of July celebrations are over and you're getting ready to go back home, I'm going to tell her myself, and I'll do it right in front of you."

"You wouldn't!" Derek breathed, his face draining of color.

"Yep, I would," Matthew said earnestly. "I really would. So you better give it some thought, Mr. Ingalls, some very serious thought." He turned and started away, waving one hand. "Cheerio, mate."

It was about six o'clock on that same July evening, when a knock sounded on the door of the cabin where Nathan and Lydia Steed lived. Lydia had her three oldest children gathered around her at the table, reading from the Book of Mormon. The baby was asleep in a simple crib in the upstairs bedroom.

"I'll get it," Emily said, swinging around and jumping down from the bench. As she went to the door, they all turned to see who it was. Emily opened it and for a moment just stood there. There was a murmur of a greeting, and Emily nodded and stepped back. Lydia got up quickly and went over. Standing on the small front porch were four people. Lydia's eyes opened in surprise when she saw who it was. "Caroline?"

"Hello, Lydia."

She craned her neck a little, looking beyond Caroline and Will, who was holding Savannah. "Did Joshua . . . ?"

Caroline shook her head quickly.

On impulse, Lydia reached out and took Caroline's hand

and squeezed it. "Please come in." She stepped back, looking at Olivia. "Hello again, Olivia."

"Hello, Mrs. Steed."

Lydia smiled warmly at her and touched her arm. "Please call me Aunt Lydia." She turned to Will. "And how are you, Will?"

"I'm fine, thank you."

Joshua had come up now too, with little Nathan trailing him. "Hello, Will," he said eagerly. On their first visit Will had paid special attention to Lydia's oldest, treating him with respect and talking to him like an adult, and Joshua had responded with open adoration, though at fourteen, Will was seven years older than Joshua.

Will grinned down at him. "Hello, Joshua. Good to see you again."

As Lydia shut the door behind them, she leaned over closer to Will, looking into Savannah's eyes. "Hello, little Savannah," she said.

"Say hello to Aunt Lydia, Savannah," Caroline said, smiling.

To Lydia's surprise there was no hesitation. One chubby little hand came up, and there was a soft, "'Lo."

Lydia laughed. "What a little doll you are!" She turned to Caroline. "She's absolutely adorable."

"And she knows it," Caroline agreed. "I'm afraid we're all spoiling her shamelessly. Not yet sixteen months and she rules the entire household."

They stood watching the baby for a moment, then Caroline looked around. "Is Nathan home?" She took a quick breath. "I would like him to take me to meet his family."

Lydia's face registered dismay. "You mean you didn't see him?"

That took Caroline aback. "See him?"

"He went to Independence."

Caroline was shocked. Will reacted to it too. "He did? When?"

"He left on Friday." Lydia looked away. "We tried to talk him out of it, but he was determined to see Joshua."

Now it was Caroline's face that was troubled. "That's not good." She looked at Will. "Give me the baby, and maybe you could take the children out and do something with the wagon."

Lydia immediately turned to her son. "Joshua, put the wagon out back, then take the horses to the pasture." She looked at Will. "You can put the team in Brother Johnson's pasture where you put them before." Then she turned back to Joshua. "You hold Nathan's hand so he doesn't get in the way."

Lydia waited until they exited, then reached out and took Caroline's arm. "Come sit down. You must be very tired."

Caroline did not deny that she was. When they were seated at the table, she looked at Lydia with genuine concern. "Joshua was furious when he came home and found that I had been here. There was no reasoning with him. I may have made a terrible mistake to push him."

Lydia shook her head firmly. "Mary Ann was so thrilled to learn that he is still here in Missouri. And about you and the children. She almost went with Nathan, but Benjamin wouldn't hear of it."

Caroline was drawing lines with her finger on the surface of the table. "What does Joshua's father think of it all, now that he knows?"

A frown darkened Lydia's eyes. "He's still angry. He called Nathan a fool for going. But that's just Father Steed. I don't even think it's the original blowup between him and Joshua anymore, but what he did to Nathan. He says that is unforgivable."

There was a touch of horror on Caroline's face. "Can you blame him for that? Joshua can't even forgive himself for it."

"Well, Nathan has," Lydia said. "And Father Steed is just going to have to learn to live with it too."

Savannah began to squirm in her mother's arms, and Caroline let her down to the floor. Immediately the little red-headed girl started around the room examining things curiously. Caroline looked back at Lydia and sighed. "I've never seen Joshua like this." There was a brief pause. "I stayed in a hotel Friday night." Anger suddenly fired her voice. "I told him it's not just his decision. His parents are Savannah's grandparents. They have a right to see her, and she has a right to know them. You're her aunt." Her voice was suddenly pleading for understanding. "Is that so wrong to want that for them?"

"Of course not." Lydia smiled, and patted Caroline's hand encouragingly. "Mother and Father Steed are going to be so excited that you've come." Then her face fell a little.

"What?" Caroline asked anxiously.

"Jessica and her husband are there. They've come for the Fourth of July celebration."

"Oh."

"I know that will be a little awkward for you," Lydia went on in a rush, "but Jessica is wonderful. I think you'll find that she holds no bitterness for Joshua. She is very happy now."

For several moments, Caroline was quiet, then finally she shrugged. "She's part of the family. And Rachel is Joshua's daughter." She took a quick breath. "It's time that I meet them all." There was a brief flicker of a smile. "But I must tell you, I've had a stomach full of butterflies the whole way up here."

Lydia smiled fully and enthusiastically now. "I know you must be starving, but Mother Steed will never forgive me if we eat over here without her knowing about it. Let's get the children and go over there right now."

Caroline blanched a little, then nodded slowly. "All right. I suppose it's time."

———— • ————

"It takes her a while to warm up to strangers," Caroline said.

Benjamin glanced at her, then went right back to looking at Savannah. "But I'm not a stranger," he said softly. "I'm her grandfather." He held out his hands, smiling gently. "Come on, Savannah. Come see your grandpa."

Savannah was eyeing Benjamin gravely with her large, dark

blue eyes. Then she seemed to make up her mind. She raised her arms and leaned away from her mother toward Benjamin.

"Ha," Benjamin said, taking her. "I told you."

"Well, I'll be," Caroline said in wonder.

Will was shaking his head. He looked at Lydia. "She never does that."

"She just wants to go exploring a little, don't you, Savannah?" Benjamin was trying hard not to show his feeling of triumph. "And Grandpa is just the one to help her do that."

He started walking slowly around the room, pointing out this and that as Savannah alternated between watching him and looking at the things he was showing her.

Caroline turned to Jessica, who stood beside her husband and daughter. Her two stepsons stood behind their father, eyeing the newcomers curiously. Caroline went down into a crouch. "And you're Rachel."

Jessica put a hand on Rachel's back and gave her a gentle push. "Go see Caroline, Rachel. She's married to your father."

Rachel stepped forward tentatively a few steps and stopped. Caroline did not try to move closer. She just smiled. "You have the prettiest brown hair, Rachel. You look very much like your mother."

"Thank you."

Caroline looked up at Jessica. "Joshua has wondered what she looks like now, how things are with you and her. Your father has kept us up to date a little bit when he received letters."

"Good," Jessica said softly. "I hope all is well with Joshua."

"It is." Caroline hesitated a moment, glancing quickly at Benjamin, who, though he seemed engrossed with Savannah, was following the conversation closely. "He's changed. He's a different man now."

Jessica took her husband's hand, then looked back at Caroline. "I don't know if Joshua ever told you, but he sent me and Rachel money."

Caroline straightened slowly. "No, he never told me."

Jessica's eyes had a faraway look as she nodded again. "Yes.

The people who brought it would never say who sent them, but I know it was him. During that first winter, after we had been driven out of Jackson County, we were living along the river bottoms. We had nothing. I don't know what we would have done without the money he sent." Finally she looked directly at Caroline. "I always knew it was his way of saying he was sorry for what had happened."

Caroline's eyes were suddenly misty. "Thank you for telling me," she whispered. "He never said anything about that."

Mary Ann's eyes were shining too. "Come," she said brusquely, trying not to let her emotions get the best of her. "Let's get some supper on. Then we want to hear all about you and your family." Her voice broke for a moment. "And more about this son of ours."

———— • ————

Rebecca was sitting next to her father, watching him feed Savannah, who was on his lap, tucked in comfortably under his left arm. Savannah would survey his plate, then lean forward. "That," she would say, pointing. And Benjamin would give her a bite of whatever it was she was pointing at.

"I think you've completely won her over," Rebecca said.

"Or vice versa," Mary Ann laughed.

Will was across the table, the youngest of those eating inside. All the rest of the children, except for the babies, had been put outside. There simply was not room inside the cabin to feed that many. Now Will was watching his little sister with amazement. "I've never seen her like this," he said to his mother.

Caroline nodded vigorously, speaking to Mary Ann. "This is definitely not the Savannah we're used to. She's never taken to anyone like this."

Mary Ann gave Benjamin an affectionate look. He pretended to be busy with his feeding chores and acted as though he had not heard. But everyone could see the pleased look in his eyes. "All of the grandchildren think Grandpa is pretty special," she said.

Matthew turned to Derek, who sat beside him. "You can bet me and Becca never got that kind of treatment."

Rebecca jumped in on that immediately. "Are you joking? It was always, 'Becca, do this,' or 'Matthew, do that.' But the grandchildren—they can do nothing wrong."

Benjamin gave them a severe look. "The Lord made grandpas to spoil grandchildren in a way that it doesn't hurt them. It's a very delicate art."

That brought a laugh from everyone. Lydia watched her father-in-law, a little awed by what had happened. She offered a quick, silent prayer of thanks for the little red-headed imp sitting on Benjamin's lap. Caroline had come here with great misgivings. Lydia herself had worried about how Benjamin would respond to meeting Joshua's wife and children, but Savannah had almost single-handedly changed all that. It had been less than two hours since Lydia had brought them over, but already any feelings of awkwardness had disappeared. Even Caroline and Jessica seemed relaxed and at ease with each other.

"I done, Gampa," Savannah said, looking up at him.

"Are you sure?"

She nodded briskly, then looked around. "Where's Livvy?"

"That's Olivia," Caroline explained. She turned to Savannah. "Livvy's outside with the other children."

Savannah started to wiggle, and Benjamin picked her up and swung her over the table and set her down. Rebecca stood up. "I'll take her out." She held out her hand. "Come on, Savannah. I'll help you find Livvy."

Immediately Savannah gave Rebecca her hand, and the two headed toward the door.

Derek got up quickly. "I'll go too," he said.

Rebecca stopped for a moment, obviously pleased. Matthew gave Derek an approving look, which the Englishman didn't see as he reached down and took Savannah's other hand. The three of them went out together.

Lydia stood up and began picking up her plate. Caroline

started to follow suit, but Lydia waved her back. "You just sit there. I didn't come fifty miles in the last two days."

Will jumped up. "I'll help"—he glanced at her quickly—"Aunt Lydia."

Her eyes widened for a moment, then her face softened with pleasure. "Why, thank you, Will."

Matthew was up too. "Tell you what," he said magnanimously, "me and Will will handle the dishes. You old folks just sit here and relax."

Mary Ann swatted at him affectionately as Lydia, Caroline, Jessica, and John all laughed aloud. But Benjamin leaned back. "If it means I don't have to help with the dishes," Benjamin growled pleasantly, "you can call me old any time you want to."

As the boys set to work and cleared the table, the adults moved to the other corner of the room and took the sofa and the chairs there. For a few minutes they sat talking lazily about the weather, about the crops, about how fast Far West was growing. They quizzed Caroline at some length about her life in Georgia and how she had come to meet Joshua.

After a lapse into silence, Benjamin gave Caroline a sidelong glance. "So Joshua wouldn't come with you?"

Mary Ann looked up quickly. That was the first time Benjamin had spoken of his oldest son by name in a long, long time. She reached out for his hand, but he avoided it.

Benjamin's question had produced sudden concern on Caroline's face. "No. He was upset with me for coming before without asking him."

"So he kicked you out of the house?"

"Benjamin!"

He waved his wife to quiet, still looking at Caroline steadily. "I asked Olivia before dinner if her father was coming too. She told me you had a big fight and you had to leave."

"I didn't *have* to leave," Caroline said defensively. "I chose to leave." It sounded pretty lame, and she knew it as well as he did. "He was angry. I couldn't reason with him. I—"

"Joshua's been angry since the day he turned sixteen," he said flatly.

"That's not fair, Father Steed." To his amazement, it was Jessica who had jumped into the conversation. "You haven't seen him in almost eleven years."

"That's right," he snapped. "Not that we haven't tried. We've written enough letters to keep the United States Post Office in business. Has he ever bothered answering? Even once?"

"He was afraid to," Caroline cried. "He's a proud man. He's afraid that you will reject him."

Suddenly, to Benjamin's surprise, Will was standing in front of him, a dish towel in one hand. "Father Steed?"

"Yes, son?"

"I know my pa has done some bad things." He looked quickly at Jessica, then back again. "He told me about them. He said he was drunk. But he's sorry. He doesn't get drunk anymore. He's changed."

Benjamin felt a stab of shame as he looked into those eyes that were filled with hurt and pride and anger all at once. He had completely forgotten that Will and Matthew were within hearing range. "I understand, Will," he said. "Thank you for telling me that."

Caroline stood and came to face her son. "Yes, thank you, Will. Your pa would be proud that you spoke up for him." She glanced at Matthew over Will's shoulder, then looked back at her son. "Would you go out and make sure Savannah is all right?"

"Yes, Mama."

"Come on, Will," Matthew said, putting away the last of the dishes. "I'll go with you."

As they left, Mary Ann shot her husband a withering glare. He ducked his head stubbornly, sorry that he had made the mistake, but not sorry for what he had said.

As the door shut, Caroline turned back to him. "Joshua has changed, Father Steed. Won't you at least give him a chance to prove that?"

He looked up, his heart aching for this woman who without question was the finest thing that had ever happened to Joshua Steed. "I wanted to do that," he said slowly. "After your first visit here, Nathan and Lydia told me all that you said about Joshua. For the first time, I felt there was a ray of hope for him. It really sounded like he had put some things behind him."

He shook his head, his mouth tightening. "And then what happens? Here come his wife and children a week later, kicked out of the house again because of that insufferable temper of his. Just like what he did to Jessica and Rachel. And you want me to believe he's changed?"

There was not a sound in the room. Every eye, except Mary Ann's, was on Caroline now. Mary Ann was staring at her hands, which were twisted together in her lap.

"It's not what you think," Caroline began. "It . . ." But then she knew it was no use. And the supreme irony was, it was her presence here that was providing the very proof that no amount of words could push aside.

Jaw set, eyes like granite, Benjamin went on in a low voice that was thick with anger. "Everything I see tells me Joshua has not changed. Not down deep. Not fundamentally." He turned to Mary Ann, his eyes wide with challenge. "And now Nathan has gone to Jackson County again. Just like before. And I swear before you and the Lord himself, so help me, if my son comes back with one hair of his head out of place, I shall go after Joshua myself."

"Joshua is your son too," Mary Ann whispered in anguish, tears trickling down her cheeks.

Benjamin shot to his feet. "No, he's not! Not after . . ." His hands came up, as if to shield himself from any further words. "No," he said again, choking suddenly. "Not anymore." And with that he turned and plunged out of the room.

Steed Cabin, Far West

Rebecca rounded the corner and stopped in surprise. Derek was leaning against the wall of the cabin. He straightened, looking a little sheepish.

"What are you doing here?" she asked.

"Just waitin'."

"At six o'clock in the morning?"

His blue eyes sparkled for a moment. "Matthew told me you like to go walking first thing in the morning."

"I—" She stopped, pleased, but peering at him more closely. "How long have you been here?"

He pulled a face. "Unfortunately, Matthew forgot to mention what he meant by 'first thing.'"

She laughed merrily. "So how long?"

He glanced up at her, then away quickly. "Since five o'clock."

She was startled for a moment, but then she gave him one of her most winsome smiles and started moving toward him again. "Then I suppose we'd better start walking, hadn't we?"

"You don't mind if I accompany you?"

She stopped short. "Derek Ingalls!"

He was dismayed at the look on her face. "What?"

"If you start talking that way again, I don't want to be with you." She walked on past him, her head turned away from him.

Hastily he fell into step beside her. "If I start talkin' what way?"

"Putting yourself down, talking like you aren't worth anything."

"Well—," he started, but she shot him such a look that he clamped his mouth shut again.

She walked quickly, her steps angry and crisp, and Derek had to stride out to keep up with her. Twice he started to say something, but then thought better of it. Gradually her step slowed again, and the firmness around her mouth softened. He watched her out of the corner of his eye, then finally dared to venture an attempt to put things right. "I talk that way because whenever I'm around you I feel that way."

She gave him a look of disbelief. "Is that supposed to be a compliment? That I make you feel inferior?"

He went on stubbornly. "I didn't say that you make me feel inferior. I was tryin' to say that I feel inferior when I'm around you. They aren't the same."

She considered that for a moment, then nodded. "All right. Why do you feel inferior when you're around me?"

They were coming to a pasture with two or three milk cows, a horse, and a small flock of sheep scattered around it. Derek stopped and walked over to the rail fence and leaned against it. Rebecca watched him for a moment, then went over to join him. "Well?" she prodded.

He took in a deep breath, searching for the right words and the courage to say them. Matthew's threat popped into his mind. He let out the breath, losing his nerve. "By the way," he said, not meeting her eyes, "did Caroline decide to go back home today?"

She shrugged. "I don't know. Last night Lydia and Mama

were still trying to talk her out of it. They feel terrible about the things Papa said about Joshua. Caroline says that's not why she wants to leave. She feels like she needs to return and work things out between her and Joshua. Lydia says it will be good for Papa if she stays until the Fourth of July. Especially for him to have Savannah around. Lydia and Mama still think that Caroline is our only hope of getting this whole thing worked out."

Derek shook his head. "Your father is such a kind man in so many ways. Yet this anger in him about your brother—it's very difficult to understand."

"I know." She was quiet for several moments, then a teasing look came in her eye. "You changed the subject on me, Derek Ingalls, and you're not going to get away with that. Why do you feel inferior around me?"

For some odd reason, an image flashed into Derek's mind. It was the image of him in the back office at the textile factory, standing in front of a very angry Mr. Morris. "You'll have until lunch to make up your mind about Mormonism," he had said. And Derek had squared his shoulders, looked him straight in the eye, and replied, "I won't need until lunch." Suddenly it struck him that that was a courageous thing he had done. It had also taken courage for him and Peter to come to America, then make their way across more than a thousand miles of country to get here. For some reason, the thought cheered him immensely. Now here he was, standing next to the woman who left him as stammering of tongue as if he were a craven coward facing a line of musketeers. It was time to call on that same courage that had helped to get him where he now stood.

He straightened and turned to face her square on. "Would you mind if I spoke to you straight out, Rebecca?" he said.

Her eyes danced mischievously. "I would find that most refreshing, Mr. Ingalls."

"Then I'll say what's on my mind." He gulped, a little abashed by his brazenness. "I don't think it was happenstance that Peter and I came to America."

The mischief in Rebecca's eyes faded.

"I don't think comin' to Kirtland and meetin' your family was happenstance either," he went on. "I feel strongly that the Lord had a hand in all of it."

"I would agree with that," Rebecca said quietly, watching him very closely now.

"Whether it was happenstance or not," he rushed on, "I know that since I first met you that day on the doorstep in Kirtland you've been on my mind a great deal, Miss Rebecca Steed."

"I have?" she said softly, her eyes shining now with something that made him glow with hope.

"Yes, you have. And whilst I seem to keep leavin' your presence over and over, I still find myself thinkin' about little else other than you." Now his countenance fell. "And yet when I do, I can't believe there's any chance you could be havin' any of those same feelings. I look at how lovely you are. You are poised and clever and witty, and I'm dull and—"

She reached up and put a hand over his mouth quickly; then, embarrassed by her boldness, she stepped back. "Don't, Derek. Please don't."

"I'm sorry," he said. "But that's how I feel when I'm around you."

She moved a step closer to him again and waited until he looked up to meet her eyes. "And what would you say if I told you I have had those same feelings? That I think about you all the time? That I was very sad when you went to Di-Ahman, because it meant I would not get to see you often?"

He stared at her in wonder. "I would say that was a very difficult thing for me to believe."

"Only because you're such a stubborn Englishman," she shot back.

He caught his breath, a little dazed. "Then, if that *were* the case, I would tell this lovely, witty, clever girl what was on my mind."

"I think that would be an excellent idea."

"I would tell her that by next spring I will have five or six acres of land cleared, plowed, and in seed. I will have a home built—not a fancy one, but big enough to see it through a few winters safely. I would tell her that I then plan to buy myself a set of Sunday-best clothes and come on down to Far West."

"For what purpose?" she asked in a half whisper.

"To go before one Benjamin Steed, Esquire, and to ask for the hand of his daughter in marriage."

She was smiling shyly now. "And if he agreed?"

"Then I would come to that daughter and ask her if she would be willing to accept an unlearned, unschooled, stubborn, mule-headed Englishman for her husband."

Rebecca turned back and leaned on the fence. "I think the answer to that question would be no."

His mouth dropped, and there was instant bafflement in his eyes.

"If he were to ask if she would accept a wise, gentle, serious-minded, hardworking Englishman who has a wonderful way with words—and who is just a tiny little bit stubborn—then I would guess that daughter just might say yes," she said.

The dismay had turned to incredulousness. "Really?" he cried.

She smiled shyly at him. "I couldn't be absolutely positive, but I think the chances are really quite excellent."

"Grandpa! Grandpa!"

Benjamin looked up from his shoveling. Young Joshua was coming across the field on the dead run, waving his arms.

Matthew was in the shallow trench they were digging to serve as the foundation for their smokehouse. He straightened, squinting against the afternoon sunshine, and watched as Joshua came sliding to a halt, puffing mightily.

"Get Grandma and come to our house right away," Joshua gasped.

Benjamin's head came up with a snap. "What's wrong? Is your father back?"

Joshua shook his head quickly. "No. Brother Joseph is at our house. He wants to talk to us. He wants all the family to come."

The relief washed over Benjamin. For an instant, he had

had visions of Nathan being returned in a condition similar to the one he had been put in when he had previously gone to Jackson County. "The whole family?" he asked.

"Yes," Joshua said. "He wants Aunt Jessica and Uncle John, Uncle Matthew, Aunt Rebecca. He said everybody."

Matthew stuck his shovel in the ground and leaned on the handle, smiling at how his nephew gulped in air between sentences.

Benjamin looked at Matthew. "Wonder what that's all about."

"Hurry, Grandpa," Joshua cried. "He's already there."

"All right," Benjamin said, holding up his hands in surrender, "tell him we're coming."

As Joshua turned to go, Benjamin called after him. "Did Caroline leave, then, or not?"

Joshua turned back, shaking his head. "Mama talked her into staying at least until tomorrow."

"Good," Benjamin said, with more earnestness than he had intended. He had said his piece last night, and his feelings had not changed; but when he learned that Caroline was thinking of leaving again, he knew it was because of what he'd said, and he regretted every word he'd uttered.

Benjamin had turned fifty-three in May. His hair was starting to thin out a little, and the gray was creeping up from the temples. When he did hard physical work, like that which they had been doing this morning, he could tell that somewhere down deep the reserves of strength were not the same as in the past. But it was all right. He was a grandfather now and was enjoying this stage of his life tremendously. He rejoiced in his family, and now Caroline and her children were part of that family. He smiled to himself as he thought about little Savannah. What a whip she was. Her and her grandpa.

So today he would keep his feelings about his oldest son to himself. He would let Caroline know what her coming had meant to all of them. And if Joshua was fool enough to drive his second family away from him, then Benjamin would be ready to provide a haven for them just as he had done with Jessica and Rachel.

"Pa?"

Matthew's voice brought him out of his thoughts. He looked up, a little sheepish. "You go get your mother and your sister. Tell Jessica and John as well. I'll put away the tools."

—◆—

To put twenty people into the one room that constituted the main floor of Nathan and Lydia's small log home was to fill it completely. Every chair, bench, and stool was either taken or saved for those still coming. The children were placed on the stairs or in the little remaining open floor space around the room. Lydia had asked Joseph if they should just let the younger children go outside and play, but Joseph had rejected that out of hand. This was to be a Steed family council, and that meant even the babies stayed so that no one would have to be absent to watch them.

By the time Benjamin and Mary Ann arrived with Matthew and Rebecca and Jessica and her family, Joseph had already been introduced to Caroline and her children. When Benjamin came in, he saw that Joseph was visiting amiably with Caroline and Will. At the sight of Benjamin, Savannah, who sat on Olivia's lap, squirmed free and toddled across to her grandpa. "Hello, little doll," he said, picking her up.

"Brother Benjamin, Sister Mary Ann," Joseph boomed, coming across to shake their hands. "Thank you for coming. I apologize for taking you away from your work."

"No bother," Benjamin said, not even trying to disguise his curiosity. "Is there a problem, Brother Joseph?"

Joseph smiled, his blue eyes unfathomable. "Well, that depends on what you mean by a problem, Brother Ben." He motioned to the chairs the family had reserved for them. "Please be seated."

As they sat down, Mary Ann gave her husband a questioning look. He raised one eyebrow. He was as baffled as she was. He tucked Savannah comfortably under his arm, then turned to Joseph.

Immediately the room quieted as the Prophet moved to the far end of the room where he could see everyone clearly. He let his gaze sweep over them slowly, which only deepened the hush. Finally he cleared his throat, and turned his eyes to Benjamin. "Brother Benjamin, I have a question for you."

"All right."

"When you die and go to the judgment bar and the book of life is opened, do you think it will be recorded anywhere that there were people on earth who prayed for you?"

That caused a ripple of surprise. Benjamin was dumfounded. What kind of question was that? "Well," he began tentatively. He glanced quickly at Mary Ann. "I suppose it will be recorded that Mary Ann prayed for me. Especially during that time in Palmyra, and when we first came to Kirtland."

Rebecca spoke out, just loud enough for her father to hear. "Mama wasn't the only one."

Lydia was nodding too.

Joseph smiled but kept his eyes on Benjamin. "Do you think that will work to your favor there?"

Benjamin was reeling a little. He had no idea where this was supposed to be going. "I would like to think so."

"I would too," Joseph said. Then instantly he changed tack. "Brother Ben, are you familiar with the parable of the unmerciful servant?" Before Benjamin could answer, the Prophet looked quickly around the room. "Now, while I may be speaking to your father and grandfather, this applies to every one here, so please listen carefully."

Benjamin's mind was racing. "Isn't that the one with the two men who both owed debts?"

"The very one," Joseph replied. "Now, I've always said that if you want to know what the parables mean, you need to ask what question or situation caused the Savior to give the parable. Does anyone recall what question was asked of Jesus that caused him to give this particular parable?"

Mary Ann raised her hand, and when Joseph nodded at her she spoke quietly, not looking at her husband. "Peter asked how many times we are required to forgive someone for their trespasses against us."

Benjamin whirled on her, his face suddenly twisting. So this was what it was about. Mary Ann had gone to Joseph and reported on him.

"That's correct, Sister Steed," Joseph said. Then his eyes went stern, even though his voice remained light. "Now, Ben, don't you be looking at your wife that way. She has not said a single word to me. So get that thought out of your head."

As Benjamin dropped his eyes away from Mary Ann's, Joseph half turned and looked at Lydia. He winked at her. It was true. Mary Ann had not said anything to Joseph. But Lydia had. She had sought him out earlier in the day and told him everything that had transpired the previous night.

"Sister Lydia," Joseph said, "could you briefly retell for the children the parable of the unmerciful servant?"

"Yes." She glanced quickly at Benjamin, not totally comfortable now with what was happening. "There were two men, each of whom owed a debt. The one owed ten thousand talents, the other a hundred pence."

"And how much is that, ten thousand talents?"

Lydia was taken aback by the question. "I don't know."

"A huge amount?"

"Yes, very large, I would imagine."

"And a hundred pence?"

"A pittance in comparison."

"Good. So what happened?"

"The first man owed the debt to his master. He went to him and begged for time to repay the debt. But the master just forgave it. He didn't have to pay any of it back."

"And then?"

"The second man was a servant also, but he owed the hundred pence to the first servant, not to the master. When he begged for more time to pay it back, the first servant showed no mercy. He was angry and threw the man into prison."

Joseph turned to little Emily, who was watching him with

wide eyes. "Emily, if you were the king who forgave the first man a great big debt, how would you feel when you found out that that same man would not forgive the other servant who owed him a little tiny debt?"

Emily's lip jutted out in a pout. "I would be very angry with him."

Joseph smiled and turned to the group. "This is a parable that even a child can understand," he said evenly.

Benjamin didn't look up. He was concentrating on helping Savannah smooth out her dress. But he knew his face was burning.

"Next question," Joseph said, swinging back to let his eyes catch Benjamin again. "Not long ago there was a man who did some terrible things to his wife. He beat her up and drove her from his house. Then he did equally terrible things to his brother."

Benjamin could not stop it. His head came up slowly, and his eyes locked with Joseph's. "In a way," Joseph went on, his eyes filled with gentleness, "these were also crimes against the whole family. They hurt the parents. They hurt the brothers and sisters. They were, in fact, crimes that would injure his future family, people he did not even know at the time."

Joseph had turned to look at Caroline and her children. Caroline's head was down, her hands rigid in her lap. The silence was total now. Even the smallest of the children sensed the tension in the room and watched Joseph carefully. Slowly now, Joseph swung back around to Benjamin. Those blue eyes with their terrible power were boring into him again. And now Benjamin was having trouble breathing.

"While the acts of this man injured many, to which of the two family members does he owe the greatest debt?"

Mary Ann was looking at Jessica. "To the wife whom he drove out," she murmured, "and to the brother whom he whipped."

"That is correct," Joseph said, never taking his eyes from Benjamin. "And if those two, to whom was owed the greatest debt, frankly forgave the man, what should that say about those to whom is owed a lesser debt?"

Benjamin could not have answered even if his mind had willed it. Savannah looked up at her grandpa, then reached up and laid her hand on his cheek. He groped for it as if it were a rope thrown to him from the top of a precipice.

The Prophet now let his eyes go to Lydia. They stopped there, and she dropped her gaze. They moved to Caroline. She couldn't bear it for more than a moment either. One by one he moved around the room. Matthew. Rebecca. John Griffith. Mary Ann. Will. Every one who had been touched by Joshua's actions and left wounded was included in that penetrating examination.

For one last time Joseph turned back to Benjamin. "How many times in the past ten years has your good wife prayed for Joshua do you suppose?"

"Hundreds," Benjamin whispered.

"And how many times have you prayed for your son, Benjamin?"

His mouth opened, then shut again, and he looked away. He couldn't bear Joseph's gaze.

Joseph's voice was soft now and filled with infinite kindness. "And at the judgment bar, when the Savior asks why there are not any of your prayers recorded in Joshua's behalf, what will you say, Benjamin? Will you tell the Man who suffered until he bled at every pore, will you tell the Man who had nails driven into his hands and feet and who hung from a cross so that all people might be saved—will you tell that Man that Joshua hurt you so terribly, he does not deserve your forgiveness?"

Benjamin felt as though he were being lashed. Blindly, he put his arms around Savannah and held her close to him. Mary Ann was crying softly. She reached out her hand for him, but he recoiled from her touch. He felt like a leper.

Joseph did not wait for Benjamin's answer. Reaching into his coat, he withdrew a book from his pocket. "Lest we think forgiveness was only a New Testament injunction, may I remind you of the following." He opened the book and turned the pages. When he had his place, he lifted the book up higher so that he could see his audience over the top of it. He began to read, clearly and with emphasis. " 'My disciples, in days of old, sought occasion against one another, and forgave not one another in their hearts.' " His voice rose sharply. " '*And for this evil* they were afflicted, and sorely chastened: wherefore I say unto you, that ye ought to forgive one another, for he that forgiveth not his brother his trespasses, standeth condemned before the Lord, for there remaineth in him the greater sin.' "

Now his voice dropped to barely a whisper. "Did you hear that, Benjamin?" he asked slowly. "Did you hear that, Sister Lydia? Caroline? John? All of you? Did you hear what the Lord said? There remains in us the *greater* sin."

He raised the book again and finished slowly. " 'I the Lord will forgive whom I will forgive, but of you it is required to forgive all men.' " He shut the book and moved slowly across the room. He dropped to one knee in front of Benjamin. "What I say to you, Benjamin Steed, I say to every one in this family who has been wronged by the actions of Joshua Steed. His crimes are terrible in the sight of God, but you have not been called to serve as his judge. Only God knows his heart. Only God can determine what is right to do in this case." He reached out and took Benjamin by the shoulder. "Do you understand that, Benjamin Steed?"

"Yes." It came out as little more than a hoarse gasp.

"Can you forgive your son for what he has done?"

Benjamin's eyes were like two holes torn out of his face. They stared wildly at Joseph, then they closed. Benjamin lowered his head. "I don't know," he whispered.

Joseph stood, nodding slowly. "I understand. I do not accept that answer, but I understand what lies behind it." Then his face grew very solemn. "Brother Benjamin, do you remember that day back in Kirtland when you came to my bedside and we talked about the destiny of the Church?"

Benjamin looked up in surprise. "Yes. Clearly."

"Well," Joseph said somberly, "that destiny still rolls on, and you, Benjamin Steed, have an important role to play in it. But as I told you then, no unhallowed hand can stop this work. This church—God's work—will prevail!" His eyes softened, and his voice dropped to a gentle whisper. "But so long as your heart is filled with bitterness, Ben, you cannot effectively carry out your part in God's great work. No unhallowed hand can stop this work." He paused, then finished slowly. "And no unhallowed hand will help move it forward."

Without further word, he turned and walked to the door. The whole group, still half in a daze, followed him with their eyes in disbelief. Was that it? Was the lesson done? Was Joseph leaving?

But as he put a hand on the latch, he stopped for a moment. "This morning has been a busy one," he said with a smile. "First Lydia came to me and raised some concerns she had about what was going on in the family. While I was still pondering on that and on what to do, I received two other visitors. I didn't know they were coming. No one here knew they were coming."

He opened the door and stepped halfway out, raising one arm to beckon. "It's time," he called. He stepped back, opening the door all the wider. A moment later a figure appeared at the door. Joseph reached out his hand and gripped the other's. They embraced.

Lydia was instantly on her feet, staring. "Nathan?" she breathed.

But before she could move, a second figure stepped through the door. Joseph stepped to him, hand extended. He pulled him further into the room. "Joshua, your family are all here. Welcome home."

Now Caroline was up, gaping, not daring to believe. Will leaped to his feet, his face infused with joy. Olivia was staring, her mouth open, her eyes rapturous. There was only one who seemed not at all surprised by the figure's appearance. Savannah wiggled free of her grandfather's grasp and slid to the floor. Arms outstretched, she trotted around the legs and the feet and the furniture that blocked her way. "Papa, Papa," she cried.

Joshua dropped to his knees and swept her up. He stood, hugging her little body fiercely to his. "Hello, sweetheart," he murmured. Then in an instant Will and Olivia were also to him. He reached out with one arm and brought them in too.

All present were on their feet now, but no one moved except Caroline. She walked toward him, as if half-numb. Joshua saw her and handed the baby quickly to Will. Then she was in his arms, and he buried his face in her hair. "Oh, dear Caroline," he whispered against her. "Can you ever forgive me? I've been such a fool."

After a moment, she pulled back. She reached up and touched his chin. "Your beard?"

"Yeah, Papa," Olivia said, looking up at him. "What happened to your beard?"

Joshua pulled free of his wife and turned to Matthew, smiling sadly. "Several weeks ago I found that my family did not know me with a beard." And then suddenly his hands were trembling. He turned to face his mother and father. "And I wanted my family to know me," he said, his voice barely audible.

With one great racking sob, Mary Ann was across the room and into his arms. "Oh, my son, my son, my son," was all she could say.

Matthew came up then, and Rebecca right behind him. Joshua reached out and touched her face. "Beautiful Rebecca," he said. "I couldn't believe it that day on the road. My little Becca grown into a lovely woman."

As they clung together there, Nathan moved over to Lydia. He slipped an arm around her waist, reaching out with his other hand to touch the baby's hand. "You're all right?" Lydia asked.

He nodded, his eyes moist. "Yes. Everything's all right now."

Suddenly Joshua turned and looked to where Jessica stood quietly waiting next to John Griffith. Rachel stood at her side, looking a little confused. Caroline, Mary Ann, Rebecca,

Matthew—in one moment they all stepped back and the room fell quiet. Joshua looked frightened, but slowly he moved across the room. His eyes did not leave Jessica's face. "Jessie," he started.

She shook her head quickly. "You don't need to say it, Joshua," she smiled. "This is enough." She turned. "I would like you to meet my husband, John Griffith."

John extended his hand, and Joshua gripped it hard. "I'm pleased to meet you, John Griffith."

John nodded, but Joshua had already turned to Rachel. His hands came up, and for a moment it looked as though he was going to take her in his arms. But her eyes were frightened, and she shrank back against her mother.

"This is your father, Rachel," Jessica said. But Rachel only pushed the harder against her.

"It's all right," Joshua said. "Joseph has invited us to stay for the Independence Day festivities. There'll be time to get to know her."

He straightened and turned. And all in the room knew that the moment had arrived. They moved back, opening the space between Joshua and his father. Benjamin had not moved from the moment he had stood up. He looked like a shattered man. His shoulders were stooped, his face old and tortured.

For what seemed like an eternity, no one moved. Then Joshua took a half step toward his father. "Pa?"

There was no answer. Benjamin just stared at him, his eyes haunted, his hands clenching and unclenching at his sides. Joseph, who had been watching all of this from the corner near the door, came forward a step. "Benjamin," he said softly, "it's time."

And with that, Benjamin Steed opened his arms and started slowly toward his oldest son. Then, with a sob that was a great cry of pain and freedom and release, he broke into a stumbling gait, and in a moment father and son were in each other's arms, clasped together in a grip that not even death itself could have broken.

Notes

Chapter One

The vision of Jesus Christ, Moses, Elias, and Elijah, which took place in the Kirtland Temple one week following its dedication, is described in the novel as it is found in Doctrine and Covenants 110 and in *History of the Church* 2:434–36 (hereafter cited as *HC*). April third in the year 1836 was Easter Sunday and Passover season.

Chapter Four

Heber C. Kimball's blessing of Parley P. Pratt is taken almost word for word from the latter's autobiography. Thankful Pratt's consumption (tuberculosis) and her ten years of childlessness are also as reported by Parley. (See *Autobiography of Parley P. Pratt*, ed. Parley P. Pratt, Jr. [1874; reprint, Salt Lake City: Deseret Book Co., 1985], p. 110; hereafter cited as *PPP Auto*.) Nathan Steed's presence is, of course, a fictional addition.

Chapters Six and Seven

In actuality Parley P. Pratt was alone on his mission to Upper Canada (now the Province of Ontario), although a Brother Nickerson did travel with him as far as "the neighborhood of Hamilton." Having Nathan Steed accompany Parley is the author's fictional device. However, the events of that mission depicted in these two chapters are as described in Parley's history. (See *PPP Auto.*, pp. 113–28.) The prayer for help in Hamilton, with its resulting offer of money and a letter of introduction to John Taylor; the coming of the Widow Walton under inspiration to the Taylor home; the miraculous healing of the blind woman; the meetings at the Patrick home, including John Taylor's reading from Acts 8—these are all as reported by Parley. Details of John Taylor's final speech when Mr. Patrick refuses to allow Brother Pratt to continue to use his home are taken from B. H. Roberts's *Life of John Taylor* (1892; reprint, Salt Lake City: Bookcraft, 1989), pp. 37–38 (hereafter cited as *LJT*).

Chapter Ten

The meeting of the sisters at Benjamin and Mary Ann Steed's house (where Parley learns that his wife has been cured) is not based on any actual meeting, but the fact that Thankful was completely cured by the time of Parley's return is a matter of record (see *PPP Auto.*, p. 129). Other details given at this point in the novel—Emma's current pregnancy and her previous losses of children, the description of Eliza R. Snow's talents, and so on—are historically accurate. Nathan's report about the conversion of the Fielding family and his account of how the woman who had been healed of her blindness finally succumbed to the pressure from her peers are as reported by Parley P. Pratt (see *PPP Auto.*, pp. 117–18, 128).

Chapter Eleven

Emma and Joseph did name their baby born on 20 June 1836 after Frederick G. Williams; and the account of the naming of Mahonri Moriancumer Cahoon reflects actual history and is how we now know the name of the brother of Jared (see George Reynolds, "The Jaredites," *Juvenile Instructor* 27 [1 May 1892]: 282).

The meeting at the temple with the brethren is not based on one specific meeting but is meant to illustrate what was beginning to happen in Kirtland at this time. Some of those depicted as being present may not have been in Kirtland at the exact time the meeting takes place in the novel. Also, records do not indicate how the Saints accepted Joseph's decision to go to Salem. Using it as a basis for some of the Saints being disgruntled is the author's interpolation. However, the figures given for the debts of the Church at this time are accurate. It is also difficult to pinpoint exactly how soon the critical spirit began to infect specific individuals. There is no question about whether men like Warren Parrish, John Boynton, and others turned against Joseph; but at what time their disaffection first began to surface remains a matter of speculation.

Chapter Thirteen

Having Newel Knight in Far West when Benjamin, Nathan, and Matthew arrive is slight conjecture on the author's part. William G. Hartley's *"They Are My Friends": A History of the Joseph Knight Family, 1825–1850* (Provo, Utah: Grandin Book Co., 1986), pp. 117–21, indicates that around this time Newel's extended family were making efforts to move to Far West, that Newel assisted in these efforts, and that he even built a cabin there into which the family of one of his brothers, Joseph Knight, Jr., moved in 1837. It therefore seemed reasonable that Newel Knight might be in the area when the Steed men arrive in October 1836. But it is likely that Newel, his wife, and their children did not actually move to Far West until early in 1838.

Chapter Fourteen

Joseph Smith did go to Salem, Massachusetts, where he met Brother Burgess, as described elsewhere in the novel. Burgess had not been there for many years and could not even identify the house where the treasure was supposed to be buried, which was a disappointment to Joseph and those with him. The revelation to which Joseph refers in this chapter of the novel is now section 111 in the Doctrine and Covenants. Five years later Erastus Snow went to Salem to preach the gospel. He baptized over 120 people, thus fulfilling the Lord's promise that there were "many people" who would be gathered out of Salem in "due time." (See D&C 111:2. See also *Church History in the Fulness of Times* [Salt Lake City: The Church of Jesus Christ of Latter-day Saints, 1989], pp. 170–71; hereafter cited as *CHFT*.)

Chapter Fifteen

The meeting of the brethren described in this chapter took place on 2 January 1837. The details are basically as reported in various sources (see note for chapter eighteen). The Kirtland Safety Society did use the bank notes already obtained by Oliver Cowdery, and wording changes (from "BANK" to "ANTI-BANKING CO.") were stamped only on those notes that conveniently allowed for such changes.

Chapter Seventeen

Thankful Pratt was able to conceive a child as Heber C. Kimball had promised in his blessing. Her remarkable experience preceding the birth of that son and her death a short time afterwards are as Parley records them in his history (see *PPP Auto.*, pp. 141–43).

Chapter Eighteen

The events leading up to and associated with the Panic of 1837 and the collapse of the Kirtland Safety Society Anti-Banking Company are summarized in several excellent sources (see, for example, CHFT, pp. 171–73; Milton V. Backman, Jr., *The Heavens Resound: A History of the Latter-day Saints in Ohio, 1830–1838* [Salt Lake City: Deseret Book Co., 1983], pp. 311–23, hereafter cited as *HR*; and Marvin S. Hill, C. Keith Rooker, and Larry T. Wimmer, "The Kirtland Economy Revisited: A Market Critique of Sectarian Economics," *BYU Studies* 17 [Summer 1977]).

Chapter Nineteen

The account of Parley's disaffection and John Taylor's response to him are accurately portrayed in the novel (see *PPP Auto.*, p. 144; *HR*, pp. 325–26; *LJT*, pp. 39–40). However, there is some evidence that Parley sought out John Taylor rather than vice versa. Nathan's role in all of this is, of course, fictional.

Joseph Smith, Sr. (usually called Father Smith by the Saints), was the Patriarch to the Church and gave patriarchal blessings to Church members in "blessing meetings." However, it is not known if Mary Fielding received a blessing from him at this time.

Chapter Twenty

For convenience in telling the story, the meeting in which Brigham Young defends the Prophet, and in which Jacob Bump tries to "lay hands" on Brigham, is placed here in the narrative, at the end of May 1837. Although some historians place this meeting at this point in time, there is evidence that it may have been held as early as February of that same year. Brigham's own account of this meeting does not specify the date. But whatever the timing, the incident is depicted as Brigham described it later (see Leonard J. Arrington, *Brigham Young: American Moses* [New York: Alfred A. Knopf, 1985], pp. 57–58). Joseph's prophecy, alluded to in this chapter, that Brigham Young would one day lead the Church is reported in *HR*, pp. 278–80.

The next three meetings described in the novel—the Sunday, 28 May, gathering during which Warren Parrish pronounces a curse on Joseph's head; the 29 May meeting in which charges are brought against some of the dissidents; and the worship services of 4 June at which Heber C. Kimball is called to go to England to proclaim the gospel—are all matters of record (see Ronald K. Esplin, "The Emergence of Brigham Young and the Twelve to Mormon Leadership, 1830–1841" [Ph.D. diss., Brigham Young University, 1981], pp. 277–79, hereafter cited as "Emergence of Brigham Young"; HC 2:484–86, 489–90; CHFT, p. 174).

Chapter Twenty-One

The depicted farewell scene between Heber C. Kimball and his family, including some of the words of his prayer, is as reported by Robert B. Thompson, newly married husband of Mercy Fielding, who with his wife would accompany Heber part of the way on his journey (see Orson F. Whitney, Life of Heber C. Kimball [1888; reprint, Salt Lake City: Bookcraft, 1992], pp. 108–9; hereafter cited as LHCK). Some sources report that Heber's children also accompanied the party to Fairport Harbor, but the novel follows the account in LHCK, which seems to imply that they did not.

Joseph's illness and the subsequent effect of Doctor Levi Richards's blessing are reported by Joseph (see HC 2:492–93). The dissenters did attribute his illness to a curse pronounced upon him by Warren Parrish, but his remarkable recovery ruled that out in a hurry. Ebenezer Robinson's statement about truth and righteousness prevailing is given in Esplin's "Emergence of Brigham Young," p. 238. This sentiment was typical of many of the Latter-day Saints who remained faithful during this period, and may partially explain why the "Truth Will Prevail" banner in England so struck Heber C. Kimball and the other missionaries when they saw it.

Chapters Twenty-Two and Twenty-Three

In chapter twenty-two, the depiction of Parley Pratt's repentance is drawn from his autobiography and other sources (see PPP Auto., p. 144; "Emergence of Brigham Young," pp. 286–88).

The events depicted in chapters twenty-two and twenty-three concerning the arrival and subsequent activities of the missionaries in Preston are told in some detail in LHCK, pp. 118–36. The seeing of the banner; the reported dreams had by some of the Reverend James Fielding's congregation in Preston; the acceptance and then rejection of the missionaries by the reverend; the race to the river; the first baptisms—all are part of this record. (See also James B. Allen, Ronald K. Esplin, and David J. Whittaker, Men with a Mission, 1837–1841: The Quorum of the Twelve Apostles in the British Isles [Salt Lake City: Deseret Book Co., 1992], pp. 26–36; hereafter cited as

MWM.) The account of the encounter with evil spirits is quoted (with some minor editorial alterations) from *LHCK*, pp. 129–31.

Chapter Twenty-Five

While Benjamin Steed's wavering between faithfulness and personal apostasy is part of the fictional story that this novel tells, the details of what was happening with many of the historical figures—David Whitmer, Martin Harris, and so on—are drawn from the accounts of those dark days in Kirtland. The attempted takeover of the temple and its resulting violence are portrayed in the novel as they are described by the Prophet's mother and others (see Lucy Mack Smith, *History of Joseph Smith by His Mother*, ed. Preston Nibley [Salt Lake City: Bookcraft, 1958], p. 241, and Eliza R. Snow Smith, *Biography and Family Record of Lorenzo Snow* [1884; reprint, Salt Lake City: Zion's Book Store, 1975], pp. 20–21; see also Karl Ricks Anderson, *Joseph Smith's Kirtland: Eyewitness Accounts* [Salt Lake City: Deseret Book Co., 1989], pp. 220–21).

Chapter Twenty-Six

The description of the progress of missionary work in England and Heber C. Kimball's activities at this time is drawn mainly from *LHCK*, pp. 137–43 (see also MWM, pp. 36–40).

The conference of 3 September 1837 is a historical event, and action was taken against many of the dissidents (see HC 2:509–11).

The action taken by Derek's boss, Mr. Morris, at the textile factory was not a widespread occurrence as far as we know, but Mr. Morris's behavior is representative of the efforts of some real-life employers and family members to coerce converts into abandoning their new religion (see *LHCK*, p. 153).

Chapter Twenty-Seven

The death of Hyrum's wife, Jerusha Barden Smith, is accurately portrayed in the novel, including her calling of the children together for a last farewell (see HC 2:519).

Chapter Twenty-Eight

The various details given in Lydia's letter to Benjamin and Mary Ann are accurate, including Joseph's call for Hyrum to marry the Canadian convert Mary Fielding without delay. The description of the precipitous flights of Brigham Young and Joseph Smith to escape death from the hands of the apostates is accurate (see *HR*, pp. 342–43).

Chapter Twenty-Nine

Oliver Cowdery was excommunicated on 12 April 1838 for the charges described in the novel. David Whitmer withdrew his name from the records of the Church before he could be excommunicated (see *HC* 3:16–19).

The part of the April 1838 revelation giving the official name of the Church is found in D&C 115:4. To this point it was commonly called the Church of Christ or the Church of the Latter-day Saints.

Chapter Thirty

The revelation designating Spring Hill in northern Missouri as Adam-ondi-Ahman is now found in D&C 116 (see also *HC* 3:34–38). The "Salt Sermon" preached by Sidney Rigdon and the letter that was produced shortly thereafter that threatened the apostates with physical violence if they did not immediately leave are matters of record (see *CHFT*, p. 191). There is no question that Joseph did not sign the letter and that he roundly condemned it once he learned of it. Some sources say that Sidney did not sign the document either. Other sources, however, claim that Sidney did sign it and that he was the one who actually wrote the letter.

Chapter Thirty-Two

Matthew's report of the circumstances surrounding Willard Richards and Jennetta Richards's meeting is drawn generally from *LHCK*, pp. 143–44 (see also *MWM*, pp. 61–62).